Approaches to emotion in Middle English literature

Manchester University Press

MANCHESTER MEDIEVAL LITERATURE AND CULTURE

Series editors: Anke Bernau, David Matthews and James Paz
Series founded by: J. J. Anderson and Gail Ashton
Advisory board: Ruth Evans, Patricia C. Ingham, Andrew James Johnston, Chris Jones, Catherine Karkov, Nicola McDonald, Haruko Momma, Susan Phillips, Sarah Salih, Larry Scanlon, Stephanie Trigg and Matthew Vernon

Manchester Medieval Literature and Culture publishes monographs and essay collections comprising new research informed by current critical methodologies on the literary cultures of the global Middle Ages. We are interested in all periods, from the early Middle Ages through to the late, and we include post-medieval engagements with and representations of the medieval period (or 'medievalism'). 'Literature' is taken in a broad sense, to include the many different medieval genres: imaginative, historical, political, scientific and religious.

Titles available in the series

32. *Riddles at work in the early medieval tradition: Words, ideas, interactions*   Megan Cavell and Jennifer Neville (eds)
33. *From Iceland to the Americas: Vinland and historical imagination*   Tim William Machan and Jón Karl Helgason (eds)
34. *Northern memories and the English Middle Ages*   Tim William Machan
35. *Harley manuscript geographies: Literary history and the medieval miscellany*   Daniel Birkholz
36. *Play time: Gender, anti-Semitism and temporality in medieval biblical drama*   Daisy Black
37. *Transfiguring medievalism: Poetry, attention and the mysteries of the body*   Cary Howie
38. *Objects of affection: The book and the household in late medieval England*   Myra Seaman
39. *The gift of narrative in medieval England*   Nicholas Perkins
40. *Sleep and its spaces in Middle English literature: Emotions, ethics, dreams*   Megan G. Leitch
41. *Encountering* The Book of Margery Kempe   Laura Kalas and Laura Varnam (eds)
42. *The narrative grotesque in medieval Scottish poetry*   Caitlin Flynn
43. *Painful pleasures: Sadomasochism in medieval cultures*   Christopher Vaccaro (ed.)
44. *Medieval literary voices: Embodiment, materiality and performance*   Louise D'Arcens and Sif Ríkharðsdóttir (eds)
45. *Bestsellers and masterpieces: The changing medieval canon*   Heather Blurton and Dwight F. Reynolds (eds)
46. *Hybrid healing: Old English remedies and medical texts*   Lori Ann Garner
47. *The heat of* Beowulf   Daniel C. Remein
48. *Difficult pasts: Post-Reformation memory and the medieval romance*   Mimi Ensley
49. *The problem of literary value*   Robert J. Meyer-Lee
50. *Marian maternity in late-medieval England*   Mary Beth Long
51. *Fantasies of music is nostalgic medievalism*   Helen Dell
52. *White before whiteness in the late Middle Ages*   Wan-Chuan Kao
53. *Literatures of the Hundred Years War*   Daniel Davies and R. D. Perry (eds)
54. *Approaches to emotion in Middle English literature*   Carolyne Larrington

Approaches to emotion in Middle English literature

Carolyne Larrington

MANCHESTER UNIVERSITY PRESS

Copyright © Carolyne Larrington 2024

The right of Carolyne Larrington to be identified as the author of this work has been asserted in accordance with the Copyright, Designs and Patents Act 1988.

Published by Manchester University Press
Oxford Road, Manchester M13 9PL

www.manchesteruniversitypress.co.uk

British Library Cataloguing-in-Publication Data
A catalogue record for this book is available from the British Library

ISBN 978 1 5261 7613 4 hardback
ISBN 978 1 5261 9584 5 paperback

First published 2024
Paperback published 2026

The publisher has no responsibility for the persistence or accuracy of URLs for any external or third-party internet websites referred to in this book, and does not guarantee that any content on such websites is, or will remain, accurate or appropriate.

EU authorised representative for GPSR:
Easy Access System Europe – Mustamäe tee 50, 10621 Tallinn, Estonia
gpsr.requests@easproject.com

Typeset
by Cheshire Typesetting Ltd, Cuddington, Cheshire

For Frank Brandsma and Sif Ríkharðsdóttir

Contents

Acknowledgements   viii
Abbreviations   x

Introduction   1
1 Words, taxonomies and translations   48
2 Embodiment and action   94
3 Performativity and performance   135
4 Audiences and affectivity   179
5 Fifteenth-century feelings   228
Conclusion   273

Bibliography   281
Index   314

Acknowledgements

I owe a huge debt of thanks to many friends and colleagues who have contributed in smaller and larger ways to the thinking in, and the writing of, this book. Thanks to Sophie Coloumbeau and Brittany Schorn for help with transcripts and data, to Anna Czarnowus for discussion, and to Pen Woods for alerting me to the possibility of a Visiting Fellowship at the Centre for Excellence for the Study of the History of Emotions at the University of Western Australia in 2016. To everyone whom I met and talked to at CHE, both in Perth and more widely across Australia, my deepest gratitude, especially to my old friend Andrew Lynch, along with Katie Barclay, Giovanni Tarentino, Paul Megna, Kirk Essary, Michael Barbezat and Jane-Héloïse Nancarrow. It was at CHE at UWA where I started working in earnest on research for this book, and the space and kindness afforded to me in those months set me on the path to rethinking emotion in medieval literature.

Jonas Liliequist organised an important conference in Umeå in 2008 that was instrumental in helping me formulate the distinctions between approaches to history and literature. Hailey O'Harrow and Stephen Spencer likewise brought a group of emotions researchers together at St Andrews University in 2022 for a very productive few days of discussion.

Monika Fludernik's work flagged up the importance of narratology for me, and I have been delighted to have the opportunity to discuss emotions in literature with her, Eva von Contzen, and Sonia Garcia de Alba Lobeira, both in Oxford and in Freiburg. Sonia's work helped shape the discussion of long-form romance in Chapter 5. Marion Turner and other colleagues in the Oxford

Acknowledgements

English Faculty have been a great source of support, as have my dear colleagues at St John's College, Patrick Hayes and Noël Sugimura. I am grateful to St John's for periods of research leave that enabled me to research, draft and finally to complete this book.

Other colleagues and friends, Guillemette Bolens, Az Brown, Stephanie Trigg, Mary Flannery, Sarah Brazil, Meritxell Risco de la Torre, Lucie Kaempfer, Hannah Piercy and Tim Bourns among them, have said many interesting things about emotions across a range of genres and literatures in papers, lectures and presentations that I have been lucky enough to listen to. Hannah Piercy and Lucy Brookes have written fascinating PhDs on emotions that I have been fortunate enough to examine, and which have left their mark on what follows. Manchester University Press have been wonderful to work with, so particular thanks to Meredith Carroll, Laura Swift and the rest of the team. The anonymous readers also made valuable suggestions; warm thanks too to them.

Finally, the book's two dedicatees, Sif Ríkharðsdóttir and Frank Brandsma, have been dear friends for more than a decade. Their wisdom, warmth, collegiality in various projects and their friendship over many years have been a source of great encouragement and happiness.

Abbreviations

AHR	*American Historical Review*
EETS	Early English Text Society
EETS OS	Early English Text Society Ordinary Series
MED	*Middle English Dictionary*, https://quod.lib.umich.edu/m/middle-english-dictionary/dictionary
OED	*Oxford English Dictionary*, https://www.oed.com
PBA	*Proceedings of the British Academy*
PL	*Patrologia Latina*
PMLA	*Proceedings of the Modern Languages Association*
SAC	*Studies in the Age of Chaucer*

Introduction

In October 2015 I listened to BBC Radio 4's regular Monday morning discussion programme, *Start the Week*.¹ Appearing on the programme were the historian Niall Ferguson, the author Jane Smiley, another historian, Gabriel Gorodetsky, and Andrew Marr, the journalist-presenter. The conversation focused on Ferguson's new book about Henry Kissinger, and Jane Smiley's novel *Golden Age*, the final novel in her trilogy 'The Last Hundred Years', which narrates a Mid-Western family history from 1920 into the very near future.² In the discussion Smiley argued that novels about history have a particular purpose, 'history and memoir tell us what happened, but novels tell us or have a theory about how it felt, and make it live for us'. Ferguson replied:

> Your characters are imaginary, Jane ... I'm not trying to disparage what you do, but we need to recognise that it's different – because these aren't real people, and you're just telling us what these imaginary people must have felt, whereas the historians ... we're trying to reconstruct past experience but from primary sources, from things that people wrote down. We're not allowed to just make it up. And that's a really important distinction.

Smiley responded, 'OK, here's the distinction between the novel and history. The historian must say that my record here is as complete as I can make it, but it's not truly complete because, if it were, then it wouldn't be accurate ... the novelist must offer a sense of completeness.' Andrew Marr intervened to ask, 'Do you accept that the novelist has a form of truth that is valid?' Ferguson replied, 'No, no, no!'³

This exchange brought into clear focus for me key issues which have clustered around the many important insights generated by the field that has become known as 'the history of emotions' when we seek to apply them to literary, particularly imaginative, texts. When what may be called 'the affective turn' in humanities studies began in the 1990s, the new focus on the role of emotion in past and present culture encompassed a number of disciplines.[4] In the mid-1980s and early 1990s the historian Peter Stearns began to frame his broadly (modern) historical and sociological investigation in terms of 'emotionology', defined as 'the standards that a society, or a definable group within a society, maintains toward basic emotions and their appropriate expression'.[5] Stearns's writing was rooted partly in his long-standing interest in family history and in his recognition of emotion as one of the motors of change within recent or contemporary cultures. His topic intersected with the work of such sociologists as Arlie Hochschild, whose classic 1983 book *The Managed Heart* was an important bellwether for the emergence of the 'affective turn'.[6]

As it has developed, that field in which Stearns and others were pioneers has become known as 'the history of emotions', in preference to such designations as 'emotion studies' or even 'emotionology', alternatives mooted in the last century. The fundamental paradigms developed as a consequence of the 'affective' or 'emotional turn' in the humanities thus have their roots in historians' praxis, for it is they who have been central to the field's growth over the last thirty years. Key figures include Barbara Rosenwein, Gerd Althoff, Damien Boquet and Piroska Nagy, in the medieval period; William Reddy, both in the French eighteenth century and then working comparatively across the medieval east and west; Monique Scheer, researching in the early modern period; Ute Frevert, in modern history; and Jan Plamper, whose meta-study of the history of 'the history of emotions' is an invaluable guide to the longer history of the various research disciplines, approaches and trends that have fused in the current field.[7]

The scholars named above, along with many more, researching at the various centres for the history of emotion across the globe, at Queen Mary University, London, the Australian Research Council Centre for Excellence for the Study of the History of Emotions in Australia, the History of Emotions Project at the Max-Planck Institute for Human Development in Berlin, and Boquet and Nagy's Les Émotions au Moyen Âge at the Universities of Montréal and Aix-Marseille, have opened up vital questions about the ways in which emotions in the past can be understood and how historical change comes about through, and concomitantly with, changes in emotional styles and repertoires, schemas and scripts (these are defined later, pp. 10–11). All these projects investigate in different ways and with different emphases how emotions have been thought about, expressed, evoked and performed over the last 1,500 years. Yet, as is foregrounded in the projects' names, they are all conceptualised in terms of strictly historical investigation.[8] No discussion of the ways in which emotion is expressed and experienced in medieval literary texts can fail to take the historians' discoveries as a starting point, nor to utilise them to scaffold distinctively literary methodological approaches. Nevertheless, literary scholars employ different and complementary methods in studying medieval emotion, in order, as Jane Smiley says, to try to 'tell us ... how it felt ... and make it live for us'. These methods, the questions that they address and the answers they provide are the topic of this book.

Below I outline the most significant among the older, larger issues which have shaped the formulation of emotion as an object of study for medieval historians and literary scholars, before I summarise the individual contributions to the debate made by key historians. I then turn to medieval models of the mind–body continuum and the place of emotion in them and consider affect theory and the related return to understanding emotion as embodied. Finally, I anticipate the ways in which this book will seek to answer the distinctive questions that literary texts raise about emotions.

What is emotion?

Everyone knows what an emotion is, until asked to give a definition.[9]

Modern studies of emotion in the pre-modern period tend to start with a disclaimer about terminology. For, as Thomas Dixon pointed out in his influential study of the 'passions', emotion is a broad and distinctively modern concept which by no means maps exactly onto the understandings of the phenomena that constituted the terms for feelings in earlier periods.[10] Elena Carrera notes that 'emotion' does not provide a universal and ahistorical set of categories; rather the term functions as:

> a practical means of examining pre-modern discussions of the prevailing medical and philosophical categories of 'passions', 'accidents of the soul', 'passions of the heart', 'movements of the soul', 'affections of the mind', 'affects' and 'perturbations', as well as descriptions, formulations and evaluations of states conventionally referred to in terms such as grief, sorrow, sadness, despair, anxiety, fear, terror, anger, wrath, pleasure and joy in Latin or in other medieval and early modern European languages.[11]

The terminology of emotion in English, including concepts such as 'feelings', 'passions', 'moods', 'sentiments' and 'affects', has often been regarded by historians either as broadly interchangeable or else (as in the case of 'passions') as pertaining to particular historical periods. Despite these reservations, most scholars working in the field settle on 'emotion' as a catch-all term for the phenomena they study, and, thus, to echo Jan Plamper, I too have elected 'to use "emotion" as a meta-concept' in this book.[12]

During the late twentieth century, philosophers and neuroscientists quietly dismantled one of western culture's long-prevailing dualities. Emotion is no longer regarded as existing 'all in the mind' – yet somehow producing physical symptoms, as René Descartes (1596–1650) argued, a position that was adopted and refined by most major philosophers of the eighteenth and nineteenth centuries.[13] In the late nineteenth century the psychologist William James (1842–1910) began the reversal of the contemporary understanding of the place of emotion within the mind–body continuum. James argued, in his own emphatic italics, '*My thesis on the contrary is that the bodily changes follow directly the PERCEPTION of the exciting fact and that our feeling of the same changes as they occur IS the emotion.*'[14] Thus, instead of the mind calculating that a snake poses a danger and the individual thus feeling fear, turning pale and beginning to shake, James argues, 'we feel sorry because we cry, angry because we strike, afraid because we tremble'.[15]

For James, the emotion is the embodied reaction alone; cognitive processing is secondary to, and caused by, physical manifestation. Psychologists were thus at the forefront of the re-evaluation of the relationship between emotion and cognition, now no longer regarded as separate domains constituted in opposition to one another. The work of Antonio Damasio and other neuroscientists has shown how intricately thinking and feeling are interconnected in the brain's neural systems.[16] Investigation of the psychology of emotion has furnished new models for understanding the processes by which, following James's insight, the complex feedback systems between sensory and other physiological stimuli, cognitive appraisal and 'action readiness' are now well understood. These have overturned the simple oppositions of mind/body that were foundational in earlier theorisations of emotion. Keith Oatley and Nico Frijda have advocated componential models in order to explain how emotional systems and subsystems appear to work.[17] They suggest that emotion can be best understood as consisting in separable parts: the perception of the emotion stimulus, neurological processing via physiological and cognitive subsystems, production of a state of 'action readiness' and behavioural outcomes. Componential theory thus proposes, in Klaus Scherer and Heiner Ellgring's formulation, that '[e]motion [is] a process that engenders cognitive activity, motor expression, physiological arousal, action tendencies and subjective feeling states'.[18]

Psychologists continue to debate about the existence of basic emotions, thought of as 'universal' and widely recognisable in facial expression, and as dependent on fixed 'affect programs' inherent in the human brain (as argued for most notably by Paul Ekman and Carroll Izard).[19] Ekman and Izard have both come to accept that culture-specific emotion display rules have an important and measurable effect on facial and other somatic expressions of emotion. A 'soft' version of basic emotion theory has thus emerged; fundamental underlying 'affect programs' are understood as 'open', subject to modification through culturally prevalent and immediate cognitive influences. Scherer and his associates, along with Oatley and Frijda, continue to argue for the componential system: emotions, particularly the more complex ones, consist in the interaction of different components activated by appraisals of the event or stimulus that elicits the emotion in question.[20] Universalist versus hard social constructionist theories have thus been modified; basic emotion advocates have scaled back the claims that certain emotions are always recognisable in cross-cultural contexts, while social constructionists now concede that the body is the primary site of pre-cognitive affect. That certain emotions – such as fear, anger, happiness, sadness and disgust – have a strongly somatic aspect chimes with a widespread folk-psychological belief that identifies strong physiological indices as showing the presence of these feelings. One further important effect of the arguments about universal versus social constructionist theorisations of emotion has been a welcome recognition of how far our traditional emotion models are western-centric, inherited from Greek and Roman philosophers, via medieval medical theorists and early modern and modern thinkers, and now incorporating psychoanalytic and psychological models. The limitations of such emotion models for non-western cultures have been foregrounded in anthropological and cross-cultural psychological enquiries.[21]

Modern philosophers have engaged with emotion in differing ways. Once the debate about the location of emotion had been resolved, as both bodily and mental, intimately bound up both with sensory stimuli and precognitive mental activity, with changing hormonal levels and speedy assessment of relevance to individual goals, models relating to different philosophical subfields emerged. One important tendency investigates the links between emotion and ethics, emphasising both cognitive and goal-oriented components. 'Emotions are not just the fuel that powers the psychological mechanism of a reasoning creature, they are parts, highly complex and messy parts, of this creature's reasoning itself', suggests Martha Nussbaum.[22] She amplifies her definition thus: 'emotions are appraisals or value judgements that ascribe to things and persons outside the person's own control great importance for that person's own flourishing'.[23] The terminology of 'appraisal', 'value judgement' and 'flourishing' aligns her model with that of Frijda and other componential-theory investigators.

Phenomenologists have focused on the embodied nature of the subject; historians of philosophy have traced changing conceptions in ancient and medieval philosophical writings.[24] With the advent of functional MRI scanners and other methods of neural imaging, neuropsychologists have been enabled to propose refinements to

Damasio's hypothesis that emotional and cognitive neural substrates are inextricable from one another within the architecture of the brain.[25] Brain-imaging-dependent theories, such as the positing of 'mirror neurons' which integrate kinetic, cognitive and emotional systems, have also had their effect on contemporary understanding of emotion.[26] The life-sciences have thus undergone their own 'affective turn', producing fresh models of human emotionality which have informed research in the humanities.

All these theorisations, however, take as their focus real people, living human subjects whose brains may be scanned and whose skin conductance may be measured. They may be questioned about their motivations and their interior sensations, and their facial expressions, utterances and behaviour may be observed and related to both to the feelings they profess and the emotional norms of contemporary cultural groups. The past however is not accessible through human bodies nor through directly elicited narratives in this way. Humanities scholars are coming to see the limitations of applying arguments from the life-sciences to textual and discursive constructions as found in medieval sources.[27] Nevertheless, as we shall see in Chapter 4, there are evolving psychological models for the ways in which humans engage with texts, whether orally performed or read silently, experienced in solitude or encountered in a collective environment. These are relevant to thinking about the ways in which specifically literary and fictional texts have different kinds of emotional impact on audiences, and thus, potentially, for investigating how change is effected in the hearts and minds of both medieval and modern audiences.[28]

History and emotion

In the mid-twentieth century historians were often inclined to accept accounts of emotions in the medieval past at face value, understanding them as displaying the irrationality and childishness ascribed to the Middle Ages by Johan Huizinga:

> All things, presenting themselves to the mind in violent contrasts and impressive forms, lent a tone of excitement and of passion to everyday

life and tended to produce that perpetual oscillation between despair and distracted joy, between cruelty and pious tenderness which characterise life in the Middle Ages.[29]

The new 'history of emotions' begins with a critique of the Huizinga position, insisting that records of the emotion displays of medieval people cannot be interpreted as reflecting what 'real people' really felt, and that medieval emotion was neither childish nor uncivilised. Rather, a nuanced understanding of contemporary medieval emotional systems and a thoroughgoing investigation into specific contexts and cultures would bring to light the rules that governed emotional display and the lexis that reflected emotions at works in texts. Yet historians' sources are never not unmediated; rather they are always representational, shaped by the preoccupations of their authors and the changing conventions of contemporary historiography. Thus, their relationship to the 'truth' must be more problematic than Niall Ferguson, in my opening anecdote, was prepared to admit. As Stuart Airlie noted in 2001, '[w]e do not have unmediated access to the past, and our own emotional responses to what it has left us offer no short cut to its perception.'[30] Airlie remained hopeful that 'investigation into the historical nature and experience of the emotions themselves' was not only desirable, but possible.[31] How this new approach to medieval history has been inflected in the intervening years is considered below.

Airlie was writing in a special issue of the journal *Early Medieval Europe*, which appeared in the wake of the important essay collection from 1998, *Anger's Past*, edited by Barbara Rosenwein. Studying history through the lens of emotion stimulated new conceptualisations and methodologies. At the forefront was Rosenwein's own methodological innovation; her interventions have been foundational in shaping the field. The key article from 2002, 'Worrying about Emotions in History', sketches the broad contours of the new approach.[32] Taking issue with the old Huizinga–Elias–Stearns paradigm of the Middle Ages as having 'the emotional life of a child: unadulterated, violent, public, unashamed', Rosenwein highlights the new cognitive psychological and social constructionist models of emotion systems as already shaping the historiography of emotion.[33] In her first monograph on the topic she introduces the concept of 'emotional communities', which is developed in detail in a series of case-studies.[34] Here Rosenwein argues that, although emotions in the past must be identified primarily through lexis, the meanings of those emotions, as understood in the broadest sense, can be uncovered through investigation of how texts circulated within 'emotional communities', 'groups in which people adhere to the same norms of emotional expression and value – or devalue – the same or related emotions'.[35] In her later book *Generations of Feeling*, Rosenwein expands her definition: 'Emotional communities are groups – usually but not always social groups – that have their own particular values, modes of feeling, and ways to express those feelings ... Larger communities will contain variants and counterstyles – "emotional subcommunities" if you will.'[36] Emotional communities then are real-world groups of people who write for, and in dialogue with, one another; in *Emotional Communities* these are clerics in early medieval Frankia, living between c. 600 and 800. Sub-communities overlap in certain social contexts and are distinct in others; they adhere to 'internalized norms that determine how we think and act and that may be different in different groups'.[37] They are of course also textual communities, as adumbrated by Brian Stock, consisting additionally of the reader or performer of a text and those who listen to the reading at a particular moment.[38]

Importantly, Rosenwein insists that the emotional norms she identifies have real-world validity and are not simply to be regarded as generic conventions, precisely because they occur across a range of (largely non-fictional) genres. In her test cases this methodology serves her well, for here she does not have to grapple, as she does in her later book, with the problematic questions of vernacularity and fictionality. In *Generations of Feeling* she extends her range: successive models of the emotions alternate with studies of successive emotional communities. These emotions are evidenced in a new set of genres – including the poetry of the troubadours (where she intersects with William Reddy) and *The Book of Margery Kempe*, as well as the Paston Letters. Many of these communities (though not of course the theorists of emotion contemporary with them) employed vernaculars, a move that opens up a different set of issues from the earlier book. Rosenwein occasionally acknowledges these but, by and large, she avoids discussing vernacular semantic fields, connotational systems and, importantly, genre.[39] Genre and genre-related emotion repertoires raise the unsettling question: are the emotions expressed in particular kinds of text merely conventional topoi with no necessary connection to real-world emotional performance? In *Emotional Communities*, Rosenwein suggests that emotional styles that recur across different kinds of text must be more than conventional, or at least that they invoke prevailing emotional norms; '[t]hey themselves were social products ... and could be drawn upon and manipulated with some freedom'.[40] 'Genres are flexible', she comments, but the difficulties presented in relating rhetoric and genre convention to real-world behaviour cannot be overcome quite so easily, particularly where predominantly imaginative and fictional forms are concerned.[41] When a romance hero weeps and faints, or a heroine tears her hair, can we extrapolate from this that real people really behaved thus in comparable circumstances?

Andreea Marculescu and Charles-Louis Morand Métivier have recently noted that Rosenwein's model does not sufficiently account for dynamism and change in discourse communities. 'Emotional norms that fabricate individual and group subjectivities are not already pre-established ... but are impacted by different discursive ruptures, negotiations and practices.'[42] This emphasis on the modification of emotional repertoires, schemas and scripts, their retooling over time to take account of larger social changes, is vitally important for the literary study of emotions since, as we shall see, literary texts work both to transmit stable emotional signifiers within genre norms, and to function as crucial vectors of expressive change. Repertoires, schemas and scripts are discrete emotional systems that operate at different scales. The emotion repertoire is the range of possible emotions available within a culture, while the emotion schema is a psychological concept. The schema is defined as 'a particular totality of primarily affectively determined modes of responses and feelings toward people and events that can be transferred onto analogous situations and similar people ... tightly integrated slot-filler structures of eliciting situations, subjective feelings, and expressive and autonomic activity'.[43] An example of a schema might be the range of situations, conscious and unconscious physiological reactions, and behaviours associated with grief. Finally, an emotion script is a term popularised by Silvan Tomkins, broadly understood as a pattern of elements that recur within an individual episode of emotion; not all of these will always be present.[44] William M. Reddy's 2001 book *The Navigation of Feeling* deals with eighteenth-century France, and thus has less direct application to the pre-modern period. Reddy is particularly interested in change in emotional repertoires, and he posits a tension between the dominant socially accepted styles of expressing emotion ('emotional régimes') enforced within the repressive world of pre-revolutionary France, and the various oppositional spaces constructed to give free rein to alternative, even revolutionary, forms of emotional expression. While Reddy's book mainly engages with larger politico-social groupings, evidence for different loci of opposition to the regime is drawn from texts written by individuals whose feelings resist dominant emotion schemas and scripts. Consequently, a key methodological construct for Reddy is the utterance. He refines J. L. Austin's concept of the speech act (see Chapter 3) as performative in function – as a means of getting things done in the world – and he coins the term 'emotive' to designate the emotionally inflected performative utterance:

> a type of speech act different from both performative and constative utterances, which both describes (like constative utterances) and changes (like performatives) the world, because emotional expression has an exploratory and a self-altering effect in the activated thought material of emotion.[45]

When an emotion is expressed in an emotive, not only does it change the world for the listener, it also affects the speaker. The emotive is 'self-exploring, or self-altering'.[46] The emotive focuses attention on an emotion which might not be apparent in the text otherwise, revealing it to the listener within the text, for the utterer and for the text-external audience. In his most recent book, Reddy stresses the similarities between the performative and the emotive, now described as 'emotional expression':

> When an emotional expression fails to elicit the expected confirming activations, it may lead to a new self-understanding. Emotional utterances are therefore similar to performatives, as described by J. L. Austin, because, like performatives, they are a way 'to do things

with words'. But they differ from performatives because of the unpredictability of their outcome.[47]

Reddy's theorisation depends on the existence of psychological interiority, a 'real self' constituted by the utterer's subjectivity. The emotive enables insight into this self. Reddy's eighteenth-century subjects did no doubt possess highly developed models of selfhood and interiority; the existence of such concepts across medieval English literature is a more contentious issue, one which will prove central to this book. Reddy extends and refines his concept, highlighting the ways in which emotives perform 'emotion management', disciplining the self to conform with the culturally available schemas for emotion episodes. He notes the 'effortful pursuit of expression to modify feeling and pursuit of feeling to modify behavior – effortful pursuit aptly dubbed "management"'. 'Navigation' finally emerges as his preferred term 'because navigation includes the possibility of radically changing course, as well as that of making constant corrections in order to stay on a chosen course'.[48] Thus, emotives become critical to the process that Sarah McNamer identifies as 'teaching [readers] how to feel', an element within the feedback loop between emotion utterances, individual feelings and performed behaviour that inculcates new emotional styles and praxis within historical contexts.[49]

The Making of Romantic Love, Reddy's next monograph, engages directly with pre-modern emotion in Southern France, India (specifically Bengal and Orissa) and Heian-era Japan.[50] He investigates the phenomenon of what in the west has become characterised as 'romantic love', but which he designates more generally as 'longing for association'. 'Whether as transgression, as norm or as ideal, the longing for association can bring partners (including sexual partners) together in more or less enduring collaborations in a wide variety of cultural contexts, but not in all.'[51] Making the argument that the constraints imposed on aristocratic life by the eleventh-century Gregorian reforms generated an emotional resistance expressed through *trobaritz* poetry, first at the court of Toulouse, then disseminated more widely across medieval France and thence much further afield, Reddy engages with this highly literary and fictional genre as if the relationship between historical actors and subjective, lyric poetry were entirely straightforward. 'In a maneuver typical of aristocratic speech, singers of love songs and tellers of love stories showed their listeners how they could quietly enjoy what they could not openly claim', he suggests.[52] While he regards poetry as accurately reflecting the ways in which men and women felt about one another in twelfth-century Occitania, occasional reservations are voiced: 'What relation the Occitan lyric had to court practices on the one hand and to Christian morality on the other has remained unsettled'; nevertheless he praises the 'excellent fit of the courtly love ideal with existing aristocratic practices'.[53]

Reddy characterises poetic discourse as 'no necessary or natural configuration. Instead, it represented a limited form of "queer performativity", in [Eve Kosofsky] Sedgwick's sense, a practice that aimed to counter the effects of "habitual shame"'.[54] Nevertheless, despite this attention to queerness, his is an oddly literalistic reading of *trobaritz* song, one that adheres to an outdated view of the poems as reflecting a highly traditional, resolutely heterosexual version of love, either frustrated or reciprocated, and keenly felt as emotionally lacerating. That the *trobaritz* adopt personas in their performances, that, as Sarah Kay has argued, the key relationship in the lady–lord–poet triangle may in fact be between the poet and his patron-lord, that *fin'amors* might be regarded, as it certainly was in England by the fourteenth century, as an elaborate, ritualistic game, crucial to ideas of courtly self-fashioning and gender performance, but with no tangible connection to actual persons' feelings or behaviour, is not a possibility that Reddy addresses.[55] Reading across other texts (chronicles, letters, court records) produced in the same period, Reddy (as Rosenwein also argues) finds 'multiple resonances between the silences and the violence of aristocratic practice, on the one hand, and the silences and abstraction of troubadour lyric, on the other'.[56] This co-option of allusive, playful and self-absorbed lyric to explore real change within an emotional regime falls foul of Reddy's failure to read literary productions as literary.[57] 'In Reddy's reading, poetry is about history: history explains poetry and poetry influences history', Peggy McCracken comments in an insightful review.[58]

In *Generations of Feeling*, Rosenwein also takes up the case of the *trobaritz*. She does not make such large claims about the actual behaviour of the aristocracy in the twelfth-century courts of Toulouse, but rather reads across from contemporary legal documents, with their emphases on fidelity, loyalty and love, and their converse, treachery and deception, to the songs. 'Love, deception, and pain: those were the intertwined themes circulating at the court of the Raimondins.'[59] For Rosenwein, the *trobaritz* poems tell us little about the feelings of actual men or women:

> The earlier troubadours had displaced all the doubts and worries about love in the counts' charters from men to women. Their poems painted women as the deceivers. Because women hardly mattered at the court of Toulouse ... this displacement made the poems both comforting and entertaining. They deflected anxieties about treachery from the political realm to the erotic.[60]

Rosenwein too sees the poetry *as poetry* as effectively irrelevant; it functions simply to confirm the important feelings in circulation in the political domain, those explained by history. In engaging directly with the lyrics in the original language, Rosenwein has to address crucial questions of vernacularity and translation; since her models for the categorisation of emotions are drawn from contemporary theologians – Ælred of Rievaulx is the most historically relevant at this point – she both recognises and sidesteps the question of how we can know which Occitan words are emotion words, and how they might map onto the Latin terms which articulate the psychological and emotional models available to the learned. At least in Occitan, etymological relation can offer clues to meaning; when Rosenwein comes to the emotion language of Margery Kempe and the Pastons later in the book, identifying lexical connotations becomes more problematic.[61]

I have dwelt at length on the work of Rosenwein and Reddy. This is, in part, because they are the most influential historians in Anglophone medieval emotion studies, but also because their approaches to the interpretation of emotion in texts are indicative of the kinds of questions that historians tend to ask of written sources. Their analyses exemplify the ways in which specifically literary questions – about rhetoric, personas, generic conventions among others – can be overlooked or sidelined. I now turn more briefly to consider work on emotion history undertaken in French and German in recent years. Piroska Nagy and Damien Boquet's collaboration has produced a number of important interventions in the field, culminating in their jointly authored book *Sensible Moyen Âge*, published in 2015.[62] Boquet and Nagy have been more open to the inclusion of imaginative literary works within the continuum of texts that they examine in their broad-ranging account of medieval emotion across the long Middle Ages. In an illuminating series of *thèses* published on the EMMA website, the two authors reflect on and engage with other historians' approaches to emotion. Here they argue that, *pace* Rosenwein, the phenomenon of emotion in texts requires more complex analysis than generating lists of emotion words, however vital a pre-condition to analysis that might be, and, with reference to Gerd Althoff's work, that the ritual and performative nature of historical emotional display should not be understood as devoid of interior significance for its subjects – nor that the emotions of those engaged in such practices are inevitably irrecoverable.[63] Medieval authors' intentions and the effects that they intended to have on their audiences are not seen as difficult to recover and interpret: 'At a second, higher level, we reap the emotional advantage inspired by readings of the old author, according to his own designs – and just like his erstwhile recipient', they claim.[64] Authorial intention and contemporary reception must be distinguished from the responses of the modern historian, and they must find ways when writing about past emotions of mediating them in their turn to readers, 'but only on condition that he [the contemporary historian] likewise demonstrates lucidity in his approach, bringing together the elements of rhetoric and of analysis to make the emotions *felt*'.[65] Given a well-grounded understanding of cultural context then, the two Francophone historians are confident that intention and reception, encoding and decoding of textual emotions can be identified, analysed and interpreted by the modern reader. This is not to suggest that the two scholars undervalue varying emotion display rules or generic differences, but rather they are inclined to regard literary and non-literary texts as situated on a continuum along which medieval audiences (and modern readers) could confidently move.

Gerd Althoff has made a major contribution to emotion studies from the 1990s onwards through his close analysis of the depictions of elite figures by historians, chroniclers and other writers. These powerful participants in public ritual deploy emotions performatively in order to achieve rational, *zweckorientiert* (end-oriented) and calculated effects in the world. Althoff has shown how social actors demonstratively harness and perform emotions in public space; these performances are preserved in the accounts of contemporary witnesses who sometimes editorialise, and sometimes simply report, the actor's behaviour and its effects.[66] In an important English-language article, Althoff makes the crucial caveat that such performances need not align with any particular interior disposition: showing anger might be necessary and strategic for a monarch quite independently of whether he was actually experiencing the somatic effects normally associated with anger.[67] In the same article Althoff notes: '[m]edieval literature, in contrast [to historical texts], offers a broader spectrum of the possible expressions of anger that stood at the disposal of kings and other people'.[68] He himself does not pursue the literary evidence in detail; taking its cue in part from his work, the investigation of emotion in medieval German literature has tended to focus on the use of emotion as *zweckorientiert*, employed for advancing plot rather than aiming at psychological characterisation.[69]

Social historians then have had much to say about the ways in which people in the medieval past behaved and felt and how changes in particular emotional repertoires might have come about as the pressure of new political formations, the rise of towns and the disastrous impact of epidemics brought about new ways of feeling – with its three riotous drinkers, Chaucer's 'Pardoner's Tale', for example, demonstrates one powerful set of responses to the Black Death.[70] A separate, though related approach is that of historians of medicine and philosophy, who have investigated the changing models of emotional systems inherited from antiquity. These were understood by medieval scholars largely as configured within the body. It is to an outline of the understanding of the mind–body continuum and a range of the successive medieval analyses of the emotions embodied within human physiological and psychological systems that I now turn.

The medieval body and mind

For most medieval thinkers, emotions are at once cognitively penetrable and somatic, which is to say that emotions are influenced by and vary with changes in thought and belief, and that they are also bound up, perhaps essentially, with their physiological manifestations.[71]

Medieval psychological models were primarily inherited from classical teaching about the body and mind, though they were also strongly inflected by theological speculation which ascribed moral value to different aspects of the system. Aristotle had located the rational, cognitive elements of human psychology within the soul, and held that the soul was to be found within the heart. Galen, writing in the second century CE, argued that reason was located in the head, while emotion and affect, along with appetites, belonged in the body, specifically the thoracic cavity, containing the heart, and stomach, liver and digestive organs. The strongly materialist four-humour theory derived from Hippocrates and developed more systematically by Galen held sway throughout the medieval period, explaining personality, disposition and changes in mood and feeling through the overarching theory of complexion. This holds that varying combinations of heat, cold, moistness and dryness account for innate character; yet complexion also changes over time as the warmth and moisture of youth are succeeded by the coldness and dryness of old age.[72] Complexion also varies by gender; women are generally thought to be colder and moister than men. Humour theory explained the biological mechanism through which complexion was determined. As summarised by Avicenna (Abu Ali Sina, c. 980–1037) in *The Canon of Medicine*, Galenic physiological theory maintained that blood was produced by the liver from the food digested in the stomach (*chyle*); the other humours – the two kinds of bile (black and yellow) and phlegm – were also generated there.[73] Complexion was also subject to astrological influences. The changing cycle of the zodiac could cause both immediate and local effects, while the position of the planets at birth had a more durative influence in explaining an individual's fundamental disposition.[74]

Conceived of as a continuum, both mind and body were affected by changes in humoral composition, the circulation of the blood and the impact of external stimuli perceived through the senses. The most influential explanatory model for the interconnected functions of mind and body was promulgated by Constantine of Africa, who had connections with the medical school at Salerno, and who can be located at the monastery of Monte Cassino in the late eleventh century. Constantine translated into Latin key sections of an Arabic-language medical encyclopaedia written by Alī ibn al-'Abbās al-Maǧūsī (Haly Abbas as he was known in the west).[75] This translation, the *Pantegni*, formed a substantial component in an important anthology of medical texts, central to the curricula taught in medieval universities' medical faculties; indeed it was used in teaching well into the early modern period. According to the *Pantegni*, the natural spirits, located in the liver and digestive organs, enabled the powers of nutrition and growth and diffused these qualities through the blood to the whole body. Blood was vivified in the heart by the air drawn into the lungs; this produced an admixture of 'vital spirit' (Latin *spiritus*; Greek *pneuma*, 'spirit'), which was further diffused through the body. In a network of arteries at the base of the brain the blood became infused with psychological powers: the 'animal spirits', those associated with *anima* (mind). This liquid was then drawn up into the brain, from where it entered the network formed by the nerves and spinal cord; here further 'special animal spirits' were produced. These spirits were transmitted along the nerves to bring about sensation, movement, thought and affect.

External sensory data were thought to be received in the front part of the brain, where *sensus communis* (common sense) was housed. These data were initially stored as images or *phantasmata* in the *imaginatio*, located in the two front ventricles, and were then transferred into the *imaginativa*, situated in the central ventricle. Here the power of *estimativa*, bringing to bear the knowledge and affect already stored in the memory, re-processed the impressions before they were finally and permanently committed to the *cellula memorialis*, the site of long-term memory located in the rear ventricle.[76] As Corinne Saunders and Charles Fernyhough note, what we would now label as cognition incorporated emotional elements into rational processing via the *estimativa* faculty.⁷⁷ Additionally, the balance of the humours could affect the image-formation processes in the anterior brain; perceptions could be skewed by a preponderance of black or yellow bile, phlegm or blood within these ventricles, just as Dame Pertelote suggests to Chauntecleer in Chaucer's 'Nun's Priest's Tale'.⁷⁸

The *Pantegni* proposed that certain emotions had medical consequences. Joy and anger, if experienced in excess, caused the vital spirits to leave the heart, directing heat to the body's extremities. Fear and distress had the opposite effect; the vital spirits moved to the heart, leaving the rest of the body cold and pale.⁷⁹ These movements could be either quick or slow: joy (*gaudia*) was a slow reaction of spirits away from the heart; anger (*ira*) was fast; fear (*timor*) was a quick centripetal motion towards the heart, while distress (*tristitia*) was caused by a slow ingress of vital spirits.⁸⁰ Two further emotions, anxiety and shame, were admitted in the *Pantegni* analysis. As we shall see, English writers, in particular Chaucer, drew on an underlying knowledge of this model to depict and account for a range of the physiological effects of emotion in their writing.⁸¹

Augustine's and Aquinas's emotion models

Augustine (354–430 CE) developed the first and most influential psychological model of emotions for the early Middle Ages. This built on, but also fundamentally critiqued, the Stoic position. 'Freedom from the emotions (*apatheia*) was in ancient times the best-known Stoic characterisation of the conditions of the good life. It was also much criticised as both impossible and inhuman', notes Simo Knuuttila; somatic indications, 'prepassions', which signalled the physiological registering of affect, were held to be suppressible through the action of reason and will.⁸² In *The City of God*, Augustine made the case for emotion as divinely created and instilled into humanity. As Jesus himself had experienced and expressed emotion in his incarnation, feelings ought not be regarded solely as *perturbationes*, 'disturbances' or 'upheavals', a term Augustine derived from Cicero.⁸³ Like the Stoics, he understood emotions as distinguished by their objects (good or evil) and their temporal orientations, whether directed towards a present or a future goal. Following Cicero, Augustine identifies delight, desire, distress (or pain) and fear as the basic emotions; other feelings are subordinate to these categories. The will is crucial to Augustine's analysis, for subjects can will themselves not to want: 'For what is desire or joy but an act of will in sympathy with those things that we wish, and what is fear or grief but an act of will in disagreement with the things that we do not wish?'[84] Thus, the object of the emotion is key to its moral inflection, and the subject can turn, or convert, to desiring the good.[85] This fourfold division is somewhat reductive, producing a matrix of approach and withdrawal, present or anticipated, that leaves no room for anger and lust. Augustine identifies these later in Book XIV as the 'irascible' and 'concupiscible' emotions, located within the irrational part of the soul and constituting a separate system from the fourfold emotion categories that he had proposed earlier.[86]

As noted above, the twelfth century saw the translation of the works of Avicenna and the rediscovery of Aristotle's key philosophical writings; as these too were translated into Latin and circulated throughout the Christian west, debate about the nature of emotion was reopened. Aristotle had in no sense produced a comprehensive theory of emotion; rather, he outlined a broadly componential, psychological model within which he located feelings. Peter King summarises Aristotle's impact on emotions thinking from the mid-twelfth century onwards as melding with 'the native medieval tradition, stemming from Augustine, supplemented by medical information from the Arabic commentators ... to produce a unique and comprehensive theory of the emotions'.[87]

As understood by medieval philosophers, Aristotle's psycho-spiritual model was constituted by four elements:

the sensitive soul, which permitted movement and sensation;
the intellective soul, where thought and volition operated;
the cognitive and apprehensive potencies, which gathered information about the world;
the appetitive potencies, which allowed the individual to engage with the world.

Both the sensitive and the intellective soul contain apprehensive and appetitive potencies, yielding four distinct psychological domains. Within the intellective soul, the cognitive and apprehensive potencies operate to permit thinking and reasoning. Appetitive potency within the intellective soul is the origin of will. The cognitive potency located within the sensitive soul enables sensation and perception – incoming stimuli – while the sensitive soul's appetitive impulses are responsible for the emotions: the *passiones animae*. It is important, as a number of commentators note, not to conflate appetitive potencies, or appetite within the sensitive soul, with the modern concept of 'drives' (hunger, thirst, for sex). Appetites for Aquinas include more subtle and complex motions of attraction and repulsion, inflected both by the objects' value and the evaluative processes within the sensitive soul.[88]

The twelfth-century Cistercian theologian Isaac of Stella (c. 1100–1170) and, following him, the Franciscan Jean de la Rochelle (c. 1200–1245) further developed Augustine's distinction between the concupiscible and irascible emotions, re-integrating them into the original Augustinian four-category model. Isaac of Stella argued:

> Affect is fourfold: as for things which we love, we either rejoice as present or hope for as future, while with respect to things which we hate we are already plunged into distress or else are in fear of being plunged into distress. And so joy and hope arise from the concupiscible power, while distress and fear arise from the irascible power.[89]

Thomas Aquinas (1224/5–1274) composed a 'Treatise on the Passions', contained within the *Summa theologica*; this proved to be the most influential and capacious discussion of the emotions in medieval thought.[90] Aquinas argued for a more extensive understanding of Aristotle's two types of cognition: sensitive cognition, he maintains, can also attend to objects within the memory and the imagination, and it contains an evaluative capacity to assess the relevance of these objects to the subject's goals.[91] Intellective cognition derives abstract and universal concepts from the data processed by sensitive cognition but, importantly, these two types of cognition are both 'simultaneous and mutually interpenetrating'.[92] Aquinas systematised and identified eleven distinct passions. The six concupiscible emotions are: love and hate, desire and aversion, and delight and distress, each produced by attraction towards or repulsion from objects, depending on whether they are perceived as good or evil.[93] The threefold structure corresponds to: (i) a perception of attractiveness or unattractiveness that produces liking or dislike; (ii) a 'striving for some sort of union' with the object of attraction (or the converse, striving to get away from the repellent thing); (iii) achieving the desired union, or failing to escape the disliked object.[94]

The five irascible emotions are produced by perceived difficulties impeding the achievement or avoidance of the liked or disliked object. These are: hope and despair – the object may be gained with effort or may be avoided only with effort; and daring or confidence and fear – emotions produced when 'striving for union', if success seems possible or, conversely, aiming for avoidance and escape, where safety seems difficult to obtain; and lastly, anger, which does not possess an obvious opposite. Anger is consequently understood as a unique case: the evil feared has come upon the subject, but attempts to overcome that evil are still perceived as worthwhile. Each basic type is capable of division into a large range of different subtypes, depending on the nature of the object or the circumstances in which the passion is produced, resulting in complex feelings such as compassion, shame or dismay.[95]

Aquinas argued that the passions (that is, emotions) must be appetitive rather than cognitive, since they are elicited by external stimuli; moreover, they are accompanied by somatic change, usually ascribed to movement of the vital spirits. Thus, as John Dryden explains, 'a passion is a psychosomatic form of concern in response to an intentional object, where to the term "concern" denotes desires, aversions, attachments, and interests'.[96] The passions are also 'cognitively penetrable, and so may be influenced by (habits of) thought and belief.'[97] That is not to say, since they remain understood as passive potencies (hence *passiones*) of the sensitive appetite, that they are under our intellectual control, only that cognition can moderate and inflect emotions; reason can be applied to them.

The intellective appetite, however, characterised above as giving rise to will, has further functions for Aquinas, in generating 'affections': 'responses to and directed toward universal objects that are capable of being understood, but not perceived'.[98] The affections have no necessary somatic concomitants (thus God and his angels also experience them); the passions of love, longing, delight, hate, aversion and sorrow all have analogues in the affections. Thus, we may feel sad to hear of a distant tragedy when it is reported in the news, exciting the affection of sorrow, but when an event affects us personally – the death of someone we love, for example – weeping, pallor, loss of appetite all indicate that passion, accompanied by predictable physiological effects, has been elicited. Moreover, the affection and the passion may both be present simultaneously.[99] The distinction between concupiscible and irascible emotions is supported by the fact that the two types can interfere with one another (an object can elicit both desire and annoyance). We may be prepared to put up with a certain amount of pain or irritation (irascible emotions) in order to achieve something that we desire. While the concupiscible emotions make sense on their own terms, irascible emotions often exist in a causal relation to them: anger can give way to delight when vengeance is achieved; fear of loss results from love of a person or object.

The later thinkers Duns Scotus (c. 1265–1308) and William of Ockham (c. 1285–1349) critiqued Aquinas, arguing that emotions are not as passive as his model suggests. Rather, they are actions of the will: we can choose to love someone. Scotus took the position that the emotions were not confined to the appetitive potencies within the sensitive soul, but they were in fact a function of the appetitive faculty – including the intellective appetite – more generally; this expansion made space for a renewed foregrounding of will as assenting to, and thus facilitating, emotions. Both philosophers took issue with Aquinas's claim that the soul is distinct from its faculties and the faculties from one another. The soul, said Aquinas, manifestly is not always engaged in thinking or willing, as it would have to be if those faculties (the cognitive and affective) were intrinsic to it. Ockham argued, on the contrary, that 'it is one and the same soul that thinks, feels, wills, and perceives'.[100] Thus, as the principle of Ockham's Razor dictates, there is no need to postulate further taxonomic categories to explain the interrelations of the psychological faculties since they are all already integrated within the soul. Absolutely central to medieval theorisations of emotion, however, is the importance of the will as generating, facilitating or repressing emotion, and a consequent understanding that passions, whether concupiscent or irascible, are intrinsically linked to humans' capacity for sin.[101]

This is only a broad-brush outline of the main contemporary theories of emotion obtaining in the later medieval period. Moreover, since theorisation of this kind was the province of theologians and philosophers, who wrote in Latin and who argued and speculated about such matters within various ecclesiastical communities and, of course, in Europe's newly constituted universities, it is hard to be sure how far such systematic analyses would percolate into the understanding of vernacular writers. William Langland had in all probability benefited from university study, and his treatment of psychological faculties in *Piers Plowman* bespeaks a thorough understanding of the psychological processes predicated by Avicenna. For other, less theologically inclined writers, the Galenic model of human physiology probably sufficed. Just so, unless they have medical or psychology degrees, most writers today possess only a general notion of how the brain and body function. Consequently, they tend to share with their readers a folk-psychological understanding of such processes and mechanisms. As we shall see, certain medieval authors foreground particular understandings of the relationships between distinct psychological faculties and feelings (made strikingly clear in the case of allegory), while others are content to leave unexplained or unexplored underlying theories of emotion and physiology, in favour of an unofficial but widely accepted set of assumptions about how mind and body interact.[102] This model could be characterised as a broadly hydraulic system, 'great liquids within each person, heaving and frothing, eager to be let out', as Rosenwein describes it, powered by the circulation of the various spirits, natural, vital and animal within the blood, as outlined above.[103] Neither Galenic medical theory nor the concomitant humoral theory have cultural validity any longer; nevertheless the hydraulic and humoral systems retain their explanatory power at linguistic and folk-psychological levels: when we describe someone as 'full of bile', 'melancholic' or 'sanguine' or we account for an angry outburst as 'a rush of blood to the head' or fear as 'blood running cold', we draw upon these deeply rooted conceptual models.[104]

Affect, the body and culture

For medieval writers, then, psychology was embodied, operating across heart and brain. The 'prepassions' of the Stoics and Cicero correspond broadly to what is now labelled 'affect', 'an unconscious, pre-discursive bodily response ... the beat of the heart; the rush of blood to the face; the flow of tears from the eyes'.[105] Brian Massumi, an influential proponent of affect theory, has suggested that the gut is also a crucial sense organ: 'the immediacy of visceral perception is so radical that it ... precedes the exteroceptive sense perception ... it anticipates the sight or sound or touch perception', registering below and before incoming sensory data, primarily as an affect of intensity.[106] In affect theory, as Stephanie Trigg notes, 'the consciousness of emotion, so often mediated by language, is seen as secondary'; as in the case of Reddy's emotives, language changes and inflects the emotion triggered by the subconscious somatic processes already under way.[107] Yet, interesting as the investigation of actual neuropsychological mechanisms is – for new insights into emotion processing within the brain regularly emerge – the relevance of neurobiology to the historical and literary study of emotions has been challenged by leading historians of emotion. For, although emotion is clearly written on and experienced in living bodies, neither historians nor literary scholars – nor indeed the contemporaries of those whose emotions are described – have or had access to the biological bodies, to the sub-attentional processes eliciting the trembling and the tears that indicated affect was at work. The past emotional self must be constituted through always already mediated manifestations, via texts or other material artefacts, created in accordance with prevailing genre conventions, sculptural styles or culturally constrained gestural repertoires.[108]

In a recent book chapter, Piroska Nagy has noted how distant the understanding of 'emotion' (broadly constituted across European languages over time, from *passio*, *affectio* or 'movements of the soul', to *sentiments*, *Gefühlen*, *Aufregung*) as studied by historians is from the object of investigation by neuropsychologists and cognitive scientists.[109] She warns against the return of a kind of biological essentialism to studies of human feeling, critiquing the emergence of a 'new paradigm [that] aims at no less than the refounding of objectivity, by challenging social and cultural constructivism ... in order to propose a new objectivity standing firm on the basis of redefined human nature, in which the biological dimension would reign supreme'.[110] Over-reliance on 'the psychology thing', as Nagy calls it, risks detaching study of emotions in the past from the complex and subtle lexis that mediates them, and from their embeddedness in particular anthropological contexts, and as subject to historical change.[111] Despite the efforts made by medical humanities projects to bridge the divide in the discipline-specific understanding of emotions – whether as largely socially constituted or as irreducible biological mechanisms – there is some truth in Nagy's perception that emotion research in the humanities has been shaped by current research funding protocols which favour the big-science approach. Neuroscience confers validity: '[r]égulièrement critiquées pour leur immaturité scientifique, les sciences de l'homme et de la société trouveraient ainsi dans les progrès des sciences du cerveau et de l'esprit de quoi garantir la légitimité de leurs pratiques' (regularly criticised for their scientific immaturity, human and social sciences thus find, in the progress made in scientific research into psychology and the brain, something by which to guarantee the legitimacy of their own practices), note Wolf Feuerhahn and Rafael Mandressi.[112]

The biological and the social must be integrated if we are to reach a holistic understanding of emotion in the past, and of how, as readers, we relate to and interpret that pastness in literary and non-literary texts. Reddy has noted that not even preconscious affect, 'visceral perception', is completely detached from inflection by culture; very recent brain research shows how 'rough sketches of stimuli are rushed forward to higher processing levels, and these higher levels respond by sending signals back down the processing chain, selectively activating likely identifications, to speed recognition'.[113] Reddy continues: 'if these findings about top-down modulation of perception continue to be confirmed, it suggests, in fact, how deeply influential our learned "cultural" background can be on every act of perception'.[114] Monique Scheer makes a parallel argument, asserting that emotions are 'something people experience and something they do. We have emotions and we manifest emotions.'[115] Biological substrates and sociological contexts then are not two radically different phenomena, to be investigated by scientists and historians respectively, but rather, claims Scheer, emotions are 'more fruitfully thought of as habits emerging where bodily capacities and cultural requirements meet'.[116] Both brain and the rest of the body are fully engaged in affect processes, from the gut-clenching sensation signalling fear to the sensation of 'jumping' when shocked. But, in practice – and here Pierre Bourdieu's concept of *habitus* becomes essential to Scheer's argument – bodies are trained through social exposure to respond in particular ways without conscious cognitive engagement or attention. '[T]hese acts are not only habituated and automatically executed movements of the body, but also encompass a learned, culturally specific, and habitual distribution of attention to "inner" processes of thought, feeling, and perception.'[117] Human bodies internalise and respond to the social scripts expected in different contexts; these are affect-related responses that – at times – contain cognitive components, as indeed Aquinas argued. Emotional manifestations are both voluntary and involuntary, as Duns Scotus and William of Ockham asserted and as ongoing neuropsychological research confirms.

Scheer's conception of emotion as practice, as a kind of *habitus* in Bourdieu's sense, opens up profitable modes of thinking about emotion: as both embodied and biological, and as socio-cultural.[118] Her insight offers a framework within which to explore the ways in which emotion happens in medieval English literature, incorporating evidence drawn from accounts of the behaviour of bodies, both imagined and real, and grounded in culturally specific practices involving the consumption and interpretation of texts as narratives and their utilisation as valued material objects.

Imaginative literature and emotions

The questions that the study of emotion in medieval literature raises are different in kind from whether we can know what people 'really' felt and whether – and how and why – that might be something that changes over time. As Julie Orlemanski suggests, '[t]he persons, situations, and worlds conjured by medieval imaginative writing were not mirrors for social reality so much as instantiations of the discursive protocols that help to constitute medieval collective life.'[119] Imaginative or fictional texts (defined in contrast to the strictly historical or didactic) represent, as Laura Ashe has argued, an innovation in Middle English (and other post-1000) literature.[120] Much had changed in the years after the Conquest; England became a trilingual culture with literatures in English, French and Latin composed for and consumed by different, yet often intersecting audiences. Aristocratic men and women – and then, increasingly, gentry and bourgeois audiences – were the patrons and consumers of romance, the genre which *par excellence* allowed free play to the fictional, to characters and stories that framed human experience differently from pre-Conquest texts and which will be central to the analysis in this book: 'emotion is the very language of romance', notes Megan Moore.[121] These texts set up, as Orlemanski minimally defines fictionality, 'a semantic mode of unearnest reference', in which audiences are not required to believe (or disbelieve) the factuality of what they hear, but rather to exercise a kind of 'cognitive provisionality' in interpreting what they heard in the light of their knowledge about human behaviour, motivation and interior dispositions.[122] What is at stake then is not historical truth in the sense argued for by Niall Ferguson above, but rather how medieval authors narrated and evoked emotion in their compositions. Consequently – and concomitantly – literary texts learned to construct fictional selves that both displayed and experienced emotion and which evoked emotion in audiences. Letters (written in Latin) purported to reveal the profoundly felt feelings of their authors; *trobaritz* lyrics intimated a highly individual experience of love (whether or not this was a skilfully crafted representation of a poetic persona).[123] Similar figurations of the individual began to emerge in Middle English writings in ways that are distinct from pre-Conquest literary depictions, 'a new kind of attention paid to interiority, to individual experience and agency, and to the unknowable realities of other people's experiences'.[124]

This recent discussion of Middle English fictionality – alongside Ashe's contention that it is precisely that fictionality which allows audiences to reflect upon and develop their own interiority by gaining insight into how other people might think and feel – revisits arguments made more than forty years ago by critics such as

Lee Patterson and David Aers.[125] In response to claims that subjectivity and individuality are distinctively early modern phenomena, closely aligned with courtly cultures of 'self-fashioning', Patterson and Aers made a robust case for the concept of the individual as already well established by the end of the twelfth century.[126] New ecclesiastical and theological injunctions had reconfigured emotional behaviour for religious and laypeople alike.[127] Processes of self-scrutiny became embedded in religious and lay behaviour through larger socio-religious innovations such as the Fourth Lateran Council's injunction (1215) that effective private confession would determine eligibility to receiving the Host at Easter mass, and the thirteenth-century turn towards affective piety. C. Stephen Jaeger has demonstrated how medieval men and women were keenly aware that public – primarily courtly – identities could both be performative, in the sense of getting things done with emotions, and be staged as performances: conscious behaviours and utterances intended to elicit particular effects.[128] Also critical to the development of ideas about the interior self and the performance of identity, as we shall see, is the history of the concept of sincerity; for once the possibility emerges of a gap between what is said and done and what is thought and felt, this will complicate and expand the ways in which interpersonal relationships and individual subjectivities are narrated.[129]

Despite the strength of the 1980s' arguments for the interest of medieval authors in representing interiority, they failed to generate a critical consensus. Counter-positions emerged: that medieval characters in many genres were 'flat'; they were simply stereotypes or conventional figures such as the *Roman de la rose*'s *La Vieille* and her many descendants, that narrators made little use of psychonarration or soliloquy. Characters in medieval stories, across genres, it has been argued, behave in ways that are entirely predictable, given the available repertoire of motifs and incidents; they function simply as a collection of signs, intended to fulfil certain kinds of narrative function: to occupy the roles of hero, villain, father or love-interest. With respect to medieval German literature, Katharina Philipowski, for example, has maintained that the main purpose of literary emotion is simply to impel the plot forwards along convincing lines, to suggest a logic of motivation, cause and effect.[130]

This position has come under increasing pressure however in recent years, through the application of new kinds of theorisation. Literary historians have begun to push back against theories of fictionality that deny its existence before the early modern period. Narratological approaches foreground the particular modes in which medieval stories are constructed; Monika Fludernik and Eva von Contzen have demonstrated that medieval literature has a range of different means for expressing consciousness, including thoughts and emotions.[131] These include, on occasion, interior focalisation, but also instances of behaviour, narratorial description, audience-directed apostrophe and free indirect speech, as well as character soliloquy. While interior complexity may be only sporadically ascribed to certain characters (at least in the earlier literature), others are clearly constructed as individual subjects with unique emotional lives (and are therefore capable of using 'emotives', 'self-altering utterances', as Reddy terms them).[132]

Historical and contextual differences between the medieval and modern prompt caution in assuming that the 'emotive indicia', as Sif Rikhardsdottir has called them, encoded in medieval texts can be easily recognised, and in assuming that their affective implications can be fully grasped.[133] Relying on claims about biological continuities in affect manifestations equally has the potential to mislead. Nevertheless, taking note of these reservations need not be construed as a counsel of despair. In their introduction to a recent essay collection on emotion in medieval German Arthurian literature, Cora Dietl and her fellow-editors have suggested that medieval texts generally offer a kind of middle way between full-blown interiority and mere narrative functionality: that medieval audiences were well versed in piecing together folk-psychology, theory of mind, the logical ascription of motivation and empathetic identification with the character in different contexts.[134] The varying forms of emotional praxis exemplified in medieval imaginative texts thus offer useful rule-of-thumb guidance as to how emotion could be depicted, invoked and deployed within particular literary traditions. Indeed, modern reading of medieval emotions, like any other reading practice, must be premised on the hypothesis that readers can understand writers' meanings, even when language and social change has occurred in the intervening period. Are the emotions that the readers or audience infer as operational within the text actually encoded into it by the authors – and if so, how? Or are emotions brought to the text by the audience who are required to fill in the gaps from their own understanding of the range of human emotional experience, as suggested by Jeff Rider?[135]

Thus imaginative texts provided important feedback in shaping social identities, in teaching their audiences not only how to feel, in McNamer's terms, but also how to perform those feelings, how to be seen to feel and how to feel specifically *Middle English* feelings.[136] Audiences come to understand new emotional formations through their encounters with texts – emotion discourse regarded as dynamic and disruptive; emotions are disseminated through literature to those who have not themselves experienced events similar to those related in the narrative through elicitation of empathetic identification. 'Literature can be viewed as an intellectual somatization of felt emotions', comment Marculescu and Morand Métivier; processes of empathy, of embodiment and of incorporation into individual and group emotion repertoires result from encounters with emotion in vernacular literature.[137]

About this book

This book is not intended as an exhaustive account of medieval emotions in Middle English literature. Rather, it aims to explore four key methods for investigating how we can identify and interpret emotion in (mostly secular) Middle English texts. These different approaches allow us to interrogate how emotion is narrated, depicted or implied in medieval writing and to hypothesise how contemporary audiences may have responded to emotion episodes in literature. The first chapter begins by asking what the lexical terminology of emotion is. Identifying the words which connote emotion at work in a text is, as Barbara Rosenwein has demonstrated, a crucial preliminary move; thus the chapter traces basic emotion words inherited from Old English and the expansion of the semantic field with borrowings from Old Norse and French. It builds on Rosenwein's model to ask how far such categorisations can map the systems in operation within particular vernacular genres, and whether they capture the dynamics of change in emotion discourse. Translated texts reconfigured the ways in which medieval readers understood literary conventions, available emotion behaviours and practices, introducing new modes for representing interior processes, charting changing emotional norms and new kinds of sensibility. Taxonomies such as the seven deadly sins and related allegorical systems foreground a primary mode of vernacular analysis of emotion-related dispositions and behaviours, offering case-studies for emotion words in action.

It is primarily through bodies that medieval authors indicate that feeling is at work. Chapter 2 explores how medieval emotion is written on bodies, when characters faint, weep, laugh, change colour or fall silent. Affect theory is utilised to explore how medieval writers understood physical manifestations of emotion as both preconscious and yet bound up in complex cognitive and interactive processes, including awareness of the function of the will. The distinction between involuntary and voluntary bodily action is shown to be critical; the unwilled operates as a tell, transmitting the character's inner state to the intradiegetic audience, not only serving the aim of plot advancement, but also producing realistic effects that elicit audience empathy. The second half of the chapter investigates deliberately performed gestures produced by social actors; a case-study of emotion gesture and accompanying vocalisation in the late cycle plays follows in chapter 4.

The third chapter considers issues of performativity and performance, asking what work emotion 'gets done' within Middle English literary texts, whether as simply advancing the plot or as performing more complex tasks. Making use of Reddy's concept of the 'emotive', the chapter examines how the gap between character interiority and external display is bridged and discusses when emotion can be construed as end-oriented performance, intended to have a particular effect on its witnesses. Concepts of sincerity and pretence, public performance and ritual are investigated in detail here; the elaboration and maintenance of the courtly persona in line with social expectation and situational pressures is explored. The chapter concludes with a case-study of a highly performative and clearly gendered emotion: *danger*.

Chapter 4 examines how medieval audiences (both intra- and extradiegetic) are emotionally affected by storytelling, by the tales embedded and related within narratives and by the literary works that real-life audiences consume. Psychonarration ascribes named, identifiable feelings to listening characters within narratives; while elsewhere narrators rely on first-person utterances in which individuals name or adumbrate their own emotional states, literary emotion is more often distributed across emotion-episodes or within emotion schemas.[138] For, as McNamer's recent discussion of *Pearl* has shown, verbal works of art are expressly designed to elicit emotion, to offer consolation, closure and catharsis.[139] Audience responses within individual texts oscillate between the twin poles posited in Chaucer's storytelling competition: the apprehension of sentence and solaas.[140] Empathy and exemplarity work to entertain and to educate; joy, laughter, sorrow and fear are brought into play through narrative techniques. Recent psychological studies of emotion and communal audience reactions – emotional contagion – provide context for the particular conditions under which medieval literary texts were most often consumed, and the neurophysiological bases for empathy are explored. These suggest that audiences and readers experience 'embodied cognition', for 'the faculty that enables us to understand actions, movements, and gestures is tied to the situated ability to infer another person's emotions, intentions, aims, beliefs, expectations and states of mind'.[141] Empathetic identification is discussed in detail; the chapter foregrounds the ways in which pre-existing audience emotion scripts and their models for understanding the feelings of others can be expanded through literary encounters and argues for emergent reformulations of ideas of the self in relation to others.

The final chapter does not propose a discrete methodological approach. Rather, it draws together two major developments in the depiction of literary emotions by the beginning of the fifteenth century. It argues that towards the end of the medieval period the ways in which authors addressed literary emotion had undergone substantial change. Authors responded to the increasing interest in other humans as thinking, feeling subjects, offering enhanced access to interiority: not just emotions, but also thoughts, memories and motivations. The long-form romance (in both poetry and prose) and the advent of printing creates space for the expanded exploration of emotion through longer dialogues, more direct psychonarration and detailed somatic affective display. These works would reach wider audiences and communicate the genre's primary emotional scripts to an expanded range of social ranks; romance's close association with historical or pseudo-historical texts worked to legitimate the production of these popular works. The fifteenth century also sees the emergence of 'autofiction'; a writing-in of fictive selves as feeling subjects whose emotionality authorises the creation of texts and opens up for the audience new possibilities for their own emotional self-fashioning across diverse social and devotional settings.

Summarising the book's larger arguments, the Conclusion weighs the relative usefulness of the theoretical and methodological strategies it employs. It foregrounds the importance of various kinds of intertextual relationships for the creation and transmission of existing and innovating generic emotional norms, as successive generations of authors and audiences explore genre-related emotion schemas as effective in communicating and producing feelings. In seeking to answer the questions raised in the book about words, bodies, performativity, audiences and change, it also identifies emerging issues that the analysis has raised. Whether they work to maintain or subvert or whether they innovate and alter existing models, emotions in literature move, educate and inform English audiences about changing ways to be human across the medieval era.

Notes

1 BBC Radio 4, *Start the Week*, 12 October 2015.
2 Niall Ferguson, *Kissinger, 1923–1968: The Idealist* (New York and London: Allen Lane, 2015); Jane Smiley, *Golden Age* (London: Picador, 2015).
3 Thanks to Dr Sophie Coulombeau of Cardiff University for her transcription of *Start the Week*. For Smiley's account of the exchange, see 'History versus Historical Fiction', *The Guardian*, 15 October 2015,

www.theguardian.com/books/2015/oct/15/jane-smiley-niall-ferguson-history-versus-historical-fiction (accessed 29 August 2023).

4 Patricia Ticineto Clough and Jean Halley, *The Affective Turn: Theorizing the Social* (Durham, NC: Duke University Press, 2007).

5 Peter N. Stearns with Carol Z. Stearns, 'Emotionology: Clarifying the History of Emotions and Emotional Standards', *AHR*, 90:4 (1985), 813–36 at p. 813; Carol Z. Stearns and Peter N. Stearns, *Anger: The Struggle for Emotional Control in America's History* (Chicago: University of Chicago Press, 1986); Peter N. Stearns, *Jealousy: The Evolution of an Emotion in American History* (New York: New York University Press, 1989). See also Stearns's discussion of his work in Jan Plamper, 'The History of Emotions: An Interview with William Reddy, Barbara Rosenwein, and Peter Stearns', *History and Theory*, 49 (2010), 237–65.

6 Arlie Russell Hochschild, *The Managed Heart: Commercialization of Human Feeling* (Berkeley, CA: University of California Press, 1983); see also Jan Plamper, *The History of Emotions: An Introduction*, trans. Keith Tribe (Oxford: Oxford University Press, 2015), pp. 118–24.

7 Barbara H. Rosenwein, 'Worrying about Emotions in History', *AHR*, 107:3 (2002), 821–45; Barbara H. Rosenwein, *Emotional Communities in the Early Middle Ages* (Ithaca, NY, and London: Cornell University Press, 2006); Barbara H. Rosenwein, *Generations of Feeling: A History of Emotions, 600–1700* (Cambridge: Cambridge University Press, 2015); Gerd Althoff, 'Empörung, Tränen, Zerknirschung: "Emotionen" in der öffentlichen Kommunikation des Mittelalters', *Frühmittelalterliche Studien*, 30 (1996), 60–79; Gerd Althoff, '*Ira regis*: Prolegomena to a History of Royal Anger', in Barbara Rosenwein (ed.), *Anger's Past: The Social Uses of an Emotion in the Middle Ages* (Ithaca, NY, and London: Cornell University Press, 1998), pp. 59–74; Gerd Althoff, 'Tränen und Freude: Was interessiert Mittelalter-Historiker an Emotionen', *Frühmittelalterliche Studien*, 40 (2006), 1–11; Gerd Althoff, *Die Macht der Rituale. Symbolik und Herrschaft im Mittelalter* (Darmstadt: Primus Verlag, 2003); and Gerd Althoff (ed.), *Formen und Funktionen öffentlicher Kommunikation im Mittelalter* (Stuttgart: Jan Thorbecke Verlag, 2001); Damien Boquet and Piroska Nagy, *Sensible Moyen Âge: une histoire des émotions dans l'Occident médiéval* (Paris: Seuil, 2015), trans. Robert Shaw as *Medieval Sensibilities: A History of Emotions in the Middle Ages* (London: Polity Press, 2018); Piroska Nagy and Damien Boquet (eds), *Le sujet des émotions au Moyen Âge* (Paris:

Beauchesne, 2009); William M. Reddy, *The Navigation of Feeling: A Framework for the History of Emotions* (Cambridge: Cambridge University Press, 2001); William M. Reddy, *The Making of Romantic Love: Longing and Sexuality in Europe, South Asia, and Japan, 900–1200 CE* (Chicago and London: University of Chicago Press, 2012); Ute Frevert, *Emotions in History: Lost and Found*, The Natalie Zemon Davis Annual Lectures (Budapest: Central European University Press, 2011); Monique Scheer, 'Are Emotions a Kind of Practice (and Is That What Makes Them Have a History)? A Bourdieuian Approach to Understanding Emotion', *History and Theory*, 51 (2012), 193–220, and Plamper, *The History of Emotions*.

8 This is not to suggest that the large-scale emotions projects have ignored literary texts entirely; see the invaluable studies from Andrew Lynch, Stephanie Trigg, Paul Megna and Stephanie Downes, working in the Australian Research Council Centre for Excellence for the Study of the History of Emotions in Australia.

9 Beverley Fehr and James A. Russell, 'Concept of Emotion Viewed from a Prototype Perspective', *Journal of Experimental Psychology: General*, 113:3 (1984), 464–86 at p. 464.

10 Thomas Dixon, *From Passions to Emotions: The Creation of a Secular Category* (Cambridge: Cambridge University Press, 2003).

11 Elena Carrera, 'Introduction', in Elena Carrera (ed.), *Emotions and Health, 1200–1700* (Turnhout: Brill, 2014), pp. 1–19 at p. 3.

12 Plamper, *The History of Emotions*, p. 10.

13 A useful overview of these developments is given in Frank Brandsma, Carolyne Larrington and Corinne Saunders, 'Introduction', in Frank Brandsma, Carolyne Larrington and Corinne Saunders (eds), *Emotions in Medieval Arthurian Literature: Body, Mind, Voice* (Cambridge: D. S. Brewer, 2015), pp. 1–10; see also Plamper, *The History of Emotions*, pp. 17–25.

14 William James, 'What is an Emotion?', *Mind*, 9 (1884), 188–205 at p. 189; see Plamper, *The History of Emotions*, pp. 174–8.

15 James, 'What is an Emotion?', p. 190.

16 Antonio R. Damasio, *Descartes' Error: Emotion, Reason, and the Human Brain* (New York: G. P. Putnam, 1994); see also Joseph LeDoux, *The Emotional Brain: The Mysterious Underpinnings of Emotional Life* (New York: Simon and Schuster, 1996); David M. Eagleman, *Incognito: The Secret Lives of the Brain* (Edinburgh and New York: Canongate, 2011). William Reddy has criticised the ways in which western-centric brain models have become naturalised in these popularisations; see Daniel M. Gross, *The Secret History of*

Emotion: From Aristotle's Rhetoric to Modern Brain Science (Chicago: University of Chicago Press, 2006), cited by Reddy in Nicole Eustace, Eugenia Lean, Julie Livingston, Jan Plamper, William M. Reddy and Barbara H. Rosenwein, 'AHR Conversation: The History of Emotion', *AHR*, 117:5 (2012), 1487–1531.

17 See Keith Oatley and Jennifer Jenkins, *Understanding Emotions* (Oxford: Blackwell, 1996); Keith Oatley, *Best Laid Schemes: The Psychology of Emotions* (Cambridge: Cambridge University Press, 1992); Nico Frijda, *The Emotions* (Cambridge: Cambridge University Press, 1986) and Nico Frijda, *The Laws of Emotion* (Mahwah, NJ: Lawrence Erlbaum, 2007). For a summary of componential model theory and alternative hypotheses, see Carolyne Larrington, 'The Psychology of Emotion and Study of the Medieval Period', *Early Medieval Europe*, 10:2 (2001), 251–6.

18 Klaus R. Scherer and Heiner Ellgring, 'Are Facial Expressions of Emotion Produced by Categorical Affect Programs or Dynamically Driven by Appraisal?' *Emotion*, 7:1 (2007), 113–30 at p. 115.

19 See for example, Paul Ekman, *Emotions Revealed* (New York: Times Books, 2003); Carroll Izard, 'Basic Emotions, Relations among Emotions, and Emotion–Cognition Relations', *Psychological Review*, 99 (1992), 561–5.

20 Scherer and Ellgring, 'Are Facial Emotions', p. 115.

21 See for example, Catherine Lutz and Geoffrey M. White, 'The Anthropology of Emotions', *Annual Review of Anthropology*, 15 (1986), 405–36.

22 Martha Nussbaum, *Upheavals of Thought: The Intelligence of Emotions* (Cambridge: Cambridge University Press, 2001), p. 3. Cf. Sara Ahmed, *The Cultural Politics of Emotion*, 2nd edition (Edinburgh: Edinburgh University Press, 2015).

23 Nussbaum, *Upheavals*, p. 4.

24 Matthew Ratcliffe, *Feelings of Being: Phenomenology, Psychiatry and the Sense of Reality* (Oxford: Oxford University Press, 2008); Peter Goldie, *The Emotions: A Philosophical Exploration* (Oxford: Clarendon Press, 2000); Jenefer Robinson, *Deeper than Reason: Emotion and its Role in Literature, Music, and Art* (Oxford: Clarendon Press, 2005); Simo Knuuttila, *Emotions in Ancient and Medieval Philosophy* (Oxford: Clarendon Press, 2004); Robert C. Solomon, *The Passions. Emotions and the Meaning of Life* (Indianapolis, IN: Hackett, 1993).

25 See for example, LeDoux, *The Emotional Brain*.

26 Notoriously, Vittorio Gallese, for example in Vittorio Gallese and Alvin Goldman, 'Mirror Neurons and the Simulation Theory of

Mind-Reading', *Trends in Cognitive Science*, 2:12 (1998), 493–501; see also Giacomo Rizzolati and Maddalena Fabbri-Destro, 'The Mirror System and its Role in Social Cognition', *Current Opinion in Neurobiology*, 18:2 (2008), 179–84; Guillemette Bolens, *The Style of Gestures: Embodiment and Cognition in Literary Narrative* (Baltimore, MD: Johns Hopkins University Press, 2012); Jean Decety and Jennifer A. Stevens, 'Action Representation and its Role in Social Interaction', in Keith D. Markman, William M. P. Klein and Julie A. Suhr (eds), *Handbook of Imagination and Mental Simulation* (New York: Taylor and Francis, 2009), pp. 3–20.

27 Piroska Nagy, 'The Power of Medieval Emotions and Change: From Theory to Some Unexpected Uses of Spiritual Texts', in Per Förnegård, Erika Kihlman, Mia Åkestam and Gunnel Engwall (eds), *Tears, Sighs and Laughter: Expressions of Emotions in the Middle Ages*, Kungliga Vitterhets Historie och Antikvitets Akademien Konferenser 92 (Stockholm: KVHAA, 2017), pp. 13–39, in particular pp. 19–21. See further discussion at Introduction, pp. 25–6.

28 See for example Keith Oatley, 'A Taxonomy of the Emotions of Literary Response and a Theory of Identification in Fictional Narrative', *Poetics*, 23 (1994), 53–74; lucidly summarised in Keith Oatley and Maja Djikic, 'Psychology of Narrative', *Review of General Psychology*, special issue 'Psychology of Narrative Art' (2017), 161–8, http://dx.doi.org/10.1037/gpr0000113 (accessed 29 August 2023); David S. Miall and Don Kuiken, 'A Feeling for Fiction: Becoming What we Behold', *Poetics*, 30 (2002), 221–4; Ed S.-H. Tan, 'Film-Induced Affect as a Witness Emotion', *Poetics*, 23 (1994), 7–32; Brian Parkinson, 'How Social is the Social Psychology of Emotion?', *British Journal of Social Psychology*, 50 (2011), 405–13.

29 Johan Huizinga, *The Waning of the Middle Ages: A Study of the Forms of Life, Thought and Art in France and the Netherlands in the XIVth and XVth Centuries*, trans. F. J. Hopman (London: Penguin, 2001), p. 9. Compare Norbert Elias, *The Civilizing Process*, 2 vols in 1: *The History of Manners and State Formation and Civilisation*, trans. Edmund Jephcott (Oxford: Blackwell, 1994), and the Stearns' rather similar characterisation of pre-modern society as lacking 'general emotional control' (*Anger*, pp. 21–3), as discussed by Barbara Rosenwein, in 'Worrying about Emotions', pp. 825–6.

30 Stuart Airlie, 'The History of Emotions and Emotional History', *Early Medieval Europe*, 10:2 (2001), 235–41 at p. 236.

31 Ibid., p. 241.

32 Rosenwein, 'Worrying about Emotions'.

33 Ibid., p. 827.
34 Ibid., p. 813; Rosenwein, *Emotional Communities*.
35 Rosenwein, *Emotional Communities*, p. 2.
36 Rosenwein, *Generations of Feeling*, p. 3.
37 Rosenwein, *Emotional Communities*, p. 25.
38 Ibid., pp. 24–5. See Brian Stock, *The Implications of Literacy: Written Language and Models of Interpretation in the Eleventh and Twelfth Centuries* (Princeton, NJ: Princeton University Press, 1983), p. 90 for a minimal definition, and Brian Stock, *Listening to the Text: The Uses of the Past* (Baltimore, MD, and London: Johns Hopkins University Press, 1990), p. 23. See also Sif Rikhardsdottir, *Medieval Translations and Cultural Discourse: The Movement of Texts in England, France and Scandinavia* (Cambridge: D. S. Brewer, 2012), p. 12, and the discussion in Chapter 5 below.
39 For more detailed critique of Rosenwein's conflation of genre with conventionality, see Chapter 1.
40 Rosenwein, *Emotional Communities*, p. 27.
41 Ibid., p. 195.
42 Andreea Marculescu and Charles-Louis Morand Métivier, 'Introduction', in Andreea Marculescu and Charles-Louis Morand Métivier (eds), *Affective and Emotional Economies in Medieval and Early Modern Europe* (New York: Palgrave Macmillan, 2018), pp. 1–16 at pp. 2–3.
43 'Emotional Schema', in Norbert M. Seel, *Encyclopedia of the Sciences of Learning*, ed. Norbert M. Seel (2012), https://doi.org/10.1007/978-1-4419-1428-6_361.
44 See Silvan S. Tomkins, 'Script Theory', in E. Virginia Demos (ed.), *Exploring Affect: Selected Writings of Silvan S. Tomkins*, Studies in Emotion and Social Interaction (Cambridge: Cambridge University Press, 1995), pp. 295–415. The acquisition of emotion scripts is an important subfield of developmental psychology; see Sherri C. Widen and James A. Russell, 'Young Children's Understanding of Other's Emotions', in Michael Lewis, Jeannette M. Haviland-Jones and Lisa Feldman Barrett (eds), *Handbook of Emotions*, 3rd edn (New York and London: Guilford Press, 2008), pp. 348–63. For a fuller discussion of the emotion script as a discrete psychological concept, see Paula M. Niedenthal, 'Emotion Concepts', in Lewis, Haviland-Jones and Barrett (eds), *Handbook of Emotions*, pp. 587–600, especially pp. 592–3.
45 Reddy, *Navigation*, p. 128.
46 Ibid., p. 100.

47 Reddy, *The Making of Romantic Love*, p. 8.
48 Ibid., pp. 115; 122.
49 Sarah McNamer, *Affective Meditation and the Invention of Medieval Compassion* (Philadelphia, PA: University of Pennsylvania Press, 2010), p. 2.
50 Reddy, *The Making of Romantic Love*.
51 Ibid., p. 6.
52 Ibid., p. 44.
53 Ibid., pp. 108, p. 206.
54 Eve Kosofsky Sedgwick, *Touching Feeling: Affect, Pedagogy, Performativity* (Durham, NC: Duke University Press, 2003), pp. 61–2; Reddy, *The Making of Romantic Love*, pp. 37–8.
55 See Sarah Kay, *Subjectivity in Troubadour Poetry* (Cambridge: Cambridge University Press, 1990); Simon Gaunt, 'Marginal Men, Marcabru and Orthodoxy: The Early Troubadours and Adultery', *Medium Ævum*, 59 (1990), 55–72, and *Gender and Genre in Medieval French Literature* (Cambridge: Cambridge University Press, 1995), and the useful review article by E. Jane Burns, 'Courtly Love: Who Needs It? Recent Feminist Work in the Medieval French Tradition', *Signs*, 27:1 (2001), 23–57.
56 Reddy, *The Making of Romantic Love*, p. 108.
57 Ruth Mazo Karras rightly notes Reddy's assumption that Duke William IX of Aquitaine 'invented' the *trobaritz* lyric, overlooking its likely relationship with Hispano-Arabic models, as argued for by María Rosa Menocal in *The Arabic Role in Medieval Literary History* (Philadelphia, PA: University of Pennsylvania Press, 1987); Peter Dronke also proposes that the lyrics take inspiration from a wide variety of earlier poems in *Medieval Latin and the Rise of European Love-Lyric*, 2nd edn (Oxford: Clarendon Press, 1999); Ruth Mazo Karras, rev. of Reddy, *The Making of Romantic Love*, *English Historical Review*, 130 (August 2015), 958–60.
58 Peggy McCracken, review of Reddy, *The Making of Romantic Love*, *Journal of Asian Studies*, 72 (2013), 681–2 at p. 682.
59 Rosenwein, *Generations of Feeling*, p. 137.
60 Ibid., p. 141.
61 These issues are discussed more fully in Chapter 1.
62 Boquet and Nagy, *Sensible Moyen Âge*, and in *Medieval Sensibilities*; see also Nagy and Boquet (eds), *Le sujet des émotions au Moyen Âge* and the special journal issue, edited by Boquet and Nagy with Laurence Moulinier-Brogi, 'La chair des émotions', *Médiévales*, 61 (autumn 2011).

63 Damien Boquet and Piroska Nagy, 'Les émotions au Moyen Âge, carnet d'EMMA', 'Historical Emotions, Historians' Emotions', https://emma.hypotheses.org/1213#_ftn4 (22) (accessed 29 August 2023).
64 Ibid.
65 Ibid.
66 Althoff, 'Empörung, Tränen, Zerknirschung', p. 72; these ideas are further elaborated in Althoff, *Die Macht der Rituale*.
67 Althoff, '*Ira regis*'.
68 Ibid., p. 60.
69 Differing theorisations of emotion in medieval German secular literature are advanced by such scholars as Katharina Philipowski, Jutta Eming, Rüdiger Schnell, and the editors of the recent essay collection Cora Dietl, Christoph Schanze, Friedrich Wolfzettel and Lena Zudrell (eds), *Emotion und Handlung im Artusroman*, Schriften der Internationalen Artusgesellschaft: Deutsch-österreichische Sektion 13 (Berlin: De Gruyter, 2017) are addressed at length in Chapter 3.
70 'The Pardoner's Prologue and Tale', in Larry D. Benson (ed.), *The Canterbury Tales*, in Larry D. Benson (gen. ed.), *The Riverside Chaucer* (Oxford: Oxford University Press, 2008), pp. 193–202. All further quotations from Chaucer are from this edition.
71 Peter King, 'Emotions in Medieval Thought', in Peter Goldie (ed.), *The Oxford Handbook of Philosophy of Emotion* (Oxford: Oxford University Press, 2009), p. 167.
72 Julie Orlemanski, 'Literary Genre, Medieval Studies, and the Prosthesis of Disability', *Textual Practice*, 30:7 (2016), 1253–72, notes (pp. 1255–6) that medieval norms of the body 'tended to form a heterogeneous set of sometimes conflicting standards', because of the centrality of flux in the Galenic humoral model.
73 See Nancy J. Siraisi, *Medieval and Early Renaissance Medicine: An Introduction to Knowledge and Practice* (Chicago: University of Chicago Press, 1990), pp. 100–11.
74 Ibid., pp. 111–12.
75 Knuuttila, *Emotions*, pp. 212–14.
76 For a succinct account of medieval models of psychology, see Corinne Saunders and Charles Fernyhough, 'The Medieval Mind', *The Psychologist*, 29 (November 2016), 880–3, https://thepsychologist.bps.org.uk/volume-29/november-2016/looking-back-medieval-mind# (accessed 2 September 2023).
77 Ibid. Knuuttila writes, 'emotions have cognitive causes, and they involve feelings, behavioral suggestions, and bodily affections'. *Emotion*, p. 225.

42 Approaches to emotion

78 Chaucer, 'The Nun's Priest's Prologue and Tale', in Benson (ed.), *The Canterbury Tales*, in Benson (gen. ed.), *The Riverside Chaucer*, pp. 252–61, lines 2923–39.
79 Knuuttila, *Emotion*, pp. 214–16.
80 This model offers interesting comparisons with Brian Massumi's arguments about 'visceral perception' (discussed later in the Introduction) as primarily registering intensity of affect in *Parables of the Virtual: Movement, Affect, Sensation* (Durham, NC, and London: Duke University Press, 2002).
81 See Lucie Kaempfer, 'Drinking Sorrow and Bathing in Bliss: Liquid Emotions in Chaucer', *Open Library of Humanities*, 4:1 (2018), 1–24, https://doi.org/10.16995/olh.227. See also the discussion of Troilus's swoon in Chapter 2.
82 On ancient and medieval theories of emotion *in extenso* see Knuuttila, *Emotions*. Rosenwein discusses Cicero and Augustine, with a particular focus on their emotion lexis, in *Generations of Feeling*, pp. 16–34; quotation from Knuuttila, *Emotions*, p. 68.
83 Augustine, *The City of God against the Pagans*, ed. Jeffrey Henderson, trans. various, 7 vols, Loeb Classical Library (Cambridge, MA: Harvard University Press, and London: Heinemann, 1957), vol. II, Books IV and V, pp. 1–277; vol. IV, Book XIV, pp. 257–407, www.newadvent.org/fathers/1201.htm. See generally King, 'Emotions', for a useful overview of the arguments made by Augustine, Aquinas and other key medieval philosophers. On Jesus's tears as signifying his humanity, see Piroska Nagy, 'Les larmes du Christ dans l'exégèse médiéval. Du bon usage de la souffrance', *Médiévales*, 27 (1994), 37–50.
84 Augustine, *The City of God against the Pagans*, vol. I, Book XIV, ch. 6, pp. 284–5.
85 Rosenwein, *Generations of Feelings*, pp. 30–1.
86 Augustine, *The City of God against the Pagans*, vol. IV, Book XIV, ch. 19, pp. 364–7.
87 King, 'Emotions', p. 174.
88 John Dryden, 'Passions, Affections, and Emotions: Methodological Difficulties in Reconstructing Aquinas's Philosophical Psychology', *Literature Compass*, 13:6 (2016), 343–50 at p. 345.
89 Knuuttila, *Emotions*, p. 228.
90 See Rosenwein's account of Aquinas's model in *Generations of Feeling*, pp. 144–68.
91 Dryden, 'Passions, Affections, and Emotions', p. 345.
92 Nicholas Lombardo, *The Logic of Desire: Aquinas on Emotion* (Washington, DC: Catholic University of America Press, 2011), p. 22.

Introduction 43

93 The distinction between emotions of approach and emotions of withdrawal is common in modern analyses of biological emotion systems. See, for example, Patrick Colm Hogan, *Affective Narratology: The Emotional Structure of Stories* (Lincoln, NE: University of Nebraska Press, 2011), p. 6.
94 Dryden, 'Passions, Affections, and Emotions', p. 346.
95 King, 'Emotions', p. 176; Dryden, 'Passions, Affections, and Emotions', p. 346.
96 Dryden, 'Passions, Affections, and Emotions', p. 345.
97 King, 'Emotions', p. 180.
98 Dryden, 'Passions, Affections, and Emotions', p. 347.
99 Dryden discusses whether our modern definitions of 'emotions' can map onto Aquinas's 'passions' *and* 'affections', arguing for the passions as 'prototypical emotions', and affections as fuzzier concepts, manifesting as borderline cases within the modern emotion system. Ibid.
100 King, 'Emotions', p. 181.
101 See Chapter 1 for vernacular taxonomies of the sins and their relationship to emotion.
102 Mary C. Flannery, 'Personification and Embodied Emotion', *Literature Compass*, 13:6 (2016), 351–6.
103 Rosenwein, 'Worrying about Emotions', p. 834. Compare Leslie Lockett, *Anglo-Saxon Psychologies in the Vernacular and Latin Traditions* (Toronto: University of Toronto Press, 2011) for a thoroughgoing account of hydraulic emotion systems in early English culture.
104 Zoltán Kövecses, building on earlier work by George Lakoff, has demonstrated that anger is regarded as a hot liquid contained under pressure within the body; fear and sorrow are also conceptualised as liquids in containers. See Zoltán Kövecses, *Metaphor and Emotion: Language, Culture, and Body in Human Feeling*, Studies in Emotion and Social Interaction (Cambridge: Cambridge University Press, 2000), pp. 20–44, developing work in Zoltán Kövecses, *Emotion Concepts* (New York: Springer, 1990).
105 Stephanie Trigg, 'Introduction: Emotional Histories – Beyond the Personalization of the Past and the Abstraction of Affect Theory', *Exemplaria*, 26:1 (2014), 3–15 at pp. 5–6.
106 Massumi, *Parables of the Virtual*, p. 60.
107 Trigg, 'Introduction', p. 6.
108 See Chapter 2 for further discussion of affect.
109 Nagy, 'The Power', pp. 19–21. Compare Plamper, *The History of Emotions*, p. 10.

110 Nagy, 'The Power', p. 21, following Wolf Feuerhahn and Rafael Mandressi, 'Introduction: les "neurosciences sociales": historicité d'un programme', *Revue d'histoire des sciences humaines*, 25:2 (2011), 3–12 at p. 9.
111 Nagy, 'The Power', p. 21.
112 See the work done by Saunders and Fernyhough, 'The Medieval Mind', and the discussion in Feuerhahn and Mandressi, 'Introduction'; citation here from p. 3. Feuerhahn and Mandressi identify the 'cognitive' or 'neuronal' turn in life-sciences as reacting against (largely French) post-modernist theories that focus on discourse as constituting reality. Translations are my own unless otherwise stated.
113 Reddy in Eustace et al., '*AHR* Conversation'.
114 Ibid.; see also Reddy, 'Courts and Pleasure: The Neuroscience of Pleasure and the Pursuit of Favour in Twelfth-Century Courts', in Naama Cohen-Hanegbi and Piroska Nagy (eds), *Pleasure in the Middle Ages,* International Medieval Research 24 (Turnhout: Brepols, 2018), pp. 131–64, and compare Robinson, *Deeper than Reason*, p. 97: 'emotions are *processes*, in which a rough-and-ready affective appraisal causes physiological responses, motor changes, action tendencies, changes in facial and vocal expression, and so on, succeeded by cognitive monitoring'.
115 Scheer, 'Are Emotions a Kind of Practice', p. 195.
116 Ibid., pp. 201–2.
117 Ibid., p. 200.
118 Cf. also Trigg, 'Introduction', on Scheer's arguments. Trigg opens up the question of how the emotion that we ourselves as scholars bring to our readings of the past can be situated, just as Boquet (above, p. 15) asserts that the historian should aim to mediate past feelings alongside our feelings about that past.
119 Orlemanski, 'Literary Genre', p. 1254.
120 Laura Ashe, 'Introduction', in Laura Ashe (ed.), *Early Fiction in England: From Geoffrey of Monmouth to Chaucer* (London: Penguin, 2015), pp. xiii–xxvi. See also *in extenso* the other articles in the special issue of *New Literary History*, 51:1 (2020), and now also Laura Ashe, '"For love and for lovers": the origins of romance', in Roberta L. Krueger (ed.), *The New Cambridge Companion to Medieval Romance* (Cambridge: Cambridge University Press, 2023), pp. 14–28.
121 Romance has been regarded as notoriously hard to define as a genre, but Finlayson's identification of chivalric ambience and heroic exploits as key motifs is among the more useful definitions. John Finlayson, 'Definitions of Middle English Romance', in Stephen

H. A. Shepherd (ed.), *Middle English Romances* (New York: Norton, 1995), pp. 428–56 at pp. 431–2; Megan Moore, 'Emotions as the Language of Romance', in Krueger (ed.), *The New Cambridge Companion to Medieval Romance*, pp. 150–66 at p. 150.

122 Julie Orlemanski, 'Who Has Fiction? Modernity, Fictionality and the Middle Ages', *New Literary History*, 51:1 (Winter 2020), 145–70 at pp. 147 and 150.

123 See, for example, the letters discussed in C. Stephen Jaeger, *Ennobling Love: In Search of a Lost Sensibility* (Philadelphia, PA: University of Pennsylvania Press, 2010), pp. 117–50; Kay, *Subjectivity in Troubadour Poetry*.

124 Ashe, 'Introduction', p. xiv.

125 Lee Patterson, 'On the Margin, Post-Modernism, Ironic History and Medieval Studies', *Speculum*, 65 (1990), 87–108; David Aers, 'A Whisper in the Ears of Early Modernists; or, Reflections on Literary Critics Writing the "History of the Subject"', in David Aers (ed.), *Essays on English Communities, Identities and Writing* (Detroit, MI: Wayne State University Press, 1992), pp. 177–203.

126 Such arguments were epitomised by Stephen Greenblatt, *Renaissance Self-Fashioning: From More to Shakespeare* (Chicago: University of Chicago Press, 1980); other classic accounts of the emergence of the 'self' in the twelfth century are Colin Morris, *The Discovery of the Individual: 1050–1200* (Toronto and London: University of Toronto Press, 1987) and John F. Benton, *Self and Society in Medieval France: The Memoirs of Abbot Guibert of Nogent* (Toronto and London: University of Toronto Press, in association with the Medieval Academy of America, 1984).

127 Ashe implies that the development of fiction is dependent upon a turn to vernacular and secular compositions, intended to instruct and entertain the nobility; Ashe, 'Introduction', pp. xxi–xxv, and Ashe, '"For love and for lovers"', p. 16, with particular reference to romance. Orlemanski, 'Who Has Fiction?', p. 153, resists any historical account that equates fiction with secularisation. Particularly with regard to aristocratic love, as Graham Williams, *Sincerity in Medieval English Language and Literature* (London: Palgrave Macmillan, 2018), p. 140, notes, before the Conquest the emotion of *love* had primarily referred to love of God. The clerics who composed the Insular French and Middle English romances consumed by the nobility were also authors and performers of the saints' lives in which powerful emotions – love, fear, anger – were staged; these works were critical to the development of the romance genre in both languages. See also

Jocelyn Wogan-Browne, *Saints' Lives and Women's Literary Culture, 1150–1300: Virginity and its Authorizations* (Oxford: Oxford University Press, 2001), pp. 91–122.
128 C. Stephen Jaeger, *The Origins of Courtliness: Civilizing Trends and the Origins of Courtly Ideals, 939–1210* (Pittsburgh, PA: University of Pennsylvania Press, 1985).
129 Williams's *Sincerity* has important implications for the development of notions of interiority.
130 Katharina Philipowski, 'Die Textualität von Gesten: Ein kleiner Beitrag zur Interdisziplinaritätsdebatte', *Journal of English and Germanic Philology*, 101 (2002), 461–77, and 'Das Gelächter der Cunnewäre', *Zeitschrift für Germanistik*, new series, 13 (2003), 9–25.
131 Monika Fludernik, 'Through a Glass Darkly: Or, the Emergence of Mind in Medieval Narrative', in David Herman (ed.), *Emergence of Mind: Representations of Consciousness in Narrative Discourse in English* (Lincoln, NE: University of Nebraska Press, 2011), pp. 69–100; Eva von Contzen, 'Why We Need a Medieval Narratology: A Manifesto', *Diegesis*, 3:2 (2014), 1–21.
132 Reddy, *Navigation*, p. 100.
133 Sif Rikhardsdottir, 'Medieval Emotionality: The *Feeling* Subject in Medieval Literature', *Comparative Literature*, 69:1 (2017), 74–90 at p. 75.
134 Cora Dietl et al., 'Vorwort der Herausgeber', in Dietl et al. (eds), *Emotion und Handlung im Artusroman*, pp. ix–xx, especially p. xi.
135 Jeff Rider, 'Positive Emotions in the Arthurian *lais* of Marie de France', *Journal of International Arthurian Studies*, 4:1 (2016), 58–68.
136 McNamer, *Affective Meditation*, p. 2; and Sarah McNamer, 'Feeling', in Paul Strohm (ed.), *Middle English*, Oxford Twenty-First Century Approaches to Literature (Oxford: Oxford University Press, 2007), pp. 241–57.
137 Marculescu and Morand Métivier, 'Introduction', p. 6.
138 Jeff Rider notes while lexical lists are useful for constructing taxonomies, they lack the nuance, the 'thick', qualitative detail that emotion narratives provide. Interrogating narratives for context is 'significantly more engaging, richer, and more useful' ('Positive Emotions', p. 68; see also p. 60).
139 Sarah McNamer, 'The Literariness of Literature and the History of Emotions', *PMLA*, 130:5 (2015), 1433–42.
140 See Colm Hogan, *Affective Narratology*, p. 103, on the cross-cultural finding that 'there are two primary purposes of verbal art ... one is

emotional; the other is didactic'. Literary works, however, do not fall into an either/or categorization; while the *story* may be entertaining on a number of levels, the theme is 'the idea communicated by works'.

141 Bolens, *The Style of Gestures*, p. 40; see also Decety and Stevens, 'Action Representation'.

1

Words, taxonomies and translations

'What were the consequences, for instance, of having *Middle English* feelings, as distinct from Anglo-Norman, Welsh, French, or Latin ones?' asks Sarah McNamer.[1] By definition, Middle English feelings must be distinct from Old French feelings, as regards the lexis used to signify them. Middle English is indeed rich in emotion words, both surviving from Old English and imported from Insular and Central French and Old Norse. How, having arrived at some satisfactory definition of emotion (as discussed in the Introduction), do we identify words pertaining to emotion? 'Denn Emotionen in Dichtungen "existieren" nur in und durch Worte' (for emotions in poetry 'exist' only in and through words), as Rüdiger Schnell remarks.[2] Barbara Rosenwein pioneered one important methodology in *Emotional Communities* and *Generations of Feeling*, assembling word lists in both Latin and vernacular languages, but the relationship between lists compiled in Latin, their vernacular counterparts and considerations of genre and register is more complicated than Rosenwein admits.[3] This chapter will focus on certain individual words and word clusters, networks and taxonomies to show how different methods of analysing lexis can illuminate the choices available to writers for directly narrating and expressing emotion in Middle English literature. It also considers what can be learned about emotion words and styles from a sample of the translations made into Middle English from Insular or Central French, to see how far Middle English emotions can indeed be considered distinctive in relation to their antecedents in earlier sources. Finally, it analyses the principal frameworks within which vernacular emotions are categorised and exemplified, in particular in the treatment of the seven deadly sins.

The lexis of emotion

Survival from Old English

Old English has a rich and varied lexis for emotion words; a good number of these have survived into modern English, although sometimes, as with OE *dream* (joy) and *fær* (sudden occurrence, which became Mod. Eng. *fear*), their meanings have radically changed.[4] The alliterative nature of Old English poetry and the importation of its alliterative and rhythmic techniques into Old English prose style resulted in a proliferation of synonymous nouns, and related adjectives, adverbs and verbs. In particular, the aesthetic demands of rhythm in late Old English prose writers such as Ælfric and Wulfstan produced doublets or pairs of words in the form of alliterating and non-alliterating collocations, a linguistic habit which continues into Middle English.

Bliss, wrap, forhtnes/forhtung (fear), *wlætta* (disgust), *sorg* (sorrow) are the most frequent Old English nominal forms associated with the so-called 'basic emotions': happiness, anger, fear, disgust and sadness are considered here. Surprise (*wundor*) is sometimes admitted to this list too.[5] However, surprise is no longer regularly considered to be a basic emotion; it has a strong cognitive component and tends to be very brief in duration, as against amazement or, indeed, wonder.[6] According to the University of Glasgow Thesaurus of Old English, *bliss* has sixteen synonyms, among which are *bliþnes, dream, eadwela, fægennes, glædnes, liss, reotu, gesælignes* and *wynsummung*.[7] These are not equally attested in nominal form; *wynsum* (adj.) (Mod. Eng. *winsome*) is more frequent than its corresponding noun. Nevertheless, *blitheness* and *fain* (now archaic) have survived into Modern English with specialised meanings, while *dream* has undergone semantic change, borrowing its meaning, though not its spelling, from Old Norse *draumr* (dream). The meaning of *sælig* has changed from 'blessed' via 'helpless' and 'innocent' to 'foolish, silly'.[8] *Wrap*'s eight synonyms for the sense 'anger' include *grama* (Middle English *greme*, from the Old Norse cognate is discussed below), a number of words such as *gebelg*, whose root relates to the idea of being swollen with rage, and *yrnes*, cognate with Latin *ira* (Mod. Eng. *ire*).⁹ *Forhtung* (fear) has a good number (15) of synonyms, the chief among them being *egelegesa* (Mod. Eng. *awe*); *wlætta* yields no synonyms in its nominal form. *Sorg* in the sense of sadness, as might be expected, has a large number (22) of synonyms, including *unbliss*, *sarignes*, *dreorignes*, *caru* and compound words formed from the also-attested simplexes *grorn* and *gnorn*. *Sarignes*, *dreorignes* and *caru* yield modern English *sorryness*, *dreariness* and *care*.¹⁰ *Wundor* (in the sense of 'amazement') has five synonyms, including *wundrung* and *færstyltnes*, glossing Latin *stupor* and found only in a Lindisfarne Gospel gloss.

Only some of these words would survive into Middle English. Michiko Ogura has explored the hypothesis that their survival may correlate with high alliterative frequency, but her results are not conclusive. The Old English survivors and the newly borrowed words from Insular and Central French remap the domain of emotion in Middle English through semantic narrowing and specialisation.¹¹ Ogura demonstrates the additions to, and supercessions of, the Old English emotion lexis by comparing the terminology in the Old English prose translation of Boethius's *De consolatione philosophiæ*, the very much shorter Old English *Metres of Boethius* and Chaucer's translation of the work from the late fourteenth century.¹² Chaucer's version contains new fifty-four emotion words, ranging from *agreable* to *vicious* (Ogura defines 'emotion words' very widely, including lexemes associated with the seven (or eight) deadly sins).

As far as the basic emotions are concerned, and again drawing on Chaucer for evidence, we find that *joie* supplements, indeed overtakes, *bliss* and *gladnes*: *blis(se)* has 42 occurrences in *The Canterbury Tales*; *gladnesse* 7, *joye* a startling 79.¹³ *Drede* (from OE *drædan* to be terrified of, to fear greatly) supersedes *forhtung*, while *fere* (from OE *fær* 'a sudden occurrence') also emerges. *Wratthe* survives, but *ire*, re-borrowed from French, is more frequent in Chaucer: *wratthe* yields 15 hits in *The Canterbury Tales*, *anger* 6, while *ire* occurs 76 times. Its frequency is in part due to the discussion of the seven deadly sins in 'The Parson's Tale', which alone accounts for 37 occurrences. *Wlate*, whether occurring as a simplex, or plus a nominal ending (-*somnesse*; -*fulnesse*;

ingnesse) is a rare word for 'disgust'; it refers also to the physical symptoms of nausea. Chaucer uses *wlatsom* (disgusting) only twice in *The Canterbury Tales*, both times as a rhetorical response to a murder in 'The Nun's Priest's Tale'. *Disgust* itself is not attested before the early seventeenth century. *Sorwe* is found 88 times in the *Tales*; *distresse* occurs 12 times; *wo* (woe) from OE *wea*, becomes very frequent in Middle English, occurring 115 times in the *Tales*.

The various historical dictionaries, thesauruses, databases and concordances now available online make it very much easier to explore individual Middle English words, along with their associations and implications. *Pleasure*, for example, is not recorded before John Gower's *Confessio Amantis* (c. 1393). The *Historical Thesaurus of the Oxford English Dictionary* allows us to trace the evolution of successive words for fear: from the Old English words *anda, egnes*, those derived from the *forht-* root discussed above, to the appearance of *fear* c. 1225, *radness* c. 1300–1400, *fleying* 1340, and *fleyednes* 1450; *crainte* appears c. 1477 and *timor* is evidenced from 1599.[14] The *Chaucer Concordance* can show us how *wo*, in 'The Knight's Tale' alone, collocates with such emotion words as *distresse, angwissh, compleynynge, criyng, torment, care* and *peyne* and contrasts with *gladnesse*. The *Dictionary of Middle English* and the *Oxford English Dictionary* note that *joye* is first recorded around 1225–30 in the *Ancrene Riwle*; the *Concordance* shows how it collocates with *honour, parfite heele* (health, well-being), *hope, gladnesse, plesaunce* and, most frequently of all in *The Canterbury Tales, blis(se)*. These tools enable us to ask and answer a whole range of questions about the etymologies, semantic domains, associations and implications of the emotion lexis of Middle English.

Dialectal differences in emotion lexis

McNamer's question cited above invites a supplementary query: are there, for example, specifically Northern medieval English feelings? The distinctive emotional lexicon of the Gawain-poet provides evidence for a partial case-study below.[15] Chaucer exploits the comedy in dialectal differences in 'The Reeve's Tale' when John, one of the

Northern clerks studying in Cambridge, explains to Simkyn the miller that he and his friend have brought the corn to be milled, because the college manciple, whose task it would normally have been, has tooth-ache: 'Oure manciple, I hope he wil be deed, / Swa werkes ay the wanges in his heed.'[16] John intends to communicate that he thinks that the manciple's suffering might be fatal, but Chaucer's predominantly Southern audience would infer, incorrectly, that John means 'wish for', anticipating the official's death with an inappropriate enthusiasm.[17] Other Northern texts, including *William of Palerne*, *Sir Gawain and the Green Knight*, *Pearl* and *The Destruction of Troy*, display this usage. The provenance of texts cannot always be reliably identified; many would have been copied and recopied by scribes from other parts of the country who might introduce dialectal changes, but it is clear that Northern texts had a different range of available lexis for emotion, drawing, for example, on Old Norse loans in preference to, or in addition to, French.

The *Gawain* manuscript uses the words *anger* from ON *angr* and *greme* from ON *gremi* (distinct from the OE-derived *gram*). *Anger* carries a variety of senses across the manuscript's four poems, reflecting the different significations of the word in Old Norse, where harm, resentment, sorrow and anger are its primary meanings.[18] Thus we find in *Pearl*: 'And loue ay God, in wele and wo, / for anger gaynez þe not a cresse' (And always love God, in good times and bad, for resentment will not do you a jot of good) (lines 342–3).[19] In *Sir Gawain and the Green Knight*, Bertilak reminds Gawain that he could have chopped off his head if he had wanted to: 'I couþe wroþeloker haf waret, to þe haf wroȝt anger' (I could have struck more angrily, to have done you harm) (line 2344). *Cleanness* pairs *anger* with *ire*, 'In þe anger of his ire þat arȝed mony' (In the fury of his anger that frightened many) (line 572). Belshazzar's queen advises calling on Daniel to interpret her husband's dreams, for Daniel had in the past calmed the temper of Belshazzar's father, Nebuchadnezzar; *Cleanness*: 'Þat is he þat ful ofte hatz heuened þy fader / Of mony anger ful hote with his holy spech' (He is the one who very often has assuaged your father / Of many heated rages with his holy speech (lines 1602–3). In *Patience*, Jonas becomes wrathful towards God: 'He wex as wroth as þe wynde towarde oure lorde. / So hatz anger onhit his hert' (He became as furious as the wind towards our lord, so rage has inflamed his heart) (lines 410–11), as also a few lines later: 'With hatel anger and hot heterly he callez' (With great and hot anger he calls out fiercely) (line 481).[20] The semantic range of *anger* in the usage of a single manuscript is strikingly demonstrated here: both the associations that the word brings with it from Old Norse – such as 'harm' – and the accrual of different kinds of nuance. These provide support for the conceptual metaphorical understanding of anger as involving internal heat and suggest that *anger* may be regarded as more violent and shorter-lasting than *ire*.

Greme, on the other hand, primarily expresses what we would identify as the modern concept of anger. Compare *Cleanness*: 'Þen ar þay synful hemself, and sulpen altogeder / Boþe God and His gere, and hym to greme cachen' (Then they are sinful in themselves and completely defile / both God and his vessels, and drive him to anger) (lines 115–16), and *Pearl*: 'Thy heued hatz nauþer greme ne gryste / On arme oþer fynger, thaȝ thou ber byȝe' (Your head is not angry and resentful / towards arm or finger, even if you wear a ring) (lines 465–6).[21] *Greme* appears widely across Northern texts; it also occurs in *Ancrene Wisse*, *The Awntyrs of Arthur*, *Havelok the Dane*, *The Siege of Jerusalem* and 'Homily 18, Second Sunday in Lent' in the Northern Homily Cycle. By contrast, it is not found at all in *The Canterbury Tales*, while its cognate, deriving from OE *grame*, occurs only once, in 'The Canon's Yeoman's Tale' (line 1403).[22] *Grame* is found only three times in *Troilus* (at I: 372; III: 1028; IV: 529), where it collocates with *travaille*, *love* and *hate*, and *manhood*.[23]

The prominence of alliteration in Northern poetic texts allows us to build up associative networks for key emotion terms in individual texts or across the works of identifiable poets.[24] Thus, to continue with *greme* and its derivatives, the *Gawain*-poet alliterates this lexeme with *God*, *gere*, *grete*, *greve*, *grucchen* and *grace* in *Cleanness*; *gryste* (as we saw above in *Pearl*); *gryndellayk* (fierceness), *grete*, *grace*, *gruche*, *grwe*, *gryndelly*, *Gawayn*, *agreved* and *gryed* in *Sir Gawain and the Green Knight*. The associative network thus includes semantically related terms such as 'grief', 'grudge', *gryndel* and *grwe* (related to Mod. Eng. *gruesome* and a distinctively Northern term in Middle English), as well as 'great' 'God' and 'grace', concepts that function as antonyms to the term under discussion. The *gr-* cluster has more members offering a close semantic fit with *greme*; *grief* and *grudge* are Old French-derived, while *gryndel* is probably connected with ON *grindill* (storm); *grwe* is not recorded in Old English but has cognates in Middle Dutch. Words that begin with the *gr-* consonant cluster may be heard as closer to the key-word than those that simply alliterate on *g*. The *gr-* words form a network of emotively marked and negatively valenced words that amplify and extend the basic emotions of sorrow and anger around which they cluster.

Glad and its derivatives, in contrast, are members of a positively valenced semantic network in the *Gawain*-poet's works. In *Sir Gawain and the Green Knight* they alliterate with *governour*, *gyng*, *Goddes*, *gef* (give), *Gawayn*, *gomnez* (games), *gomenly*, *god* (good), *godmon*, *Cleanness* contributes *glam* (cheerful noise) and *glod* (glided), *god* (good), *gest*, *gay*, *God* and *grone*. In *Pearl*, where the word occurs quite frequently, not always as an alliterating stress, it chimes with *glory*, *glace* (glides), *gome* (man), *Grece*, *glentes* (glances), *gloryous*. *Patience* in contrast yields only *unglad*, alliterating with *glam* and *glod*. The poet alliterates on the *gl-* consonant cluster where he can, but is also content to use *g-*, expanding the network to include phonically more loosely connected words and facilitating a wider semantic range that, significantly, includes both God and Gawain as important members. Exploring these alliterative networks both within the work of a single poet and more widely across the larger alliterative tradition would allow us to extend the lexical study of emotion beyond mere word lists so that we can map the ways in which distinctively literary techniques (with their particular attention to the interface of sound and semantics) express different emotional nuances.

This brief examination of selected emotion words in medieval English has been of necessity partial; it suggests effective methods for investigating individual words rather than offering, as Ogura attempts to do, a survey of linguistic and semantic change across the whole emotions domain. The presence of such words is the clearest indicator of emotion in literary texts; a narrative voice will often employ them for psychonarration ostensibly to provide necessary information to advance the plot. In *King Horn*, for example, once Horn has been taken in as a foundling by the King of Westernesse, the narrator tells us that everyone loves him, 'and mest him luvede Rymenhild' (line 252).[25] Indeed, 'Heo luvede so Horn child / That negh heo gan wexe wild' (lines 255–6). Rymenhild feels *soreghe*, *pine* and *wo* (lines 265; 267), and orders her father's steward to summon Horn to her chamber.[26] Athelbrus the steward feels *in herte wo* and thinks this *gret wunder* (lines 279, 282); he fears that Rymenhild intends some harm to the young man: namely, to *misrede* him. Athelbrus therefore fetches one of Horn's companions to Rymenhild instead. With passionate intensity (she *wexe wild*, line 300), the girl puts her arms around the young man and declares her love. Athulf quietly reveals his true identity, and she flies into a rage with the steward, threatening him with both *schame* and hanging. Athelbrus prostrates himself and apologises, mentioning the risk of the king's anger (*wrathe*) if Rymenhild were to *pleie* with Horn as she had evidently been ready to do with Athulf, and asks her to abate her *tene* (fury). He promises to fetch Horn, and Rymenhild becomes *blithe* once more.

In this episode, the emotions at work are clearly named and largely predictable. Nevertheless, the comparatively simple language suggests that more complex feelings and cognitions are at work, requiring the audience to make assumptions about the characters' internal conditions. The shorthand phrase *wexe wild* gestures towards the kind of full-blown passion that, in the later romance *William of Palerne* for example, will trigger a long, densely emotive soliloquy addressing all the symptoms of Ovidian love-madness. The steward fears that Rymenhild's summons represents a threat to Horn – but what sort of danger might *misrede* designate? Athelbrus's explanation in the face of the princess's fury, that he feared she would make advances to Horn and trigger the king's anger, seems plausible, given the behaviour he has just witnessed, but it is not clear that this was the peril he anticipated. While the audience knows what Rymenhild has in mind and that her pretence of illness masks genuine lovesickness, Athelbrus moves from suspicion to placation, and finally, cooperativeness. Although *King Horn* cannot lay claim to great psychological complexity in its depiction of emotions, it nevertheless makes use of narrative voice, psychonarration and a sporadic access to characters' hidden feelings that anticipates more substantial explorations of interiority in later romances.

Rosenwein's word lists and mystical lexis

In *Emotional Communities* Barbara Rosenwein investigated the emotional lexis of a number of emotional communities in seventh- and eighth-century Francia. In *Generations of Feeling* she expands her investigation to include samples of emotional communities from 600 to 1700. She relies on her original methodology: generating lists of emotion words: 'Because emotions are inchoate until they are given names, emotional vocabularies are exceptionally important for the ways in which people understand, express, and indeed "feel" their emotions.'[27] Her extended sample now includes vernaculars (Occitan, Middle English, early modern French) and a larger range of genres than are examined in the previous book. Tracing emotion in vernacular languages is more fraught than noting the occurrences and contexts of Latin emotion words, as established in *Emotional Communities* and expanded here by attending to the topic in a series of writers in medieval Latin. Rosenwein acknowledges translation issues to some extent, but also firmly rejects what looks like a common-sense method, identifying words that are assigned to the semantic field of emotion in the modern language: 'The troubadours [subject of her chapter 4] allow us to confront a new – vernacular – vocabulary. But how can we determine which words had emotional force for them? The worst answer would be to look for analogues to modern English emotion words!'[28] Rather, Rosenwein's method is to find words which are associated with the locations of emotion: the mind, soul and body, but primarily the heart, feelings' principal seat. This method presents one way of approaching emotion systems in vernacular texts, but it risks failing to identify other emotion terms that do not collocate closely with the heart and overlooking emotion states not named as such, but which can be inferred from speech, gesture or other kinds of behaviour within more evidently literary contexts.

Rosenwein's analysis of Margery Kempe's emotional style identifies Margery's extrovert and expressive emotional behaviour as constructed in opposition to more decorous norms that dominated in her particular community. Although Margery tends to alienate others through her dramatic behaviour and her propensity to talk about spiritual matters, she nevertheless cultivates supportive networks of people (very often women) who understand her behaviour as justified by the intensity of her feeling and the apparently involuntary nature of her actions. A loosely constituted group of confessors and friars encourage Margery's own unique spirituality, and they use their own emotional literacy – awareness of the contemporary mystical emotion repertoire – to educate Margery in developing her own emotional styles. *The Book of Margery Kempe* has a vivid lexis of emotion; the work's quasi-autobiographical nature enables the reporting of her shifting interior states, affording multiple insights into the way in which Margery verbalises her feelings, her behaviour, both willed and involuntary, and other people's responses to her; the *Book*'s depiction of emotion is examined in detail in Chapter 5 below. Rosenwein generates a substantial list of emotion words for Margery Kempe by selecting those which are associated with *herte* and their synonyms and antonyms.[29] This offers a useful starting point for emotion analysis, clearly exemplifying Margery's 'melodramatic emotional style', such as her propensity to weep 'ful plentevowsly and ful boystowsly' for hours at a time.[30] While Rosenwein's list is extensive, it is not exhaustive. *Solas*, for example, is not included, though its collocate *co(w)mfort* is; *solas* is an important term not only for Margery's relationship with Christ (p. 383), and the paradoxical feelings she experiences when others rebuke her (pp. 43; 97), as also for the emotional responses that the *Book* is meant to engender in the reader (p. 41). Other emotion words in Margery's repertoire repay a closer look.

Labour is a key term with a range of complex emotional associations. So, for example, when Margery suddenly becomes subject to lechery – just when she thought that her sexual desire had been extinguished – she is tempted by a man 'whom sche lovyd wel'. He importunes her in somewhat threatening language as they are going into church. Turning over his approach in her mind during the service, Margery is troubled, 'labowrd wyth the mannys wordys'

(p. 68), This vivid term, suggesting the effortfulness that anxiety produces, first occurs in the *Book* with Margery's first pregnancy, culminating in and closely connected with the 'labowr sche had in chyldyng' (p. 52). The word recurs not only throughout this episode but also whenever she relates her battles with madness, demons, doubt and (sexual) temptation (pp. 55; 64; 327). Margery also employs *labowr* for the anxiety she experiences when she anticipates that she is about to embark on one of her bouts of loud crying: 'evyr it schuld labowryn in hir mende mor and more' (p. 166), for crying is in itself 'labowr' (p. 338). In Rome, a group of women who are concerned by the effects of just such a crying episode seek to give her 'solas and comfort' after 'hir gostly labowr'. *Labowr* and its derivatives are synonymous with *vexacioun* (pp. 281; 316). In Book II, however, *labowr* is employed only in relation to physical effort – the hard work of the elderly woman's arduous journey across Northern Europe, for at this stage of Margery's career, her propensity to experience such intense emotion episodes seems to have receded. The semantic associations of *labowr* mark Margery's powerful feelings as grounded in her initial traumatic pregnancy and childbirth, and they underline the exhausting physicality of performing, and indeed in trying to repress and control, her emotional style.[31]

Another important emotion term is *languren*, 'to languish, to suffer'.[32] Jesus tells Margery early after her conversion that, despite her wish to die soon and to be received into heaven, she must 'abyden and languren in lofe' (p. 79), bearing witness in the world. *Languren* has powerful spiritual implications. One Palm Sunday, Margery is listening to a sermon, delivered by a doctor of divinity, 'and he rehersyd oftyntyme thes wordys "Owr Lord Jhesu langurith for lofe"' (p. 337). The phrase derives from the Song of Songs 2:4–5; 5:8, where the bride declares that she languishes with love, 'Quia amore langueo'. By the fifteenth century the phrase had been widely adopted in Middle English vernacular lyric. Although it could be employed to signify the secular lover's desire for his lady, it occurs most frequently in Marian hymns.[33] Sometimes the biblical tag operates as a refrain, making ambiguous play with the identity of the poet's beloved, sometimes it is voiced by Mary herself, the bride whose love for the bridegroom makes the Incarnation possible. In the remarkable lyric 'In the vaile of restles mynde', the poet hears a mysterious voice lamenting in these words; as he ascends a hill he finds a bloodied Christ sitting beneath a tree.[34] Christ relates how he has loved his spouse, the wayward and errant mankind, how he has suffered violence for her, and although she still runs away from him, he continues to languish for her, offering the wound in his side as a nuptial chamber where they can unite in love.[35] The poem deftly shows how the topos of Christ the Lover-Knight, known from at least c. 1200, where it appears in *Ancrene Wisse*, meshes with both the erotically charged refrain of the secular love-lyric and the allegorical understanding of Christ and his beloved.

The fourteenth-century Yorkshire contemplative Richard Rolle translates and glosses the phrase *amore langueo* ('I languysshe for luf') in *The Form of Living*, a guide to the religious life probably composed for Margaret Kirby, an anchoress, a text that Margery very likely knew.[36] For Rolle, however, in keeping with the aims of his text, it is the devout addressee who aspires to languish in love for God; when all 'comfort and solas' is excluded from the heart, save in Jesus Christ alone, 'Þan may þou hardyly [boldly] say: "I languysshe for luf"', Rolle admonishes his interlocutor.[37] No wonder, then, that on Palm Sunday, as she contemplated Jesus's entry into Jerusalem, in order to redeem his beloved spouse from the clutches of the Devil, Margery found herself so powerfully affected by these words from the pulpit. Given her long-held fears about the implications of her married state for her hopes of heaven, and with her highly eroticised feelings for Christ, the doctor of divinity's repetition of 'Owr Lord Jhesus langurith for lofe' kindles in Margery an answering 'fir of lofe', which, when she can no longer keep it 'clos wythinne hir brest', bursts out with the usual roaring and weeping. This reaction to the ritual of Palm Sunday climaxes in an elaborated vision of the events of the Passion. In an aside to this passage, Margery notes in this passage that she sometimes hears 'gret sowndys and gret melodiis wyth hir bodily erys' which confirm her belief that it is 'ful mery in hevyn'; this engenders in her 'ful gret languryng and ful gret longyng' to go there (p. 338). *Langor* is a powerful trigger for Margery's deeply felt anxieties about her still-desiring female body and the recurrent challenges of redirecting that desire towards the manhood of Christ so as to achieve reassurance and release from her fears.

Julian of Norwich, in contrast, employs *langor* mostly to describe the illness which triggered her visionary experiences, although twice in the *Shewings* she uses the noun to express the longing of mankind for God. 'For al this life and this langor that we have here is but a poynte', she notes, evoking the early vision in which she saw God 'in a poynte'.[38] In her interpretation of the parable of the servant, however, Julian makes clear that Jesus shares in humanity's *langor* for salvation: 'For the langor and desire of al mankynd that shal be savid aperid in Jesus, for Jesus is al that shal be savid, and al that shal be savid is Jesus.'[39] Another key emotion term associated with Julian, *homely*, is given a distinctive application by Margery. Shortly after Margery's mystical marriage to the Godhead, Jesus explains that he desires to share with her the intimacy that a wife shares with her husband. 'For it is convenyent the wyf to be homly wyth hir husbond. Be he neveyr so gret a lorde and sche so power a woman whan he weddyth hir, yet thei must ly togedir and rest togedir in joy and pes' (p. 196). So, he adds, 'most I nedys be homly wyth the'.[40] When Jesus meets Mary Magdalen after the resurrection, and warns her not to touch him, she realises with 'hevy cher' that she may no longer be *homly* with him as she had been before (p. 356). Margery's identification with Mary Magdalen, 'hys trewe lover' (p. 323), is both strong and competitive; she yearns to be worthy so that she can be as sure of his love as Mary (p. 325).

Jesus's exemplification of the significance of being *homly* comes some way into the *Book*, where it fleshes out the promise made in chapter 1, that the *Book* will relate how Jesus was 'homly in hyr sowle'; here with the implication of 'at home, comfortable' (p.44).[41] When, shortly after her visit to Julian in Norwich, Margery seeks further counsel from an anchorite at Lynn about her difficulties with her temporary confessor, he explains the confessor's point of view: knowing Margery to have been until recently a sinner, the priest cannot believe that God should 'ben homly wyth yow in so schort a tyme' (p. 125). There are other instances of *homlyness*: in Assisi, a Friar Minor is astonished at Margery's privileged relationship with God, 'for to be so homly wyth God be lofe and homly dalyawnce' (p. 180) is unexampled, he says. Yet St Birgitta (Bridget), although a Swedish princess, had cultivated *homlyness* with all her acquaintances in Rome (p. 204), showing a 'lawhyng cher' to all who would speak to her.[42]

These three English mystics thus draw upon a range of different words denoting the emotions produced by desire for God. Margery's lexis is the most varied: her emotional life spans the whole gamut of feelings from despair to ecstasy. Rolle and Julian focus rather on the positive: on love, grace, comfort and joy. By the fifteenth century, particular emotion words were freely crossing genres, bringing the connotations and associations of lyric, homily and drama into other kinds of writing – autobiographical, didactic, mystical – effecting the reassurance of lay-people, men and women alike, that salvation was possible, if they could train themselves to feel sufficiently and correctly.

Categorising emotion: the deadly sins

Regrettably, no systematic taxonomies of emotion have been preserved in Middle English vernacular texts.[43] Although writers such as Ælred of Rievaulx, St Thomas Aquinas and, in France, Jean Gerson were writing in Latin about emotions throughout the period, vernacular writers did not embark on categorising and analysing medieval modes of feeling.[44] One exception is Reginald Pecok, writing c. 1445, who lists eight bodily passions, located in the heart and closely tied to the senses: 'passional love, hate, desijr, drede, gladness, sorynesse, reuþ, schame'; these have eight spiritual counterpart passions located 'in þe ouerer appetite or wil'.[45] Popular, however, since they were useful for preachers and for those offering pastoral care, were analyses and typologies of the seven deadly sins, and the corresponding cardinal virtues. 'The emotions and the virtues-vices tradition had always been two sides of the same coin', observes Rosenwein.[46] The early English cleric Alcuin composed in 799 or 800 the widely circulated and translated *De virtutibus et vitiis liber* (*The Book of Virtues and Vices*), which serves as an early model.[47] Alcuin's virtues either are associated with religious practice or are classifiable as behaviours: wisdom, faith, charity, hope and enthusiasm for reading are his first headings, while patience, humility, compunction and fear of God might variously be considered as kinds of positive emotion. Alcuin identifies eight principal vices: pride, greed, fornication, avarice, anger, weariness (*accidie*), sorrow and *cenodoxia* (vainglory).[48] The book concludes with brief discussion of the four principal virtues: prudence, justice, fortitude and temperance, none of which constitute emotions, though they may be associated with certain affective states. Rosenwein has recently suggested that, nonetheless, Alcuin's treatise 'was as much about emotions as it was about morality, like the modern authors [of self-help books], Alcuin assumed that understanding and mastering emotions was the key to happiness'.[49]

Alcuin's eight vices were gradually pared back to seven in the post-Conquest period. *Accidie* mutated into sloth, sorrow (*tristitia*) disappeared; *cenodoxia* was absorbed into pride; gluttony and lechery continued along with anger. Avarice might alternate or overlap with envy and covetousness; sometimes the inclusion of two of these three terms would expand the total of principal sins back to eight. Which of these sins might we consider to be emotions? Anger, clearly; its visibility in medieval culture has generated a number of important historical studies.[50] Pride and envy, perhaps, while sloth, gluttony and lechery seem closer to behaviours or dispositions. This standardised cultural conspectus of the deadly sins underlies not only such Christian treatises as Chaucer's 'Parson's Tale', which offers a good number of insights into particular manifestations of the sins, but also the dramatisation of Reason's sermon in William Langland's *Piers Plowman*. John Gower's *Confessio Amantis* likewise organises Amans's confession under the heads of the sins, defined and imagined primarily in relation to erotic love; this move underlines the extent to which the sins, their constituent parts and antitypes, and emotions overlap in the construction of aristocratic masculine identity.

'The Parson's Tale', drawing on two well-known handbooks, Raymond Peñaforte's treatise on penance and William Peraldus's account of the seven deadly sins, is the final tale of *The Canterbury Tales*. As the pilgrims near Canterbury, the Parson reminds his companions of the journey through life and the heavenly goal, figured by the cathedral city so near at hand. Pride '[is] the general roote of alle harmes', he avers (following the now traditional

Gregorian order), when he has finished his introductory disquisition on penance. He lists the 'twigges' that spring from that root as:

> inobedience, avauntyinge, ypocrisie, despit, arrogance, inpudence, swellynge of herte, insolence, elacioun, inpacience, strif, contumacie, presumpcioun, irreverance, pertinacie, veyneglorie, and many another twig that I kan nat declare.[51]

Although the multiple divisions and subdivisions of the seven deadly sins section seem rather stiff, the Tale contains striking details, from the capacity of the proud to indulge in 'semblable wast of clooth in vanitee / ... costlewe furrynge in hir gownes ... the superfluitee in lengthe of the foreside gownes, trailynge in the dong and in the mire' (p. 300) to the conduct of elderly and impotent lechers, 'thise olde dotardes holours, yet wol they kisse, though they may nat do, and smatre hem' (p. 318). They are demeaningly compared to dogs, 'for an hound, whan he comth by the roser or by othere [bushes], thugh he may nat pisse, yet wole he heve up his leg and make contenaunce to pisse' (p. 318).[52] Sinful behaviour is exemplified and brought vividly to life through such colloquial observation, contributing significantly to writers' imaginative repertoires of emotion-related indicia and permitting the audience to recognise and interpret particular actions as pertaining to invisible, internal emotional states.[53]

William Langland's personification of the sins is highly performative and altogether more vivid than the Parson's account, for as Suzanne Conklin Akbari notes, 'Personification not only makes an abstraction visible, it makes it alive.'[54] In Passus V of the B-text, Reason preaches a sermon to 'the feld ful of folk', the whole realm and the king himself, urging chastisement and asceticism. Picking up on the anxieties generated by the prominence of Lady Mede in the preceding Passus, in his opening remarks he focuses on extravagant female clothing and idle children, advocating as remedy patriarchal violence, administered by husbands and fathers.[55] Repentance now steps forward in the role of confessor in order to hear the people's accounts of their sins and to offer spiritual counsel, penance and absolution. First, in line with the ranking of sins noted above, Pernele Proud-herte prostrates herself and vows to respond humbly to insult: 'now wol I meke me and mercy biseche / For al that I have hated in myn herte' (V: 69–70). Pride, the 'queen of all evils', as Alcuin observes,[56] is closely associated with hatred for others. Envy's comic account of his own behaviour reveals his lack of self-knowledge. When Repentance tells him that he must be sorry, he replies that he is seldom anything else, 'And that maketh me thus megre, for I ne may me venge' (V: 127) Envy's long account of his misdeeds, his scowling, deprecating, his 'chidynge and … chalangynge … bakbitynge and bismere and beryng of fals witnesse' (V: 87–8) anatomises envious behaviour throughout the community, in the market-place or at church, meeting neighbours on the street or when shopping among London merchants. Envy is lean, pale and shrivelled, like a leek left too long in the sun, but at the same time swollen with rage, biting his lips and clenching his fists: vivid images of physical markers of emotion.

Wrath comes forward next, eyes glazed with rage, snivelling and hanging his head – not symptoms we would currently associate with anger – and explaining how he infiltrates religious houses in order to sow dissension through gossip and untruths, 'Til "Thow lixt!" and "Thow lixt!" lopen out at ones / And either hitte oother under the cheke; / Hadde thei had knyves, by Crist ! hir either hadde kild oother' (V: 161–3); astonishingly, these furious figures are nuns.[57] 'Wrath does not embody anger, but engineers it in others', suggests Paul Megna; in the B-text the rage Wrath produces operates to inflame the regular clergy, but not, significantly, the laity nor yet friars.[58] Covetousness has beetle-brows, thick lips and bleary eyes, all features of old age; wearing torn, old clothes, he teaches merchants how to commit various frauds and deceits. Covetousness's activities stretch to usury and pawn-broking, the new financial practices which the emerging fourteenth-century cash economy encouraged. He comes close to despair when he reviews his behaviour, and almost hangs himself, but is encouraged by Repentance to hope for mercy. Up to this point, Repentance's exhortations appear to be broadly successful in eliciting contrition and intention to reform.

Langland's intention here is of course didactic: '[t]he personified emotion exhibits the symptoms and performs the gestures associated with that particular emotional state, enabling readers to imagine the sensory experience and practice of that emotion', notes Mary Flannery.[59] Glutton's initial attempt to go to church and seek absolution is derailed when he is greeted by the local tavern-keeper, Beton the Brewstere, '"I have good ale, gossib," quod she, "pepir and pione ... and a pound of garleek"' (V: 303–5). Glutton gets thoroughly drunk, swears and staggers about, goes home and collapses into bed, where he has an *accidie* (a fit of sloth) and spends the weekend sleeping it off. The language of disgust infuses the description of Glutton's behaviour, after pissing 'a Paternoster-while' and farting loudly and noxiously, he vomits profusely: 'And koughed up a cawdel in Clementes lappe / Is noon so hungry hound in Hertfordshire / Dorste lape of that levynge, so unlovely it smaughte!' (V: 355–7). Finally, Sloth, half-asleep, bleary-eyed and belching, confesses that he remembers very little Christian teaching, being better versed in 'rymes of Robyn Hood and Randolf Erl of Chestre' (V: 396); he has been a priest these thirty years but can barely read a line of Latin. Sloth promises to go to church more regularly, pay back everyone to whom he owes money and then go on pilgrimage to Rome, certainly not the action of an idle man – if indeed he follows through. Langland completes his analysis of the sins with Sloth, though Robert the Robber comes forward next to proclaim his crimes. Amplifying Sloth's intention to undertake a pilgrimage in penance, the field of folk swear to go on a collective pilgrimage, on a journey to seek out Truth; this is when Piers the Plowman enters the scene.

Langland's detailed depiction of five of the seven deadly sins vividly illustrates the social contexts – the pub, the market-place, the convent garden – where emotion visibly plays out in the interplay of the sinful self and others. The series of memorable vignettes demonstrates typical emotion-related behaviours, such as swearing, falling asleep, forgetting or gossiping, for, as Flannery observes, 'personification gives emotion a body, a face and a personality'.[60] The portraits elaborated in Langland's taxonomy allows the audience to recognise both themselves and their neighbours, and thus to understand emotional states as a kind of *habitus*, not just a transient feeling, but rather a disposition and a marked set of congruent behaviours. The physical characteristics associated with each sin are shown; affect is crucial to the sins' accounts of themselves, as their interior states are written clearly on their bodies as corpulence, pinchedness, pallor, eye-impairments, snivelling or bleariness. Sinful identities are fully integrated into emotional linguistic subsystems: Envy participates in an associative network of linguistic emotional behaviours – backbiting and bearing false witness, challenging and chiding – denoted by terms which often alliterate with one another, and with semantically related words. Thus, alliterating associative chains link together *bismer* (scorn); *bolneth* (swells); *bitter*; *blame*; so too *loveless* chimes with *luther* (vicious), *lye*, *loure* and *lakke* (disparage). Langland shows too how the more important emotions produce and reinforce one another; gluttony leads to *accidie*, pride is linked with hatred, while envy is closely associated with anger, a by-product of the excess gall that swells the body with its bitterness.[61]

Personification allegory is an important genre in Middle English imaginative writing. Alongside *Piers Plowman* Flannery considers the translated *Romaunt of the Rose* and John Skelton's late *Bowge of Court* (perhaps composed c. 1480), and she concludes by suggesting that, as well as demonstrating 'the embodied nature of emotional practice', personification allegory can also furnish vital evidence for material depictions of emotion and for gesture and movement, as well as for context and social interaction.[62] Moreover, in the personification of one particular emotion, such as Sorrow in *The Romaunt*, not only are Sorrow's key behaviours and traits laid bare, but the figure is also described in terms of what she cannot experience – the cluster of happy, joyful feelings which sorrow necessarily excludes. The *Romaunt/Roman*'s author(s) show(s) 'a vision of how emotions work, particularly in relation to one another: emotions like sorrow may coexist alongside others like anger, but they also have clear contraries from which they are mutually exclusive'.[63] Emotion systems and the related subsystems of behaviour, disposition and gesture can thus be analysed both through the taxonomies of allegory as genre and through the associative lexical networks – as we saw in the works of the *Gawain*-poet above, constituted by alliteration, rhymes and collocations in poetry and prose.

Translation and adaptation

Poets in late medieval England could choose between three languages when they embarked on a composition. 'Were particular languages associated with particular forms of emotional and social governance in late medieval England?' asks Stephanie Downes, discussing the decisions of John Gower and Charles d'Orléans to compose lyrics of love and loss in a language which was not their mother tongue.[64] Language choice radically affects the ways in which the poets construct 'a feeling self'.[65] As Downes notes, for Charles d'Orléans to compose in English was to compose in the language of his captors; for Gower, conversely, French would be a 'natural, courtly choice for poetry', especially if he aimed to address an aristocratic audience.[66] Downes offers a thoughtful analysis of the ways in which the two poets composing in a second language frame their own and other figures' emotional subjectivities. Charles d'Orleans's English lyric sequence, a meditation on the death of a female beloved, often translates his own French lyrics; yet he occasionally switches the gender of the addressee, and, as Downes shows, makes use of verbal similarities across the two languages to pun, or to evoke bilingual associations.[67] 'Restoring literary expressions of emotion to the multilingual contexts in which they were written and received intensifies our understanding of the range of emotional vocabularies in the past', she concludes.[68]

When fictional texts cross the linguistic boundary in Middle English literary history, they generally move between a type of French into English. Such *mouvance* (in Paul Zumthor's terms) can be complicated by other real or imaginary intermediate versions.[69] Marie de France claims that she first planned to translate material from Latin into *romanz*, but since so many others had already done this, she decided rather to rewrite the tales preserved by the Bretons in their (Breton-language) *lais* in Insular French verse. More than one poet then translated some of them into Middle English. These processes of transmission and adaptation create new emotional communities; emotions are conceptualised differently by the authors and audiences for whom the text was composed in the original language and by the re-mediator and the new audience created by the act of translation. Sif Rikhardsdottir's work on romance in Old French, Middle English and Old Norse has demonstrated the ways in which emotion schemas must be reconfigured for new audiences.[70] She questions the 'premise ... of the stability of emotional representation and categorisation across cultures. If emotions are to a great extent culturally defined, and therefore unstable and shifting, how does one translate emotional behaviour for an audience that conceives those emotions (or the literary representation of a particular emotion) differently?'[71] Rikhardsdottir emphasises how translation entails the adaptation of the source text's signifying systems in order to make the new text signify for the target audience, a move which often lays bare the ideological processes at work in both texts.

Rikhardsdottir framed her 2012 book in terms of 'reading communities', akin to Brian Stock's concept of the 'textual community'.[72] Crucially, she extends the original definition – rather as Rosenwein does in formulating the emotional community – beyond those persons sharing texts with one another in the same historical moment.[73] In Rikhardsdottir's definition, the reading community includes 'the person (or persons) instigating the translation and subsequent copying of the text as well as those for whom the text was translated or copied [a kind of implied reader], and ultimately the groups of audiences who actually read and preserved those texts'.[74] The addition of an implied audience and readership to the model is an important one, for translators make their changes, retool their emotional system, to make them legible for the immediate consumers of their texts, not necessarily for the audience of the actual text which comes down to us and which happens to have survived in particular circumstances.[75] So, for example, the hypothetical audience who would have encountered the English version of *Lai le Freine* that we still have (preserved only in the Auchinleck manuscript) would differ both from the implied audience that its original translator had in mind, as well as, of course, from the aristocratic audience for whom Marie originally composed.[76] Just as an 'emotional community' already possesses an emotional repertoire, comprising a series of emotion schemas and of scripts, made up of individual 'emotive indicia' and derived from previous consumption of similar texts, so a 'reading community' will develop a set of genre-specific emotion repertoires, derived from the texts that they share across space and time; these are not only 'Middle English feelings', but specifically 'Middle English *romance* feelings'.

'Genres are inherently ideological constructs; the formal and structural features of a text do not produce aesthetic effects that can be divorced from content and thereby from ideology, but on the contrary they signal participation in a discursive framework that implies a worldview with a heavy ideological investment', notes Simon Gaunt.[77] These ideological implications equally shape genre-specific emotional norms; not only are imported scripts modified to arouse the target audience's emotion but, over time, they also affect the development of emotion simulations and scripts within the target culture's literary polysystem, to use the theorist Itamar Even-Zohar's terms.[78] The Middle English genre system, drawing on generic kinds both inherited from Old English and imported from French, is by no means static. While different vernacular religious genres became popular across a broad social spectrum through the growth of affective lay piety, the originally French fictional genres that were the staples of aristocratic literary consumption in the twelfth century found new audiences among the gentry and mercantile classes over the next centuries. Just as the generic polysystem develops both in parallel with and in interaction with the ideologies of the social polysystem, so too, when the emotional subsystems of a particular genre are translated into a new language, they do not become ossified. Rather, as the indigenous polysystem shifts and flexes to accommodate fresh imported works alongside original English compositions, the genre's emotional repertoire incorporates and prioritises new 'emotive indicia' while downplaying or critiquing older values or those associated with a different social stratum.

Thus when Chrétien de Troyes's romances, Marie de France's *lais* or other romances originally composed in Insular and Central French are translated into Middle English, the adaptor makes allowances for an English audience's internalised understanding of what would constitute appropriate emotion scripts, an audience that is already used to native emotion models. Comprising a range of 'emotive indicia', these are, as in the *King Horn* passage discussed above, expressed through the available emotion lexis, surviving from Old English or newly borrowed. The Middle English translations were composed significantly later than their source texts, their emergence reflecting the growing status of the English vernacular as a literary medium. The reasons for this emergence are complex and multi-faceted. Reading and listening comprehension of French must have been on the wane, particularly as Central French, although widely spoken at the English court, began to diverge markedly from the insular variety. The extension of literacy to the gentry and bourgeoisie, in particular to women and girls, may have fuelled demand for vernacular versions of Chrétien's and Marie's poetry. Chaucer notes in 'The Nun's Priest's Tale' that women have a particular taste for Arthurian romance (lines 3211–12). Poems such as *William of Palerne*, *Partonope of Blois* or *Sir Tristrem* had French exemplars which very likely were no longer well understood by English audiences of non-noble rank. For new gentry and bourgeois reading communities the production of such translated texts reinforced their acquisition of and fluency in romance's particular emotional repertoires. Learning to recognise and to write Middle English feelings effectively involved first, listening to and reading Insular and Central French romances, and subsequently evolving new kinds of emotion scripts for native Middle English compositions. Below I examine adaptation strategies in emotion episodes in three translations or versions of twelfth-century *lais* and romances.

Translating Yvain or Le chevalier au lion

In *Yvain* (c. 1170), Chrétien de Troyes illustrated with comic acuity how the *nouveaux riches* might use romance texts as a guide to appropriate social behaviour. When Yvain comes to the Castle of Dire Adventure (Chateau de Pesme-Aventure) he discovers that the castle-owner's fortunes appear to be founded on a silk-manufacturing sweatshop.[79] With tears trickling down her face, one of the incarcerated girls explains the women's plight to the astonished knight. Yvain finds the proprietor lounging in his orchard, listening to his daughter read a romance to him; he is greeted with extravagant hospitality and served far too much food at dinner: 'De mes tant que trop en y ot' (line 5435). Yvain is unpleasantly surprised the next morning when his previously courteous host demands that he fight two demons; if he is victorious, he must marry his daughter and take over his lands. His defeat of the demons allows Yvain to obtain the captives' release; the lord's enraged and churlish reactions when Yvain politely declines his daughter's hand suggests that the castellan still has much to learn about courtliness.[80] Through his juxtaposition of the romance-reading scene, the overabundance of courses at dinner and the surly behaviour of the host, Chrétien implies that those who lack innate *gentillesse* will not be able to acquire it through listening to romances, though they may learn to simulate it up to a point. Romance teaches and instils courtliness; courtliness demands the consumption of romance: this understanding creates an ideological feedback loop that instructs new audiences how to evaluate character motivations and feelings with reference to new genre-specific emotion-scripts.

Some one hundred and fifty years later, Chrétien's poem was translated into Middle English, in a broadly faithful version known as *Ywain and Gawain*.[81] Its new reading community was probably located among the gentry, whose comprehension of Central French could not be guaranteed. Chrétien's emotive indicia are sometimes curtailed, sometimes more clearly flagged for the English audience: thus the 'Chateau de Pesme-Aventure', with its implications of chance, opportunity and adventure, becomes the 'Castel of Hevy Sorrow' (line 2933).[82] In the French text the unhappy maidens weep moderately, and they also cast their eyes downwards, ashamed of their wretched appearance: 'Si s'enbronchent toutes et pleurent' (line 5204). The lowered-eyes detail is omitted in English, replaced by a hyperbolically sorrowful display: the women 'weped al / Als thai wal al to water fall' (lines 2975–6). Chrétien's subtle criticism of the castellan's vulgarity is also played down. The household still treat Ywain handsomely, and there must be some audience uneasiness in registering the connection between enforced female labour and the 'ful riche wedes' (line 3107) and the 'serk and breke ... soft as the sylke' (lines 3103, 3105) that the knight is offered to wear. The dinner, though 'ful really' (royally) (line 3112) served, is not as ridiculously lavish and draws no narratorial comment. In the new context the castellan's consumption of romance narratives no longer functions as a marker of social ambition; his performance of hospitality seems to reflect the social norms pertinent to its English reading community.

So too the English host is less brusque than his French counterpart, begging Ywain not to be offended that he cannot be permitted to leave when he wishes: 'Tak it to na greve' (line 3127). All the same, like the castellan, and indeed his porter, he uses an inappropriately familiar 'thou' to his guest. In the battle with the demons Ywain is hard pressed. 'De honte et de crieme escaufés' (sparked by shame and fear) (line 5584), he defends himself well but he cannot overcome his foes. Yvain's companion-lion too, locked in an outbuilding to prevent his participation in the battle, has a sad and troubled heart: 'a son cuer dolent et trouble / Li leons' (lines 5590–1). Growing enraged, 'esrage vis et forsenne' (line 5606), the lion is spurred by his fury to escape by digging under the door; the English lion is sad too, but he does not become furious. *Ywain and Gawain* amplifies Ywain's fears about his situation just before the lion breaks out: 'Sare he douted to be ded' (line 3236). While Chrétien does not mention the accompanying damsel's reponses to the hero's peril, *Ywain and Gawain* focalises situation-appropriate emotions of despair and sorrow through the girl, who models a dramatic, thoroughly empathetic reaction to Ywain's plight: 'And also his damysel / Ful mekil murnyng made omell / And wele she wend he sold be slane' (lines 3237–9).

In Chrétien's account, Yvain's victory elicits great *joie* (joy), the pre-eminent communal emotion that signals the restoration of courtly order after chaotic adversity. In *Ywain* the happiness is more muted: the lord and lady simply embrace the knight. Although the English lord is somewhat peevish when Ywain refuses his daughter's hand, the dialogue is much reduced. The substantial, churlish speech with which French Yvain is given permission to depart is rendered briskly and indirectly; deliberate rudeness is replaced by pragmatism: 'The lord saw it was no bote / Obout that mater more to mote. / He gaf him leve oway to fare' (lines 3327–9).

Many elements within the individual emotion-episodes of the French and Middle English versions of *Yvain* remain the same. Beyond the English text's curtailment of longer stretches of Chrétien's direct speeches (such as Laudine's lament for her husband) and of narrative asides (as in the discussion of love when Yvain catches sight of Laudine), it is difficult to characterise systematically the emotional adjustments made by the English translator. Small tweaks, omissions or expansions are made moment by moment to fine-tune the elicitation of the new reading community's responses. The changes made in the episode discussed here smooth out Chrétien's social satire and amplify the emotional response of the girl to the hero's moments of danger; they scale back the lion's ferocity and play down certain other emotions – courtly joy at the fall of the demons and unseemly anger at Ywain's refusal to wed the daughter. Poking fun at the ostentatious consumption of romance and the arriviste castellan's excessive performance of aristocratic behaviour may have seemed inappropriate for the translator's target reading community, and the tone is tempered accordingly.

Reworking Le conte du Graal: Sir Perceval *and* 'The Tale of Sir Thopas'

The other Chrétien romance that survives in a loose Middle English version is *Perceval: ou le conte du Graal*. As *Sir Perceval of Galles*, it is preserved, like *Ywain and Gawain*, in a single manuscript, one which, even more clearly than the compendium represented by Cotton Galba E. ix, was intended for a particular household.[83] Here too, comparison between Chrétien's handling of Perceval's arrival at king Arthur's court and the Middle English version's recasting of the scene shows marked alteration as the later text assimilates unusual motifs to more familiar plotlines, a fundamentally revised emotional repertoire and a very different imagining of the courtly context.

In *Le conte du Graal* Perceval rides into Arthur's hall immediately after the Red Knight has committed the outrage of snatching the king's goblet and splashing its contents over the queen; his aim is get himself knighted immediately.[84] The standard romance welcome schema dictates that the young man should dismount, enter the hall, formally greet the king, be acknowledged in turn, state his boon and have it granted; all these conventions are radically subverted in Perceval's performance.[85] Chrétien's account offers considerable emotional detail: as the newcomer enters, the king remains silent, lost in thought and brooding over the insult he and the queen have sustained, while the courtiers chatter away among themselves. Perceval rides straight into the hall, oblivious to the emotional temperature; nor can he even identify the king. The usual greeting ritual fails entirely; the king does not respond to the young man until his hat is knocked off by the nose of Perceval's horse. Then Arthur apologises profusely, and explains that he has just suffered an outrageous insult and that he fears that the queen may die, so angry and outraged is she. Perceval takes absolutely no notice of the king's account, but immediately demands to be knighted. The depth of the king's sorrow and anxiety is indicated by his failure to respond to the newcomer; the indifference of the court to his silence suggests other, different possibilities: that they lack sympathy for the king's unhappiness and the insult to the queen, or, more likely, that they are politely trying to pretend that the outrage has not happened in order to save communal face.[86] A complex emotion scenario is under way, yet Perceval remains unaware of, or indifferent to, it, locked into his own naïve and idiosyncratic emotional schema.

Evidently composed for a gentry audience with no particular sense of the etiquette attendant on entering the royal presence, the Middle English *Sir Perceval* casts the arrival in the hall very differently.[87] The normative welcome script is still subverted, but to deliberately comic effect. Perceval's behaviour – riding up to the dais and coming so close that his horse is able to kiss the king's face – occasions amazement all round. This Arthur is not preoccupied by his own thoughts, for he has not yet been insulted by the Red Knight but is as surprised as anyone else. He weeps openly when he sees Perceval, for the young man reminds him of his dead brother-in-law, slain fifteen years earlier by the Red Knight and who has never been avenged. This was in fact Perceval's father, as the audience, but not Perceval himself, knows. Perceval could not care less about the king's emotions nor about this ancient history, '"Sir, late be thi jangleyng / Of this I kepe nane!"' (lines 575–6), he commands rudely. *Sir Perceval* immediately assimilates Chrétien's subtly subversive arrival-at-court episode to the vengeance soon to be undertaken – albeit unwittingly – for Perceval's father. Unlike the preoccupied French king, Arthur fulfils his royal function correctly; he does not ignore the newcomer, but simply does not get the chance to greet him before the horse's muzzle is shoved in his face. The sorrow he feels when he sees his nephew is both appropriate and comprehensible in narrative terms. Arthur's weeping for a beloved lost kinsman carries a very different resonance from his pensive withdrawal in the face of a remarkable insult in the source text and the dramatic claim that the queen may die of humiliation.

The variant generic conventions of English metrical romance with respect to French courtly romance norms strongly inflect the scene's emotional praxis.[88] Many questions have been raised about what kind of knowledge of the French original the author of *Sir Perceval* had, given the very different narrative framing he employs, but it is clear that the English poet makes use of a distinctive and dramatic emotional repertoire (see further discussion in Chapter 4), and that the courtly ideology and behavioural schema that Chrétien expects his audience to have internalised is replaced by a less rarefied but by no means less emotional script. Given its preservation context *Sir Perceval* may even, as Phillipa Hardman has suggested, have been composed for young readers and listeners, its emotions recalibrated for a youthful, household audience who might have appreciated Perceval's insouciance and directness.[89]

Sir Perceval intimates emotion largely through gesture and bodily responses, not through narrative comment or psychonarrative. This convention, along with other generic emotion characteristics, is guyed in Chaucer's 'Tale of Sir Thopas' in *The Canterbury Tales*, where Perceval is invoked by name.[90] Perceval's adventures, perhaps even as related in an antecedent version to that found in the Thornton Lincoln manuscript (Lincoln Cathedral Library, MS 91), must have been well enough known for the metropolitan author to regard them as an appropriate object for parody, for what were by now romance clichés abound in Chaucer's poem. Sir Thopas is afflicted by a mysteriously undirected 'love-longyng', deciding that the elf-queen, of whom he had dreamed the previous night, is the only creature worthy of his love. Like the *Yvain* castellan, Thopas listens to performances of romance as he is armed for battle, sending for 'geestours for to tellen tales ... Of romances that been roiales / Of popes and of cardinales, / And eek of love-likynge' (lines 846–50). These should instil in him appropriate feelings of courage and derring-do.[91] The story breaks off with the host's highly critical intervention, just as Sir Thopas is directly compared with Sir Perceval. The poem is short – just over 200 lines – but nevertheless it pokes fun at metrical romance's key emotion tropes: vague love-longing, sudden love for a supernatural lady, a problematic performance of courageous defiance of the enemy and, tellingly, the instrumental practice of listening to romances to heighten the hero's performance of chivalric identity. Chaucer makes knowing use of the emotion scripts of contemporary metrical romance in his mock-modest personal entry in the pilgrims' tale-telling contest.

Adapting Lai de Lanval and Sir Launfal

In the late fourteenth-century *Sir Launfal* Thomas Chestre produces a new version of the tale first found in Marie de France's *Lai de Lanval*. He introduces substantial plot-episodes and elaborates certain scenes for an implied audience with a different understanding of the romance emotion repertoire from that familiar to the *Lanval* audience.[92] Chestre's work is based on the earlier English *Sir Landevale* rather than directly on Marie's; some motifs are drawn from the Old French *Graelent*, and a now-lost source may have provided the two tournament episodes that separate the initiating of the taboo and its breaking.[93] A comparison between *Lanval* and *Sir Launfal* shows how the two English poets adapted first Marie's text and then the version preserved in *Sir Landevale* to make legible the feelings, both publicly expressed and privately experienced, in this emotionally eventful story.

Like Marie's other *lais* and Chrétien's romances, *Lanval* makes considerable use of psychonarration. When Lanval is arbitrarily ignored in the king's distribution of gifts at Pentecost, he is extremely distressed: 'Ore est Lanval mult entrepris / mult est dolenz, mult est pensis' (Now Lanval is very embarrassed / very unhappy, very anxious).[94] The knight tactfully withdraws from the court, claiming that his father is on the point of death. *Sir Launfal* motivates the exclusion more clearly; it is the queen, thoroughly disliked by all the knights because of her sexual reputation, who deliberately decides to exclude Launfal from the gift-giving at her wedding: '[t]hat grevede hym many a sythe' (line 72).[95] Launfal's continuing misery anticipates the straitened circumstances he now faces, for while the well-meaning king sends his two nephews with Launfal, this kindly gesture accelerates his financial embarrassment. In the *lai*, the encounter with the fairy mistress follows almost immediately on Lanval's departure. Chestre adds a new episode that compounds the social implications of the knight's misery and shame. When Launfal seeks lodgings for himself and his companions with his former servant, now the Mayor of Caerleon, he confides his loss of favour to the Mayor. The Mayor's consequent temporising about offering accommodation causes Launfal to laugh ironically at his change of tone: 'Thereof he hadde scorne inowgh' (line 116). When the fairy mistress sends her damsels to fetch Lanval to her tent, as Jeff Rider observes, Marie does not describe the young man's feelings, but rather expects the audience to infer and supply the appropriate emotional response from their own emotional repertoires.[96] Chestre subjects his hero to additional humiliations: being abandoned by the king's nephews and his horse falling over in the mud, 'wherefore hym scorned many men' (line 215). Already 'yn sorow and sore' (line 229) when he saw the girls approach, Launfal 'began to syche' (line 249). This response is multivalent: we assume that in his filthy, tattered clothes he scarcely dares address the damsels; at the same time, he longs to regain his place in a courtly society where men and women mix freely together.

The emotions expressed by both knight and lady in their love-tryst in the tent are broadly similar in English and Insular French, but as Marie's Lanval departs from his beloved the next morning, his emotional state is complicated:

Suvent reguarde ariere sei.
Mult est Lanval en grant esfrei;
de s'aventure vait pensant
e en sun curage dotant.
Esbaïz est, ne set que creire;
il ne la quide mie a veire. (lines 195–200)

(Often glancing behind him, Lanval is very troubled; he thinks about this adventure and wonders in his heart. He is amazed and does not know what to think; he dares not believe that this is true.)

Lanval's doubts are set at rest by his discovering the complete transformation of his fortune back at his lodgings. Chestre, in contrast, omits any idea of doubt or wonder in his hero's mind; he is simply 'glad and blythe' (line 358). Feelings of wonder are displaced onto the churlish Mayor who responds to his former master's new prosperity with astonishment and obsequious friendliness; the shame that coloured their earlier exchanges is now transmitted to the Mayor as Launfal rebukes him for his earlier rudeness.

The contretemps between knight and queen are staged similarly in the two texts, though Chestre downplays the direct accusation that Lanval is interested in young men rather than women. French Lanval retreats to his chamber, where he realises the consequences of breaking the taboo: 'pensis ... e anguissous' (anxious and miserable), he 'se pleigneit e suspirot, / d'ures en altres se pasmot; / puis li crie cent feiz merci' (he laments and sighs / from time to time he swoons and cries for mercy a hundred times) (lines 340; 343–5). Launfal's expression of his misery is similarly violent and is notably self-directed. The Insular French verbs *debatre* (beat) and *se detraire* (torment oneself) are elaborated and particularised:

> He bet hys body, and hys hedde ek
> And cursede the mouth that he wyth spek
> Wyth care and greet dolour
> And for sorow yn that stounde
> Anon he fell aswowe to grounde. (lines 751–5)

The climax of the trial with the approach of the fairy lady's maidens evokes different emotions in the two versions. The emissaries give Lanval's ally Gauvain some hope: 'Mult fu haitiez' (He was very glad) (line 483), even though his friend does not recognise them. When the lady finally appears and vindicates her beloved, no words are exchanged between them. 'Lanval l'oï, sun chie dresça, / bien la cunut, si suspira. / Li sans li est muntez el vis' (Lanval heard her, lifted his head / he recognised her and sighed / the blood mounted to his face) (lines 609–11). Speaking only to himself, he exclaims that this is indeed his *amie*; now that he has seen her again he does not fear death. Once the lady has declared the truth, he acts. Waiting on the mounting-block as she rides out of court, he leaps up behind her and they depart to Avalon, never to be seen again.

Marie's audience must infer the hero's emotional turmoil: Lanval's joy, his hope that his life may be saved and that he may be forgiven. All this is going on in the background while the court and the audience's attention is focused on the lady, removing her mantle and showing off her beauty. Once the judges have acquitted Lanval, he takes a risk – is he forgiven? – and makes that dramatic leap onto the palfrey behind his beloved.

In *Sir Launfal*, Gawain is not so visibly cheered by the girls' appearance; since Launfal does not recognise them, he registers their arrival only 'with drery thoght' (line 895). When Triamour appears, however, Launfal's interior emotions are clearly displayed as he cries out to the bystanders with open emotion – poised between joy, hope and terror – 'Her ... comyth my lemman swete! / Sche myghte me of my balys bete, / Yef that lady wolde!' (lines 970–2). Maintaining narrative tension, Triamour makes no direct answer to him. Once the queen has been blinded, Triamour is ready to depart. May Launfal go too? *Sir Landevale* here adds a substantial exchange between knight and lady (lines 503–24) in which Landevale begs her pardon; *Sir Launfal* wisely reverts to the silence of Marie's version. Has he been forgiven? The appearance of his fairy servant Gifre and his own horse gives him his answer; he leaps onto his horse and rides away alongside his lover. The English thus lacks the tightly loving embrace with which Lanval clings to his lady on their single mount; the drama is reduced, normality restored, and given the poet's observation that Launfal returns to the human world to joust one day a year, it is clear that he does not entirely reject his emotional ties with his former life as he does in the French text.

The emotional schemas in Chestre's version are not markedly different from Marie's in the main shared emotion episodes. In places, *Sir Launfal* is more reticent, modelling a lower-key response to royal disfavour and hinting at the knight's feelings, when he sighs at the sight of the maidens. Marie has moments of delicacy: the instant when Lanval rides away from his lady, torn between uneasiness at the supernatural intervention and marvel at his sheer luck, or the silence between lady and knight at the climax that summons forth Lanval's powerful leap up onto the horse. In the scenes after Triamour's disappearance and at the poem's climax Chestre gives more insight both into Launfal's feelings and into those of his fellow-knights: cycling through despair and joy, sympathy and mistrust. *Sir Launfal* seems likely to have been composed for a gentry audience, for a rather different set of emotional and social assumptions are in play than those of the high nobility of Henry II's court.[97] The Mayor's urban bourgeois respect for money and status is treated as contemptible, while the sexual morals of the royal court and Arthur's gullibility come into question. Most obviously, the new scenes involving Launfal's tournament exploits, first in Caerleon, where he successfully recuperates his chivalric status, and then in jousting against the giant Lombard knight Sir Valentine, aided by Gyfre, his invisible squire, award the knight an unfair advantage that would have been viewed as problematic by a noble audience: 'neither character nor narrator appears concerned about negotiating fourteenth-century chivalric codes governing combat or tournament', comment Laskaya and Salisbury.[98]

Chivalric homosocial bonds retain their value, however. Marie emphasises the communal feeling among Lanval's fellow-knights that he should not abandon himself to his grief: 'mult l'unt blasmé e chastié / qu'il ne face si grant dolur, / e maldiënt si fole amur' (they blamed him very much and chastised him for making himself so miserable and cursing his mad love) (lines 410–12). They manifest their concern by coming to see him every day, making sure that he continues to eat and drink, so as not to make himself ill. Chestre compresses this concrete expression of chivalric affection into 'everych man therfore was wo / That wyste of that tydynge' (lines 827–8). Yet the English poet is interested in the politics and emotions of knightly solidarity. Thus, Sir Hugh and Sir John keep their promise to Launfal to conceal his plight from the royal court, even though their lean appearance and tattered clothes are noted by the king. That the chivalric community has already taken a dislike to the queen strengthens their apprehension that the queen must certainly be in the wrong, even if Launfal cannot produce his mistress to show the truth of his remarks, and they work hard on his behalf. While Launfal waits for the day of the trial he is paralysed by misery: 'Greet sorow and care yn hym was lyght / Hys hondys he gan wrynge' (lines 821–2), and he would 'gladlyche' (line 826) have died: a state which makes other sorry for him. The Earl of Cornwall indeed is in the process of trying to negotiate a compromise – exile – when the first of Triamour's outriders appears. Modes of translation and adaptation thus transmit a constellation of emotion scripts across the different versions of romance narratives preserved in the two languages, producing significant variation within genre-specific emotional systems. Such emotional repertoires – exemplifying sorrow, joy, fear, anxiety, among other feelings – continue to develop within the genre even when writers and poets are separated from their readers and audiences by a century or more of social change. As the late medieval English romance audience diversifies, so too the generic polysystem changes; men and women of lower social ranks now collect and consume a kind of fiction that had emerged to entertain and educate the high courtly society that it generally depicts. Romance genre conventions, operating through specific emotion lexis and formulas and via emotion scripts, enable quite complex delineation of characters' interior psychologies. As the translated texts influence and modify the existing genre system, so genre-based emotion repertoires evolve. Such changes are easier to demonstrate in Old Norse, where certain *Íslendingasögur* (sagas of Icelanders) composed in the thirteenth century show clear influence from the new romance emotional repertoire, imported through Norwegian translations of Marie de France and Chrétien.[99] In Middle English, the direct effects of translated romances on indigenous emotion systems are more difficult to instantiate because of the paucity of surviving English literary composition in the hundred and fifty years following the Conquest. Nevertheless, the augmentation of Old English heroic and epic emotions, publicly performed and expressed, with private feelings, related through psychonarration, and a somewhat sporadic access to characters' interior emotional processes is a defining feature of the Middle English romance genre.[100]

Conclusion

Words are the essential starting point for the literary analysis of emotion. Middle English adds to its substrate of surviving Old English emotion words a significant number of borrowings from

Old French and Old Norse, expanding and nuancing the semantic field of emotion. Word lists help in identifying the most obvious place where emotion is at work; close study of collocation allows us to build up associational patterns and related phonic and aesthetic effects. Emotion taxonomies are lacking in vernacular imaginative literature, but the model of the seven deadly sins, particularly as creatively repurposed by Langland and Gower in personification allegory, enables us to reconstruct the connotations, associations and delimitations of certain emotions, work that invites audiences to consider how everyday, socially embedded behaviour adheres to or transgresses their own and their community's emotion norms.

Translation studies make abundantly clear that while many Middle English words for individual emotions are acquired from French, English translators and adaptors work with particularised models of audience emotional knowledge in order to retool their stories for new reading communities. Modifications occur at the level of emotive indicia within particular episodes, or in larger assumptions about the relationship between emotions and social rank; consequently, emotions associated with courtly identity are less nuanced in those English texts intended for reading communities who are unlikely ever to imitate or interpret aristocratic behaviour in their own lived experience. Genre-specific emotion repertoires develop, most significantly in romance. These comprise emotion lexis, schemas, conventional behaviours and a range of narratological devices, such as psychonarration or soliloquy. Changes in the social constitution of audiences and consequent ideological shifts modify these repertoires, enabling emotional scripts to migrate between genres, as in the case of Margery's susceptibility to a phrase popularised in contemporary lyric; innovative emotion scripts are registered and likely to be practised by different social constituencies. As we shall see in the chapters that follow, romance (defined very loosely as 'noble men and women doing things'), along with the genres with which it hybridises, notably pseudo-history, hagiography and tragedy, is the most productive genre in Middle English for the exploration of changing narratological approaches and emotional styles.

Andrew Lynch has recently urged that the presence of emotion in literary texts is very often not signalled by the kinds of 'emotion words' under investigation in this chapter, whether uttered by a narrator or by characters themselves.[101] Rather, he suggests, 'the quality of emotions is to be looked for in the extended and multi-centred forms of narratives, with their details of the movements of bodies, words and objects in particular environments, rather than in abstract taxonomic tables'.[102] The next chapter addresses the ways in which emotion is depicted at work in textual bodies, and the complex relationship between the will, the body and individual subjectivity.

Notes

1 McNamer, 'Feeling', p. 248.
2 Rüdiger Schnell, 'Gefühle gestalten: Bausteine zu einer Poetik mittelalterlicher Emotionsbeschreibungen', *Beiträge zur Geschichte der deutsche Literatur und Sprache*, 138 (2016), 560–606 at pp. 560–1.
3 Rosenwein, *Emotional Communities; Generations of Feeling*.
4 See Alice Jorgensen, Frances McCormack and Jonathan Wilcox (eds), *Anglo-Saxon Emotions: Reading the Heart in Old English Language, Literature and Culture* (Farnham: Ashgate, 2015).
5 Michiko Ogura, *Words and Expressions of Emotion in Medieval English*, Studies in English Medieval Language and Literature 39 (Frankfurt am Main: Peter Lang, 2013), distinguishes between Old English expressions of 'a troubled state of mind' and 'a blissful state of mind' and lists them at pp. 16–17.
6 In recent psychological study, 'surprise has been re-assessed as a cognitive state, because, unlike most emotions, it can be positive or negatively valenced'. M. Foster and M. Keane, 'Why Some Surprises are More Surprising than Others: Surprise as a Metacognitive Sense of Explanatory Difficulty', *Cognitive Psychology*, 81 (2015), 74–116 at p. 75.
7 *Old English Thesaurus*, https://oldenglishthesaurus.arts.gla.ac.uk.
8 See *OED*, s.v. 'silly'.
9 The prevalence of 'swelling' as a somatic effect associated with anger is considered in Chapter 2.
10 Ogura, *Words and Expressions*, pp. 341–5, gives a useful list of Old English poetic formulas with emotion words.
11 Ogura summarises thus the changes that had taken place by the beginning of the early modern period: 'Not a few words are replaced

by native or foreign words: e.g. *(ge)belgan* by *be angry, anda* by *envy, (ge)lustfullian* and *(ge)winsumian* by *rejoi*ce, *gefea* by *joy, frofor* by *comfort* … *Irre*, being borrowed from Latin and then reinforced by French, was replaced by *anger*, though a native *wraðe* survived. *Lufu* and *lufian* remained in use without rivalry, while *hatian* ousted an Anglian synonym *feogan*, and a polysemous *teona* was replaced by *anger, grief, envy, reproach*, etc., according to context.' *Words and Expressions*, p. 127.

12 Ibid., p. 29. See for an extensive discussion of *joie*, in particular in *Troilus and Criseyde*, but also more generally in Middle English, Lucie Kaempfer, 'Finding Joy in *Troilus and* Criseyde' (DPhil thesis, University of Oxford, 2018), pp. 47–73.

13 These figures are drawn from the no longer available *Chaucer Concordance* at the University of Maine. The database for *The Canterbury Tales* contains considerable duplication, and the totals generated by the database for each word are unreliable. Where I give figures from the *Concordance* I have counted them myself. See now the Johns Hopkins University Middle English Concordance, which gives entries for Chaucer and Gower: https://middleenglish.library.jhu.edu/search.

14 Ogura, *Words and Expressions*, p. 23.

15 See Anita Auer, Denis Renevey et al., 'Introduction: Setting the Scene, Interdisciplinary Perspectives on the Medieval North of England', in Anita Auer, Denis Renevey et al. (eds), *Revisiting the Medieval North of England* (Cardiff: University of Wales Press, 2019), pp. 1–12 for discussion of the cultural distinctiveness of the medieval North; and Joseph Taylor, *Writing the North of England in the Middle Ages: Regionalism and Nationalism in Medieval English Literature* (Cambridge: Cambridge University Press, 2022).

16 Geoffrey Chaucer, 'The Reeve's Prologue and Tale', in Benson (ed.), *The Canterbury Tales*, in Benson (gen. ed.), *The Riverside Chaucer* (Oxford: Oxford University Press, 1988), pp. 78–84, lines 4029–30.

17 J. R. R. Tolkien, 'Chaucer as a Philologist: *The Reeve's Tale*', *Transactions of the Philological Society* (1934), reprinted in *Tolkien Studies*, 5 (2008), 109–71, and Simon Horobin, 'J. R. R. Tolkien as a Philologist: A Reconsideration of the Northernisms in the "Reeve's Tale"', *English Studies*, 82:2 (2001), 97–105.

18 Thanks to Dr Brittany Schorn of the Gersum Project for providing useful information about anger. See www.gersum.org/database?search%5Bkeyword%5D=anger (accessed 29 August 2023).

19 All the following quotations from the works in the *Gawain* manuscript are given in text and are cited from Malcolm Andrew and Ronald Waldron (eds), *The Poems of the Pearl Manuscript*, 5th edn (Liverpool: Liverpool University Press, 2007). The works in the manuscript may or may not all be composed by the same person, but the linguistic usages across the four poems are strikingly consistent.

20 See Ogura, *Words and Expressions*, pp. 58–61 for discussion of the '*Gawain*-poet' and preferences for alliteration or rhyme and or alliteration and rhyme, for Old Norse-derived and Old French-derived emotion words.

21 Cf. also *Cleanness* lines 947–8: 'Þe grete God in His greme bygynnez on lofte/ To wakan wederez so wylde'; *gremen* (verb) 'to anger' also occurs in *Cleanness* at lines 138 and 1347. *Grame*, from OE *gram*, occurs only twice in the manuscript: *Patience* line 53; *Gawain* line 2502.

22 Geoffrey Chaucer, 'The Canon's Yeoman's Prologue and Tale', in Benson (ed.), *The Canterbury Tales*, in Benson (gen. ed.), *The Riverside Chaucer*, pp. 270–81.

23 Geoffrey Chaucer, *Troilus and Criseyde*, ed. Stephen A. Barney, in Benson (gen. ed.), *The Riverside Chaucer*, pp. 471–585.

24 Compare Maria Elena Ruggerini's investigation of similar alliterative and associational networks in Old English and Old Norse. Maria Elena Ruggerini, 'Alliterative Lexical Collocations in Eddic Poetry', in Carolyne Larrington, Judy Quinn and Brittany Schorn (eds), *A Handbook to Eddic Poetry: Myths and Legends of Early Scandinavia* (Cambridge: Cambridge University Press, 2016), pp. 217–31, and Maria Elena Ruggerini, 'Word … soðe gebunden (*Beowulf*, line 871a): Appreciating Old English Collocations', in Marco Battaglia and Alessandro Zironi (eds), *Dat dy man in all landen fry was: studi filologici in onore di Giulio Garuti Simone di Cesare* (Pisa: Pisa University Press, 2017), pp. 141–64.

25 *King Horn*, in Ronald B. Herzman, Graham Drake and Eve Salisbury (eds), *Four Romances of England: King Horn, Havelok the Dane, Bevis of Hampton, Athelston* (Kalamazoo, MI: Medieval Institute Publications, 1997). Line numbers are given in text.

26 Bellisent in *Amis and Amiloun*, Josiane in *Bevis of Hampton* and, with the aid of a confidante, Melior in *William of Palerne* are equally forthright in declaring their love.

27 Rosenwein, *Generations of Feeling*, p. 4.

28 Ibid., p. 119. See in contrast, however, Andrew Lynch, '"What Cheer?" Emotion and Action in the Arthurian World', in Brandsma,

Larrington and Saunders (eds), *Emotions in Medieval Arthurian Literature*, pp. 46–63, who notes: 'Nevertheless, many modern names for 'emotions' – love, hatred, fear, pity, anger, envy, joy – are found in medieval texts, and seem to have been considered operative in daily life, though they may well have meant something different in the very different material and conceptual realms medieval people inhabited' (p. 48).

29 Are these actually Margery's words or those of her amanuensis? Rosenwein argues, rightly, that even if the *Book* is in effect co-composed with the man who wrote it down, he and Margery are members of the same emotional community, and share their understanding of emotion words, *Generations of Feeling*, pp. 194–5, n. 104.

30 All quotations from the *Book* are taken from *The Book of Margery Kempe*, ed. Barry Windeatt (Harlow: Longman, 2000), here p. 79, and hereafter cited in text.

31 Julian of Norwich's preferred term for the labour of childbirth, evidenced in Julian of Norwich, *The Shewings*, ed. Georgia Ronan Crampton (Kalamazoo: Medieval Institute Press, 1994), Part III, line 2494 (https://d.lib.rochester.edu/teams/publication/crampton-shewings-of-julian-norwich), and, by association, for other kinds of effortful emotion-charged activity, is *travel*.

32 Richard Rolle, 'The Form of Living', in S. J. Ogilvie-Thomson (ed.), *Richard Rolle: Prose and Verse* (Oxford: Oxford University Press, 1988), pp. 3–25; Claire Elizabeth McIlroy, *The English Prose Treatises of Richard Rolle* (Cambridge: D. S. Brewer, 2004).

33 See, for example, 'O excellent sovereign, most semly to se', in MS Bodleian 12653 (www.dimev.net/record.php?recID=3882) and in Maxwell S. Luria and Richard L. Hoffman (eds), *Middle English Lyrics* (London and New York: Norton, 1974), pp. 42–4; 'In a tabernacle of a tour', in Karen Saupe (ed.), *Middle English Marian Lyrics* (Kalamazoo, MI: Medieval Institute Publications, 1997), no. 79, and 'Upon a lady mi love is lente' (no. 80) (https://d.lib.rochester.edu/teams/publication/saupe-middle-english-marian-lyrics) both address the Virgin Mary, though her identity is ambiguous in the opening stanzas.

34 Susanna Greer Fein (ed.), *Moral Love Songs and Laments* (Kalamazoo, MI: Medieval Institute Publications, 1998), https://d.lib.rochester.edu/teams/text/fein-moral-love-songs-and-laments-in-a-valley-of-this-restless-mind.

35 See Christiania Whitehead, 'Middle English Religious Lyrics', in Thomas G. Duncan (ed.), *A Companion to the Middle English Lyric*

(Cambridge: D. S. Brewer, 2005), pp. 96–119, especially pp. 104–5. Whitehead draws attention (n. 33) to the shifting gender implications of Christ's presentation.
36 See Windeatt's discussion of the influence of Rolle's idiom on the *Book* in 'Introduction', in *The Book of Margery Kempe*, p. 11.
37 Rolle, 'The Form of Living', line 494.
38 Julian of Norwich, *The Shewings*, ed. Crampton, Part III, line 2679; Part I, line 427.
39 Ibid., Part II, lines 2016–18.
40 Compare also the view expressed by Jesus, 'it longyth to the wyfe to be wyth hir husbond and no very joy to han tyl sche come to hys presens' (p. 101).
41 We might compare the discussion of the cushions with which Margery furnishes her soul in order to welcome the Trinity: *The Book of Margery Kempe*, ed. Windeatt, p. 373.
42 On the implications of late Middle English *chere* see Lynch, '"What Cheer?"', pp. 62–3.
43 Philippa Maddern, '"It is Full Merry in Heaven": The Pleasurable Connotations of "Merriment" in Late Medieval England', in Cohen-Hanegbi and Nagy (eds), *Pleasure in the Middle Ages*, pp. 21–38, notes some lists and glosses in Reginald Pecok, Bartholomaeus Anglicus and the *Promptorium parvulorum* (pp. 21–2).
44 See Rosenwein, *Generations of Feeling*.
45 Reginald Pecok, *The Donet*, ed. Elsie Vaughan Hitchcock, EETS OS 156 (Oxford: Oxford University Press, 1921), p. 37.
46 For an account of the cardinal sin tradition, see Richard Newhauser and Susan J. Ridyard (eds), *Sin in Medieval and Early Modern Culture: The Tradition of the Seven Deadly Sins* (York: York Medieval Press, 2012), in particular Newhauser's introduction. Quotation from Barbara Rosenwein, 'Taking Pleasure in Virtues and Vices: Alcuin's Manual for Count Wido', in Cohen-Hanegbi and Nagy (eds), *Pleasure in the Middle Ages*, pp. 167–79 at p. 173.
47 Alcuin, *De virtutibus et vitiis liber ad Widonem comitem*, in PL 101, cols 613–38. See Clare A. Lees, 'The Dissemination of Alcuin's *De virtutibus et vitiis liber* in Old English: A Preliminary Survey', *Leeds Studies in English*, n.s. 16 (1985), 174–89, for example.
48 The list of eight deadly sins derives from the monk John Cassian (c. 360–465), whose works were required reading in Benedictine monasteries. See Carole Straw, 'Gregory, Cassian, and the Cardinal Vices', in Richard G. Newhauser (ed.), *In the Garden of Evil: The Vices and Culture in the Middle Ages* (Toronto: Pontifical Institute of

Medieval Studies, 2005), pp. 35–58, and Lester K. Little, 'Pride Goes before Avarice: Social Change and the Vices in Latin Christendom', *AHR*, 76:1 (1971), 16–49. Cassian's list begins with gluttony, the sin which, in reductive terms, caused Eve to take the apple, and arranges them in intensifying order of seriousness, culminating in pride as the most serious. In *Moralia in Job*, Gregory the Great reshapes the list, adding envy; he also regards pride as the first and most serious sin, an ordering which Alcuin follows. See here Rosenwein, *Emotional Communities*, ch. 3.

49 Rosenwein, 'Taking Pleasure', p. 169.
50 See Rosenwein (ed.), *Anger's Past* and her further comments in *Emotional Communities*, pp. 12–13 and 41.
51 Chaucer, 'The Parson's Prologue and Tale', in Benson (ed.), *The Canterbury Tales*, in Benson (gen. ed.), *The Riverside Chaucer*, pp. 287–327 at p. 299. While the Parson notes pride as chief sin, the Pardoner famously identifies avarice as the root of all evil (line 334). See Little, 'Pride Goes before Avarice', for a full account of the alternative evaluation.
52 As Wenzel notes, the dog-and-rosebush image is not in Peraldus, but rather in two English adaptations of Peraldus which he entitles *Quoniam* and *Primo*, models closer to whichever version(s) Chaucer used among his sources for the Tale. Siegfried Wenzel, 'The Source for Chaucer's Seven Deadly Sins', *Traditio*, 30 (1974), 351–78 at p. 377.
53 See Richard G. Newhauser, 'The Parson's Tale and its Generic Affiliations', in David Raybin and Linda T. Holley (eds), *Closure in the Canterbury Tales: The Role of the Parson's Tale* (Kalamazoo, MI: Medieval Institute Publications, 2000), pp. 45–76.
54 Suzanne Conklin Akbari, *Seeing through the Veil: Optical Theory and Medieval Allegory* (Toronto: University of Toronto Press, 2004), p. 10, cited from Flannery, 'Personification and Embodied Emotion', p. 353.
55 William Langland, *Piers Plowman: The B-Version*, ed. A. V. C. Schmidt (London and Toronto: Everyman, 1978), V: 10. All subsequent references are taken from this edition and are cited in text.
56 Rachel Stone, 'Translation of Alcuin's *De virtutibus et vitiis liber* (Book about the Virtues and Vices', *The Heroic Age: A Journal of Early Medieval Northwestern Europe*, 16 (2015); Book 27, §34, https://www.heroicage.org/issues/16/stone.php (accessed September 2023).
57 For an insightful discussion of the sins and the specific impairments of vision associated with them in contemporary manuals, see Virginia

Langum, 'Langland's Diseased Vision', *Avista Forum Journal*, 19:1 (2009), 42–5.
58 Paul Megna, 'Langland's Wrath: Righteous Anger Management in *The Vision of Piers Plowman*', *Exemplaria*, 25:2 (2013), 130–51. Megna argues that in the A-text, Wrath is omitted from the 'Confession', because the younger Langland was still working out the distinctions between righteous anger, sinful wrath, and wrath as a species of envy (p. 137); the poem is 'always already ambivalent about anger' (p. 138). Cf. the distinction made between righteous and sinful anger by Chaucer's Parson in 'The Pardoner's Prologue and Tale', p. 305.
59 Flannery, 'Personification and Embodied Emotion', p. 353.
60 Ibid., p. 352. Cf. Scheer, 'Are Emotions a Kind of Practice': '[e]motional practices can be carried out alone, but they are frequently embedded in social settings. Other people's bodies are implicated in practice because viewing them induces feelings. These effects are stored in the habitus, which provides socially anchored responses to others' (p. 211).
61 See Virginia Langum, *Medicine and the Seven Deadly Sins in Late Medieval Literature and Culture*, The New Middle Ages (New York: Palgrave Macmillan, 2016).
62 Flannery, 'Personification and Embodied Emotion', p. 359.
63 Ibid., p. 355.
64 Stephanie Downes, 'How to be "Both": Bilingual and Gendered Emotions in Late Medieval English Balade Sequences', in Susan Broomhall (ed.), *Authority, Gender and Emotions in Late Medieval and Early Modern England* (Basingstoke: Palgrave Macmillan, 2015), pp. 51–65 at pp. 51–2.
65 Ibid., p. 51.
66 Ibid., p. 52.
67 Ibid., pp. 60–2.
68 Ibid., p. 62.
69 Paul Zumthor, 'Intertextualité et mouvance', *Littérature*, 41 (1981), 8–16, in particular p. 13.
70 Rikhardsdottir, *Medieval Translations and Cultural Discourse*; see also Sif Rikhardsdottir, 'Translating Emotion: Vocalisation and Embodiment in *Yvain* and *Ívens Saga*', in Brandsma, Larrington and Saunders (eds), *Emotions in Medieval Arthurian Literature*, pp. 161–79.
71 Rikhardsdottir, 'Translating Emotion', p. 172.
72 See Stock, *The Implications of Literacy*, 1983), p. 90 for a minimal definition, and Stock, *Listening to the Text*, p. 23, where he suggests

that the 'textual community' consists of the reader or performer of a text and those who listen to the reading at a particular moment.
73 Rosenwein, *Emotional Communities*, pp. 24–5.
74 Rikhardsdottir, *Medieval Translations and Cultural Discourse*, p. 12.
75 Rikhardsdottir, ibid., notes that translations may continue to encode information about the original textual community for whom the source text was composed as well as about the target audience for the translation.
76 The poem is uniquely, if rather poorly, preserved – it lacks an ending – in Edinburgh, National Library of Scotland, Advocates 19.2.1 (known as the Auchinleck manuscript), fols 261ra–262a. The dialect of the poem is Southern, with some East Midland features, much like Chaucer's, and thus does not differ substantially from the likely Auchinleck audience's own language variant.
77 Simon Gaunt, 'Romance and Other Genres', in Roberta L. Krueger (ed.), *The Cambridge Companion to Medieval Romance* (Cambridge: Cambridge University Press, 2000), pp. 45–59 at p. 46; compare Gaunt, *Gender and Genre*, pp. 3–10.
78 Itamar Even-Zohar, 'Polysystem Theory', *Poetics Today*, 11:1 (1990), 9–94. For a valuable account of genre and Middle English romance, framed in terms of a 'generic contract', see Kevin S. Whetter, *Understanding Genre and Medieval Romance* (Aldershot: Ashgate, 2008), pp. 9–33, and Alastair Fowler, *Kinds of Literature: An Introduction to the Theory of Genres and Modes* (Oxford: Clarendon Press, 1982), pp. 59–105, on the kinds of features included in generic repertoires (though emotion or feeling is not one of them).
79 Chrétien de Troyes, *Le chevalier au lion ou le roman d'Yvain*, ed. David F. Hult, in Michel Zink (gen. ed.), *Chrétien de Troyes: Romans* (Paris: Livre de Poche, 1994), lines 5503–53. All further references are given in text.
80 See Stephen Knight, *Arthurian Literature and Society* (London: Macmillan, 1983), pp. 91–3.
81 Preserved only in London, British Library, MS Cotton Galba E. ix, fols 4r–25r; the poem's date of composition is thought to be early fourteenth century, while the manuscript dates from about a century later.
82 Citations from *Ywain and Gawain*, in Mary Flowers Braswell (ed.), *Sir Perceval of Galles and Ywain and Gawain* (Kalamazoo: Medieval Institute, 1995), http://d.lib.rochester.edu/teams/publication/braswell-sir-perceval-of-galles-and-ywain-and-gawain. All subsequent references to these poems are given in text. Whetter, *Understanding Genre*,

remarks: 'it is a critical commonplace that *Ywayne and Gawayne* shortens and steers away from Chrétien's concern in *Le chevalier au lion* with emotion, psychologizing and courtly love' (p. 68).
83 See Mary Flowers Braswell, 'Introduction', in *Sir Perceval of Galles*, in Braswell (ed.), *Sir Perceval of Galles and Ywain and Gawain*, http://d.lib.rochester.edu/teams/text/braswell-sir-perceval-of-galles-introduction. The romance is preserved in Lincoln Cathedral Library, MS 91, the Lincoln 'Thornton manuscript', written in a Northern dialect in the fifteenth century by Robert Thornton of East Newton. See Susanna Greer Fein, 'The Contents of Robert Thornton's Manuscripts', in Susanna Greer Fein (ed.), *Robert Thornton and his Books: Essays on the Lincoln and London Thornton Manuscripts* (York: York Medieval Texts, 2014), pp. 13–65, and other essays in that volume.
84 Chrétien de Troyes, *Le conte du Graal*, ed. Charles Méla, in Michel Zink (gen. ed.), *Chrétien de Troyes: Romans*, lines 900–71. For a discussion of Old French and Old Norse transformations and emotion lexis in *Le conte du Graal and Parcevals saga*, see Carolyne Larrington, 'Learning to Feel in the Old Norse Camelot?', *Scandinavian Studies*, 87:1 (2015), 74–94.
85 See Carolyne Larrington, '"Wyȝe, welcum iwys to þis place!": Emotions in the Schemas for Arrival, Return and Welcome at the Arthurian Court', *Journal of International Arthurian Studies*, 4:1 (2016), 92–103.
86 John Burrow identifies such behaviour as 'civil inattention', the polite turning of a blind eye. See John Burrow, *Gestures and Looks in Medieval Narrative* (Cambridge: Cambridge University Press, 2002), pp. 83–4.
87 *Sir Perceval of Galles*, lines 481–576, in Braswell (ed.), *Sir Perceval of Galles and Ywain and Gawain*.
88 Rikhardsdottir notes, 'emotional representation … reflects generic dispositions that one must assume audiences would have recognised and to which they would have responded'. 'Translating Emotion', p. 178.
89 Phillipa Hardman, 'Popular Romances and Young Readers', in Raluca Radulescu and Cory J. Rushton (eds), *A Companion to Medieval Popular Romance* (Cambridge: D. S. Brewer, 2009), pp. 150–64.
90 Chaucer, 'The Prologue and Tale of Sir Thopas', in Benson (ed.), *The Canterbury Tales*, in Benson (gen. ed.), *The Riverside Chaucer*, pp. 212–16, lines 915–16. See Chapter 4 below for further discussion of 'Sir Thopas'.
91 The alliterative pairing of 'romance' and *real* (royal) also occurs in *Ywain and Gawain*, line 3089. Popes and cardinals, particularly in the

plural, seem somewhat unlikely characters to appear in romance; the inclusion of the cardinals may be driven by rhyme.

92 *Sir Launfal*, in Anne Laskaya and Eve Salisbury (eds), *The Middle English Breton Lays* (Kalamazoo, MI: Medieval Institute Press, 1995), https://d.lib.rochester.edu/teams/text/laskaya-and-salisbury-middle-english-breton-lays-sir-launfal. All references to this poem are given in text.

93 See Laskaya and Salisbury's 'Introduction', ibid., https://d.lib.rochester.edu/teams/text/laskaya-and-salisbury-middle-english-breton-lays-sir-launfal-introduction#7. A text of *Sir Landevale* (with *Lanval*) is printed in A. J. Bliss (ed.), *Sir Launfal* (London: Nelson, 1960), pp. 105–28. Following references to this poem are given in text.

94 *Lanval*, in *Lais de Marie de France*, ed. Karl Warnke, trans. with notes by Laurence Harf-Lancer (Paris: Librairie Générale Française, 1990), lines 33–4. Further citations from this edition are given in text. For a persuasive reading of the *lai* as investigating anxieties associated with patronage networks, particularly where a woman offers patronage, see Laurie A. Finke and Martin B. Shichtman, 'Magical Mistress Tour: Patronage, Intellectual Property, and the Dissemination of Wealth in the "Lais" of Marie de France', *Signs*, 25:2 (2000), 479–503.

95 Corinne Saunders, 'Mind, Body and Affect in Arthurian Romance', in Brandsma, Larrington, Saunders (eds), *Emotions in Arthurian Literature*, pp. 31–46 at pp. 39–40; see also Lynch, '"What Cheer?", pp. 56–9. In *Sir Landevale*, Landevale simply spends too generously at court and falls into debt, necessitating his withdrawal (lines 21–30).

96 Rider, 'Positive Emotions', p. 65; Rider uses 'emotionology' meaning 'emotional repertoire' in a different sense from that outlined by Stearns and Stearns, 'Emotionology' and discussed at length in Plamper, 'The History of Emotions: An Interview', pp. 261–5.

97 A. C. Spearing characterises the poem as 'more concrete and dramatic but less capable of elegance and abstraction … [*Sir Launfal*] reflects a lower level of courtly manners and a narrower understanding of courtly values.' A. C. Spearing, *The Medieval Poet as Voyeur: Looking and Listening in Medieval Love Narratives* (Cambridge: Cambridge University Press, 1993), p. 106.

98 Laskaya and Salisbury, 'Introduction' in *The Middle English Breton Lays*. Bliss (ed.), *Sir Launfal*, p. 25, ascribes the tournament material, not entirely convincingly, to an anecdote found in Andreas Capellanus.

99 See Larrington, 'Learning to Feel'.

100 See Whetter, *Understanding Genre*, pp. 63–98.
101 Andrew Lynch, 'Positive Emotions in Arthurian Romance: Introduction', *Journal of International Arthurian Studies*, 4:1 (2016), 53–7.
102 Ibid., p. 56.

2

Embodiment and action

A young man has been shut in a smallish room for nearly twenty-four hours, his presence concealed from the rest of the household, for he hopes to meet privately the woman whom he loves, and to consummate their relationship. At last, his accomplice alerts him that the time to emerge is at hand, but when he enters the chamber where the lady is in bed, he finds her in a state of distress. He kneels by her bedside, offering words of greeting, then sits on the edge of the bed. But his beloved has been told (falsely) that he has come to the house so late at night because he is jealous of her supposed relationship with another man. The lady declares that she is faithful to him, that there is no truth in the allegations, and castigates jealousy as a feeling that has no place in true love. She swears her innocence, then, weeping, she hides her head under the sheets. Sensing that the much-anticipated encounter has gone disastrously wrong, the young man feels 'aboute his herte crepe ... the crampe of deth' (III: 1069–71). Cursing the original plan, perceiving that the lady is now 'wroth', instead of being receptive to sexual advances, he blurts out his blamelessness for the stratagem, then faints. The woman and man, in panic, rub his wrists and palms; she whispers words of encouragement in his ear, and at last he regains consciousness. Soon the couple are deep in conversation, swearing their love for one another, and before long they are making love with mutual enjoyment, while the accomplice tactfully absents himself.

The young man is, of course, Troilus, and his swoon – the subject of much critical discussion – has been read in multiple ways. The longed-for union with Criseyde is at hand and yet Pandarus's inventive fiction has provoked anger and unhappiness in her. Troilus has no courtly emotion script that will serve him in these circumstances.

> Ther-with the sorwe so his herte shette,
> That from his eyen fil ther not a tere,
> And every spirit his vigour in-knette,
> So they astoned or oppressed were.
> The feling of his sorwe, or of his fere,
> Or of ought elles, fled was out of towne;
> And doun he fel al sodeynly a-swowne. (III: 1086–92)

This passage closely describes the physical mechanisms by which the faint is precipitated. Sorrow *shette* Troilus's heart, preventing him from shedding tears. The vital spirits which circulate throughout the body have contracted back within the heart, evidencing both shock and fear: the kind of physiological response predicted by Galenic medicine and discussed in the Introduction.[1] Shortly afterwards, as a result of Pandarus's and Criseyde's ministrations, Troilus recovers, 'and gan bet mynde and reson to hym take / But woonder sore he was abayst, ywis' (III: 1121–2). Once rationality returns, he realises that all is not lost and he can assuage Criseyde's anger and unhappiness, though he is notably embarrassed by his own temporary loss of internal control.[2]

The physical mechanisms causing Troilus's swoon would have been clear enough for medieval audiences, but the implications of his loss of consciousness, his emotional lability in these stressful circumstances, have been very much open to debate.[3] Jill Mann situates the swoon within the 'proces' through which Criseyde has come to trust that Troilus will not seek to assert mastery over her, a 'proces' which now threatens to founder on Troilus's supposed 'jalousie'. For Troilus can neither deny the truth of the story which Pandarus has spun and of which he had no previous knowledge nor – given Criseyde's reaction – insist that his jealousy is well founded. Mann is sympathetic to Troilus's situation: '[w]e not only can, but need to, respond directly to the emotions and instincts involved', she argues, appealing to an empathetic understanding of Troilus's collapse.[4] Much like David Aers's explanation of Troilus's swoon as caused by confrontation with Criseyde's physicality as a living, breathing woman rather than the imagined love-object, Mann's account depends on reading the poem with a novelistic realism that we should treat with caution.[5] Since the 1980s, other scholars have analysed the swoon as evidence for alternative readings of Troilus's masculinity, most arguing for its integration into a historicised understanding of medieval emotional norms. Swooning belongs to romance's genre-specific emotion repertoire and consequently can be read as an entirely appropriate response to overwhelming feeling: 'an aristocratic hero's proper reaction to his own emotions of shock, guilt and compassion for Criseyde's tears', as Judith Weiss observes.[6] Alternatively, other readers have associated the swoon with Troilus's other behaviours – his frequent bouts of weeping, frenetic tossing and turning and other violent displays of passion when his love appears hopeless or thwarted – adducing it as evidence that Troilus's performance of masculinity is defective.[7]

Chaucer relays relevant information about the circumstances of Troilus's swoon. He has been subjected to hours of unusual physical hardship, immured in the *stuwe*; he is in a state of emotional lability before he even enters Criseyde's chamber, and thus his physiological reaction to the dilemma that Pandarus has involved him in is entirely explicable in contemporary medical terms. But the poet does not employ psychonarration here to make explicit the cognitive and emotional processes at work in the hero's imagined body, thus leaving open the scene's interpretative possibilities. What is certain is that Troilus feels some emotion very deeply: 'swooning is a paralinguistic marker of sincerity for men in late medieval romances', observes Graham Williams.[8] Clues to the social meaning of the incident are offered by the immediate context. When Criseyde asks him on his recovery, 'Is this a mannes game? / What, Troilus, wol ye do thus for shame?' (III: 1126–7), although she softens her words with an embrace, she unwittingly echoes Pandarus's rallying and jocular admonition to the nervous young man he releases from the *stuwe*, 'Thou wrecched mouses herte / Artow agast so that she wol the bite?' (III: 736–7). That he himself is *abayst* on coming round and that Criseyde also invokes shame opens up within the text itself the possibility that his subjection to intensely felt affect produces audience responses of embarrassment for him.

As John Burrow reminds us, '[u]nlike real people, persons in texts have no inaccessible insides, nor can they harbour intentions beyond what their author states or implies.'[9] Persons in texts do not possess physicality; their embodiment depends on the author-narrator's decision to represent in language the whole or various parts of bodies. Self-evidently, the responses of other characters to emotion or affect displays performed by bodies within literary texts can tell us a certain amount about emotional norms – or at least norms for that particular genre, even if those norms are not generalisable to actual historical circumstances. We can investigate 'emotive indicia', 'the emotive configurations embedded within the framework of the text'; as Sif Rikhardsdottir goes on to acknowledge, although our readings must take into account the 'historical and ideological contingencies of medieval emotionality', we must keep in mind our own historical situatedness.[10] Where psychonarration is lacking, or where (as in *Troilus*) an author only intermittently reveals what a character is feeling, audiences are dependent on direct speech and bodily signs to interpret characters' emotional states. Very often emotion is written – or writes itself – on the medieval body in ways to which we must attend if we are to comprehend this important signifying subsystem for emotion in Middle English literature. This system, which bridges the gap between the interior and exterior in ways that are highly various in their legibility, is the focus of this chapter.

Affect and the body

Certain theories of emotion, classical, medieval and modern, identify preconscious physical reactions as an integral stage to certain kinds of emotions; such reactions, so evolutionary psychologists would argue, confer adaptive advantage in responding to threats within the environment.[11] These reactions quickly become available to consciousness; top-down semantic processing offers immediate, interim identifications according to pre-existing schemas, feeding rough-and-ready outlines, 'sketchy candidates in search of a match', back to the body, to hormonal, circulatory and visceral systems.[12]

In Nico Frijda's terms, this enhances a person's 'action readiness', and the subject acts appropriately: taking evasive action or approaching the external stimulus, having assessed the relationship between the event and the subject's 'goals'.[13] Thus, particularly as regards the so-called basic emotions, such as fear, anger and happiness, somatic signs manifest themselves prior to cognitive appraisal, and thus, by extension, beyond conscious control or suppression. As Joanna Bourke notes: 'frightened people cannot escape physiological signs of terror. Frightened people possess a body – witness the trembling of limbs and hysterical gait of the survivors of disasters.'[14] How the sensations accompanying fear are interpreted by those who experience them and those who witness them is, she suggests, socially constructed and variable:

> although the emotion of fear cannot be reduced to the sensation of fear, nevertheless, it is not present without sensation. In noting that the body is not simply the shell through which emotions are expressed, the social constructivists are correct. Discourse shapes bodies. However, bodies also shape discourse.[15]

'Affect' has emerged as the preferred term in talking about exactly the physiological, or physical, aspects of emotion which will be the focus of the first half of this chapter.[16] Affect can be understood, so Stephanie Trigg defines it, as 'the embodied, sensate aspect of mental and emotional activity', and 'can range from bodily, cerebral or endocrine activity (a blush, a glance, a tear, a quickening of mental activity or a heartrate) to broader unconscious desires, or the network of forces that drive, motivate and connect minds and bodies with other bodies and bodies in the social world'.[17] To flag up the importance of bodies as feeling in this way is not to downplay or ignore the different constructions that subjects, literary characters and audiences place upon physical symptoms of feelings, for as Trigg suggested in an earlier article, 'in contrast to the unconscious or pre-discursive emphasis of affect theory "emotion" emerges with a more specialised sense, referring to the way we experience, narrate, and perform what we feel'.[18] While the physiological and physical indices of affect must logically pre-exist cognitive processing (even as, as Scheer and Reddy note, the body is always already subject to, and implicated within, culture), as readers we do not have access to the bodies of the past (and even less to the bodies of past fictional persons).[19] What we encounter in textual sources must then be affects 'as they are processed, described, and performed by human subjects'.[20]

In later medieval physiological models, affect is thought to be located in the heart; from there it suffuses the very core of the individual: 'hyt ys membre principal / Of the body', Chaucer observes.[21] Despite a growing medical understanding that the brain had an important part to play in the regulation of both emotion and cognition, such terms as *anima*, *animus*, *mens*, *cor* and *corpus* were used quite interchangeably in both medical and non-medical texts. As outlined in the Introduction, Galen had located cognition and perception in the brain, as responding to the environment through the sense organs chiefly located on the head. Nevertheless, Avicenna's *Canon of Medicine*, known in the west from the twelfth century, declared that the soul, the seat of emotions, was attached to the heart.[22] The 'embodied cardiac soul' is central to *The Book of Margery Kempe*; as Rosenwein and Victoria Blud register, Margery's mystical and visionary experiences are consistently located within her heart.[23] Witnessing priests performing the quasi-dramatic rituals associated with the deposition and burial of Christ one Good Friday, Margery imaginatively identifies with the Virgin Mary. This empathetic focalisation and vivid remembering 'ocupiied þe hert of þis creatur'. Although Margery's *mende* and her 'gostly eye in the syght of hir sowle' are also involved, the heart is the locus of the vision's initiation; there is no reason to suppose that the *gostly eye* is located anywhere else.[24] The intense physicality of Margery's experience is made particularly clear in this instance; in addition to her usual crying aloud, 'wex sche al blew as it had been leed and swet ful sor' (p. 276).[25]

Love at first sight demonstrates the operation of affect: metaphorised as piercing by Cupid's arrow, entering through the eye, but lodging in the heart.[26] At the instant of impact, the victim realises that something physical has occurred, but not exactly what. A speedy affective chain reaction is triggered. Thus in *Troilus*, although Cupid's dart strikes Troilus *sodeynely* (I: 209), its affect becomes operational only a few lines later, when his glance falls upon Criseyde: 'And sodeynly he was therwith astoned ... Therwith his herte gan to sprede and rise' (I: 274, 277). At lines 305–6, 'sodeynly him thoughte he felte dyen, / Right with hir look, the spirit in his herte'. Cognitive processes then come into play; Troilus resolves to feign normality for several hundred lines until he can find some privacy to consider what has happened to him. Chaucer's detailed description of the affect process lays bare how the stimulus (the sight of Criseyde) impacts upon Troilus's sense organ – the eye – and then the vital spirit reacts within the heart. Both are dependent on that first 'visceral perception', as Brian Massumi terms it; the gut-level feeling produced by Cupid's arrow, preconscious and intense, that signals and catalyses profound emotional reaction.

In *The Parliament of Foules*, as Cupid forges and files his arrows, Will, his daughter, tempers them in the nearby well (lines 211–17).[27] Chaucer thus vividly allegorises the Augustinian dictum that feelings are intricately bound up with operation of the will (*voluntas*), with a cognitive processing stage that follows swiftly on the initial onset of affect. Cognitions quickly act to temper somatic responses, particularly in the humorally well-balanced body. In 'The Knight's Tale', Theseus's first response to discovering Palemon and Arcite doing battle over Emelye is so furious that he trembles with rage, 'he for ire quook and sterte' (line 1762).[28] After his wife and sister-in-law, moved by *pitee*, kneel to him in intercession Theseus reframes the men's behaviour as typical of lovers rather than as unconscionable defiance: 'And although that his ire hir gilt accused, / Yet in his resoun he hem both excused' (I: 1765–6). David Aers astutely notes that Theseus's initial responses in 'The Knight's Tale' are frequently intemperate and wrong-headed – or, rather, instantaneous and emotional, – until reason prevails, as he registers the perspectives of others present in the scene.[29]

Augustine draws an important distinction within the body's display of affect between those signs which are not intended to signify (though they may indeed signal affect to an observer) and those which are so intended; these include primarily utterances, but also gestures, looks and other forms of non-verbal communication.[30] With a slightly different nuance, Reddy distinguishes between 'those expressions – verbal, gestural, facial and so on – that derive directly from conscious, intentional "decisions" made in the full light of attention, from other expressions that occur inadvertently or with only partial awareness'.[31] Certain somatic effects then are not under the control of the will and thus express – betray even – congruence between a character's inner feelings and outward demeanour. Other deliberately produced physical signs are intended to communicate or to disguise emotion, opening up the possibility that insincerity may be in play, and that the character's interiority is at variance with their observable performance. I begin with the bodily signs of affect understood as least under conscious control – changing colour and trembling – before considering more ambiguous emotion manifestations: smiles, laughter and weeping.

Blushing and other colour changes

A change of facial colour, blushing or paling, implies affect for both text-internal characters and audiences. Philippa Maddern discusses a fifteenth-century courtesy book that warns young men about the conclusions others may draw if a youth blushes in response to hearing bawdy tales, 'lyghtnes of word in halle ne boure'. Onlookers might conclude that 'þe trespas þou hase wroȝht', mistaking the young man's embarrassment for shame at his own past misbehaviour.[32] *Sir Gawain and the Green Knight* offers several instances of blushing that exemplify how the colour change can signal a complex cluster of emotions. Most notable is Gawain's powerful reaction to the Green Knight's revelation that he knows of Gawain's failure to hand over the girdle the previous evening. Gawain's response shows the interaction of cognitive and physical processes. First, he stands 'in study' (line 2369), processing what he has just heard, 'so agreued for greme he gryed withinne' (so upset for *greme* he shuddered inwardly) (line 2370).[33] This moment in which Gawain takes in the multiple facets of his deception lasts, in his own subjective experience, 'a gret whyle' (line 2369). The feeling of time passing is both embodied and variable in comparison to objectively reckoned clock-time: temporality a matter of individual proprioception.[34] Meanwhile, Gawain's body is registering a visible response: 'Alle þe blode of his brest blende in his face, / Þat al he shrank for schome þat þe schalk talked' (lines 2371–2). So, in fact, the 'gret whyle' extends only for as long as it takes the knight to work out what he might say; once he speaks he quickly slips into the language of confession and repentance, a discourse that Bertilak also adopts. This facial reddening recurs when Gawain reports his adventure back at Camelot: 'Þe blod in his face con melle, / When he hit schulde schewe, for schame' (lines 2503–4). Again, the blush is generated by cognitive activity along with his feelings as he seeks the words to communicate his failure to the court.

The hydraulic pressure of Gawain's blood, moving from his *brest*, site of the organ of feeling, the heart, into his face, signals affect and makes legible his emotions; a similar quickening in circulation can be inferred in the second instance. *Schame* is identified as the primary emotion in play, but in the confrontation with Bertilak Gawain's response is also explicitly linked to *greme* and with its Old English-derived cognate *grame*, when he is back at Camelot. *Greme*, as discussed in Chapter 1, is a complex emotion-term that conflates shock, anger, embarrassment and sorrow. In the scene in Camelot, Gawain's storytelling is infused with sadness: *grame* alliterates with *gref*; the knight *tened* and *groned* as he reached the story's climax.[35] The substitution of *grame* for the earlier *greme* seems significant here. Gawain's repeated rehearsals to himself of his failure during his long ride back from Hautdesert have solidified his feelings about his adventure as combining sorrow and shame. The knight's apparently instant physical and verbal reaction to Bertilak's revelation is differently inflected when he must now narrate his experience to the court, a task understood as more cognitively and emotionally complex.

Blushing occurs earlier in the poem, associated again with shame and anger. When the Green Knight laughs scornfully at the court's failure to respond to his challenge, he elicits from Arthur a shame reaction identical to that manifested by Gawain at the poem's end:

þat þe lord greued.
Þe blod schot for scham into his schyre face   [bright]
and lere;   [countenance]
He wex as wroth as wynde. (lines 316–19)

Arthur, though, can expunge his shame through action, leaping to his feet, advancing to stand by the Green Knight and accepting his challenge.[36] The narrator assures the audience of Arthur's internal emotional state of wrath – a proper response for a king *greued* by the insult to his court. Arthur's display of anger is controlled, although the aggression and authority in his speech is clear. '[T]he experience and bodily performance of shame are closely associated with social authority', observes Stephanie Trigg; the king's shame is purged by the exercise of that authority. Arthur deals effectively with the Green Knight; at the poem's end, he also acts decisively to nullify the effect of the shameful green girdle, transforming it into a 'sign of social unity' to be worn openly on the body.[37]

Becoming pale is diagnostic of hidden emotion: in particular, the sorrow of frustrated love. *The Erle of Toulous* concerns a calumniated wife, the Empress Beulybone, falsely accused of adultery by two wicked knights who have both fallen in love with her.[38] The knights decide to conspire together after one recognises in the other the signs of secret love-languishing and challenges him to explain his leanness and deathly pallor:

> 'Methynkyth thou fadyste all away,
> Os [as] man that ys clongyn in clay,
>   So pale waxeth thy blee!'   [colour]
> Then seyde that other, 'Y make avowe,
> Ryght so, methynketh, fareste thou,
>   Whysoevyr hyt bee.' (lines 493–8)[39]

So too, in *Troilus and Criseyde*, Pandarus claims that he overheard the prince lamenting his love in the palace garden; when he approached Troilus, the young man quickly tried to disguise his emotions:

> though that he for wo was pale and wan,
> Yet made he tho as freshe a countenaunce
> As though he shulde have led the newe daunce. (II: 551–3)

Pandarus's account is complicated here by the fact that his tale of Troilus's disclosure does not square with the narrator's earlier account of the prince's revelation to his friend. Overhearing a love-lament in a beautiful garden is conventional in romance; interrogating a miserable young man in his darkened bedroom is not. Just as the evil knights in *The Erle of Toulous* suspect that they share the emotional cause of their common languishing, so Pandarus (and his creator) produces a more appropriate story for Criseyde, embellished with culturally appropriate signs of affect.[40]

Pallor is also produced by shock, as blood and its vital spirits rush from the face into the heart.[41] At the conclusion of *Emare*, the heroine sends her son to ask her father, the Emperor, visiting at the papal court of Rome, to come to see the daughter whom he had consigned to sea in an open boat many years earlier. At this summons, 'the Emperour wax all pale' (line 1009); although he has already repented of his action, he is shocked to discover that there may be a remedy for his crime.[42] Intense pallor can shade into greenness, a more dangerous hue, signalling even stronger physical affect. The Man in Black encountered by the dreamer in *The Book of the Duchess* is both pale and green in hue 'for ther no blood ys sene / In no maner lym of his' (lines 488–99).[43] Criseyde is already pale with sorrow when the lovers meet in Book IV, but when she swoons, her face becomes both pale and 'grene' (IV: 1154). These complexional colours now come to characterise Criseyde. Troilus imagines her as pale and green in the Greek camp (V: 243). Criseyde's pallor recurs when she is contemplating how to return to Troy (V: 708), but once audience access to Criseyde's thoughts and feelings is withdrawn, after she misses the deadline of the tenth night, somatic signs of her affect also vanish. Pallor remains associated with Troilus until the poem's end.

Blueness of face offers a striking example of the historical variations in how affect is mediated. Where now we would understand 'his face darkened' as presaging anger, and 'his face turned blue' as a physiological indicator of a dangerous lack of oxygen, caused by some imposition on the subject's body, blueness's metaphorical and literal implications are encoded differently in Middle English semantics. We saw above how Margery Kempe turned 'blew as it had been leede' when moved by her intense Good Friday vision. Elsewhere in the *Book* she records how, in similar fits of loud crying, her body would twist to and fro, turning both 'blewe and blo as it had be colowr of leed' (p. 220). *Blo*, 'dark, discoloured, black-and-blue, livid', is a hue often associated with the dying Christ in Middle English lyric.[44] *Blo* has an early metaphorical association with sadness: in Henry Lovelich's *Merlin* (c. 1450) and the *Prose Merlin* from a similar date, Brittany is consistently designated *Breteygne bloye*. Lovelich explains the epithet as commemorating an internal physiological effect suffered by the Bretons when many of their kinsmen died in a *gret mortalyte*, after the death of Lancelot: 'Bloye breteygne hit was clepyd .... and why bloye? ... For here hertes bothe *blw* and blak they were ... for here frendis dethis' (lines 10220–4).[45] Emotional pressures within the heart produce not only legible indicators of affect on the face, but also a lastingly invisible internal discoloration that characterises the Bretons collectively.

Changes in facial colour are thus associated with shame, shock and sorrow in varying degrees within the romance affect repertoire. Explanation through psychonarration is not usually necessary; romance authors generally rely on audience understanding of the feelings that are written on the face through movement of the vital spirits to or from the heart.

Trembling

Trembling is a powerful sign of negative affect: both of anger and fear. In 'The Knight's Tale', Theseus trembles with rage when he finds the Thracian princes duelling in the forest. So too the Summoner 'lyk an aspen leef ... quook for ire' (III: 1667) in response to the Friar's Tale. In an ironic prolepsis, Troilus quivers in fury at the very sight of Diomede, come to escort Criseyde away from Troy (V. 36). His wrathful reaction is produced by his sense of impotence, and he sublimates his frustration into a series of rhetorical questions about why he does not act to prevent Criseyde's departure. In the Monk's list of tragedies, Belshazzar (Baltasar) 'for feere ... quook and siked' (VII: 2204) when the mysterious hand writes on the wall. In female characters, trembling consistently denotes fear; Criseyde's heart 'quaketh' when she is weighing up the implications of allowing herself to love Troilus (II: 809). A little earlier in the book (II: 302), Pandarus warns his niece neither to be afraid (*agast*) nor to tremble nor to change her colour, outlining a cluster of emotional manifestations all associated with the fear that he expects a woman in Criseyde's position to display.

A similar preconscious reaction is Gawain's flinching from the Green Knight's first strike. Bolens argues that '[t]he specific narrativization of Gawain's little flinch shows that his identity is a performance, highlighting as it does the effort involved in achieving a perfect correspondence between behavior and identity'.[46] The autonomic response cannot be suppressed by Gawain's determination to wait bravely for the blow; his chivalric 'idealised identity' is shown as dissociated from Gawain's 'social performance'.[47] Yet, in a move that typifies the poem's inherent ambivalences, if the flinch invites us to conclude that there is indeed 'a flaw in the system of social mastery', at the very next moment, Gawain demonstrates that he can indeed control his autonomic responses, when at the second swing of the axe he successfully suppresses his instinct to quail.[48] His self-control is figured by a simile comparing him to a stone, or rather, says the poet, a tree-stump, anchored in rocky ground by a hundred roots (lines 2292–4). Now Gawain has 'hert holle', the Green Knight can proceed, the assailant declares. While the Green Knight's earlier taunt about Gawain's cowardice elicited anger (*greme*), Arthur's knight now speculates that fear lodges in his opponent's own breast: 'I hope [think] that thi hert arwe[quails] wyth thyn awen selven' (line 2301).

Further examples of trembling – as an appropriate response to a vivid account of hell in *Sawles Warde*, for example – could be multiplied across Middle English genres, both religious and secular.[49] It signals strong negative emotional arousal within the somatic response system; whether the emotion in play is understood as fear or anger is conditioned by the context. Authors, particularly Chaucer, frequently employ psychonarration to specify exactly which passion has been aroused, for the potentiality for trembling to signal either proper knightly aggression or timorous anxiety has serious consequences for the performance of honour in the chivalric contexts of romance.

Laughter and joy

Laughter occupies an interesting intermediate position between involuntary somatic response and deliberate gesture, as a behaviour that can be unwilled or deliberately performed, signifying differently in either case. As explored in Umberto Eco's *The Name of the Rose*, laughter was regarded by church authorities as indecorous and inappropriate.⁵⁰ The Benedictine Rule is clear that monks should not be 'ready or quick to laugh' (*non sit facilis ac promptus in risu*). Speech should be modulated so that it does not provoke hilarity with *verba vana aut risui apta* (words that are foolish or likely to cause laughter).⁵¹ From the early ninth century onwards, commentators elaborated on the Rule's proscriptions, suggesting that laughter is in fact natural to man: only excessive laughter need be avoided. Hildemar of Corbie argues that *verba risui apta* (words that cause laughter) can be harnessed for good if used by the wise. Laughter within the cloister is acceptable as long as it is not the loud belly-laugh of the laity. Hildemar's defence of laughter makes possible the telling of jokes for didactic purposes: in sermons or collections of exempla.⁵² For laughter puts an audience in a good mood, making it more receptive to teaching, though this strategy had to be used in moderation if it were not to attract criticism: 'Non disse Cristo al suo primo convento: / Andate, e predicate al mondo ciance' ('Christ did not say to his first congregation / "Go and preach idle nonsense to the world"'), says Beatrice, tartly, in *Il Paradiso*, complaining that 'Ora si va con motti e con iscede /a predicare, e pur che ben si rida, / gonfia il cappuccio e più non si richiede' ('Now preachers ply their trade with buffoonery and jokes, their cowls inflating if they get a laugh, and the people ask for nothing more').⁵³

Despite these clerical reservations, there is plenty of laughter in medieval literary texts: its significance inflected by questions of social rank, gender and context, as well as genre.⁵⁴ It is a complex social behaviour involving, as a minimum, two correlates: the actor who causes laughter and the one who laughs, a bond which may be triangulated by a third party: the butt of the joke. As Andrew James Johnston points out in his reading of Chaucer's 'Miller's Tale', there are important interpretative differences between Alisoun's laughter at Absolon who has just kissed her bottom (a straightforward expression of satisfaction at a successful trick) compared with the crueller laughter of the Oxford townsfolk at poor John's plight at the end of the Tale, left with a broken arm and a clerically delivered diagnosis of madness, the apparently good-humoured laughter of the pilgrim company at the story, and indeed our laughter as the external audience.⁵⁵ As Johnston notes, unlike us and the intradiegetic pilgrim listeners, John's neighbours do not know the whole story; 'Our laughter is occasioned by the skilfully composed fabliau in its entirety, while theirs derives merely from a feeling of superiority rooted in social power structures, power structures upheld and strengthened by their very laughter.'[56] That John's injury occasions laughter instead of sympathy is indeed rooted in a sense of superiority: the neighbours have already formed a view of him much like that of the narrator, as a foolish old artisan who has married a wife too young for him and who deserves his fate. Moreover, the clerks among them, who may be privy to Nicholas's ingenious plan, laugh from a position of intellectual as well as social superiority. That sense of superiority percolates out into the frame text as Oswald the Reeve takes offence at the mocking of a character with whom he identifies on the grounds of shared social status.

Laughter is rarely about – or only about – something funny. It engages closely with anxiety: about social control, individual honour and status, and gender attributes. In literary contexts – as this Chaucerian instance exemplifies – internal and external audience responses complicate interpretations. Chaucer's pilgrim-narrator draws attention to the range of responses to the Tale: 'Diverse folk diversely they seyde, / But for the moore part they lough and pleyde' (lines 3857–8). The laughter and chatter of the nobility, the clerics, the women and the lower-ranked pilgrims stem from different perceptions of humour in the Tale: the different positionings of these imagined selves in relation to the story's protagonists. But no one, so we are assured, is upset by it, except Oswald the Reeve.

Laughter in fabliau invites interpretations grounded in differences in gender and social rank; wives laugh at husbands or unsuccessful would-be lovers; clerks laugh at those they trick; the nobility laugh at the pretensions of lower social ranks. Laughter in other genres is associated with heroic or Christian confidence, with superior knowledge. In 'The Second Nun's Tale', St Cecilia laughs in the face of her tormentor, Almachius, when he demands that she sacrifice to idols or renounce Christianity: heroic laughter showing defiance in the face of death and predicated on certainty of winning a martyr's place in heaven.[57] The disguised Bevis of Hampton laughs knowingly when other people enquire about his fate (lines 1305; 2135; 2167). When a former friend asks how he has fared since they last met (line 1991), Bevis is prompted to detail his hardships with ironic laughter.[58] A Saracen laughs pointedly when the young Bevis reveals his ignorance of the fact that it is Christmas Day (line 599). In romance as in epic, laughter is appropriate when exulting over one's enemies: Bevis invades a mosque on a feast-day, kills the imam, casts the idols (!) into a ditch and 'lough hem alle ther to scorn' – whether inwardly or openly is unclear, since there seems to be no living witness (line 1358); he laughs too when he hears how the Emperor has accidentally killed his own son (line 3116).

Other instances of laughter in romance are more in tune with modern perceptions of when laughter is appropriate. Havelok is cheerful company in the workplace, 'lauhwinde ay and blithe of speke' (line 947); Launfal laughs quietly to himself when he receives the boastful tournament challenge from Sir Valyntyne (line 540).[59] Laughter does not express joy, and thus tends not to be a key element in romance endings. When Orfeo and Heurodis return to their kingdom, their people express their happiness through music as Heurodis is formally conducted into her city. The narrator exclaims at it: 'With al maner menstraci – / Lord! ther was grete melody!' (lines 589–90). Earlier, Orfeo laughs (line 314) when he sees the fairy hunt – a major turning point as he abandons his static grief for recuperative action. Most often, the romance happy ending is accompanied by weeping at the sorrows endured, with swoons and embraces, rather than individual displays of exuberant joy.

Laughter runs through *Sir Gawain and the Green Knight*, for instance, but it is notoriously hard to interpret, particularly in communal court scenes. After the Green Knight has picked up his head and ridden noisily away, the tension in the hall dissipates:

What þenne?
The kyng and Gawen þare
At þat grene þay laȝe and grenne'. (lines 462–4)

Grenne has unpleasant implications in Middle English.[60] Its primary meaning is 'to bare the teeth, grimace or snarl', a definition supported by comparisons to animals, particularly dogs; secondary meanings are 'to gape', and 'to sneer, scoff, laugh unpleasantly; (of teeth): to be set in a grin'.[61] Laughter which shows the teeth implies scorn, rather than good humour, an effect compounded by the preposition 'at', emphatically placed at the start of the line. Gawain and the king laugh at the Green Knight – but he has already left.

I suggested above that in addition to the speaker who cracks a joke and those who laugh, we should pay close attention to the butt of the laughter. In *Sir Gawain and the Green Knight*, exactly *what* or *whom* laughter is directed at, beyond the speaker, often remains obscure. When Bertilak learns the identity of his guest he laughs, apparently with delight: 'When þe lorde hade lerned þat he þe leude [man] hade, / Loud laȝed he þerat, so lef [pleasant] hit hym þoȝt' (lines 908–9). On first reading or hearing, the audience takes Bertilak's cheerful response at face value; he is indeed glad, as is the rest of his household, that they will host so distinguished a guest over Christmas. Only later, when Bertilak's true stake in the various games is revealed, does the audience re-evaluate the laughter as having a sinister undertone. That laughter can be insincere or conceal other emotions is clear from the first laugh in the poem; when the court are playing at forfeits for kisses before the New Year feast: 'Ladies laȝed ful loude þoȝ þay lost haden / And he þat wan was not wroþe' (lines 69–70). The Green Knight laughs mirthlessly and aggressively, as noted above, when at first no one seems keen to take up his challenge (line 316). Bertilak's castle – again on first reading or hearing – is full of laughter, from the jovial host's good-humoured entertainment of his guest to the peals of laughter that accompany his wife's visits to Gawain's bedchamber; this laughter is interpreted as mediating quite different emotional effects on a second hearing.[62] Now the laughter of the Hautdesert folk will strike the audience as unpleasantly knowing: in particular when Bertilak laughs as Gawain reveals his destination, and when he prevails on his guest to take part in the Exchange of Winnings (lines 988; 1068). By contrast, Gawain's answering laughter is innocently open and cheerful. He laughs *gomenly* (merrily) when he hears that the Green Chapel is nearby (line 1079), and he and Bertilak laugh heartily both when sealing the Exchange of Winnings agreement and when it is fulfilled on the first day (lines 1113; 1398).

The poem's final burst of laughter, close to the poem's end, echoes Gawain's and Arthur's uncomfortable mirth at the end of the first Fitt. Gawain relates his adventure and its shame-filled dénouement: 'Þe kyng comfortez þe knyȝt, and alle þe court als / Laȝen loude þerat' (lines 2513–14). When knight and monarch laughed earlier, it was at the vanished Green Knight; when Bertilak laughs on hearing his guest's name, þerat identifies the fact as cause of the laughter (line 909). When the court laugh þerat here however, the butt of the laughter remains undefined. Critics have argued for two opposed possibilities: that the court laugh at Gawain, suggesting that he is over-reacting to the business of the girdle, or that they laugh in sympathy with him, uncomplicatedly rejoicing at his safe return.[63] Absent a clearly designated object for at, or other bodily manifestations such as grinning, we cannot be sure of what makes the court laugh and what that might mean. The equivocal emotional behaviour that Gawain's return elicits must be integrated into the poem's broader interpretative framework: how we hear the laughter depends on how we read the court and its understanding of chivalry.

Joy and laughter, along with singing, dancing and conversation, are closely aligned in communal courtly contexts, as Lucie Kaempfer argues; strongly associated with women, this conventional courtly behaviour bears no necessary relation to emotion.[64] In Malory, Helen Cooper notes, laughter is 'open. It is ... most often a collective experience, shared both by characters in the work, and, by extension, readers.'[65] When Guenevere finds Dinadan's dressing in women's clothes so hilarious that she falls from her chair, helpless with laughter (I: 530), the amusement is both good-humoured and shared by all present. Dinadan has willingly taken on the role of butt, 'for he was a grete skoffer and a gaper, and the meryste knyght amonge felyship that was at that time lyvynge' (I: 526), and the laughter that he provokes is both affectionate and a marker of communal rejoicing, expressing a powerful sense of identity and belonging.[66]

Tears

Tears bear witness to emotion in process; they are powerful and efficacious, as well as essentially ambiguous, for much depends on who weeps – and why.[67] Galenic teaching holds that they arise from an excess of moist humours, which is why women are more prone to weeping, being colder and wetter than men. Central to the practices of later medieval piety, scenes of weeping, quintessentially at the Passion, were depicted in painting or sculpture; devotional texts, sermons and lyrics repeatedly evoked the Virgin's tears. Such media encouraged, indeed constrained, the audience, reader or beholder to weep too, for emotion is contagious. Bodily affect works both within and across bodies, most powerfully through representationality.[68] Although Margery Kempe may weep whenever she thinks of the Passion, her bodily symptoms of emotion intensify when she is actually at Calvary or when she sees a crucifixion scene.

Direct narratorial comment, aiming at the elicitation of emotion, is not uncommon in devotional texts. In his *Mirour of the Blessed Life of Jesus Christ*, composed in the early fifteenth century, Nicholas Love urges emotional responses upon his audience, changing, as Michelle Karnes notes, the direct imperative address to the reader found in his sources, to an inclusive 'we', distancing author and meditator from the immediate scene while intimating a shared and compelling emotional response.[69] Love enjoins empathetic somatic performance. 'Miche owht we to wepe & to haue compassion with him, for he wept þis day ful sore' is how he introduces his account of the circumcision, insisting on an immediate audience response to the infant Christ's pain.[70] The scene's emotional impact is intensified through vivid description of the Virgin's own tears at her son's suffering, one that goes well beyond the authority of the Gospels and directly models the compassionate response demanded above:

> For wele mowe we wit, þat when she sey hir louely sone wepe, she miȝt not withhold wepyng, þan mowe we ymagine & þenk how þat litel babe in his modere barme seyeng hir wepe, put his litel hande to hire face, als he wold not þat she shold wepe, & she aȝeynward inwardly stired & hauyng compassion of þe sorrowe & þe wepyng of hir dere son, with kissyng & spekyng, comforted him as she miȝt.[71]

From *Ancrene Wisse* and other 'AB works' onwards, clerical authors had increasingly emphasised intra- and extradiegetical emotional display in lay devotional texts as crucial to the development of self-regulation, devotional self-fashioning and the centralising of compassion as a key Christian virtue.[72] These early Middle English writings taught their audiences how to cultivate and to perform their interior dispositions with regard to God and other members of their communities. Texts composed for the guidance for enclosed religious were the forerunners of the kind of popular vernacular guides exemplified by Love and no doubt consumed by Margery Kempe. Similarly, clerical authors, especially the chaplains in noble households, took up questions of self-discipline and moral development in romance, in particular the penitential romances, hybridising romance with hagiography. This subgenre is constituted by narratives which 'explore the nature of remorse and rehabilitation, learning and growth, by focusing on the sinner's awareness of his guilt and his relationship with God'.[73] But, as Andrea Hopkins emphasises, the penitential romances were not different in kind from other romances; they are preserved in the same manuscript compilations and addressed similar themes to both metrical and courtly romances.[74] Vernacular theology and romance together taught aristocratic, gentry and bourgeois readers that emotion was a key domain for assessing the individual's relationship with God and with the larger social community; empathetic tears were an important index of shared social values.

Foregrounded as an appropriate emotional response to a range of textual situations and in situations which open up questions of the interaction of will and body, weeping is the most multivalent of the bodily expressions of affect deployed in Middle English texts.[75] 'Tears are not to be understood as evidence, but merely as signifiers, which require interpretation, a process which inevitably risks misinterpretation', suggests Simon Meecham-Jones.[76] Can people force themselves to weep or prevent themselves from weeping? John Burrow observes that 'a cynical Scottish poet' and doubtless plenty of other medieval writers expressed the opinion that women could weep on cue.[77] A late medieval anti-feminist lyric warns of women: 'they can wepe oft and all is a sleit, / and when they list the teere is in the ey'.[78] Margery Kempe's community is often sceptical of the sincerity of her weeping, and the suggestion is frequently voiced that she is merely an attention-seeker rather than a holy woman blessed with the gift of tears.[79] Pandarus voices the possibility that a lover can weep on cue, when he urges Troilus, writing his first letter to Criseyde: 'Biblotte it with thy teres eek a lyte' (II: 1027). Troilus does indeed bathe his signet with his tears before sealing the letter, though the narrator has not described him as weeping while he composes. Yet Troilus's tears stamp the authenticity of his feelings onto his letter, 'through appealing to physical (pre-linguistic) signs of emotion, even as these tears are artfully arranged', suggests Antony Bale.[80] But, as Meecham-Jones emphasises, Troilus's tears may not be under the control of the will: 'Should Troilus's tears be understood as an involuntary act or as a choice he makes, as an act of will or a response to compulsion? ... if his tears are not to be read as an expression of his intention, then their interpretation becomes opaque.'[81]

From the Proem to Book I of *Troilus* onwards, Chaucer complicates these physical manifestations of sorrow. In his first stanzas, he asks the Fury Tisiphone to help him compose 'thise woful vers, that wepen as I write' (I: 7).[82] It is not the narrator, nor his audience, but poetry itself that weeps, while in the next stanza Tisiphone is begged to induce 'a sory chere', suitable to a 'sorwful tale' (I: 14), leaving unspecified whose face(s) – author and / or audience – will assume a miserable expression.[83] Chaucer's strategy is one of indirection: tears of grief circulate freely between author, audience, characters and the text itself. Once he has fallen in love with Criseyde, Troilus freely vocalises his paradoxical feelings in song, soliloquy, in internal speech to Criseyde and direct address to the God of Love. Yet, despite the *sorwe* that love produces, it is not until I: 543, just before Pandarus finds him 'bywayling in his chambre', that Troilus is said to shed tears. When at last they come, they come in excessive quantities: 'neigh ... he in salte teres dreynte', so the narrator tells us in a striking hyperbole.

Troilus's tears are usually shed in private, or – in Book IV – in company with Criseyde. When the lovers meet here the narrator offers an odd, little excursus – absent in Boccaccio – on the unusual, even unnatural, composition of the tears the two lovers shed: 'As bittre weren, out of teris kynde, / For peyne, as is ligne aloes or galle' (IV: 1136–7).[84] So bitter are the tears that 'in this world there nis so hard a herte / That nolde had rewed on her peynes smerte' (IV: 1140–1). Bitterness not only permeates the lovers' tears, but is imagined as percolating the audience's bodies, stinging even the hard-hearted into sympathy. Chaucer's conceit again complicates the circulation of emotion through the characters' bodies, the narrator's sentiments and the expected physical responses of the audience.

Albrecht Classen observes: 'that tears speak a unique language in symbolic terms and aim for a subtle communication would be self-evident, but literary evidence lends itself exceedingly well to explore the complexity of the phenomenon much further and to reveal the multivalence of crying in a myriad of unique contexts'.[85] Consider the case of Sir Launcelot's famously ambiguous tears at the healing of Sir Urry. Launcelot, Malory tells us in an extremely rare aside, speaks 'secretely' to God as he prays for Urry's relief. While the court rejoices, 'ever Sir Launcelote wepte, as he had bene a chylde that had bene beatyn' (I: 868) There is much critical divergence over why Launcelot weeps; a number of readers have assumed that the image of punishment suggests that Launcelot is aware of his own sinfulness and unworthiness, and that his tears are those of repentance.[86] Yet it is clear that – although the narrative hurries on ('And so I ... overlepe grete bokis of sir Launcelot') (I: 869) in order to reach Aggravaine's revelation – Launcelot does not in fact repent, any more than he did when he confessed in rather loose terms to his regard for Guenevere during the Grail Quest (I: 696). His tears are rather tears of relief, first, that he remains apparently the best knight in the world – a title lost to his son during the Grail Quest, but now publicly restored to him. Second, he weeps because, as he had beseeched God in his internal address, his 'symple worship and honesté' have indeed been saved.[87] God has refrained from openly castigating or humiliating him, but rather, just as Jesus tacitly assents to Isolde's tricksy circumvention of religious ordeal in Gottfried's *Tristan*, the Lord has shown mercy both to Urry and to Launcelot.[88] Launcelot's reluctance to expose himself before an already faction-ridden and gossiping court hints at his otherwise well-concealed anxiety and fear of shame. We would be wrong however to understand these tears as signifying guilt, compunction or an uneasy conscience – the emotional states normally associated with repentance.[89] By capitulating to Arthur's insistence ('Sir, ye muste do as we have done' (I: 866)) that he must share the chivalric community's endeavour to heal one of their own, Launcelot has risked a public shaming which would have threatened his core knightly identity, and he has got away with it. Significantly, the Urry-episode follows the battle against Sir Mellyagaunce in the 'Tale of the Knight of the Cart'.[90] That time too, the two lovers escape public exposure and shaming, thanks to Mellyagaunce's obtuseness and Launcelot's shrewdness. While Launcelot gets off scot-free again, his luck will shortly run out.

Emotionally ambivalent as Launcelot's tears are, one component in his weeping may be joy. Joyous tearfulness is prevalent in religious texts; Margery Kempe's tears commingle sorrow at Christ's suffering and joy at his assurances of salvation. The gift of tears, which Margery shares with a good number of other medieval female mystics, is a reason for rejoicing.[91] Holy men and women frequently weep for joy on others' behalf, celebrating the repentant sinner now received into heaven.[92] In romance, joyful tears are occasionally shed at the happy ending to a sorrowful tale. It is not when Orfeo reveals his identity to his faithful steward and the court that people weep, but rather when Heurodis makes her formal entry into the city to be received by her husband, now washed, shaved and reclothed. 'For joie thai wepe with her eighe / That hem so sounde y-comen seighe.'[93] The restoration of order to the community, the return of the king and queen, public rejoicing rather than private happiness elicit tears of unalloyed joy.[94] There is thus no weeping when Emaré and her son are restored to her husband and father, nor at the conclusion to other metrical romances that involve family reunion or the reunion of lost lovers, however much hardship and suffering has been endured. When Emaré's husband weeps, it is because the boy who serves him at table reminds him of his own lost son who shares the young squire's name (lines 877–84).

In Chaucer's hands, the moral tale, closely related to hagiographic romance, depicts its protagonists as weeping, apparently with joy, once the catharsis of the ending is under way. At the close of 'The Man of Law's Tale', there is a scene comparable to the close of *Emare*.[95] When Alla sets eyes on his long-lost Custance, he weeps, 'that it was routhe for to see' (II: 1052); Custance remains silent, 'her herte shet in hir distresse / Whan she remembred his unkyndenesse' (II: 1056–7). Then, just as in the case of Troilus discussed at the beginning of this chapter, she swoons. In fact, neither husband nor wife weeps for joy; their tears are elicited by the recollection of the sorrow they have endured. Custance remembers the order of banishment for her and her son, issued, she believes, by her husband. Alla's tears acknowledge his recognition of the wrongs done to her. Both husband and wife embark on formal complaints about their lots, but, once the truth has been revealed, they recover their spirits. When they kiss one another 'an hundred tymes' (II: 1074), the involuntary emotional sign is replaced by the classic, willed gesture of reconciliation. Similarly, when Custance is reunited with her father, she falls at his feet and begs not to be sent away once more. This paradoxical 'pitous joy' is embodied in weeping and swooning and resolved in kissing; wrongs committed by accident are forgiven, and a joyful family reunion ensues, symbolised by the kisses lavished on the child Maurice, hope of the future.

Equally complex emotions are at stake in the conclusion of 'The Clerk's Tale'; once again 'pitous joy' is invoked. Grisilde swoons twice and weeps 'pitously' (lines 1080–2), kissing and embracing her newly restored children.[96] Although joy is intuited at some level, it is scarcely unalloyed by memory of the tribulations survived; moreover the onlookers also weep at the spectacle of Grisilde's emotions. Traumatic physiological effects – the heart closing off from the vital spirits and the concomitant swoon – suggest that tears shed at moments of intense joy reflect back on past misery rather than present happiness. Boquet and Nagy note how the communal rejoicing at the conclusion of civil peace in the late Middle Ages is often prefaced by the shedding of copious tears by the main parties in the negotiations, as they recall wrongs done and lives lost. So too in the moral tales memory intensifies affect, signalled by dramatic somatic responses to past injustices and suffering. These must be acknowledged; forgiveness must be sought and granted before the full joy of reunion with loved ones can be entered into. This process of narrative resolution has strong parallels with that late medieval master-sacrament: penance. Both demand acknowledgement of wrongs done, repentance, forgiveness, restitution and absolution, eliciting the emotions of guilt, shame and sorrow, before the bliss of living 'happily ever after' or dying in a state of grace is attained.

Deliberate gesture: kissing, kneeling, smiling

Examples of gesture as non-verbal communication are surprisingly rare in Middle English literature; Burrow suggests that oral performance may have suppressed the notation of emotion signifiers and gesture, because the performer could be relied upon to supply them as the occasion demanded.[97] Nevertheless, medieval texts are not devoid of gestures with emotional significance though the rules of display, the social interpretation of such moves within the texts and the inferences drawn by the audience differ considerably from the emotional repertoires available in modern genres. Consequently, the significance of such gestures can be lost on the modern reader.[98] Leading an honoured guest by the sleeve and by the right hand is a gesture which reflects respect; disregarding the convention should shock an audience. In Chrétien de Troyes' *Le chevalier de la charette* Meléagant, ever discourteous and impatient of courtly custom, leads the kidnapped queen into his castle by the *left* hand.[99] In *Sir Gawain and the Green Knight* Morgan also leads Lady Bertilak 'bi þe lyft honde' (line 947), reflecting her superior status vis-à-vis the younger woman, a detail that should alert the attentive listener that the old lady may not be quite what she seems. When Malory stipulates that Guenevere leads Launcelot 'by the bare hond' (I: 850) after he arrives at Mellyagaunce's castle, that intimate gesture, placing skin next to skin, anticipates the sexual expression of love that will follow that night.

Kissing is a common gesture of friendliness, given impetus by the church custom of exchanging the kiss of peace. Burrow notes how foreign travellers to late medieval England were struck by the frequency of social kisses; one observer comments that kisses are preferred to handshakes.[100] Kissing is thus a friendly greeting among men and women, and it is offered across genders without necessarily signalling erotic attraction. Sir Gawain 'kysses' Lady Bertilak 'comlyly' and 'lappez hir a lytel in armez' (lines 973–4) on first meeting her. Kindred habitually kiss on meeting, particularly after traumatic separation; in Malory, Launcelot and Ector de Maris weep, embrace and kiss when they are reunited after Launcelot's recovery from his madness (I: 655). Sagramowr, son of the King of

Galys and Emaré, greets his grandfather, the Emperor, with a kiss though the older man does not yet know his identity (line 993). Indeed, all the visiting lords kiss the handsome young boy in greeting (lines 994–5). Kisses of peace and reconciliation are also crucial to romance endings, as noted above; the Earl of Toulouse and the Emperor, who has greatly wronged him, 'lovely can ... kysse' towards that romance's ending.[101]

The default social gesture becomes charged in certain contexts; Gawain's politesse towards his hostess on second reading anticipates the desire sparked in her visits to his bedchamber. Likewise, the implications of the kisses given by Gawain to Bertilak go beyond the merely social.[102] 'Gawain renders each kiss he has received, and in the manner in which he received it: 'sauerly and sadly' (with relish and solemnly). 'The kisses were seductive, erotic in their first instance: are they now?', asks Carolyn Dinshaw.[103] The longed-for lover's kiss that Absoloun hopes to obtain in 'The Miller's Tale', chewing spices to make his breath sweet, ends up thoroughly misdirected; his appalled reaction reframes for the audience the anticipation that preceded it. In 'The Summoner's Tale', the friar 'chirketh as a sparwe' when he sweetly kisses Thomas's wife.[104] The comparison evokes lechery, reputedly characteristic of both sparrows and friars; the sound itself is harder to interpret – does it signal lip-smacking lust or is it the equivalent of the polite modern air-kiss?[105] Certainly the friar shows little further interest in the woman, except in offering suggestions as to what he would like to eat for dinner.

Kneeling is a clear marker of humility, submission and supplication. Criseyde kneels to Hector in order to gain sanctuary in Troy after her father's defection (I: 110); Troilus falls to his knees and embraces Pandarus (I:1044) when the latter agrees to help him in his suit, an action that ill befits a prince. Pandarus kneels and praises the gods with ringing rhetoric as Criseyde consents to be Troilus's lady (III: 3032). Kneeling is essential to the performance of love-service, marking the lover's formal declaration of submission to the will of his lady. So Troilus kneels at Criseyde's bedside when he enters the chamber in Pandarus's house (III: 95), a social inversion that alarms Pandarus: '"Nece, se how this lord kan knele!' (III: 962), such that he fetches a cushion to make

Troilus's position more comfortable. Once their relationship is consummated there is no more kneeling.[106] In *The Legend of Good Women*, the affair between Dido and Aeneas is initiated by his kneeling to her in the cave (lines 1232–3) and concluded (lines 1311; 1314) by Dido kneeling, both before altars and before her lover; at last, she prostrates herself at his feet, begging him to not break his oaths to her.[107]

Subversion of the kneeling ritual is intended to shock. Late in the *Morte Darthur*, Guenevere must seek a champion to defend her in the affair of the Poisoned Apple. None of the knights is prepared to take her cause on, for they all believe her guilty. An increasingly anxious queen pleads with Bors for aid, but he merely rebukes her for her ill-treatment of Launcelot (I: 796–7). Guenevere acknowledges her fault. 'And therewith she kneled down upoon both hir kneys and besought sir Bors to have mercy uppon her.' At this moment Arthur enters. 'And than sir Bors toke hir up and seyde, "Madam, ye do me grete dishonoure"' (I: 796). A queen being forced to kneel to a knight to beg him for service is entirely contrary to chivalric convention. The king's entrance embarrasses Bors into reacting to her gesture, and he raises her up. Caxton labours this point through expansion: 'Ryght so cam kynge Arthure and founde the queen knelynge *afore sir Bors*' (I: 797).[108] It is only after the king requires Bors to defend his wife, 'for the love ye owghe unto sir Launcelot', invoking his obligations, not to king or queen, but to his cousin, that Bors agrees to act. Since a modern audience associates kneeling with pleading it may fail to note this serious *bouleversement* of medieval social hierarchy.[109]

Malory reframes his sources completely in his construction of this scene. In the *Stanzaic Morte* the emotional ambience is agonising in its intensity: the queen kneels and pleads movingly for support before a succession of knights, each of whom brusquely rejects her request.[110] In the *Mort Artu* the queen sends for Bors and Ector and promptly kneels to them, weeping. As soon as she has finished speaking, Bors helps her to his feet and weeps too in sympathy, offering her immediate reassurance that a better champion than he will be found. Bors's reaction is the courteous, correct, but also humane, one; that Ector is also included in the queen's address doubtless increases the pressure on him to behave properly.[111] Malory's Bors, in contrast, risks being seen as boorish.

Sometimes overlapping with laughter, smiling is an ambiguous and deliberate emotional gesture. As Burrow notes, medieval English (and French) authors rarely qualify their descriptions of smiles further than suggesting that a character might smile 'a lytel' or 'with lyppes smal laȝande', actions quite distinct from the fullthroated laughter of the sort discussed above.[112] Windeatt comments that there is a smile of superior knowledge, epitomised in *Troilus* where characters recognise that their interlocutors are being disingenuous.[113] So, when Criseyde begins to press Pandarus on Troilus's capacities to speak eloquently about love, 'Tho Pandarus a litel gan to smyle / And seyde, "By my trouthe, I shal yow telle"' (II: 505–6); later, Criseyde teases her uncle by pretending that she will not write to Troilus, but rather he must give her answer for her, and 'gan to smyle' (II: 1159). Cassandra too, as Burrow observes, smiles when Troilus comes to consult her about his disturbing dreams (V: 1457).[114] Given her prophetic gifts, Cassandra's smile intimates an ironic knowledge: she knows both what the dream means and that her brother will not believe her. Not all smiles betoken knowledge: Troilus's smiling (surely more akin to smirking) at those of his retinue who are foolish enough to fall in love (I: 194) is rather a marker of ignorance.

Troilus's spontaneous smile when Pandarus comes to tell him in the chamber at Deiphebus's house that Criseyde is coming up to see him will soon moderate into anxiety. 'The olde wyf' in 'The Wife of Bath's Tale' smiles in amusement at her husband's unwillingness to consummate their marriage (line 1086).[115] Her smile too indicates knowledge: of who she really is and how the knight may be able to release himself from the uncomfortable position of sexual constraint in which he finds himself. Elayne of Astolat's expression as the barge bearing her corpse rolls at the Westminster riverbank is quietly mysterious: 'she lay as she had smyled' (I: 829).[116] What – if she is smiling – does Elaine smile at? Malory's smiles, as Helen Cooper astutely notes, are 'a code for secret or privileged knowledge ... a one-sided recognition, an inward thought'; 'the smile is not social, not shared, but as it is visible, it requires an explanation'.[117] Elayne's smile is multivalent, implying perhaps the end of her suffering, consummation, even salvation, but, ultimately, asserts Cooper, '[i]nterpretation in this case is disabled at source; finally the emotions of the dead are beyond speculation.'[118]

Unlike the involuntary signals of affect discussed earlier, gesture is not always reliable as an index of a character's interiority. Not only can characters act insincerely, performing in such a way as to suggest emotions they do not feel and intentions they do not harbour, fiction's gestural systems that are thoroughly embedded in particular social contexts become inappropriate or meaningless as customs and conventions change. This affects the legibility of gesture over time; they become differently understood, as purely metaphorical, as in 'tearing one's hair', or pathologised: scratching the face in grief. Although trembling, swooning and colour changes are physiologically produced by the movement of vital spirits, indicia such as weeping or laughter open up larger questions of congruence with regard to characters' motivation and interiority; neither entirely involuntary nor completely falling under the individual's control, the ambiguity of tears and laughter allows medieval authors to complicate the ways in which the body communicates subjective processes.

Conclusion

The somatic modes through which medieval bodies register emotion in literary texts are generally legible, even to modern audiences. Genre determines some of the variance in how characters' faces, gestures or bodies indicate which emotions are at work in a particular context or expressed through particular scripts. Nevertheless, characters within texts – and, we surmise, their audiences – are usually confident that they read these indicia correctly. It is possible to adduce some evidence from contemporary illustration and sculpture to support theorisations of somatic emotional display, although a holistic approach to the positioning of the whole body in context is advisable.[119] That bodily stance, facial expression, tears and colour changes were regarded in medieval society as reliable indicators of internal psychological processes is supported by the evidence Philippa Maddern adduces: that a chin jutting forward denotes anger; repeated weeping, unhappiness; a joyful face at a marriage, consent – and is understood as such in courts of law.[120]

Secular and religious texts draw upon somewhat different emotion repertoires, yet the textual indices of emotion as written on the body are largely consistent across generic boundaries. Unhappiness is signalled by weeping, bowing the head, raising the hands to the face or wringing the hands. Fear results in the loss of colour as blood drains away from the face, the vital spirits rushing into the heart and by trembling. Anger is shown by facial reddening, and, as Maddern's witnesses show, with *vultu pretenso* (the face jutting forward).[121] Shame is also indicated by blushing (without the thrust-forward chin). Context and motivation remain crucial; authorial psychonarration is sometimes employed to clarify which emotions exactly are in operation, particularly when the physiological signs are ambivalent, as when a noble man begins to tremble. Blushing modestly at one's own thoughts or the insinuations of others, as Criseyde frequently does, is different in implication from the fiery flush of shame that Gawain experiences at the Green Knight's revelation. Happiness is less clearly marked: tears of joy, as we have seen, are surprisingly rare. Smiling and laughing may indicate pleasure, but equally may signify complex cognitive processes: knowledge withheld, or social dominance triumphantly confirmed. The hydraulic physiological model of humoral circulation which increasingly centres emotion in the heart explains the swoons and physical collapse that accompany emotional extremes across different kinds of Middle English writing.

All these are primarily involuntary somatic expressions of emotion, adduced by authors to particularise and make credible the emotions thought appropriate or normative in the narrative situation. Other bodily actions fall under the heading of behaviour; they are deliberately willed and performed movements: kneeling, kissing, embracing, taking by the hand. Nevertheless, the connotations of such actions are clearly understood by those who perform them and those who receive or witness them. Gestural norms can of course be subverted for plot purposes; the kisses exchanged in *Sir Gawain and the Green Knight* bear a range of different meanings for characters and audience, depending on who is kissing whom, while the comedy of Absolon's 'misdirected kiss' ('The Miller's Tale', lines 3733–9) derives from the mismatch between the young clerk's delighted expectation, the romantic implication of permitting a wooer a kiss and the exaggerated disgust with which Absoloun responds to intimate contact with the beloved.[122] Alisoun's contemptuous vocalisation, 'Tehee' ('The Miller's Tale', line 3740), compounds his humiliation.

The suggestion of affect through gesture or somatic signs can often be achieved through a minimal allusion to one well-recognised physical indicium; the audience can imaginatively supply the additional signs and probable gestures that complete the emotion script appropriate to the narrated. A. C. Spearing notes how efficiently *King Horn*'s 'synecdochic narrative style' works: a 'single gesture stands for fuller (and imagined) emotional responses'.[123] When Rymenhild unbolts her door and catches sight of the drowned body of the messenger she has sent to Horn to warn of her impending marriage to King Modi, the detail 'hire fingres he gan wringe' (line 82) is, as Spearing observes, enough for the audience to provide from their own 'emotionology' – and their knowledge of the genre-appropriate emotion repertoire – her thoughts and feelings and to intuit further unnarrated physical signs of grief.

Bodily signs and gestures allow, note Boquet and Nagy, 'la théorisation savante, la cartographie des émotions [qui] éclairent la nature de la peur ou de la honte dans telle ou telle situation, et son usage tant par l'auteur d'un texte que par son protagoniste' (knowing theorisation, the mapping of emotions [which] illuminate the nature of fear or of shame in such and such a situation, as much for the text's author as for his protagonists).[124]

When read with 'une vision cognitive et constructiviste' (a cognitive and constructivist view) and in a well-understood context, the somatic signs explored in this chapter offer strong, if not always unequivocal, evidence for the signalling and significance of emotions in medieval literary texts.[125] Author and audience collude in creating fictional characters inhabiting fictional bodies that are congruent with the thoughts, feelings and motivations produced by context and plot. However, congruence cannot always be taken for granted: dissimulation of emotion was easily imaginable. Characters who pretend about their emotional states include such diverse figures as '[t]he smylere with the knyf under the cloke' (line 1999), whom Chaucer pictures in the temple of Mars in 'The Knight's Tale'; May, in 'The Merchant's Tale', who weeps so convincingly when she declares her faithfulness to Januarie, even while she signals to Damyan to start climbing the pear-tree; or Gower's hypocritical lover who counterfeits the physiological effects of lovesickness as part of his campaign to seduce a female victim: 'The colour of the reyni mone / With medicine upon his face / he set'.[126] In response, Amans hastily assures Genius that he himself demonstrates the converse case: 'my corage / Hath ben mor siek than my visage' (I: 715–16). Even before she leaves Troy, in Lydgate's account, Criseyde's doubleness is signalled through the perennial misogynist observation that women can cry at will:

As wommen kan falsly teris borwe –
In her herte though ther be no sorwe –
Lik as thei wolde of verray trouthe deie.
Thei can think oon and another seie.[127]

The strategic deployment of emotive indicia could thus trump the 'natural' movements of the humours and the spirits within the body, an understanding that problematises the connections between affect, will and motivation. The performative function of emotions, in getting things done in the textual world, as key drivers in the advancement of plot, and the deliberate and self-conscious deployment of emotion-related behaviour, emotion as performance, expand our understanding of what emotions are good for in imaginative writing, and are the focus of the next chapter.

Notes

1 See Introduction, p. 24; cf. Barbara Rosenwein, 'Worrying about Emotions', pp. 834–6, and Zoltán Kövecses, 'Emotion Language: A New Synthesis', in Zoltán Kövecses, *Metaphor and Emotion, Language, Culture, and Body in Human Feeling*, Studies in Emotion and Social Interaction (Cambridge: Cambridge University Press, 2000), pp. 182–99, in which he elaborates the emotion-as-force metaphor (not necessarily in liquid form).

2 See Elizabeth M. Liggins, 'The Lovers' Swoons in *Troilus and Criseyde*', *Parergon*, 3 (1985), 93–106 for comparison of Troilus's

and Criseyde's swoons and their treatment with contemporary medical sources. Liggins prosaically notes the effects of confinement in a small, probably over-warm room and lack of food as contributing to Troilus's collapse (p. 96).
3 Jill Mann, 'Troilus' Swoon', *Chaucer Review*, 14:4 (1980), 319–35.
4 Ibid., p. 322.
5 David Aers, *Community, Gender and Individual Identity: English Writing 1360–1430* (London: Routledge, 1988), pp. 129–32.
6 See the most recent interventions in this debate, Barry Windeatt, 'The Art of Swooning in Middle English', in Christopher Cannon and Maura Nolan (eds), *Medieval Latin and Middle English Literature: Essays in Honour of Jill Mann* (Woodbridge: Boydell and Brewer, 2011), pp. 211–30, who sees the swoon as a kind of self-absenting (p. 212); Megan G. Leitch, 'Sleeping Knights and "Such Sorow-Makynge": Affect, Ethics and in Malory's *Morte Darthur*', *Arthurian Literature*, 31 (2016), 83–100, discusses the multivalent nature of swooning as 'due to uncomfortable emotions', ranging (in Malory) from sorrow to blood-loss to empathy to sexual frustration and hysteria (understood in a Galenic sense; p. 98); Judith Weiss, 'Modern and Medieval Views on Swooning: The Literary and Medical Contexts of Fainting in Romance', in Rhiannon Purdie and Michael Cichon (eds), *Medieval Romance, Medieval Contexts* (Cambridge: D. S. Brewer, 2011), pp. 121–34, quote from p. 134.
7 See the extensive discussions in Tison Pugh and Marcia Smith Marzec (eds), *Men and Masculinities in Chaucer's* Troilus and Criseyde (Woodbridge: D. S. Brewer, 2008), especially Gretchen Mieszkowski, 'Revisiting Troilus's Faint', pp. 43–57.
8 Williams, *Sincerity*, p. 146.
9 Burrow, *Gestures and Looks*, p. 3.
10 Sif Rikhardsdottir, 'Medieval Emotionality', p. 75.
11 See the discussion in the Introduction and, for an evolutionary psychological explanation, for example, John Tooby and Leda Cosmides, 'The Past Explains the Present: Emotional Adaptations and the Structure of Ancestral Environments', *Ethology and Sociobiology*, 11 (1990), 375–424.
12 William Reddy, in Eustace et al., '*AHR* Conversation'. See also Jenefer Robinson, *Deeper than Reason*, pp. 41–2, and for further elaboration of new understandings of top-down processing systems and 'preconscious' emotions, see now Reddy, 'Courts and Pleasure', p. 139.
13 Nico Frijda, 'The Laws of Emotion', *American Psychologist*, 43 (1988), 349–58, reprinted in Jennifer Jenkins, Keith Oatley and

Nancy Stein (eds), *Human Emotions* (Oxford: Wiley-Blackwell, 1988), pp. 270–87.
14 Joanna Bourke, 'Fear and Anxiety: Writing about Emotion in Modern History', *History Workshop Journal*, 55 (2003), 111–33 at p. 122.
15 Ibid., p. 123.
16 For a useful introduction to affect theory, see Glenn Burger and Holly Crocker, 'Introduction', in Glenn Burger and Holly Crocker (eds), *Medieval Affect, Feeling, and Emotion* (Cambridge: Cambridge University Press, 2019), pp. 1–24.
17 Stephanie Trigg, 'Affect Theory', in Susan Broomhall (ed.), *Early Modern Emotions: An Introduction* (London: Routledge, 2017), pp. 10–13 at p. 11.
18 Stephanie Trigg, 'Introduction', p. 7.
19 See Introduction, and Scheer, 'Are Emotions a Kind of Practice'; Reddy, in Eustace et al., '*AHR* Conversation'.
20 Stephanie Trigg, 'Introduction', p. 7.
21 Geoffrey Chaucer, *The Book of the Duchess*, ed. Colin Wilcockson, in Benson (gen. ed.), *The Riverside Chaucer*, pp. 329–46, lines 495–6.
22 Eric Jager, *The Book of the Heart* (Chicago: University of Chicago Press, 2000), p. xv; see also Heather Webb, *The Medieval Heart* (New Haven, CT: Yale University Press, 2010).
23 Victoria Blud, 'Emotional Bodies: Cognitive Neuroscience and Mediaeval Studies', *Literature Compass*, 13:6 (2016), 457–66, gives a lucid overview of the impact of increasingly cardiocentric models for the soul in Middle English texts. See also Rosenwein, *Generations of Feeling*, pp. 195–9.
24 Blud, 'Emotional Bodies', p. 462. Here with reference to *The Book of Margery Kempe*, ed. Windeatt, p. 275.
25 See later in Chapter 2, pp. 104–5.
26 I owe this observation to Anna Czarnowus.
27 Geoffrey Chaucer, *The Parliament of Fowls*, ed. Larry D. Benson, in Benson (gen. ed.), *The Riverside Chaucer*, pp. 383–94.
28 Geoffrey Chaucer, 'The Knight's Tale', ed. Larry D. Benson, in Benson (gen. ed.), *The Riverside Chaucer*, pp. 37–66. See further discussion of trembling below in Chapter 2, pp. 105–6.
29 David Aers, *Chaucer* (Brighton: Harvester, 1986), pp. 24–32.
30 Augustine, *De doctrina christiana*, ed. R. P. H. Green (Oxford: Oxford University Press, 1996), II: 1–7; Burrow, *Gestures and Looks*, pp. 2–3.
31 Plamper, 'The History of Emotions: An Interview', pp. 241–2.

32 F. J. Furnivall (ed.), *Early English Meals and Manners*, EETS OS 32 (London: Oxford University Press, 1868), p. 187. Cited from Philippa Maddern, 'Reading Faces: How Did Late Medieval Europeans Interpret Emotions in Faces?', *Postmedieval*, 8:1 (2017), 12–34 at pp. 20 and 25.
33 All citations from Andrew and Waldron (eds), *Sir Gawain and the Green Knight*, in Andrew and Waldron (eds), *The Poems of the Pearl Manuscript*; references are given in text.
34 Thanks to Guillemette Bolens for this point.
35 See the discussion of *grame* as an Old English-derived variant in Chapter 1.
36 Bolens takes a different view: 'Arthur's kinesic reaction is at once vehement and inadequate. The challenge is not to do battle but rather to meet a specific and unusual test: chop off the head of the consenting, or rather demanding, challenger. By reacting inappropriately, the king exposes himself and endangers his worthiness.'. *The Style of Gestures*, p. 126.
37 Stephanie Trigg, '"Shamed Be …": Historicizing Shame in Medieval and Early Modern Courtly Ritual', *Exemplaria*, 19:1 (2007), 67–89 at p. 76.
38 *The Erle of Toulous* is probably a late fourteenth-century composition. It is preserved in a number of important fifteenth- and sixteenth-century compilation manuscripts: Bodleian 6922 (Ashmole 61), Bodleian 6926 (Ashmole 45), Cambridge Ff.2.38 and Lincoln Cathedral Library, MS 91 (Thornton).
39 *The Erle of Toulous*, in Laskaya and Salisbury (eds), *The Middle English Breton Lays*, http://d.lib.rochester.edu/teams/text/laskaya-and-salisbury-middle-english-breton-lays-erle-of-tolous.
40 See Williams, *Sincerity*, pp. 192–3.
41 Maddern, 'Reading Faces', pp. 20–1.
42 *Emare*, in Laskaya and Salisbury (eds), *The Middle English Breton Lays*, http://d.lib.rochester.edu/teams/text/laskaya-and-salisbury-middle-english-breton-lays. Further references are given in text.
43 Chaucer, *The Book of the Duchess*, ed. Wilcockson, lines 488–99. See Robert G. Benson, *Medieval Body Language: A Study of the Use of Gesture in Chaucer's Poetry*, Anglistica 71 (Copenhagen: Rosenkilde and Bagge, 1980), p. 23.
44 See *MED* references *ad loc.*
45 Henry Lovelich, *Merlin*, ed. E. A. Kock, Part I, EETS Extra Series 93 (London: Kegan, Paul, 1904). Cf. Geoffrey Chaucer, *Compleynt of Mars*, ed. Laila Z. Gross, in Benson (gen. ed.), *The Riverside Chaucer*,

pp. 643–7, line 8 'wyth teres blew' (glossed by its editor as 'livid'). 'Black and blue' as the result of beating is found as early as the Harley lyrics from around 1325, again in connection with Christ's suffering body. See 'Iesu, swete is þe loue of þe', in Karl Böddeker (ed.), *Altenglische Dichtungen des Harl. 2253* (Berlin: Weidemann, 1878), p. 199.
46 Bolens, *The Style of Gestures*, p. 156.
47 Ibid., p. 161.
48 Ibid.
49 See Chapter 4.
50 Umberto Eco, *The Name of the Rose* (London: Picador, 1984), pp. 79–83. See also Boquet and Nagy, *Sensible Moyen Âge*, pp. 303–4.
51 *Benedictine Rule*, 7.59; 4.53; https://www.intratext.com/IXT/LAT 0011/ (accessed 29 August 2023).
52 For an overview of ecclesiastical attitudes to laughter, see Olle Ferm, 'Laughter and the Medieval Church', in Förnegård et al. (eds), *Tears, Sighs and Laughter*, pp. 166–81, and Wim Verbaal, 'Bernard's Smile and the Conversion of Laughter', in the same volume, pp. 193–215.
53 Dante Aligheri, *Il Paradiso*, Canto XXIX, lines 109–10; 115–17. Cited from Princeton Dante Project, https://dante.princeton.edu/dante/pdp/commedia.html. Boquet and Nagy observe that while the jokes deployed in exempla may sometimes be subversive, more often they entrench social inequality: 'Ce qui fait rire certains auditeurs fait honte à d'autres' (that which makes some audience members laugh makes others ashamed). *Sensible Moyen Âge*, p. 341.
54 Manuel Pfister, 'Introduction: A History of English Laughter?', in Manfred Pfister (ed.), *A History of English Laughter: Laughter from Beowulf to Beckett and Beyond* (Amsterdam and New York: Rodopi, 2002), pp. v–x, especially pp. v–vii.
55 Andrew James Johnston, 'The Exegetics of Laughter: Religious Parody in Chaucer's *Miller's Tale*', in Pfister (ed.), *A History of English Laughter*, pp. 17–33, here pp. 18–20.
56 Ibid., p. 19.
57 Benson, *Medieval Body Language*, p. 46.
58 *Bevis of Hampton*, in Herzman, Drake and Salisbury (eds), *Four Romances of England*, http://d.lib.rochester.edu/teams/text/salisbury-four-romances-of-england-bevis-of-hampton. Further references are given in text.
59 *Havelok*, in Herzman, Drake and Salisbury (eds), *Four Romances of England*, https://d.lib.rochester.edu/teams/text/salisbury-four-rom

ances-of-england-havelok-the-dane; *Sir Launfal*, in Laskaya and Salisbury (eds), *The Middle English Breton Lays*.
60 See *MED*, s.v. 'grennen'.
61 Ibid. Benson, *Medieval Body Language*, p. 16, notes Hate's aggressive grin 'for dispitous rage' in the Middle English translation of the *Roman de la rose* (line 156).
62 For Lady Bertilak's laughter, see lines 1207; 1212; 1290; 1479; 1757; significantly, on the second day, 'Þay laȝed and layked longe' (line 1554).
63 See Martin Stevens, 'Laughter and Game in *Sir Gawain and the Green Knight*', *Speculum*, 47 (1972), 65–78. For a reading critical of the court's attitude, see Patricia Clare Ingham, *Sovereign Fantasies: Arthurian Romance and the Making of Britain* (Philadelphia, PA: University of Pennsylvania Press, 2001), p. 133. For positive assessments of the laughter as re-integrative, see, for example, A. C. Spearing, *The Gawain-Poet* (Cambridge: Cambridge University Press, 1970), p. 230; and David Aers, 'Christianity for Courtly Subjects: Reflections on the *Gawain*-Poet', in Derek Brewer and Jonathan Gibson (eds), *A Companion to the Gawain-Poet* (Cambridge: D. S. Brewer, 1997), pp. 91–101 at pp. 99–100.
64 See Albrecht Classen, 'Laughter as an Expression of Human Nature in the Middle Ages and the Early Modern Period: Literary, Historical, Theological, Philosophical, and Psychological Reflections. Also an Introduction', in Albrecht Classen (ed.), *Laughter in the Middle Ages: Epistemology of a Fundamental Human Behavior, its Meaning and Consequences* (Berlin and Boston, MA: De Gruyter, 2015), pp. 1–140 at p. 14. Compare Lucie Kaempfer's observations of Blanche (in *The Book of the Duchess*) and Criseyde's performance of laughter, in 'Finding Joy in Chaucer's *Troilus and Criseyde*', pp. 194–6.
65 Helen Cooper, 'Afterword: Malory's Enigmatic Smiles', in Brandsma, Larrington and Saunders (eds), *Emotions in Medieval Arthurian Literature*, pp. 181–8 at p. 185.
66 Sir Thomas Malory, *Le Morte Darthur*, ed. Peter J. C. Field, 2 vols (Cambridge: D. S. Brewer, 2013), I: 861–9. All further references are to this edition and are given in text.
67 Maddern, 'Reading Faces', p. 26; Elina Gertsman, 'Preface: "Going they Went and Wept": Tears in Medieval Discourse', in Elina Gertsman (ed.), *Crying in the Middle Ages: Tears of History* (New York and London: Routledge, 2012), pp. xi–xx at p. xi.
68 See Piroska Nagy's discussion of Angela de Foligno and Lukardis of Oberweimar in 'The Power', pp. 28–33; on emotional contagion, see Chapter 4.

69 Nicholas Love, *Mirror of the Blessed Life of Jesus Christ*, ed. Michael G. Sargent, Garland Medieval Texts 18 (New York and London: Garland, 1992); Michelle Karnes, 'Nicholas Love and Medieval Meditations on Christ', *Speculum*, 82:2 (2007), 380–408.
70 Love, *Mirror of the Blessed Life*, ed. Sargent, p. 41.
71 Ibid.
72 Williams, *Sincerity*, pp. 146–7; McNamer, *Affective Meditation*.
73 Andrea Hopkins, *The Sinful Knights: A Study of Middle English Penitential Romance* (Oxford: Clarendon Press, 1990), p. 199.
74 Ibid., pp. 197–8.
75 See Chapter 4 for extended discussion of audience emotion responses.
76 Simon Meecham-Jones, '"He in Salte Teres Dreynte": Understanding Troilus's Tears', in Katrina O'Loughlin, Andrew Lynch and Stephanie Downes (eds), *Emotions and War: Medieval to Romantic Literature* (Basingstoke: Palgrave Macmillan, 2015), pp. 77–97 at p. 90.
77 Burrow, *Gestures and Looks*, p. 4.
78 'Against Women' (no. 133), in R. T. Davies (ed.), *Medieval English Lyrics: A Critical Anthology* (London: Faber and Faber, 1999), p. 239.
79 Rosenwein, *Generations of Feeling*, pp. 198–9.
80 Antony Bale, 'Afterword: Three Letters', in Burger and Crocker (eds), *Medieval Affect, Feeling, and Emotion*, pp. 203–17 at p. 209.
81 Meecham-Jones, '"He in Salte Teeres Dreynte"', p. 90.
82 See Lucie Kaempfer, 'Drinking Sorrow and Bathing in Bliss'.
83 See on *Troilus*'s opening stanzas, and on Middle English literary tears more generally, Stephanie Trigg, 'Langland's Tears: Poetry, Emotion, and Mouvance', *Yearbook of Langland Studies*, 26 (2012), 27–48 at p. 31.
84 These tears are even more bitter than those shed by Myrrha, whose transformation into a tree made her weep tears of myrrh (*Troilus*, IV: 1139–40); see Ovid, *Metamorphoses* 10:298–502, in *Metamorphoses II*, ed. Jeffrey Henderson, trans. Frank Justus Miller, 2nd edn, rev. G. P. Goold, Loeb Classical Library 43 (Cambridge, MA: Harvard University Press, 1984), pp. 84–99, and notes in Benson (gen. ed.), *The Riverside Chaucer*, p. 1048.
85 Albrecht Classen, 'Crying in Public and Private: Tears in Medieval German Literature', in Gertsman (ed.), *Crying in the Middle Ages*, pp. 230–48 at p. 231.
86 See Kevin S. Whetter, 'Weeping, Wounds and Worship in Malory's *Morte Darthur*', *Arthurian Literature*, 31 (2016), 61–82 at pp. 76–8 for a recent survey of critics discussing the episode.

87 Compare Whetter, who reads Launcelot's reaction as constituted by 'tears of earthly emotion, principally relief and gratitude' (ibid., p. 77). However, he interprets the function of the weeping somewhat differently, as fundamentally a form of 'sympathetic healing' which 'actively reinforces Launcelot's heroic stature' (p. 78). Cf. Earl R. Anderson, 'Malory's "Fair Maide of Ascolat"', *Neuphilologische Mitteilungen*, 87 (1986), 237–54 at p. 249, n. 24.
88 Gottfried von Strassburg, *Tristan*, XXIV: 15733–6, https://www.hs-augsburg.de/~harsch/germanica/Chronologie/13Jh/Gottfried/got_tr00.html.
89 See Stephanie Trigg, 'Weeping Like a Beaten Child: Figurative Language and the Emotions in Chaucer and Malory', in Burger and Crocker (eds), *Medieval Affect, Feeling, and Emotion*, pp. 25–46.
90 The Mellyagaunce episode is discussed in detail in Chapter 3.
91 Studied by Piroska Nagy, *Le don des larmes au Moyen Âge. Un instrument spirituel en quête d'institution* (Paris: Albin Michel, 2000).
92 See William M. Aird, 'The Tears of Bishop Gundulf: Gender, Religion, and Emotion in the Late Eleventh Century', in Cordelia Beattie and Kirsten A. Fenton (eds), *Intersections of Gender, Religion and Ethnicity in the Midde Ages* (Basingstoke: Palgrave Macmillan, 2011), pp. 62–84 for an early example of the practices of affective piety.
93 *Sir Orfeo*, lines 591–2, in Laskaya and Salisbury (eds), *The Middle English Breton Lays*, http://d.lib.rochester.edu/teams/text/laskaya-and-salisbury-middle-english-breton-lays-sir-orfeo.
94 Cf. Maddern, 'Reading Faces', at p. 27, who mentions the joyful tears of the people of Arras on learning that peace had been established between the Duke of Burgundy and the King of France. See also Boquet and Nagy, *Sensible Moyen Âge*, p. 316.
95 Geoffrey Chaucer, 'The Man of Law's Prologue, Tale and Epilogue', in Benson (ed.), *The Canterbury Tales*, in Benson (gen. ed.), *The Riverside Chaucer*, pp. 87–104.
96 Geoffrey Chaucer, 'The Clerk's Prologue and Tale', in Benson (ed.), *The Canterbury Tales*, in Benson (gen. ed.), *The Riverside Chaucer*, pp. 137–53. Benson, *Medieval Body Language*, p. 49, notes Grisilde's tearlessness throughout the tale until this point, even when her children are taken from her and she is humiliatingly dispatched back to her father's house.
97 Burrow, *Gestures and Looks*, p. 182.
98 Ibid., p. 49. See Benson, *Medieval Body Language* for a thorough account of gesture in Chaucer.

99 Burrow, *Gestures and Looks*, p. 49.
100 Erasmus recounts in a letter of 1499, 'When you arrive anywhere, you are received with kisses on all sides, and when you take your leave they speed you on your way with kisses ... The world is full of kisses.' Burrow, *Gestures and Looks*, pp. 32–3.
101 *Erle of Toulous*, line 1196, in Laskaya and Salisbury (eds), *The Middle English Breton Lays*.
102 See Carolyn Dinshaw, 'A Kiss Is Just a Kiss: Heterosexuality and its Consolations in *Sir Gawain and the Green Knight*', *Diacritics*, 24 (1994), 204–26.
103 Ibid., p. 206. The homoerotic implications of the kiss between the two men are unthinkable in the poem's production context, Dinshaw argues, although the modern reader may well read the poem as working to contain the deviant within an insistently heterosexual discourse.
104 Geoffrey Chaucer, 'The Summoner's Prologue and Tale', in Benson (ed.), *The Canterbury Tales*, in Benson (gen. ed.), *The Riverside Chaucer*, pp. 126–36, line 1804.
105 Benson, *Medieval Body Language*, pp. 72–7, offers a detailed reading of gesture in 'The Summoner's Tale'.
106 Ibid., p. 29.
107 Geoffrey Chaucer, *The Legend of Good Women*, ed. M. C. E. Shaner, in Benson (gen. ed.), *The Riverside Chaucer*, pp. 587–630.
108 Field incorporates Caxton's reading in his text: Malory, *Morte Darthur*, ed. Field, II: 697.
109 Cf. Burrow's discussion of Arthur's failure to bid Launcelot and Guenevere to rise when Launcelot formally returns the queen to him at Carlisle: *Gestures and Looks*, p. 21.
110 *Stanzaic Morte Arthur*, lines 1318–1426, in Larry D. Benson and Edward E. Foster (eds), *King Arthur's Death: The Middle English Stanzaic Morte and Alliterative Morte Arthure* (Kalamazoo, MI: Medieval Institute Press, 1994), https://d.lib.rochester.edu/teams/publication/benson-and-foster-king-arthurs-death.
111 Norris J. Lacy et al. (eds and trans.), *Lancelot-Grail: The Old French Arthurian Vulgate and Post-Vulgate in Translation*, 5 vols (New York: Garland, 1993–6), vol. IV, p. 117; Jean Frappier (ed.), *La mort le roi Artu: roman du XIIIe siècle* (Geneva: Droz, 1964), p. 102.
112 Burrow asks pertinently whether it is the lexis of smiling and laughter that changes in English and French, or the behaviour to which the words refer – are display rules different in the medieval period so that

characters laugh where we are more likely to smile? (*Gestures and Looks*, pp. 76–7).
113 Barry Windeatt, 'Gesture in Chaucer', *Medievalia et Humanistica*, new series, 9 (1979), 143–61 at p. 161, n. 12.
114 Burrow, *Gestures*, p. 126.
115 Geoffrey Chaucer, 'The Wife of Bath's Prologue and Tale', in Benson (ed.), *The Canterbury Tales*, in Benson (gen. ed.), *The Riverside Chaucer*, pp. 105–28.
116 Cooper, 'Afterword', pp. 181–8.
117 Ibid., p. 185.
118 Ibid., p. 187
119 See Elina Gertsman, 'The Facial Gesture: (Mis)Reading Emotion in Gothic Art', *Journal of Medieval Religious Cultures*, 36:1 (2010), 28–46, and Mia Åkestam, '"I Felt Like Jumping for Joy": Smiles and Laughter in Medieval Imagery', in Förnegård et al. (eds), *Tears, Sighs and Laughter*, pp. 214–38.
120 Maddern, 'Reading Faces'.
121 Ibid., pp. 24–5.
122 Geoffrey Chaucer, 'The Miller's Prologue and Tale', in Benson (ed.), *The Canterbury Tales*, in Benson (gen. ed.), *The Riverside Chaucer*, pp. 66–77. See Dinshaw, 'A Kiss Is Just a Kiss'.
123 A. C. Spearing, *Textual Subjectivity: The Encoding of Subjectivity in Medieval Narratives and Lyrics* (Oxford: Oxford University Press, 2005), pp. 46–7 at p. 47.
124 Damien Boquet and Piroska Nagy, 'Pour une histoire des émotions', in Nagy and Bouquet (eds), *Le sujet des émotions au Moyen Âge*, pp. 15–51 at p. 38.
125 Ibid., p. 38.
126 John Gower, *Confessio Amantis*, vol. I, ed. Russell A. Peck and Andrew Galloway (Kalamazoo, MI: Medieval Institute Press, 2006), I: 692–4;, http://d.lib.rochester.edu/teams/publication/peck-confessio-amantis-volume-1.
127 John Lydgate, *Troy Book: Selections*, ed. Robert R. Edwards (Kalamazoo, MI: Medieval Institute Press, 1998), III: 4277–80, http://d.lib.rochester.edu/teams/publication/edwards-lydgate-troy-book-selections.

3

Performativity and performance

Getting things done with emotion

Emotion does not occur in a vacuum: the feeling subject perceives, processes – within both preconscious and cognitive systems – and responds, whether at a physiological level or expressively, through verbal or other behaviours. The focus of this chapter will be on that expressive level, on investigating how literary characters 'get things done' with emotions: how emotions function as performatives. This formulation deliberately refers to J. L. Austin's seminal 1962 book *How to Do Things with Words*, in which the idea of the performative is first developed. Austin's arguments have been refined in different ways in emotions scholarship, not least through the realisation that emotional performatives are very often non-verbal. Performativity also overlaps with performance: the expression of an emotion undertaken with an eye to an (often text-internal) audience and intended to affect both individuals and collectives. The concepts of performance and performativity thus open up questions of character motivation and interiority: are the emotions depicted in the text (whether directly or indirectly) simply linguistic signs whose employment is largely driven by the imperatives of plot? Against this argument, dissimulation, pretence and doubleness, all relatively common features in Middle English imaginative texts, are closely connected with performativity and performance, implying that certain characters are imagined as possessing an interiority that can be concealed both from other characters and from the audience. There are of course 'flat' characters who are not generally imagined as having inner lives – damsels, servants, labourers, for example – contrasted with more central characters with interiority to which the audience is granted frequent, if not constant, access. Nevertheless, a consensus has emerged that medieval audience members were well aware that they themselves had an interior life that was not always on external display to the social groups of which they were members, and that literary persons might also be imagined as equipped with an interiority whose workings might become salient at different points within a narrative.[1]

The concept of emotional performativity frames emotions as always occurring within social space, opening up questions about how writers utilise emotion in speech and action in differing Middle English genres and varying discursive situations to fulfil a range of aesthetic, narrative and audience-focused, empathetic purposes. This chapter concludes with a case-study of one of the most interesting and understudied emotional performatives: *danger*. This behaviour is highly gendered in its performance and in its affective purpose and expected responses; understood as socially indispensable, it is nevertheless regarded as highly frustrating and is thus easily harnessed to contemporary misogynist discourses.

Performatives, performance and emotives

The philosopher J. L. Austin was the first to identify a class of sentences which he described as 'performative utterances', or 'performatives' for short. These are sentences with 'humdrum verbs in the first person singular present indicative active', which are not true or false ('constative') in Austin's terminology.[2] '[T]o utter the sentence … is not to *describe* my doing … it is to do it.'[3] Austin's examples include: 'I take this woman as my wedded wife', 'I name this ship', 'I bequeath this watch' and 'I bet you sixpence' as constituting the acts of marrying, naming, bequeathing and betting; to these can be added such acts as: promising/swearing/vowing, commanding, cursing and blessing. The utterance is the key element in the performative, but Austin adds the important rider that 'it is always necessary that the *circumstances* in which the words are uttered should be in some way, or ways, *appropriate*'.[4] Thus the bet must be accepted by someone, the ship will be named only if the speaker has been designated to name it, the marriage will require other conditions – consent, the previously unmarried status of both parties – to be effective. The necessary accompanying conditions are generated by social context; here vital questions of power, authority and intention come into play. In his second lecture, Austin elaborates the conditions of appropriateness, showing that there must 'conventionally' be agreement that the speech act functions as such, that it has been uttered correctly and completely, and that – importantly:

> where the procedure is designed for use by persons having certain thoughts or feelings ... then a person participating in and so invoking the procedure must in fact have those thoughts or feelings, and the participants must intend so to conduct themselves, and further must actually so conduct themselves subsequently.[5]

Thus, when someone promises someone else something, they must intend at the time of promising to keep the promise and must subsequently do so. If they do not, the performative will be 'unhappy'; that is, it will fail. Failure may also be caused by lack within the circumstances or formula. I cannot simply walk up to a ship with a bottle of champagne and re-name it whatever I like; the priest may bungle the words in the baptism service. While the constitution of the other necessary conditions has generated scholarly discussion, the 'thoughts and feelings' aspect of the performative has been most productive in emotion research.

In an significant analysis of the Middle High German poem *Das Nibelungenlied*, Elaine Tennant defines the performative as follows: 'an underlying cultural convention the characteristics of which are sufficiently unambiguous to permit members of the culture in which it obtains to recognise individual realisations of the convention as belonging to the performative category of that convention'.[6] Moreover, as Austin had also noted, the performative must sound or look like a performative to those who witness it: 'any individual realisation of a performative convention must exhibit enough recognisable features of that convention for members of the culture in which it obtains to identify it and assign it to the same convention'.[7] Tennant's argument converts the performative into a transhistorical concept, emphasising that different cultures will have different categories within which performativity is possible. In an earlier essay, Tennant lists some of the performatives available in medieval culture.[8] As we might expect, these include all Austin's categories as listed above, but also more culturally specific speech acts, such as 'blessings and curses; insults, commands, requests, and refusals of same, vows of ... feudal and military allegiance, clerical and secular investiture; proclamations of excommunication and banishment; and the like'.[9] Tennant's catalogue highlights the crucial condition: the possession of the requisite authority to assure the success of performatives. Only priests have the power to carry out ecclesiastical performatives; lords may command where subordinates may not; kings may invest subordinate aristocrats with particular noble ranks. The performative must command social support and be recognised and accepted as such by those who hear it. Thus, through attention to the identities of those who make use of performatives and how they are performed, as well as to their particular contextual functions in historical texts, valuable evidence is gained for the social norms and dynamics operational within those texts, and the cultures to which they bear witness.

Also analysing *Das Nibelungenlied*, Kathryn Starkey offers a useful refinement of Tennant's understanding of the performative as essentially verbal: 'Emotional gesture can stand in lieu of words to express reactions, and sentiments, but also to make statements and elicit changes in a state of affairs', she notes.[10] Starkey discusses the ways in which Brunhild's smiles signify differently before and after her marriage for, as seen in the last chapter, the smile is particularly effective in signalling unexpressed sentiments; its appearance invites witnesses to draw particular conclusions or to press for further information (see Chapter 2, pp. 121–2). Starkey elaborates her understanding of performatives, as 'function[ing] to affect socially recognised states of affairs, changing the status of someone or something'; these may include 'displays of emotion as political statements'.[11] They can moreover be 'spontaneous, affective, and possibly even unintended or unconscious'.[12] The related concept of performance is defined by Starkey as 'self-conscious presentation or action undertaken with the knowledge that someone is watching', implying 'a self-conscious distance between the enactment and the motivation ... or intent'.[13] Performance is calculated, undertaken for effect (although not only for effect), and it often occurs in public space, incorporating elements of ceremonial and ritual. Knights who appear at King Arthur's court to ask for a boon or to offer an adventure often incorporate marked performance elements into their self-presentation, as discussed below.

William Reddy expands the valence of the performative by outlining the concept of the 'emotive'. This he defines as 'a type of speech act different from both performative and constative utterances, which both describes (like constative utterances) and changes (like performatives) the world, because emotional expression has an exploratory and a self-altering effect in the activated thought material of emotion.'[14] An emotive is an utterance such as 'I am angry' or 'I am not afraid' or 'I am in love with you'; these 'do things to the world', specifically changing the apprehensions of both the listener and the speaker. Importantly, that changed state becomes present to the speaker's attention.[15] Emotives are thus 'both managerial and exploratory', Reddy explains; they cannot be unconscious or unintended, though they may reveal something that has only just been realised by the speaking self.[16] Once uttered, emotives may dissipate the emotion they express, but just as often they trigger a search for confirming evidence, intensifying the underlying feeling. Emotives may be non-verbal: tears rolling down the cheeks may alert the subject to their own unhappiness. Like the performative, the emotive cannot be 'true' or 'false', but rather it is either 'efficacious' as a barometer of an internal emotional state, or 'ineffective'.[17]

Reddy's idea of the emotive is well grounded within his study of eighteenth-century France in *The Navigation of Feeling*. In this book he utilises a good number of sources which do indeed reflect the interior states of those either conforming to, or resisting, the existing 'emotional régime', defined as '[t]he set of normative practices and the official rituals, practices and emotives that express and inculcate them; a necessary underpinning of any stable political regime'.[18] The emotive has been hitherto regarded as less useful for analysis of medieval literary texts, for the speaking self that interrogates its emotional state after uttering an emotive must be possessed of a degree of interiority, of self-reflectiveness that has generally been regarded as uncharacteristic of the earlier fictional productions of the period. Katharina Philipowski has argued, '[i]m Gegensatz zu

Menschen sind Figuren nicht dazu in der Lage, zu verdrängen, zu lügen oder zu sublimieren, denn das setzt eine psychische Struktur vǫraus, die höchstens derjenige haben kann, der den Text verfasst, nicht aber die Figure, die er schafft' (in contrast to people, characters are not in a position to suppress, to lie, or to sublimate, for that presupposes a psychological system which that person who composes the text possesses to a high degree, but not the characters whom he creates).[19] Yet, while people in medieval texts do not have subconsciouses which they sublimate or repress, they certainly lie, dissimulate and deceive. Monika Fludernik has traced the evidence for characters represented as undertaking self-reflexive analyses of their own 'meta-emotions', often in soliloquies, adducing examples from *King Horn* and 'The Knight's Tale'.[20] These demonstrate that 'Middle English displays much more extensive narrative depictions of subjectivity and interiority than it is usually credited with.'[21]

Chaucer's characters, particularly in *Troilus and Criseyde*, tend to behave in ways that recall the emotive, as exploratory and self-altering. In Book II, after hearing from her uncle of Troilus's love for her, Criseyde is exposed to a number of chance events that work upon her emotional state: Antigone's song, the song of the nightingale and her dream of the eagle. Thus, by the next day, when she is required by Pandarus to compose her first letter to Troilus, Criseyde's emotional state is in flux even as she writes. The narrator summarises the process for us: she begins by thanking Troilus quite conventionally for his good wishes and categorically refusing to bind herself in love, but by the end of the letter, as she explores her feelings in greater depth, she is ready to offer more: 'as his suster, hym to plese, / She wolde fayn to doon his hert an ese' (II: 1224–5). The shift under way in Criseyde's emotional orientation is recognised by Pandarus, who presses his advantage: urging that she should no longer remain aloof, except as far as modesty and reputation demand: 'al wolde ye the forme of daunger save' (II: 1243). Almost immediately, Troilus appears below her window, as will be discussed later.[22]

In Malory's version of Lancelot and Guenevere's final conversation at Amesbury, the idea of the emotive as 'managerial' is crucial. Both lovers say what they must in order to discipline themselves, to control the powerful emotions of guilt, hope, love, regret and no little anger at stake in the scene (I: 932–4).[23] The lovers' meeting is witnessed by Guenevere's nun-companions; the queen is no longer surrounded by the close female intimates who were privy to the lovers' meetings within the Arthurian court, but by a silent, perhaps more judgemental, but not unsympathetic audience. Guenevere swoons three times – a clear paralinguistic marker of emotion – when she sees Launcelot. At first, she will only speak about him to her women, emphatically acknowledging their shared love and consequent guilt: 'thorow oure love that we loved togydir is my moste noble lorde slayne' (I: 932). When she does address Launcelot directly, Guenevere employs a consistent – and insistent – second-person singular pronoun rather than the courtly second-person plural that the couple have habitually used. She declares that her sole concern now is 'to gete [her] soule hele'; this announcement works not only to steel her in her purpose to exclude Launcelot from her future life, but also to set the emotional key in which she will speak. The queen deploys performatives – requiring and beseeching – to exact from her lover the undertaking that he will never come to see her again; these are accompanied by imperatives – that he depart to his own country 'and there take the a wyff' (I: 933). Thus Guenevere manages both her own responses to Launcelot and his responses to her, for she schools him in the new emotion scripts he will promise to adopt in response to her: those of penance and prayer.

For his part, Launcelot is forced to revise his hopeful expectation that he might now have 'had [her] into my owne royame' (I: 933). He begins with the tender epithet 'Now, my swete madame', an adjective that Malory rarely uses, one which bespeaks an intimacy between the lovers which the text has not hitherto shown just when it must be abandoned.[24] Not without a pointed rejoinder about the enduring love he has borne her and his consequent failure in the Grail Quest, Launcelot gradually adopts the queen's dispassionate language, accepting her decision and promising that he too will withdraw from the world. Heartbreaking though it is, the exchange is dignified and measured; with emotions kept firmly under control, it ends with Guenevere's categorical refusal to grant her lover one final kiss. That the conversation is framed by swooning and weeping on either side bears witness to its emotional aspects: the struggle to manage the emotions in play at this decisive moment of parting and the effort involved in establishing a new emotional status quo of conversion and resignation, redirecting those feelings towards God.

Performatives, performance and, to a lesser extent, emotives are thus useful conceptual tools for the exploration of emotion and its expression in medieval literary texts. For Middle English literature, like the Middle High German examples analysed by Tennant and Starkey, asks us always to be alert to the gaps between what is said by characters or done by bodies and the factors which underpin them. Authors thus gesture towards the psychological processes and suggestions of interiority of the kind that Reddy discusses. While performatives allow the modern reader insight into medieval social and cultural processes, both public and private, the concept of performance opens up possibilities of pretence and insincerity, of a mismatch between internal feelings and action. Emotives, although harder to identify in most Middle English literary genres, suggest emerging ideas of interiority, not only those associated with the soul and its relation to God, but also, in romance in particular, with the proto-psychological exploration of characters' emotional and cognitive processes.

Performance and performativity in *Troilus and Criseyde*

Performance and performativity may pull in different directions within a single text, operating paradoxically, even ironically. In Book II of *Troilus and Criseyde* performativity, performance and, indeed, the emotive as discussed earlier all come into play. Chaucer departs considerably from his source material in Boccaccio in order to explore the thematics of emotion as mediated through differing stagings and as underpinned by varying textual and authorial motivations. In the first scene I discuss, Pandarus and Troilus organise an affective – and effective – performance for Criseyde's benefit: Pandarus will deliver a letter from Troilus to Criseyde at her house, and then he will, as if by chance, draw Criseyde over to the window past which Troilus will be riding, 'in thy beste gere' (II: 1012), Pandarus advises. And indeed, Troilus comes into view: 'ysee who cometh here ryde!' says Pandarus, giving his niece a metaphorical nudge in the ribs (II: 1253). Troilus's appearance induces the appropriate emotional somatic effects in the lady: she 'wex as reed as rose' (II: 1256). Criseyde feels, so the narrator tells us, pity for him but she says nothing; rather she fences with Pandarus, offering brief, if emphatic answers – 'Nay, *by my trouthe*' (II: 1281, my italics). From Criseyde's blushing Pandarus seems to infer her internal cataloguing of Troilus's many excellent qualities; he 'felte iren hoot, and he bigan to smyte' (II: 1276), asking rhetorically whether the prince must die of lovesickness simply because his beloved lacked 'routhe', pity for him. Pandarus thus picks up exactly on Criseyde's emotional state: for she does indeed feel 'routhe of his distresse' (II: 1270); he invokes the very emotion that she is experiencing, so the psychonarration informs us. This lexical congruence suggests that Pandarus is indeed an astute and reliable reader of emotions.

Yet whatever the performative effects of Troilus's appearance, Criseyde's actual performance is of the gendered emotion behaviour characterised as 'danger' – refusal to engage and looking away. These are actions deemed appropriate to a modest woman when apprised that some man is in love with her.[25] Pandarus raises the emotional temperature by reconfiguring and renaming her emotional response as inappropriate, as 'shame' and 'folie' (II:1286). This done, Pandarus heads home, 'and right for joye he felte his herte daunce' (II: 1304). While his emotion is expressed metaphorically, it is nevertheless clearly locatable as a movement of spirits within the heart, the seat of feeling. He thinks that the staged performance – Troilus's ride-by – has had the desired performative effect, perceiving that progress is under way in their shared masculine project. He is however unaware (as the audience is not) that he cannot take the main credit for the change under way in Criseyde's feelings.

For, as Jill Mann has analysed, Chaucer (but not Boccaccio) has already anticipated the men's clever, conspiratorial staging of their performance.[26] Criseyde had already caught sight of Troilus from her window on the previous day, an entirely chance glimpse, entirely lacking the premeditation of performance (II: 643–69). On this earlier occasion, Troilus is not in his 'beste gere', but simply returning from battle with 'helm to-hewen' and 'sheld to-dasshed'

(II: 638; 640). As the crowd cheer him, it is Troilus who 'wex a litel reed for shame' (II: 645). This unanticipated appearance has a much more powerful performative effect on Criseyde than the one discussed above. Its emotional impact is swift and striking. 'Who yaf me drynke?' (II: 651), she asks, pulling in her head; and she blushes in response both to his blush, and to her own internal thought processes, as detailed by the narrator. For Criseyde, the question that she asks herself crystallises how she is beginning to feel: it functions as an excellent example of an emotive, revealing to speaker and text-audience alike that affect of a particular kind is at work: an 'affective intoxication', as Williams comments.[27] Criseyde feels as if she has been given alcohol, or perhaps a love-potion (as in the Tristan story). The sight of Troilus converts her pre-existing emotional arousal – for Pandarus's news, imparted that very morning, that the prince of Troy loves her has left her in a highly labile state – into a new emotional configuration. Her exclamation focuses attention, for an imagined listener, for Criseyde herself as the speaker of the emotive and for the extradiegetic (or external) audience, on a nascent feeling which is not otherwise apparent. The Chaucerian narrator is quick to intervene, to raise – and dismiss – the question of whether Criseyde falls in love rather quickly, and to assure the audience that this is merely the beginning of the 'proces and … good servyse' (II: 678) by which Troilus wins her love.

Somatic indices of feeling are highlighted in both scenes: primarily blushing, but also the internal surge of joy felt by Pandarus as his scheme gets off to a promising start. Cognition is key within the narratological handling of the second encounter; the audience is privy both to Pandarus's conniving and to Criseyde's inadvertent viewing of Troilus and its earlier effects upon her, and it can make use of that knowledge to interpret action and dialogue in both scenes. In play is the variance between what the three principal actors know, and what they think they know, and what they do not know, but the audience does. Social convention ('emotionology') is also crucial to Pandarus's staged scene; Troilus's proper behaviour, acknowledging the lady, not looking self-confident, but rather anxious, 'with dredeful chere' (II: 1258) and changing facial colour, is intended to reassure Criseyde, to lay the groundwork for further exchanges between them. This is not to say that his appearance of the previous day was not equally a performance: of quiet pride and modesty, but it was undertaken to demonstrate his courage and service to the people of the city, rather than to display those qualities to the woman he loves. That it should engender *routhe* (II: 664) in Criseyde – the emotion which is rekindled by Troilus's greeting the next day, and explicitly named by Pandarus – signals that for Troilus, a performative, spontaneous and unconscious though it is, is nevertheless in play.

Public performance and ritual

The distinction between performance and performativity, between public ritual and private feeling, is central to the understanding of emotion as primarily social in medieval texts. Medieval culture sees ritual and ceremony as an important mode of getting things done, as performative in the sense outlined above. Very frequently emotion plays a crucial role in such public performances.[28] Gerd Althoff concludes that in medieval public rituals, people could express sadness, joy, anger and contrition with considerable intensity, without feeling that they had to align the strength of their expressions with their own internal feelings.[29] So the expression of collective joy at the acclamation of a king is to be interpreted not as 'spontanen Emotionen, ... sondern von einem gezielten Versuch, die Dynamik des Rituals für die eigenen Zwecke zu nutzen' (spontaneous emotion, but rather as a targeted attempt to make use of the ritual's dynamics for their own purposes).[30]

Such examples might be multiplied from historical texts; the authors who record occasions of ritual emotion write in conformity to cultural norms of what is appropriate, where questions of sincerity and authenticity simply do not arise. Froissart's account, drawn from Jean le Bel, of King Edward III's and Queen Philippa's Calais performance of royal anger, queenly intercession and the assuaging of the king's wrath not only is, as Paul Strohm has shown, a textbook example of an emotional performance producing performative effects, but moreover is extremely unlikely to have happened in anything like the circumstances that Froissart and his source describe.[31] Queen Philippa, highly pregnant, kneels before the king and begs mercy for the six hostage-burghers whom he has sworn to behead in retaliation for the city's resistance to him. 'The centrality of femininity, and the implications of humility and weakness that attend it, are additionally emphasised by such elements as the kneeling posture that reveals Philippa's sympathetic self-identification with the threatened and oppressed', Strohm observes. The queen's intervention allows the king to conclude his performance of regal anger with a strategic amelioration of his verdict by granting her request. 'We must imagine the Edward of this account well pleased, for without any disrespect to the force of his male ire, his wife has contributed a supplementary perspective that will enhance the repute of his kingship.'[32]

This example of emotional performance and its performative effectiveness within Froissart's text and, apparently, in a real-world context underlines the importance of understanding performance in literary texts in a similar light. We must beware of assuming that performances are inauthentic or insincere, and of thinking that because powerful emotions are in evidence, there cannot, at the same time, be strategic or performative interests in play. The coexistence of performance and performativity complicates the audience's apprehension that the emotion performed is either adequate or inadequate as an expression of an interior state. Jutta Eming expands on these arguments, which are foregrounded in much German research into medieval emotion. Like Althoff she sets aside questions of sincerity and authenticity, emphasising that in medieval texts the quality of 'theatricality' is not associated with such negative terms as '"exaggerated", "artificial" and "simulated"'.[33] Rather, argues Eming, '[r]itualized expression communicates and authenticates emotions through an ostentatious styling of the body, through facial expression, gesture, movement, voice and speech'.[34] In imaginative texts, theatricalised ritual has very little to do with the 'natural', or even, necessarily, the physiological, but is rather produced by narrative demands and aesthetic criteria. Genre, therefore, is critical to the ways in which performance and performativity can be understood.

Later medieval romance offers the clearest cases in which authors choose to include evocations of interior processes in their literary characterisations. Here it becomes possible to assess the alignment between internal and external: as when Gawain weeps on his return to court when narrating his adventure, or when Criseyde promises to return to Troy on the tenth night after her departure. 'Questions of affective sincerity versus linguistic performance are perhaps most acute when it comes to Criseyde's commissive speech acts to Troilus, e.g. when she pledges she will find a way to return', observes Williams, and he notes how the narrator takes a whole stanza to assure the audience of her *good entente* (IV: 1416), anticipating the 'unhappy' outcome of this particular promise.[35]

In a thoughtful reading of the ending of Chrétien's *Yvain*, Frederic Cheyette and Howell Chickering argue that for a contemporary – twelfth-century – audience the conceptualisation and language of lordship, of lovingly entered-into bonds of service guaranteed by verbal promises, also forms a key component in the expression of romantic love; the categories of 'political' and 'erotic love' that 'for us today are two different areas of feeling were only two different aspects of a single emotional category'.[36] By the end of the poem, when the husband and wife are reconciled, and love is re-established: '"Love" here does not refer to the subject's interior feeling but to what one receives externally from another. It is thus more public and social than private and "romantic".'[37] The expected words are uttered, appropriate postures, such as Yvain's kneeling to his lady, are adopted. The performance of all these emotion scripts does not so much express as actually constitute the emotions of anger and love at stake in the situation. The Middle English *Ywain and Gawain* does not differ greatly from the Old French exemplar at this point, although, in keeping with its author's clear interest in contemporary legalism, it makes use of English legal terms in framing Ywain's performative.[38] Ywain also kneels to his lady; Lunete urges her to acknowledge him by raising him up:

'Take up the knight, madame, have done
And, als convenand betuix us was,
Makes his pes faste or he pas.'[39]

At this point, Alundyne does not yet know the knight's name; she reiterates her earlier promise to bring about a *saghtelyng* (settlement) between 'the knight of the lion' and his lady. When Ywain's identity is revealed, she is taken aback and rebukes Lunete briefly, but, in similar terms to the French, accepts 'That I have said, I sal fulfill' (line 3993). Ywain apologises in highly formal terms, acknowledging his *foly* in passing his *terme-day* and his *trispase*, and asking for mercy, which *by Goddes law* he should be granted (lines 3995–4004). For her part, Alundyne agrees that she will abide by the earlier-mentioned *saghteling*; Ywain takes her in his arms, and their marital love is renewed. Just like the twelfth-century French audience discussed by Cheyette and Chickering, the fourteenth-century English audience recognised how the emotions of lordship and service, of erotic and marital love, are woven together within the emotion script required to terminate feud and create a settlement.[40] Legal language is closely allied to the discourse of feudal service, a rhetoric that is always central to the construction of aristocratic love-relationships during the courtship phase. In 'The Franklin's Tale', Chaucer implies that the conceptualisation of love within marriage is indeed normally understood as differently constructed from the models that underlie the wooing process. Once wed, the husband exercises 'lordship' over his wife, but Arviragus and Dorigen, exceptionally, agree that for them the dynamic of unmarried love will continue to pertain. He shall 'hire obeye, and hir wyl in al / As any lovere to his lady shal' (lines 749–50).[41] In *Ywain and Gawain*, as in *Yvain*, the rupture between husband and wife can similarly be healed by the recognition that the reiteration of the obligations of service can reset the love-relationship, with a new understanding and set of expectations.

Arthurian romance recognises another kind of highly ritualised behaviour as typical: that of the newcomer approaching the king's hall. As many sources relate, Arthur refuses to eat on major feast-days until something remarkable has occurred. This convention opens up the court to novelty and adventure, that which is normally excluded is allowed inside under the conditions of the feast.[42] The dramatic entrances staged by the Green Knight in *Sir Gawain and the Green Knight* and by Sir Gareth in 'The Tale of Sir Gareth', and the extraordinary incursion of the knight with hart, brachets and lady who intrudes upon Arthur's wedding feast are highly conventional performances (see Percyvell's subversion of the entrance and greeting ritual, discussed in Chapter 1).[43] The knights' performances are intended to capture the king's and court's attention, to exert pressure to grant a boon or accept a challenge. Without a striking entrance performance, a knight can vanish among the throng: his hopes of royal notice and welcome unfulfilled, Sir Balin, who has already been imprisoned and released by Arthur, lurks unnoticed among the other courtiers. Both poor and from Northumbria, he struggles to find a role at court until he unexpectedly achieves the adventure of the sword with strange hangings. Thereupon he attracts the king's praise and notice and elicits a formal welcome.[44] There is limited emotional investment for those who theatricalise their entrances; primarily they hope that the ritual may function as a successful performative and enhance the performer's status in the courtly world. Yet the performance elicits other more strongly marked emotions – surprise, fear, joy, anger – in the court itself. We saw in the last chapter how the Green Knight's elaborate staging of confrontation and disrespect provoked Arthur's royal anger; the mediation of acceptance and rejection, of welcome and of welcoming back in romance, are bound up in highly ritualised and conventional behaviours.

Malory offers a brilliant variation on the theatricalised arrival-at-court motif with the barge-journey of the dead Elayne of Ascolat (I: 828–30). Rejected by Launcelot, she gives detailed instructions to her grieving father and brother as to the disposal of her body. She dictates a letter, to be bound fast to her hand, and orders that she be placed in a barge that will bear her downriver to Westminster. There the letter is removed and brought to the king to be read publicly. In contrast with the scenes from *Troilus* discussed above, where the narratological framing gives the audience a privileged insight of the motivations and plot factors in play, Malory's audiences (both intra- and extradiegetic) have no idea what is in the letter. External listeners and readers are left in suspense as to whether Elayne's words will accuse or vindicate Launcelot, and whether the letter's content will exacerbate the queen's jealous rage, which has already led to her banning Launcelot from her presence. In fact, Elayne's letter defuses the situation, making clear that her love was not reciprocated and that she died 'a clene mayden' (I: 827). While 'the kynge, the queen and all the knyghtes wepte for pité of the dolefull complayntes' in the letter, when Launcelot is summoned to listen to the letter, his appeal to the dictum that 'love muste only aryse of the hearte selff, and nat by none constraynte' wins assent (I: 827). Both king and queen acquit Launcelot of blame; Launcelot recuperates, even increases, his 'worshyp' by ensuring Elayne is buried 'worshypfully' (I: 830). The spectacle devised by the girl focuses all attention on her after death, eliciting compassion and pity from all who hear the letter read (not, strikingly, from viewing the body, which simply occasions *mervayle*). Elayne's self-staging thus, like the entrances of living knights, serves to get her complaint a royal audience, and to elicit pity at her fate from the court and the audience alike. But it does not change much in the courtly world; rather it restores the relationship between the queen and her knight and asserts the primacy of the homosocial bond between Launcelot and Lavayne, Elayne's brother, over erotic or sibling relationships.[45]

Negotiating performativity and performance: Launcelot and the ladies

Performance is, as we have seen, often co-present with performativity: highly self-conscious and undertaken with deliberate regard to the effects that words spoken or actions taken will have on others present within a scene. When a character seeks to uncouple performance from its performative effects, the situation must be carefully negotiated so that all parties are clear about the meaning of the principal's behaviour. In Malory's version of the 'Knight of the Cart' adventure, Launcelot finds himself imprisoned in Mellyagaunce's dungeons, having fallen through an oubliette during a tour of the castle (I: 855–7). He needs to escape in order to champion Guenevere in a trial by combat; the queen is required to answer the charges of infidelity with one or more of the wounded knights who shared her quarters when Mellyagaunce kidnapped her. Launcelot's food is brought in his cell by a lady who importunes him every day to sleep with her; if he consents, she will release him in time to rescue the queen. Launcelot is adamant that he will not compromise his principles, even when she invokes the threat of shame if he were to fail the queen in her hour of need. Finally, on the very day of the battle the lady moderates her demands: 'Sir Launcelot, bethynke you, for ye are to hard-harted. And therefore, and ye wolde but onys kysse me, I shuld delyver you and your armour and the beste horse that was within sir Mellyagaunce stable' (I: 856). Launcelot deliberates. 'As for to kysse you, ... I may do that and lese no worshyp. And wite you well, and I understood there were ony disworshyp for to kysse you, I wold nat do hit' (I: 857). Launcelot is very careful to specify that the kiss is merely a performance, empty of performative signification; it does not dishonour any of his previously made vows, and no erotic or any other kind of emotional bond is formed in acceding to her request. The kiss is purely instrumental; and soon he is riding 'all that ever he myght walop' (I: 857) to the court to combat Mellyagaunce and rescue the queen. The lady has raised the emotional temperature in the dungeon by invoking shame ('disworshyp'), but Launcelot's timely arrival for the combat lifts the shame that the court was feeling that the queen's champion had apparently failed her. Indeed, that anxiety quickly modulates into a vicarious shame felt by the onlookers when Launcelot reveals his opponent's duplicity: 'they were all ashamed on his behalffe' (I: 858), though the villain himself is consistently and notoriously shameless (I: 858–60).

Launcelot's careful deliberation in his 'cave' allows him to conclude that while he may enact emotionally significant behaviour as a performance it shall have no performative effect, and he declares as much to the lady. Both parties are thus clear about the transactional nature of the gesture. Launcelot may kiss without expressing anything thereby; the lady gains perhaps a strangely fleeting satisfaction of the desire that she claims to feel – and becomes instrumental in the rescue of Guenevere from the consequences of the queen's own expression of sexual desire. The question of the lady's actual feelings is left unresolved. Most probably she has little investment in the sexual consummation she demands; rather she simply intends to probe the strength of Launcelot's love. Given her origins in Chrétien's 'Knight of the Cart' material, as mediated through the Vulgate *Lancelot*, she represents a variant of the many damsels who test Lancelot's sexual resolve in the earlier narratives.

Much earlier in his career in Malory, Launcelot had previously been incarcerated by four enchantress-queens, led by Morgan le Fay, who demanded that he take one of them as his mistress and made open reference to his relationship with the queen (I: 193–6).

In this episode Launcelot is again released from his dungeon by a woman, who effects his liberty on the promise – willingly made and duly kept by the knight – that he will fight on the side of her father, King Bademagu, in a tournament to be held the following week.[46] Launcelot's actions here are strictly performative; he makes and keeps a promise while the erotic temptation motif is displaced onto the four queens, whose demands brook no compromise. That Mellyagaunce is Bademagu's son, and that the damsel who releases Launcelot on this occasion is thus Mellyagaunce's sister confirms the origin of this imprisonment and female-engineered release complex in Chrétien's *Le chevalier de la charette*. There, the seneschal's wife and Meleagant's sister are both instrumental in Lancelot's release from the tower where the seneschal has imprisoned him. The seneschal's wife has erotic intentions (although Lancelot bargains her down to a straightforward promise to return); Meleagant's sister acts in exchange for chivalric service previously rendered.

Usually Malory represents Launcelot as deft and determined in his dealings with women, though he can – as in his own Tale – be deceived by them when they invoke chivalric norms in order to entrap him.[47] His scrupulosity about interrogating the meaning of his behaviour falters however in his dealings with Elayne of Ascolat, where his understanding of what constitutes performance and what is performative becomes disastrously blurred. Malory's staging of Elayne's behaviour is very different from the versions he found both in the *Mort Artu* and *Stanzaic Morte Arthur*.[48] The 'Tale of the Fair Maid of Ascolat' is so narrated that the audience is immediately made privy to Elayne's feelings when she sets eyes on her father's guest: 'ever she behylde sir Launcelot wondirfully', the narrative voice notes, revealing that 'she was so hote in love' that she asks Launcelot to wear her token at the tournament (I: 806–30). Launcelot abandons his customary caution in dealing with women who ask boons of him, since the sleeve she offers will function as a disguise. His first response, 'Damesell, ... and if I graunte you that, ye may sey that I do more for youre love than ever y ded for lady or jantillwoman' (I: 806), opens the door to misunderstanding; even as Launcelot utters it, he expects not to grant her the favour. After he changes his mind, he unwisely reiterates, 'Never dud I erste so much for no damesell' (I: 806). No wonder then that Elayne feels that love has been invoked between them ('for youre love'). For Launcelot, any performative dimension to his behaviour is 'unintended and unconscious' (in Starkey's terms), but Elayne interprets the giving of the sleeve precisely as a performative. 'Youre love' does not necessarily mean 'love of you', but rather 'for your sake'; it is an ambiguity that Elayne will later exploit when Gawain arrives, claiming more than once of the knight who owns Lancelot's shield that is now in her keeping that 'he ys my love' (I: 815).[49] Gawain understands that Elayne loving Launcelot does not necessarily entail reciprocal feelings on the knight's part, but the detail of the acceptance of the sleeve seems to persuade him. By the time his news has been processed at court, Guenevere construes Gawain's report to the king that the 'Fayre Maydyn of Ascolat lovith hym mervaylously well' (I: 817) as a report that it is 'mervayle to telle of the grete love that ys betwene the Fayre Maydyn of Astolat and hym' (I: 818), no matter what Bors might say in Launcelot's defence.

Elayne later tracks down the injured Launcelot in the hermitage, where she shrieks and swoons at the sight of his wounds (I: 819). He kisses her; for him the performance of a friendly and courtly gesture, for her yet another confirmatory performative, re-establishing the love that she believes must surely obtain between them. Launcelot takes to his horse too early in his convalescence, reopens his wound and is brought back to the hermitage unconscious; Elayne kisses him 'and dyd what she myghte to awake hym' (I: 823). Launcelot's cousin Bors, who witnesses this, has already warned Launcelot that Elayne loves him, for which Launcelot – as he will say more than once to her male kinsfolk – expresses regret: 'that me repentis' (I: 821). The knight does his best to manage Elayne's emotions sensitively when she confronts him with her demand for marriage, but to no avail. Her declaration, 'Alas than ... I muste dye for youre love' (I: 826), functions as a powerful emotive; in uttering it Elayne makes clear to the audience – her brothers and father and Launcelot – and to herself what the outcome of his refusal will be.

Elayne's interiority is suggested by Malory through a range of narratological devices: psychonarration, a range of appropriate gestures and somatic indices, and the young woman's own careful and truthful negotiation of her emotional position in her utterances. Her dialogue with Launcelot and her impassioned outburst to her confessor – 'Am I nat an erthely woman?' – constitutes a remarkable defence of the 'fervent love' that brings her to her death (I: 827–8). Faced with a considerably more complex character, more highly elaborated from the young women that Malory found in his sources and exercising her own subjective appraisal of Launcelot's emotion scripts, the knight fails to make the key distinction between performance and performativity that will soon prove so crucial in Mellyagaunce's dungeon. The romantic implications of Launcelot's acceptance of the sleeve, his throwaway comment that this is a unique event and his invocation of the concept of love, however obliquely, when he does so, seem to Elayne to be confirmed by his kiss when he sees her again; all these emotion-inflected actions, (mis)interpreted as performative in nature, contribute powerfully to Elayne's catastrophe.

Sincerity, pretending and authenticity

Medieval aristocratic life entailed a range of different kinds of courtly performance, both as depicted in literary texts and in actual lived experience: 'Literary characters express chivalric commitment through the poetics of a genre; historical knights are similarly engaged in a rhetoric of experiences. It is on this citational plane of performance that instances of chivalric behavior meet and influence one another', remarks Susan Crane.[50] Thus when characters go to lengths to perform publicly a particular emotion, we should not assume that that their behaviour is merely strategic – though strategy may indeed be involved. That they know how to perform effectively does not negate the emotional content or the performative effect.

A performance may nevertheless be intended to deceive onlookers; in ritual and ceremonial contexts, a performance that conforms to communal norms can function effectively to maintain social identity and to project a particular emotional state, even as the audience is aware of a lack of congruence with the individual's interior condition. Public penitence, as we shall see in Chapter 4, raises questions about future intentions not to trespass again, at the same time as it seeks to deflect anger and solicit forgiveness. In *William of Palerne*, a mid-fourteenth-century translation of a

French romance from around 1200, the Queen of Spain is confronted with her stepson, Alphouns, whom, many years before, she had transformed into a werewolf. The werewolf threatens to tear her to pieces but is restrained by the hero. The queen falls to her knees in front of the beast, admits what she has done, apologises for the wrong, promises redress and begs for mercy; she swears by God never to harm Alphouns again and, weeping, asks William and the other lords present to intercede for her. Now she prostrates herself in front of the wolf; her words, but most of all her actions, elicit *reuthe* (line 4414), weeping and woe from all the onlookers. William must ventriloquise the voiceless wolf, so it is he that offers forgiveness, on condition that Alphouns be immediately restored to human form. The queen transforms Alphouns in a private chamber; once human he does not offer further recrimination, but rather expresses shame at his nakedness. The queen inspects him to ascertain that he is indeed a man once more and helps him into a bath in an intimate scene that works to guarantee her future good will towards and acceptance of her husband's heir.[51] Once William has brought his friend suitable clothing, Alphouns's re-integration into human society can begin. The queen's physical actions – kneeling to, then prostration before a wild beast – perform again that disturbance of natural order that she instigated when she turned a prince into a wolf, and they open up the possibility that this may be reversed. Despite their knowledge of her past wickedness, the sight of a queen grovelling to a werewolf produces pity in the onlookers and intensifies the pressure on William to forgive her. The poet has told us that the queen was terrified – 'wax neiȝ of her witt' (line 4346) when the werewolf looked set to attack her – and 'was gretli glad' (line 4383) that William restrained him. Thereafter the queen's feelings are of much less interest than her exemplary speech and courteous actions. As one of the few identifiably courtly romances preserved in Middle English, *William of Palerne* generally concurs with Crane's argument: 'Public appearance and behavior are thought not to falsify personal identity but, on the contrary, to establish and maintain it.'[52]

Text-internal audiences are ready to accept performances as performative, as signalling a congruence between interior states and public declaration; text-external audiences may also, as in the

Queen of Spain's case, be willing to accept such thoroughgoing confession and repentance as heralding a change in feelings and future intentions. In *Sir Tristrem*, however, the audience has ample knowledge of Ysonde's passion for Tristrem and is interested to see how the queen will manage the oath-ordeal in which she must swear her innocence of adultery. To swear a false oath is a serious offence in the eyes of God and men so, rather than perjure herself, Ysonde devises an elaborate plan. This enables her to swear that the beggar-man (the disguised Tristrem) who carried her to the ship on which she was to cross the Thames to Westminster for the ordeal-ceremony 'ferli neighe ... wan' (came very close) to her private parts as he stumbled with her in his arms.[53] No other man, except her own husband, had come so close, *sothe thing* (truly), she avers. And so Ysonde 'hath sworn hir clene / that miri may', comments the narrator, admiring her ingenuity and untroubled by her duplicity – and encouraging his audience to do likewise.[54]

In Book IV of *Troilus and Criseyde*, Calchas, Criseyde's father, decides to take advantage of the capture of a good number of Trojan prisoners to negotiate his daughter's transfer to the Greek camp. In pursuit of this aim he performs his paternal grief before the Greek ambassadors. Calchas knows very well what this ought to look like, and so 'with a chaunged face hem bad a boone' (IV: 68). He reminds his Greek audience in highly emotional terms of what he has given up in order to bring them the 'comfort' of his prophecy that they will have victory, berates himself, 'O sterne! O cruel father that I was!', for leaving the sleeping Criseyde behind when he made his moonlight escape from the city, regretting that he did not bring her with him 'in hire sherte', and finally offers a reassuring reprise of the prophecy of Greek victory.

> Tellyng his tale alwey, this olde greye,
> Humble in his speche and in his lokyng eke,
> The salte teris from his eyen tweye
> Ful faste ronnen down by either cheke,
> So longe he gan of socour hem biseke
> That, for to hele hym of his sorwes soore,
> They yave hym Antenor, withouten moore.
>
> But who was glad ynough but Calchas tho? (IV: 127–35)

The old man's physical posture emphasises his humility as suppliant to the politicians' good will, and he weeps as he speaks. Once the ambassadors agree to his request, he immediately cheers up. The change in demeanour is immediate, taking effect across the stanza break.

By calling attention to his *chaunged* appearance, by separating out the rhetorical appeal of the speech from the physical performance of emotion and – particularly – by the speed with which Calchas displays a very different emotion when his boon is granted, Chaucer stages the father's emotion in a way which, with typical Chaucerian indirection, intimates the element of conscious performance, of theatrical gesture and posture in Calchas's behaviour. This is not to say that Calchas is either insincere or pretending about his feelings; rather that he is aware of how performance and performativity interact. It comes then as mildly shocking for the audience, some five hundred lines later, to learn from the narrator that Criseyde could not care less about the father who left her so dangerously exposed in Troy when he defected: 'Criseyde … / which that of hire fader roughte / As in this cas, right nought, ne whan he deyde' (IV: 666–8) (Criseyde, who cared absolutely nothing for her father in this case, even if he were to drop dead).

Once the news of the Trojan parliament's agreement to the exchange is public knowledge, Criseyde's female friends come round to congratulate her on being reunited with her father, expressing paradoxical emotions of *pitous joie* (IV: 683): sorrow that they will lose their friend, and what they believe to be empathetic happiness, resonating with the emotion that Criseyde ought to be feeling at the prospect of rejoining her father. Chaucer nicely delineates Criseyde's emotional condition and her lack of clear affect. In one of the earliest examples of emotional absence in English literature, her body is present in the chamber with her sympathetic friends, but her heart and her mind (*advertence*) are not engaged.

> Tho wordes and tho wommansshe thynges
> She herde hem right as though she thennes were;
> For God it woot, hire herte on othir thyng is.
> Although the body sat among hem there,
> Hire advertence is alwey elleswhere (IV: 694–8)

Criseyde produces a competent social performance contrasting with a psychonarration that intimates a very different emotional interiority. The next stanza registers the intensity of the passion that Criseyde feels – her heart is burning while she listens to the imbecilities of the women (*vanyte*, repeated twice) who seek to console her. They completely misinterpret Criseyde's sorrow – which eventually breaks out in tears – as sadness that she must leave her good friends (the women themselves) behind. The narrator briskly calls them *fools*, well-meaning though they are, even though they shed empathetic tears with Criseyde: 'ech of hem wepte ek for hire destresse' (IV: 721). The narratological staging of the gap between internal and external is expertly achieved: the different characters' behaviours, the account of their interior thoughts, and the narrator's (and thus the audience's) superior understanding of all the emotions at play in the situation are produced and maintained through fictionality, offering a series of overlapping perspectives which are a key generic feature of romance. Once her companions have left, Criseyde retreats to her chamber, where she performs all the conventional behaviours of female grief: tearing her hair, sobbing, wringing her hands and turning pale (IV: 736–42). 'Criseyde has by this point morally graduated from the socially-minded reader of linguistic scripts for love and devotion to becoming saint-like (*of martire*) in that her suffering resembles a hagiographic scene', comments Williams.[55]

Medieval authors make use of various strategies to suggest the sincerity of the emotions that their characters are represented as feeling.[56] These include such narrative tools as the inexpressibility topos; the narrator of *Sir Orfeo* exclaims that no one could relate the suffering of Orfeo in exile: 'Lord! who may telle the sore / This king sufferd ten yere and more?'[57] The author of *William of Palerne* claims he cannot do justice to the city's performance of joy when the Emperor of Greece enters Rome: 'soþli to say, þeiȝh I sete euer, / I schuld nouȝt telle þe merþe þat maked was þere' (lines 1622–3). Here of course, where communal emotion is evoked, public performance and interior feeling need not be aligned. When Alphouns the now disenchanted werewolf is reunited with his father, the King of Spain, and his half-brother: 'No tong miȝt telle treuli þe soþe / þe joye þat was wrouȝt wiþ lasse and with more' (lines 4558–9).

Joy is imputed generally to the Palerne court who witness to the reunion, rather than represented in exclamation or gesture. This is courtly joy, elicited by the restoration of the status quo, but also – and in contrast to the performance of the citizens of Rome when the Emperor of Greece arrives – it suggests a contagious, sincerely empathetic happiness, generated by the powerful emotion felt by the parents, the King of Spain and the Queen of Palerne, who are reunited with their long-lost children.

Chaucer's Man of Law appeals to his audience's own experience in asking them to compare Custance's fear as she faces the charge of having murdered her friend Donegyld to a man on his way to execution: 'Have ye nat seyn sometyme a pale face / Among a prees, of hym that hath be lad / Toward his deeth'? (lines 645–7).[58] Interior monologues – soliloquies – and direct speech also contribute to the authenticity effect, along with the employment of conventional, spontaneous, somatic gestures – colour changes, trembling and swooning, as we saw in the last chapter, for in these spontaneous indicia of affect, the body does not lie. Yet general assumptions about characters' sincerity are not without their exceptions; the conversations between Lady Bertilak and Gawain within the intimate space of the bed-curtains make skilled play with different kinds of pretending. From the moment at which Gawain, glimpsing the lady's stealthy entrance into his bedchamber, pretends to be asleep so that he can wake up and appear to be surprised, 'let as hym wondered' (line 1201) the poem focuses on courtly emotional performance that bears little relation to the two characters' internal dispositions. Gawain laughs and jests, though his appointment with the Green Knight is never far from his mind. The lady, on first hearing, seems genuine in her protestations of love, but the poet unexpectedly raises a question about her sincerity: 'and ay þe lady let lyk a hym loued mych' (line 1281).[59] That suggestion, though glancing, changes the audience's perception of the emotional stakes in the scene, alerting some members, at least, to interpret what is happening in relation to similar scenarios in the Arthurian intertextual universe. Relevant comparators may be the kinds of romance episodes in which a knight's resolve is tested (as in the Launcelot-scenes discussed above), or the conventional French characterisation of Gawain's irresistibility, a trait that underpins episodes in which ladies fall in love with him from afar and vow their virginity to him.[60]

Troilus's self-conscious dramatisation of his own misery in Book V, imagining how pitiable he must look to others in his grief, authenticates his emotional state to his own satisfaction.

> And of hymself ymagened he ofte
> To ben defet, and pale, and waxen lesse
> Than he was wont, and that men seyden softe,
> 'What may it be? Who can the sothe gesse
> Why Troilus hath al this hevynesse?'
> And al this nas but his malencolie,
> That he hadde of himself swich fantasie. (V: 617–23)

Projecting his internal belief that his appearance has dramatically changed – he thinks he has lost weight and looks pale – onto concerned onlookers, Troilus imagines that people are talking anxiously about him. He thus conjures up for himself a sympathy for his misery that he can otherwise elicit only from Pandarus. The Chaucerian narrator, as elsewhere, offers a humoral explanation for Troilus's imaginings about himself: his *malencolye*, which both causes and is intensified by his psychological suffering. The authenticating somatic signs of grief are ironically undercut by the narratorial comment. Does the prince's healthy young body actually show signs of the tumult of his inner state? Chaucer's psychonarration complicates our apprehension of how far Troilus's interior turmoil affects his capacity to perform noble, heroic masculinity, particularly on the battlefield. Troilus's miserable imaginings of the pity with which he is regarded here can be read as contrasting with that earlier scene, discussed above, when, despite his agony of lovesickness, Criseyde first caught sight of him looking handsome and confident as he rode victorious through the streets of Troy.

The case of Danger

Danger is a gendered, highly performative and performance-oriented, emotional behaviour ascribed to, indeed perhaps imposed upon, noble women. It is a concomitant of the emotional schema of courtly *fin'amor*, coming into play when a noble or gentry woman receives romantic advances from a man. She is conventionally expected to resist his attentions – neither to accept his love nor to allow physical or extended contact – until such time as he may be said to have won her love through his service. *Danger* then calls provocatively into question the alignment between male courtly behaviour, the rhetoric of love and the responses of the recipient – and the relationship of all these to the textual notion of the self. '[I]n other words, one had to have the in-group knowledge and skills to perform and compose expressions of this love, but also fulfil ideo-affective conditions that were not absolutely confirmable in the external world', notes Williams.[61] How can the sincerity value of the lover's performance be measured? What factors determine the strength and duration of the lady's performance of *danger*, and how do *danger*'s performative aims effect changes in social relationships in the textual world?

Danger is consistently personified as masculine in love-allegory – and consequently in the Chaucerian texts that draw upon this mode – the *Legend of Good Women* (Text F, line 160) and 'Merciles Beaute' (line 16), though Skelton depicts the figure as 'chief gentlewoman' in *The Bowge of Court* (see pp. 170–10).[62] He also appears in William Dunbar's *The Golden Targe*.[63] In most of these later allegorical poems *Danger*'s characteristics are shaped by the highly influential personification depicted in the *Roman de la rose*.[64] There *Danger* is an ugly churl, a version of the uncivilised Wild Man. In Chaucer's description, expanded from that of Guillaume de Lorris:

> Full gret he was and blak of hewe,
> Sturdy and hidous, whoso hym knewe
> Like sharp urchons his her was growe   [hedgehogs]
> ...
> His nose frounced, full kirked stood   [wrinkled, crooked]
> He com criand as he were wood.
>
> (*Romaunt of the Rose*, B, lines 3133–5; 3137–8)

Danger keeps company with Shame, Fear and Wikked-Tunge (Gossip), all of whom are obligated to protect the Rose's honour. Despite the Lover's early success in ingratiating himself with Bialacoil (Fair-Welcome), Danger drives him away. With flattery and politesse, and with the help of Fraunchise (Openness) and Pité (Pity), Danger is temporarily overcome and permits the Lover to approach more closely: 'Daunger is daunted and brought lowe' (line 3602). This provisional victory is followed by further setbacks, ranging Shame and Fear against Fraunchise and Pité, until Danger is at last put to flight by Venus's fiery brand.

The lady's propensity to say 'evere "nay"', as John Gower puts it, is gradually overpowered by love and its concomitant qualities, Fraunchise and Pité, whether these are externally allegorised or embodied in the lover.[65] Social reputation is key to the triggering of *Danger*, as the *Roman* shows: fear of gossip about the lady's honour and anxiety that she will be thought unchaste and shameless if she gives any encouragement to the importunate lover. In love-allegory the protagonist can neither understand nor sympathise with the churlish Danger for he is closely aligned with, indeed is implicated in producing, masculine feelings of frustration and aggression. The lover may not directly blame his lady for her refusals or reluctance; rather the ethic of service means that he must bear these in good part. His suppressed anger and impatience, what we might today call a sense of entitlement, are thus projected onto the low-ranking, club-wielding figure, whose churlish appearance always offers a paradoxical reassurance: that he will eventually be put in his place by a properly deployed courtliness when performed by the lover-hero.

Indeed, as discussed by Mary Flannery, in Jean de Meun's continuation of the *Roman*, Amis (Friend) advises the lover that he should simply pluck (*cuillir*) the Rose at his pleasure, for the furious outcry that *Dangier*, *Honte* (Shame) and *Poor* (Fear) will set up is only feigned: 'mais que feintement s'en corroucent' (they only pretend to become angry).[66] Surprisingly then, sexual violence is recommended as a possible strategy, not by an allegorical figure with a name like Rashness or Intemperance, but by an experienced and worldly-wise friend to the Lover. As Flannery observes, this points to fear of violence as one component affecting the lady's performance. The allegorisation of frustrated desire and impatience, as excised from the Lover and projected onto the person of Danger, enables a more positive focus on the protagonist's emotional state, and on the processes through which he learns self-control: the capacity that will overcome the psychological qualities embodied by his opponent.

John Gower's late fourteenth-century poem *Confessio Amantis* promotes Danger from the status of *villain*. For although his earlier, violently protective role, so argues Elliot Kendall, aligns him with 'long-sighted conservative principles', defending aristocratic interests in the transmission of power and property through women and marriage, his uncivilised nature makes him impossible to integrate within a reformed praxis of erotic love moderated by effective courtly performance.[67] No longer laying about himself wildly with an iron club, Danger is reconceived as, in Kendall's words, 'a civilised and powerful noble servant'. He smoothly bars the lover's access to the lady, taking private counsel with her to make sure that she keeps the interloper at bay, patrolling her innermost apartments. As the officious Danger interposes himself between the petitioner and his lady, he encloses her in a kind of stickiness that means Amans can gain no purchase: 'he hath mi ladi so englued / Sche wol noght that he be remued' (III: 1553–4).[68] Amans is furious with Danger (for this is the Book of Wrath) and longs to expel him from the household, giving voice to a peevish wish 'that he were in som wise slain' (III: 1576). He later moderates this to the hope that he might at least lose his high-ranking office: 'So that Danger, which stant of retenue/ With my ladi, his place mai remue' (VIII: 225–6), and Amans petitions Venus, so effective in the *Roman de la rose*, to aid him against his implacable enemy.

In Book V, Danger appears again, now as a *wardein* (a role also undertaken by chamber-servants), guarding the lady's intimate space from unauthorised intruders; he operates within the very household domains that Amans would claim as his own.[69] He is suggestively charged with the role of keeping her treasure, 'under lock and under keie, / That no man mai it stele aweie' (V: 6621–2), and thus he prevents Amans from entrance – for any purpose whatsoever – into this restricted area. Kendall notes rightly how the 'aristocratic becomes polarised in the poem across Amans and Danger's rivalry'; the new form of the personification reflects not only the woman's 'repudiation of Amans's *fin'amor*, but a separate version of the aristocratic'.[70] Danger's portrait here meshes with contemporary courtly anxieties about who controls access to the monarch or the lord. Resentment is engendered by the officials who stood in the way of supplicants seeking royal or magnate notice, in addition to the usual masculine emotions of erotic frustration and longing. Amans's opposition to the good order and respectability that Chamberlain Danger represents is couched in violent and excessive language; were Danger not there to prevent him, he would indeed forcibly break into the lady's chamber and attempt to steal 'som thing of love' (V: 6681), as he readily admits. Again, the threat of masculine violence subtends the allegory.

Gower's tale of Iphis and Araxarathen in Book IV (Sloth) exemplifies in more detail the components of *Danger* in performance. Iphis, a king's son, has fallen in love with a low-born girl. Despite his excessive protestations of love, the girl is 'with resoun ... restreigned'; she eschews him for 'drede schame' and is careful to preserve her virginity.[71] Despite the gifts, messages and speeches that Iphis delivers she continues to resist him. He falls into despair and commits suicide outside his beloved's house, chiding before he dies: '[t]hi Daunger' which 'schal to maye mo / Ensample be fore everemo' (IV: 3589–90). As Iphis perishes he claims that he does not know whether his death will bring her joy or sorrow. In fact, Araxarathen is stricken by guilt and herself prays for death; the gods turn her into a stone. Iphis embodies one particular emotional state: that of the individual lover who cannot cope with the destabilising effects of *Danger* on his masculine identity. His performance of the desiring male fails as a performative and he blames the woman for this failure. Genius relays the changing perspective of the community: first, *as sche scholde*, which registers and praises the girl's modest, shamefast response to the prince, but he sums up with a double-edged verdict: 'He was to neysshe [*soft*] and sche to hard / Be war forthi hierafterward' (IV: 3681–2). The girl behaves exactly as she should, and yet as she should not; a familiar misogynist double-bind.

In contrast to the male-gendered, lesser-ranking personifications of *Danger* represented in the allegorical texts, in those narratives where, as here, *danger* is invoked as an emotional behaviour, it is perceived as entirely within the woman's control. Thus, it can have a complex performative function, enhancing the lady's reputation for modesty and virtue, while testing the lover's resolve. In the *Book of the Duchess*, to the Man in Black's faltering declaration of his feelings, the lady 'sayde nay / Al outerly'.[72] This is a successful performative, resulting in the lover's enhanced schooling in virtue and self-control so that finally she becomes willing to grant him mercy. In other texts the performance aspect is foregrounded. If *danger* is nothing but 'countrefet disdeyn' (IV: 2161), as Lydgate cynically suggests in the context of Criseyde's rather sudden decision to grant 'merci' to Diomede, it should be easy to counteract and neutralise.[73] For, so Lydgate opines, as in Criseyde's case, with sufficient encouragement or through changing circumstances, a woman easily can be persuaded to abandon it: 'So that the wynde be redy and the tyde, / Passage is ay, whoso list to passe' (IV: 2158–9). Employing a contemporary comparison that recasts women's love as commodity, Lydgate suggests that it is less straightforward a task to exchange crowns or ducats with the Italian bankers in Lombard Street – who are extremely keen to do business – than it is to get women to drop their *danger*, abandon their former *trouthe* and grant their favour to a new lover (IV: 2148–59). Lydgate's analysis focuses on the deliberate nature of *danger* as emotion praxis:

> Right as Cryseyde lefte Diomede
> Of entent to sette hym more afire,
> As this wommen kyndely desyre,
> Whan thei a man have brought in a traunce,
> Unevenly to hange him in balaunce,
> Of hope and drede to lynke hym in a cheyne,
> Ay of the fyn unsure of bothe tweyne,
> To dryve him forthe yeres hem to serve
> And do no force wher he lyve or sterve:
> This is the fyn of Lovis fyri rage.
> And for she wolde have hym in servage,
> She lokkid hym under swiche a keye
> That he wot nat wher to lyve or deye (III: 4854–66)

The performance is an *entent*, designed to bring its victim out of equilibrium – 'Unevenly to hange him in balaunce'. The lover's intemperateness is figured by the language of fire and flame: his helplessness by binding and locking up, while the woman is indifferent to his well-being, seeking only to extract further *servage* from him.

In *Troilus* we find Pandarus acknowledging the social inevitability of the performance of *danger* by his niece, at the same time as he urges her to rein it in; he employs the extreme rhetoric of imminent death – his own and Troilus's – to discourage her. At this stage in Book II, it is a rhetorical stratagem he thinks of as highly effective: 'Lat youre daunger sucred [sugared] ben a lite / That of his deth ye be naught for to wite' (II: 384). This is an entirely pre-emptive move, coming before the lovers have even exchanged letters. Later in the same book, Pandarus seeks to reassure Troilus, who despairs of progress in the affair. Whenever *Kynde* (Nature, Kindness) succeeds in eliciting *routhe* in Criseyde, this emotional development is constantly thwarted by 'Daunger', who 'seith, "Nay, thow shalt me nevere wynne!"' (II: 1376). Elsewhere, however, chiming with Lydgate's cynical view of women, Chaucer contrasts the honourable and loving behaviour of Anelida, Queen of Armenia, towards her lover, Arcite of Thebes, with the discipline enforced upon him by Arcite's new beloved for whom he abandons Anelida. Chaucer's account of the *newe lady*'s behaviour is couched in terms similar to Lydgate's.

> Her daunger made him bothe bowe and bende,
> And as her liste, made him turne or wende;
> ...
> And for she yaf him daunger al his fille,
> Therfor she hadde him at her owne wille.[74]

The new love-object's behaviour is effective in binding Arcite to her; Anelida loses her lover because, so the poem implies, she is too humble and loving adequately to perform *danger* in such a way as to keep her lover in doubt about her feelings for him. Nevertheless, the narrator approves her stance, pities its outcome and criticises Arcite for his fickleness. Anelida is trapped by her own goodness and open-heartedness.

That *danger* was regarded as essential emotion behaviour for young, marriageable women is borne out by an account given by the Knight of the Tour-Landry, as translated by William Caxton in the late fifteenth century. The young knight was sent to meet a possible wife, but he felt he had to reject her because of her forwardness: of her lack of *danger*.[75] The behaviour of which the Knight complains seems comparatively mild, little more than a gentle flirtatiousness: she picks up on and plays with one of the standard rhetorical tropes of *fin'amor*. The young people are talking about prisoners in the context of the Hundred Years War. The young Knight says he would rather be her prisoner than be captured by the English; she replies that she has recently seen someone (sc. the Knight himself) whom she would like to take prisoner, and she would keep that man 'as dereworthy as her owne body'. It is this that seems to be too bold: is it the mention of 'body' that signals an absence of suitable modesty? To the Knight, the girl's lack of reserve is alarming: 'what shall I say, she loued me enough and had her eye quyck & lyght / and she was ful of wordes'.[76] His father agrees that the girl's behaviour shows 'ouer grete malepertnes & the lyght manere' and the match is not pursued.[77] Nor is the Knight surprised, he claims, when, shortly afterwards, she loses her reputation ('she was blamed') and then dies. As a father, the Knight strongly warns his daughters against failing to perform the approved *danger* behaviour whenever a suitor might come to visit them.

Danger is clearly understood in these texts both as a performative and as a socially enforced performance; it maintains female reputation and buys the woman time until she can decide whether the love is seriously offered and whether she can or should reciprocate it. Yet the suitor resents the behaviour, to a greater or lesser extent; and he further resents the fact that he may not openly challenge or complain about *danger*, except in conversations between men, as in Amans's confession to Genius, or Chaucer and Lydgate's conversational criticising of the practice in their addresses to their readers. For, despite the cultural insistence that courtly masculinity must overcome women's shamefastness, as Flannery argues, a countervailing social convention insists on the value of *danger* in testing out sincerity and moral self-control.[78] Male authors sympathise rather with the poor lover, bound fast in chains of desire and aflame with love, who is dangled by the lady as her plaything, all the while seeking to persuade her of his merits and his good intentions. The young woman who dispenses with *danger* and presses her own suit on a young man, like the Knight's would-be fiancée or Belissent, the duke's daughter in *Amis and Amiloun*, may unleash unforeseen and potentially tragic plot consequences.

Danger thus locks the medieval woman into a formidable double-bind.[79] Her position of resistance and rejection is regarded as inauthentic by the man whom her reserve keeps at arms' length. But what if she genuinely does not care for her suitor? Malory explores this dilemma early in the *Morte Darthur* where the lady Ettarde exhibits a thoroughgoing *danger* towards the brave knight Sir Pelleas who is anxious to win her love (I: 130–6). According to genre rules, Pelleas should have merited Ettarde's favour by winning a tournament and awarding his prize to her as the fairest lady present. But Ettarde will have none of Pelleas, and although he has followed her into her own territory and jousts regularly with her knights to showcase his prowess, she 'is so prowde that she had scorne of hym' (I: 132). Other ladies, the text tells us, disapprove of Ettarde's conduct towards Pelleas: 'all ladyes and jantyllwomen had scorne of hir that she was so prowde' (I: 131). Pelleas confides his situation to Gawain, invoking the ameliorating quality that the *Roman de la rose* associates with the overcoming of *danger*, with 'I truste she woll have pyté uppon me at the laste', and he adds that Ettarde 'rebukyth me in the fowlyst maner' whenever they meet (I: 132). Ettarde is altogether more friendly towards Gawain, who promises to intervene to gain her favour for Pelleas but ends up seducing her himself. The impasse can only be resolved, not entirely satisfactorily, through magical intervention. The Damesel of the Lake enchants Ettarde so that she falls in love with Pelleas and enchants Pelleas so that he no longer loves his former lady. Ettarde now dies of sorrow, and Pelleas and the Damesel become lovers.

The term *danger* is not invoked by Malory in this account, but it seems clear that Ettarde's behaviour approximates to a *danger* that is sustained beyond what the chivalric community regards as reasonable. Pelleas has amply shown his courage and continued to love his lady faithfully, despite her treatment of him. She ought to now have mercy on him, according to the emotional systems at work in romance's depiction of courtly gender ideology. Tellingly, it is other women who articulate and enforce the emotional norms: both the women who are shocked that Ettarde does not accept Pelleas' love at the tournament and the Damesel of the Lake. What should be a finite performance of *danger* completed by the granting of mercy becomes entirely performative, reiterating Ettarde's unaltering dislike of her suitor. Since Ettarde will not change her mind and feelings; they are changed for her through an interpellation that ends in a punitive madness and death.

Malory notably rescripts the story he found in his source in the Post-Vulgate *Suite*; there Pellias is low-born, and the lady Arcade rejects him specifically on those grounds: 'il n'estoit pas de tel lignage que elle le deust amer' (he was not of such a lineage that she could love him).[80] It is Gauvain who labels Arcade 'orgueilleuse' and 'villaine' (arrogant and ignoble) (II: 405) for failing to return Pellias's love. Arcade falls passionately in love with Gauvain, and he with her. Once the couple are discovered in bed by Pellias, Gauvain renounces the relationship and commands Arcade to take Pellias as her lover instead. Arcade does indeed wed Pellias. Her arrogance has, it seems, been dissipated by her own experience of love, but she does not burn with erotic passion for Pellias as she did for Gauvain. In this version, male figures – Gauvain, the lord who relays Pellias's story to him, and Arcade's councillors and barons – school the lady into abandoning her emotional resistance to Pellias. Once she has allowed herself to love another man, the possibility of feeling or persuasively performing *danger* becomes excluded. Although the text makes no explicit reference to it, Arcade's honour now needs recuperation; her no-longer-virgin status – although that is knowledge restricted to the three main protagonists – may also be instrumental in recalibrating her sense of her own worth and the relative distance in social status between her and her suitor.

Anatomised in extreme form in Andreas Capellanus's *De arte honeste amandi* (c. 1180), the ideology of *fin'amor* necessarily problematises the woman's position. For, if the task of the man is, as Toril Moi suggests, to persuade the lady of his lovableness – through the proxies of courageous deeds, generosity, physical appearance and courtly skills – his primary method of approach is through language.[81] As Moi notes, in Andreas Capellanus, 'it is the lover who does most of the talking; the lady, although obviously capable of quick repartee, limits her remarks to shrewd criticism of the lover's points, and hardly ever instigates a new topic of her own'.[82] Consequently, there is no linguistic space for the lady to express her own desire, to negotiate around her performance of *danger* and to hint that it has been overcome. Rather, she 'remains a curiously cold, distant and enigmatic creature whose love is perceived as a capricious and unreliable entity precisely because we, as well as the lover, suspect her of having no passion at all, deprived as she is of a discursive initiative of her own'.[83] Moi's arguments focus on Andreas Capellanus's primer for the courtly lover; although the text's function and context remain contentious, her observation is a telling one. For, as we have seen, the practice of *fin'amor* leaves little space for the lady either to affirm her own feelings – which would be contrary to the socially enjoined *danger* behaviour and would risk being 'blamed' like the Knight of the Tour-Landry's acquaintance – or to express her enduring lack of desire in any terms that the lover is prepared to hear or accept. The 'cold, distant and enigmatic creature' must always be assumed to be dissembling, to be in conscious control of her own responses and to be deliberately performing the withholding of love.

The tension between performance and performativity in *danger* – the implication that *danger* is always provisional and is at some level feigned (and when it is not it must be punished) – opens up this emotional complex to productive investigation. Whether *danger* is something that women 'really' feel, or do not feel; whether it is something they must perform, or they choose to perform; whether it is performatively effective in testing the lover's sincerity or aggrieves and annoys him, and how it can be distinguished from actual dislike: all these positions are brought into play in the texts analysed here. *Danger* is strongly associated with particular social ranks: primarily aristocratic and gentry; Alisoun in 'The Miller's Tale' performs a rather cursory version for comic effect, swiftly overcome when Nicholas 'gan mercy for to crie / And spak so faire, and profred him so faste / That she hir love graunted atte laste' (lines 3288–90). As an allegorical character *Danger* can be crude and menacing, or smoothly effective, and he is difficult, even impossible to overcome (except by flattery, gifts and money or by noble deeds, patience and self-restraint); the concept leaves little room for female agency. When women exercise that agency, it can operate only between highly delimited boundaries. The changing social role occupied by the personification is of interest: Gower's *wardein* and Skelton's depiction of Danger as 'chief gentlewoman' to Lady Saunce-Peere, in *The Bowge of Court* show how *danger* performance becomes integrated into evolving aristocratic contexts. When imagined as operative within a courtly setting, the wild man's club is superseded by a chain of office and a set of keys; in *The Bowge of Court*, by verbal rebuke and frowning: 'And with that worde on me she gave a glome /With browes bente and gan on me to stare / Full daynnously, and fro me she dyde fare.'[84]

The tension between performance and performativity in *danger* – the implication that *danger* is always provisional, can never finally, in Austin's terms, prove 'happy' – opens up this emotional complex to productive investigation. Socially enjoined and policed, both deprecated and admired, *danger* offers a fascinating case-study in the ways in which performance, performative, gender and rank intersect in medieval imaginative literature.

Conclusion

Concepts of performativity and performance have proved to be useful tools for analysing the ways in which emotionally motivated words and actions and their effects are framed within Middle English fictional texts. At the most reductive level, they advance plots by providing narrative motivation and action; they make things happen within the story. They have a key role in constructing the imagined secondary worlds of different genres, filling in the details of the social norms that obtain in particular contexts: be that Troy, the Arthurian court, Palerne or the psychological internal landscapes of personification allegory. Most importantly, performativity and performance work to bridge the gap between the internal and external, to communicate how an imagined interiority might impact upon speech and action in a range of discursive contexts. These concepts allow the audience to relate what individuals do or say within the narrative to the ways in which they are imagined as feeling or thinking. In romance in particular, conventionalised and moralised responses, such as the performance of classical Ovidian love-symptoms, of chivalric rage and aggression or female mourning, are developed in authors such as the *Gawain*-poet, Chaucer and even Malory into subtler, more densely imagined insight into human thoughts and feelings.[85] Access to interiority via performativity is often intermittent, or – as in *Troilus* – manipulated by the narrator in order to vary the focalisation of the story; here emotives may offer a confirmatory meta-analysis on changes within the emotional self. These moves allow medieval authors to develop their modes of characterisation from relatively 'flat' to creating – not fully realised psychological characters of the kind found in the modern realist novel – but persons who are recognisable as complex in their humanity, and who subsequently invite and enable empathetic identification from audiences and readers. The range of techniques that medieval authors employed to elicit empathetic responses in their audiences, and the surviving evidence for audience identification and emotion are the subject of the next chapter.

Notes

1 Frank Brandsma has suggested (personal communication) that, just as audiences assumed that literary characters had noses, even if their noses were not mentioned, so they must have assumed that such characters possess the mental and emotional attributes that generally pertain to humans.
2 J. L. Austin, *How to Do Things with Words*, in J. O. Urmson and Marina Sbisà (eds), *The Works of J. L. Austin* (Oxford and New York: Oxford University Press, 1976), p. 5.
3 Ibid., p. 6.
4 Ibid., italics in the original.
5 Ibid., p. 15.
6 Elaine Tennant, 'Prescriptions and Performatives in Imagined Cultures: Gender Dynamics in Nibelungenlied Adventure 11', in Jan-Dirk Müller and Horst Wenzel (eds), *Mittelalter: Neue Wege durch einen alten Kontinent* (Stuttgart: S. Hirzel, 1999), pp. 273–316 at p. 288.
7 Ibid., p. 288.
8 Elaine Tennant, 'The Protection of Invention. Printing Privileges in Early Modern Germany', in Gerhild Scholz Williams and Stephan K. Schindler (eds), *Knowledge, Science and Literature in Early Modern Germany* (Chapel Hill, NC: University of North Carolina Press, 1996), pp. 7–48.
9 Ibid., p. 29.
10 Kathryn Starkey, 'Brunhild's Smile: Emotion and the Politics of Gender in the *Nibelungenlied*', in C. Stephen Jaeger and Ingrid von Kasten

(eds), *Codierungen von Emotionen / Emotions and Sensibilities in the Middle Ages* (New York and Berlin: De Gruyter, 2003), pp. 159–73 at p. 161. Cf. Kathryn Starkey, 'Performative Emotion and the Politics of Gender in the *Nibelungenlied*', in Sara S. Poor and Jana K. Schulman (eds), *Women and Medieval Epic: Gender, Genre and the Limits of Masculinity* (London and New York: Palgrave Macmillan, 2007) pp. 253–71 at p. 257.

11 For example, royal anger, as discussed by Gerd Althoff in his 1996 article 'Empörung, Tränen, Zerknirschung' and revisited in '*Ira regis*' in Rosenwein's *Anger's Past* collection.

12 Starkey, 'Brunhild's Smile', pp. 163–4.

13 Ibid., p. 163.

14 Reddy, *Navigation*, p. 105.

15 Ibid., p. 105.

16 Plamper, 'The History of Emotions: An Interview', pp. 241–2.

17 Reddy, *Navigation*, pp. 106; 108.

18 Ibid., p. 129.

19 Philipowski, 'Die Textualität von Gesten', p. 471. Cf. Philipowski, 'Das Gelächter der Cunnewäre', and Starkey, 'Brunhild's Smile', p. 161 and note 5, who asserts that 'emotions arise from an external state of events in which a character finds him or herself and not as part of a psychological process'; they are principally motivated by narrative and plot. See in particular contra this position, Sif Rikhardsdottir's arguments in 'Medieval Emotionality', discussed in the next chapter.

20 Monika Fludernik, 'Through a Glass Darkly'.

21 Ibid., pp. 77–9.

22 See the detailed discussion of *daunger* later in this chapter.

23 I am grateful to Andrew Lynch for drawing my attention to the relevance of this scene to Reddy's concept of the emotive.

24 On Launcelot's unique use of the adjective *swete*, see Terence McCarthy, 'Malory's "Suete Madam"', *Medium Ævum*, 56 (1987), 89–94.

25 See below in this chapter for further discussion of *danger* as both performative and performance, particularly in relation to its sincerity.

26 Jill Mann, 'Chance and Destiny in *Troilus and Criseyde* and the *Knight's Tale*', in Piero Boitani and Jill Mann (eds), *The Cambridge Companion to Chaucer* (Cambridge: Cambridge University Press, 2004), pp. 93–111.

27 Williams, *Sincerity*, p. 193. Williams offers a shrewd reading of Criseyde's emotional repertoire across the poem (pp. 191–202).

28 See Gerd Althoff's two important articles 'Empörung, Tränen, Zerknirschung' and 'Tränen und Freude'.

29 Althoff, 'Tränen und Freude', p. 7. Note however Schnell's argument that in cases where public penance is at stake, the inner state of mind must be aligned with the external performance for the sacrament to be efficacious: Rüdiger Schnell, 'Medialität und Emotionalität. Bemerkungen zur Lavinias Minne', *Germanisch-Romanische Monatsschrift*, 55:3 (2005), 267–82 at pp. 271–5. So too Williams, *Sincerity*, pp. 19–23, argues that Christian sincerity originates in the bringing into alignment of 'internal emotions' and 'externalized language'.
30 Althoff, 'Tränen und Freude', p. 10.
31 Paul Strohm, *Hochon's Arrow: The Social Imagination of Fourteenth-Century Texts* (Princeton, NJ: Princeton University Press, 1992), pp. 99–105.
32 Ibid., pp. 102; 103.
33 Jutta Eming, 'On Stage: Ritualized Emotions and Theatricality in Isolde's Trial', *Modern Language Notes*, 124 (2009), 555–71 at p. 555.
34 Ibid., p. 556.
35 Williams, *Sincerity*, p. 196.
36 Frederic L. Cheyette and Howell Chickering, 'Love, Anger, and Peace: Social Practice and Poetic Play in the Ending of *Yvain*', *Speculum*, 80 (2005), 75–117 at p. 108. See also Stephen D. White, 'The Politics of Anger', in Rosenwein (ed.), *Anger's Past*, pp. 127–52; Frederic L. Cheyette's 2001 study, *Ermengarde of Narbonne and the World of the Troubadours* (Ithaca, NY: Cornell University Press, 2001), and William Reddy's account of 'love-as-passion' in *The Making of Romantic Love*.
37 Cheyette and Chickering, 'Love, Anger, and Peace', p. 113.
38 Keith Busby, 'Chrétien de Troyes English'd', *Neophilologus*, 71 (1987), 596–613 at p. 606, and A. B. Freedman and N. T. Harrington (eds), *Ywain and Gawain*, EETS OS 254 (Oxford: Oxford University Press, 1964), pp. xxvi and 130–1.
39 *Ywain and Gawain*, in Braswell (ed.), *Sir Perceval of Galles and Ywain and Gawain*, lines 3968–70.
40 Williams, *Sincerity*, pp. 188–9, notes that Middle English translated romances often retain or add a deontic modality (*must* or *shall*) when translating 'I love you': '*must* and *shall* make the speech act much more like a commissive in a traditional sense of loving, i.e. a promise "to honor" or "to serve" the addressee in the future, rather than the more fully expressive, epistemic speech act that seems foregrounded in the French' (p. 189). Alundyne and Ywayne make frequent use of *sal* (shall) to add this dimension to their exchange.

41 Geoffrey Chaucer, 'The Franklin's Prologue and Tale', in Benson (ed.), *The Canterbury Tales*, in Benson (gen. ed.), *The Riverside Chaucer*, pp. 177–89.
42 See Aisling Byrne, 'The Intruder at the Feast: Negotiating Boundaries in Medieval Insular Romance', *Arthurian Literature*, 27 (2010), 33–57, and Aisling Byrne, 'Arthur's Refusal to Eat: Ritual and Control in the Romance Feast', *Journal of Medieval History*, 37 (2011), 62–74.
43 For Arthur's wedding-feast adventure, see Malory, *Morte Darthur*, ed. Field, I: 81–98; Larrington, '"Wyȝe, welcum iwys to þis place!"'.
44 See Carolyne Larrington, 'Sibling Relations in Malory's *Morte Darthur*', in David Clark and Kate McClune (eds), *Blood, Sex, Malory: Essays on the* Morte Darthur, special issue of *Arthurian Literature*, 28 (2011), 57–74 at pp. 60–3.
45 Larrington, 'Sibling Relations', pp. 70–1.
46 Carolyne Larrington, *King Arthur's Enchantresses: Morgan and her Sisters in Arthurian Tradition* (London: I. B. Tauris, 2006), pp. 60–70. Bademagu's daughter first demands a 'rash promise' or *don contraignant*, to which Launcelot trustingly accedes. The 'rash promise' or 'rash boon' is a particularly binding form of speech act that puts notable pressure on chivalric conceptualisations of honour and shame.
47 See Cathy la Farge, 'Launcelot in Compromising Positions: Fabliau in Malory's "Tale of Sir Launcelot du Lake"', in Clark and McClune (eds), *Blood, Sex, Malory*, pp. 181–97.
48 See Larrington, 'Sibling Relations', pp. 68–9, and Amy Brown, 'Lancelot in the Friend Zone: Strategies for Offering and Limiting Affection in the *Stanzaic Morte Arthur*', in Mary C. Flannery (ed.), *Emotion and Textual Media*, Early European Research 13 (Turnhout: Brepols, 2018), pp. 75–97.
49 See Terence McCarthy, 'Did Morgan le Fay Have a Lover?', *Medium Ævum*, 60 (1991), 284–9 at p. 287.
50 Susan Crane, *The Performance of Self: Ritual, Clothing, and Identity during the Hundred Years War* (Philadelphia, PA: University of Pennsylvania Press, 2002), p. 2.
51 G. H. V. Bunt (ed.), *William of Palerne* (Groningen: Bouma's Boekhuis, 1983), lines 4327–543. Hereafter references are given in text.
52 Crane, *Performance*, p. 4.
53 *Sir Tristrem*, in Alan Lupack (ed.), *Sir Lancelot of the Laik and Sir Tristrem* (Kalamazoo MI: Medieval Institute Publications, 1994), line 2274, https://d.lib.rochester.edu/teams/publication/lupack-lancelot-of-the-laik-and-sir-tristrem.

54 Ibid., lines 2278–9. Contrast Gottfried von Strassburg's treatment of the parallel scene where the poet's comments seem intended to invite his courtly audience to reflect on the morality of such oath-swearing. *Tristan*, XXIV: 15733–40.
55 Williams, *Sincerity*, p. 195.
56 See Schnell, 'Gefühle gestalten', pp. 600–6. Schnell's analysis is grounded in Middle High German texts; Fludernik, 'Through a Glass Darkly' comes to similar conclusions about the representation of characters' feelings within their imagined consciousness.
57 Thorlac Turville-Petre, *Description and Narrative in Middle English Alliterative Poetry* (Liverpool: Liverpool University Press, 2018), p. 30; Fludernik, 'Through a Glass Darkly', p. 85; *Sir Orfeo*, lines 263–4, in Laskaya and Salisbury (eds), *The Middle English Breton Lays*.
58 Fludernik, 'Through a Glass Darkly', pp. 92–3, adduces also the unique (in Middle English) extended simile in 'The Knight's Tale' (lines 1635–48), when Palemon and Arcite face off against one another in the duel. The change of facial colour as they realise that one or other of them is likely to die is rendered in virtual direct speech.
59 Tracing the use of *let* in this sense throughout the poem also reveals Arthur pretending not to be surprised at the turn of events after the Green Knight's departure and Gawain acting as if he will not flinch at the Knight's first stroke (though in fact he does).
60 See Carolyne Larrington, 'English Chivalry and *Sir Gawain and the Green Knight*', in Helen Fulton (ed.), *Blackwell Companion to Arthurian Literature*, ed. Helen Fulton (Oxford: Blackwell, 2009), 252–64 and Carolyne Larrington, 'Mourning Gawein: Cognition and Affect in *Diu Crône* and Some French Gauvain-Texts', in Brandsma, Larrington and Saunders (eds), *Emotions in Medieval Arthurian Literature*, pp. 123–41 at pp. 132–5.
61 Williams, *Sincerity*, pp. 173–4.
62 See John Skelton, *Bowge of Court*, www.skeltonproject.org/bowge/.
63 William Dunbar, *The Golden Targe*, line 223, in John Conlee (ed.), *William Dunbar: The Complete Works* (Kalamazoo, MI: Medieval Institute, (2004), https://d.lib.rochester.edu/teams/publication/conlee-dunbar-complete-works.
64 Ernest Langlois (ed.), *Le roman de la rose*, 5 vols, Société d'anciens textes français (Paris: Firmin-Didot, 1914–24), vol. I, p. 148, lines 2920–50; translation by Charles Dahlberg, *The Romance of the Rose*, 3rd edn (Princeton, NJ: Princeton University Press, 1971), pp. 71–2, lines 2920–50. Geoffrey Chaucer, *The Romaunt of the Rose*,

ed. Larry D. Benson, in Benson (gen. ed.), *The Riverside Chaucer*, pp. 685–767, lines 3130–8.
65 John Gower, *Confessio Amantis*, vol. II, ed. Peck, trans. Galloway (Kalamazoo, MI: Medieval Institute Press, 2013), IV: 2813.
66 See Mary C. Flannery, 'The Shame of the Rose: A Paradox', in Jenny Chamarette and Jennifer Higgins (eds), *Guilt and Shame: Essays in French Literature and Cinema* (Oxford: Peter Lang, 2010), pp. 51–69 at p. 60; Langlois (ed.), *Le roman de la rose*, line 7682.
67 Elliot Kendall, 'Chamberlain Danger: The Social Meaning of Love-Allegory in the *Confessio Amantis*', *Medium Ævum*, 76 (2007), 49–69 at p. 53.
68 Gower, *Confessio Amantis*, vol. II, ed. Peck, trans. Galloway. All references are given in text.
69 John Gower, *Confessio Amantis*, vol. III, ed. Peck, trans. Galloway (Kalamazoo MI: Medieval Institute Press, 2004), V: 6614–52.
70 Kendall, 'Chamberlain Danger', p. 54.
71 Gower, *Confessio Amantis*, vol. II, ed. Peck, trans. Galloway, IV: 3530–4.
72 Chaucer, *The Book of the Duchess*, ed. Wilcockson, lines 1243–4.
73 Lydgate, *Troy Book:*, ed. Edwards. Further references are given in text.
74 Geoffrey Chaucer, *Anelida and Arcite*, ed. Vincent J. Dimarco, in Benson (gen. ed.), *The Riverside Chaucer*, pp. 375–81, lines 186–7; 195–6.
75 William Caxton (trans.), *Book of the Knight of the Tour-Landry*, ed. M. Y. Offord, EETS Special Series 2 (Oxford: Oxford University Press, 1971), ch. 12, pp. 27–8.
76 Ibid., p. 27.
77 Ibid., p. 28.
78 See now Mary C. Flannery, *Practising Shame: Female Honour in Later Medieval England* (Manchester: Manchester University Press, 2020), pp. 90–114, particularly on feigning shamefastness and its relationship to *Danger* in Lydgate's *Troy-Book*.
79 Compare, for a slightly different view of the female double-bind, Flannery, 'The Shame of the Rose', p. 53: 'medieval women ... occupied an impossible position, expected to adhere to honourable ideals of female shamefastness while ideals of masculine behaviour read this shamefastness as something to be overcome – if necessary, through force'.
80 Gilles Roussineau (ed.), *La suite du Roman de Merlin*, 2 vols (Geneva: Droz, 1996), vol. II, pp. 392–425 at p. 403. My translation. Further references are given in text.

81 Toril Moi, 'Desire in Language: Andreas Capellanus and the Controversy of Courtly Love', in David Aers (ed.), *Medieval Literature: Criticism, Ideology and History* (Brighton: Harvester, 1988), pp. 11–33.
82 Ibid., pp. 23–4.
83 Ibid., pp. 24–5.
84 Skelton, *Bowge of Court* (c. 1500), lines 79–82, http://www.skeltonproject.org/bowge/.
85 For an early discussion of the Gawain-poet's treatment of the intermittent access given to Gawain's thoughts and feelings, see Spearing, *The Gawain-Poet*, pp. 174; 202; see also David Aers's discussion of the parallels between Gawain's interiority and the depiction of private space in Hautdesert, in *Community, Gender and Individual Identity*, pp. 163–6.

4

Audiences and affectivity

Literary texts, as I suggested in the Introduction, are specifically designed to produce emotion in their audiences and readers; such emotion effects are highly variable, ranging from laughter to horror to tears to rage. Audience emotion is usually elicited by various degrees of empathetic engagement with the characters within the text; as we shall see below, this is an area which has been of considerable interest to psychologists. Audiences can also, or concomitantly, respond positively or negatively to the aesthetic and stylistic qualities of a literary text. Here useful parallels with film theory can be invoked; at the same time as audience members empathise with the characters in a film, they also think and feel critically about the film itself as art, as entertainment and as representative of its particular genre. Collective audience effects will also come into play; if everyone else in the audience is laughing, or shuddering, or weeping, individual reactions will also be affected.

Narrative itself, as medieval moralists well knew, could be more persuasive than direct preacherly didacticism: 'Multi enim incitantur exemplis, qui non moventur praeceptis' (many are stirred by examples who are not moved by precept), asserts Jacques de Vitry.[1] Anne M. Scott has noted this sentiment as one to which Chaucer's Pardoner apparently subscribed, calculating that his Tale will move his pilgrim-audience to penitence where mere exhortation may not.[2] Intradiegetic features cue audiences to respond to, and with, emotion. These may inhere in the work's style, its narratological organisation and its formal qualities. Generic convention plays an important role; opening lines that set a dream-vision in the spring prime audiences to anticipate revelations about love;

luxurious, courtly interiors suggest nobility of sentiment; sulphurous smells and crackling flame invoke the fear of hell-fire. Romance makes notable use of what Frank Brandsma has characterised as 'mirror characters', text-internal audiences whose reactions to events model, and may even help to elicit, appropriate emotional responses in those who hear or read the texts.[3] Writing in the ways in which attentive readers should react to the words they hear or read through apostrophe, exclamatory tags or narratorial comment is by no means limited to religious texts.[4]

Authors, audiences and readers depend on textual cues, on discourse effects to make feelings or to be made to feel.[5] Whether modern audiences and readers are made to feel the same feelings or to feel in the same way as medieval audiences felt is, of course, a debatable question. Sif Rikhardsdottir maintains that, while we must 'acknowledge and seek to tease out the subtleties of historical and ideological contingencies of medieval emotionality', 'this can best be done by conceding our own historicity in our re-enactment of medieval emotionality'.[6] We modern readers cannot claim unerringly to reconstruct medieval emotional responses in ourselves, although the methodologies and arguments outlined in this chapter suggest that by triangulating our readings with text-internal audience responses or by conceding some ground to biologically based arguments about embodied cognition and its relation to affect, some approximation to contemporary audience effects may be attained. Nevertheless, we can – indeed must – rely on our shared humanity and a sense of cultural and readerly continuities to unpack how Middle English texts feel and mean. For, as Guillemette Bolens acutely notes, 'l'interface entre le texte et son destinataire, [c'est le] seul espace auquel nous avons effectivement accès dans notre effort de compréhension des émotions médiévales' (the interface between the text and its intended audience [is] the only space to which we have effective access in our efforts to understand medieval emotions).[7] It is that space, that interface, which this chapter will explore. It begins by outlining contemporary psychological theorisations of empathy and their medieval counterparts, attending to the important distinction between those emotions produced by characters and events, and those elicited by the aesthetic and artistic effects that encode the literary narrative. It continues by exploring the stylistic and structural techniques that seem most conducive to producing audience emotion, and then examines some arguments for the existence of mirror neuron networks; these appear to offer a basis for theories of embodied cognition that intersect with some of the claims made for empathy in the consumption of literary texts. So-called 'mirror characters' and other techniques for modelling and guiding audience emotions, as in the framed story-collection or produced by romance's propensity to embed stories within larger narratives, are also considered. The chapter concludes with a case-study of the evidence for particular audience responses to late-medieval cycle dramas, raising some larger questions about the production of emotion in specific cultural contexts.

Empathy and the 'paradox of fiction'

Psychologists of emotion such as Keith Oatley, Raymond Mar, Maja Djikic and their associates have long been interested in how fiction engages the emotions of its audiences or readerships.[8] Indeed, Oatley defines fictional narrative as 'that mode of thought in which the planful agent, on meeting vicissitudes, experiences emotions'.[9] In an important article, Mar and Oatley argue that the experience of reading or hearing a story should be understood as analogous to a computer simulation: 'as a kind of simulation that runs on minds [which] will extend our understanding of selves in the social world'.[10] The narrative's context, language, aesthetic effects and thematic structuring all work to elicit mental world-building activity on the part of its consumers, and it communicates information about the social worlds in which they live. Mimetic representations of real-world emotions are created within the imagined space. The audience mentally run a simulation of the characters' experiences, an exercise that is strongly determined by the text's particular focalisation, and thus audience members come to share in the emotions encoded in the text, those created by the 'vicissitudes' experienced by the 'planful agent'.[11] The reading or hearing experience is thus integrated into an immersive process of identification for, as Oatley and Djikic stress, audiences and readers need to run such 'simulations to understand complexes in which several factors interact'.[12]

These simulations are more multifarious than straightforward identification with the hero or some other character; Oatley and Djikic propose that 'a work of literary art is a piece of externalised consciousness ... which readers can take in and make their own' and that this 'enables readers, partly by means of foregrounding, not just to understand their emotions in relation to themselves and others but to explore, further understand, develop, and transform them'.[13] Consuming literary texts, then, modifies the individual's own emotional configuration and capacity to hypothesise what is in the minds of others, in ways that can be determined through self-report and other psychological measures.[14]

Simulation theory offers one kind of explanation for what occurs when audiences immerse themselves in a fictive world. At the same time, as explored by numerous critics, audiences are well aware that the persons with whom they identify, and whose vicissitudes they share, are not real in the way that the person sitting next to them in the hall, chamber or theatre is real. In a well-known article, Colin Radford and Michael Weston analyse the paradox of emotional responses to fictive characters, placing a good deal of emphasis on the distinction between historical people, to whom events are believed 'really' to have happened, and such figures as Mercutio in Shakespeare's *Romeo and Juliet*. Radford and Weston suggest that the experience of emotion on hearing of the fates of persons who lived in the past is more explicable and 'natural'.[15] Radford thus identifies one of the peculiar conditions of much medieval imaginative literature: that it represents itself as, at some level, history. Thus, it may be understood as 'true'; its literary reproduction is authorised by its utility in teaching moral lessons to which an emotional audience reaction may be regarded as an appropriate and desirable literary aim.[16]

The paradox of fiction – emotional response to literary characters who demonstrably are not real in the way the person sitting next to you is real – may be resolved, as Ed Tan has argued, by making a clear distinction between the kinds of emotion aroused by events within the work of art's fictive world, and the emotions produced by the art itself as art: he designates the first as (fictive) F-emotion and the second as (artefact) A-emotion.[17] Tan writes specifically about film, but his findings are of relevance to the reception of literary texts also, particularly in those medieval contexts where textual consumption was a communal experience. Tan distinguishes between emotions produced within the fictive world and those produced by the artefact itself. He emphasises the importance of the diegetic effect: the sense that one is present within the world of the film as an invisible witness, one who may wish to intervene in the action, to warn or to reprehend, but yet who can have no actual effect on the unfolding narrative.[18] This diegetic effect may be less marked in the experience of listening to or reading a story, yet audiences still become imaginatively immersed in the story-world (as we shall see below), and experience the breaking-off of the tale as annoying – in terms of both plot resolution and aesthetic enjoyment. Attention to the story generates reward on both levels; the audience experiences empathetic emotion, understood as 'an emotion in the viewers [sc. audience] that is stimulated by the construed significance of the situation to some fictional character', and cognitive reward, as plot-focused narrative questions are finally resolved.[19] At the same time, aesthetic patterns and structures will also achieve some kind of closure: rhymes are completed, numerological designs (as in *Pearl*) are worked through, structural devices such as threefold adventures or trials are achieved, and recurrent systems of imagery are felt as pleasurable for those audience members who notice them.[20]

If we apply Tan's model to *Sir Gawain and the Green Knight*, it is evident that the poem exploits the audience expectation of completion on both fictional and aesthetic levels. In artistic terms, the poem's ending is enormously satisfying; the repetitions and echoes of the opening stanza in the closing lines, of 'þe segge and þe assaute' at Troy and the role of Brutus in the founding of Britain bring the verbal patterning full circle.[21] Yet at the narrative level, as many readers have noted, the story ends ambivalently.[22] Gawain's emotions on returning to the court and relating his adventure are met with laughter as discussed in Chapter 2 (pp. 110–11): whether this is sympathetic rejoicing that Gawain has come through his ordeal or uncomprehending merriment that refuses to acknowledge the knight's subject position is a matter of audience interpretation. Closure in the fictional world is effected according to the generic conventions of Arthurian romance; the knight returns from his adventure, having learned from his experiences, and is re-integrated into the courtly community, yet the audience's empathy with Gawain, seeking to communicate his conflicted emotional state to those who remained behind, resists an easy narrative resolution. The result is dissonance, of a kind that seems likely to have opened up opportunities for audience response and discussion in its original performance contexts, as much as in the contemporary classroom. In other more conventional Middle English romances, however, fiction-related and artefact-related emotions are equally rewarded. The hero and heroine are united and produce numerous children to continue the dynasty, as in *Havelok the Dane*, *Horn*, *Bevis of Hamtoun* and similar tales.[23] Romance and hagiography hybridise in one important romance subgenre; here the fiction concludes with a turn to God and a retreat from worldly affairs, as in *Floris and Blancheflcur*. In *Amis and Amiloun* the two friends' births on the same day are satisfyingly paralleled by their simultaneous deaths and their burial in the same grave.

Building on the work of Tan and others, David Miall and Don Kuiken argue that the emotions produced by reading differ from the basic emotions: 'anger, fear, or sadness are less likely to occur during reading than are the subtle and fugitive feelings that are not so readily named'.[24] Although anger, fear and sadness can of course be produced as empathetic emotions, as responses to characters within texts, they are of a much shorter duration than those feelings when elicited in non-literary circumstances. Miall and Kuiken distinguish between evaluative, narrative and aesthetic feelings (responding to formal features of the text) and – the focus of this particular article – self-modifying feelings: those 'that restructure the reader's understanding of the textual narrative and, simultaneously, the reader's sense of self'.[25] Miall and Kuiken particularly emphasise the unfolding nature of audience emotional responses as a narrative develops; their experimental method (essentially reader commentary) 'captures the temporally unfolding *experience* of a text rather than its consummating *interpretation*'.[26] Analogy is key to their theorisation of the processes involved in understanding audience emotional effects: audiences draw analogies between different kinds of affective schemas, for a situation that evokes emotion will recall (often in structural terms) an analogous situation that creates the same feelings. Metaphorical systems, allowing the recognition of subtextual emotional implications across the narrative, produce related affective responses at different points in the text.

These hypotheses propose that the consumption of fiction is a kind of simulation that elicits a spectrum of different kinds of feeling. These feelings are different from those encountered outside the reading-listening experience; they are briefer, less intense, and are elicited not only by events within the text, but also by the literary qualities of the text itself. Fiction consumption, Miall and Kuiken argue, has a vital adaptive function: it teaches and informs audiences about the ways in which other people think, feel and behave, and can have a transformative effect on its hearers. On a folk-psychological level, it is regarded as beneficial to children's psychological development (whether medieval or modern) to be taught from the earliest age to listen to stories, to think about their implications and to respond both to what the story relates and the skill with which it is told. The mechanisms by which empathy effects are enabled are neural networks common to primates, and thus are biological in origin; yet such networks are powerfully configured by learning and socialisation.

Mirror neurons and mirror characters

How is empathetic audience reaction produced within the bodies of readers or listeners – and is the empathy mechanism a universal biological phenomenon? Recent discoveries in neuroscience have opened up the possibility that our responses to visual and aural narratives are underpinned by neural substrates within the primate brain that contain specialised 'mirror neurons'.[27] When a motor act is performed (for example, biting an apple) certain neurons fire; the same neurons fire when an action is observed when being performed by others. This 'mirror-mechanism' is found in the premotor and posterior parietal areas of the brain, operating as a network rather than at a particular location. The debate around the functions of mirror neurons in humans has been wide-ranging, and much remains to be confirmed.[28] In summary, however, a consensus has emerged that mirror neurons are instrumental in 'action understanding': not simply registering that another being is moving, but hypothesising the goal of that movement. There seems also to be a – not necessarily causal – relationship between mirror neuron networks and speech perception. Since the premotor cortex is also involved in processing language relating to action, cerebral connections between seeing, visualising, reading about and hearing about actions may be made in such a way as to account for certain sensations of affect and empathy. Whether input mode is critical – whether hearing about action has the same effect as witnessing it or reading about it – is currently unclear. However, there is more general agreement that empathy, along with other forms of social cognition, is related to mirror neuron functions. Vittorio Gallese claims that 'brain imaging evidence shows that whenever we witness the emotions or sensations experienced by others, some of our brain regions display mirror activation'.[29] In two articles co-written with Hannah Wojciehowski, Gallese expands his intuition that 'our capacity to empathise with others might be mediated by embodied simulation mechanisms, that is, by the activation of the same neural circuits underpinning our own agentive, emotional, and sensory experiences'.[30] Gallese and Wojciehowski argue that humans experience their social world as 'embodied simulation ... internal non-linguistic "representations" of the body-states associated with actions, emotions, and sensations within the observer, as if he or she were performing a similar action or experiencing a similar emotion or sensation'.[31] These arguments for embodied cognition thus intersect with the theorisations of Oatley and Mar, providing a neural basis for their simulation mechanisms.[32]

Embodied cognition theory has been productively taken up by Guillemette Bolens, whose study investigates the connections made between the motoric systems to which mirror neuron networks belong, other sensory receptive networks and the representational systems used in mental imagery: 'modality-specific systems underlie the representation of knowledge', she asserts.[33] Bolens centres her analysis on perception of movement, defined as kinesic intelligence, and proprioception, 'the felt sense of owned embodiment'.[34] Through a close reading of *Patience* she shows how Jonah's experience in the belly of the whale is profoundly and strangely corporeal, depending on 'a kinesis of visceral movement', a 'fantasmatic viscerality' in which 'Jonah perceives haptically and olfactically the inside of another body from within this very body'.[35] In the listening medieval audience, as with modern readers, embodied cognitive systems are activated to facilitate mental representation: the cognitive and affective experience of the feel and smell of the whale's guts, of the absence of visuality in the infernal darkness. Here it is primarily sensory systems that are set to work, impelling the audience to the paradoxical imagining of an embodiment that instantiates what it is like to inhabit a human body that is inside another non-human body.

In her analysis of *Sir Gawain and the Green Knight* Bolens foregrounds the motoric systems, drawing attention to the kinesic and proprioceptive forces involved as Gawain prepares to withstand the Green Knight's blow. Gawain glances sideways as the axe descends on his bare neck and he 'schranke a lytel with þe schulderes for þe scharp yrne' (line 2267). Bolens observes, '[t]he specific narrativization of Gawain's little flinch shows that his identity is a performance, highlighting as it does the effort involved in achieving a perfect correspondence between behavior and identity'; yet that effort 'stumbles on the embarrassing surplus of kinesic expressiveness'.[36] It is however exactly the audience's own shiver of recognition, our shared shrinking from the swinging axe, that opens up for us the gap between the human and the idealised, the debate about how Gawain's humanity and his courtly identity might intersect that Bertilak takes up in his revelatory exchange with the knight after the third blow which nicks Gawain's neck. There the verb *schrank* is employed again, in a slightly different usage: 'þe scharp schrank to þe flesch þurh þe schyre grece' (line 2313), in a phrase recalling the beheading that the Green Knight himself underwent in Fitt One. There the alliteration, running across two lines, adds aural intensification to the kinesic: 'þat þe scharp of þe schalk schyndered þe bones, / And schrank þurȝ þe schyire grece, and schade hit in twynne' (lines 424–5). The semantic and kinesic difference between the shoulders shrinking at a feared touch and the crunching slice through flesh, fat and bones is telling here; the audience can scarcely help feeling Gawain's flinch, but we can only visualise, rather than experience in our own bodies, the violence of the severing blade.

The reader or listener's haptic sensory system responds to textual details of touch in complex ways. When at last Troilus holds the naked Criseyde in his arms:

> Hire armes smale, hire streghte bak and softe,
> Hire sydes longe, flesshly, smothe, and white
> He gan to stroke (III: 1247–9)

Does the listener or reader register this scene in terms of touching or being touched? Empathetic identification may be gendered or may escape gender and generate the possibility of different kinds of queer pleasure-taking. As Carolyn Dinshaw argues for the kisses received and delivered in *Sir Gawain and the Green Knight*, 'we are thus on complex and difficult terrain with the kisses in Fitt III circulating erotic power'.[37] Resistance to the heteronormative interpretation of the text is to be found, she suggests, 'in the practice of reading, in constantly queerying the text', but also in each audience member's individual embodied cognition about where pleasure might lie.[38] McNamer has demonstrated how such embodied identifications are key to affective piety's strategies for eliciting compunction.[39] To see Christ's torment, his mocking and scourging and his suffering on the Cross in civic drama cycles invites empathetic identification with the Virgin and St John, and with Christ himself; the recitations, in Middle English religious lyrics, in which Christ describes his pain and explains why he has willingly undergone cruel death for humanity's salvation are designed to evoke compunction and contrition.

It may be argued that embodied cognition theory takes insufficient account of critical distance, of audience awareness that the character is 'just made up', as discussed above (pp. 182–3). Nevertheless, the embodiment hypothesis goes some distance towards explaining how and why audiences might experience sorrow, fear, anger or joy, while remaining cognitively aware that the literary characters with whom they empathise are simply a collection of signs, of marks on the page. However powerful the theory's explanatory value, it must be weighed against a folk-psychological approach to individual emotion responses. To read about or to see a film about a murder being committed produces feelings which depend strongly on techniques of focalisation. If an audience shares in any way the feelings experienced by the murderer – of exhilaration, of horror, of sorrow – these are a highly attenuated and fleeting version; a differently focalised version of the same events will elicit powerful emotional identification with the victim. So, for example, in Chaucer's 'Franklin's Tale', the focus suddenly shifts from Dorigen's own profound distress at her plight now that the feared rocks are indeed 'awey' to her husband Arveragus's emotions on learning of his wife's rash promise to his squire. Arveragus listens to Dorigen's account and answers her calmly, 'with glad chiere, in freendly wise' (line 1467). Yet, immediately after offering his advice, 'he brast anon to wepe' (line 1480). The audience must switch from empathy with the suffering Dorigen, to astonished admiration of Arveragus's 'glad chiere', registering the self-control required for him to maintain a steady demeanour while he advises his wife, to identification with the damage to his sense of honour and the misery that causes him. The varied critical responses to this scene suggest that the demand for rapid switches in empathetic identification can result in a failure of empathy with one or other character. Compare, for example, two popular and radical readings of the Tale. Stephen Knight's view of Arveragus is severe: 'Resolution of the feudal threat comes from husbandly firmness, action, feeling and control, and concern for the external world of honour. The wife goes and comes, like a "thing" at last.'[40] Jill Mann argues rather that 'Arveragus relinquishes his own claims so that she [Dorigen] may meet the ones she has created. So far from depriving her of her freedom, Arveragus's action means that she must take full responsibility for it; her husband's refusal to forbid her to keep her promise deprives her of the alibi of male coercion.'[41]

The neurological approach to empathy mechanisms outlined above might seem irrelevant to a consideration of medieval emotions. The medical models of cognitive and affective mechanisms which had explanatory force in the medieval period and which, as discussed in the Introduction, incorporated the concept of localised function within the brain had no viable models to explain the production of empathy. Nevertheless, contemporary theorisations of neuropsychology and the affective domain seem to strengthen the arguments for a biological substrate to emotion. On the one hand this would allow us to assume, as discussed above (p. 180), that basic emotional responses – laughter, tears, anxiety, horror, disgust – to medieval literary texts are shared by medieval and modern audiences, a move that appears to discount social, historical and generic contexts in favour of a more universal biological emotional model. Yet, if mirror-neuron theorists agree on anything, it is that primate mirror-neuron networks are created through imitation and learning, that neural connections are developed from infancy in response to different kinds of social conditioning.[42] Most of us would not now willingly witness an execution that involved the culprit being burned at the stake; the spectacle would probably evoke horror, fear and disgust. If we believed fervently however that it was better for the victim to burn in this world than the next, and if such burnings were commonplace and our witnessing of them habitual, then our emotional response might be very different. Empathy, it seems, can be best understood as an interaction between biological and socio-cultural mechanisms; in these respects it should be understood as an important learned behaviour.

The unnuanced or instrumental adoption by humanities scholars of (neuro)scientific theoretical methods has not always been illuminating for historical or literary investigations.[43] Notwithstanding the pro and contra arguments about mirror neurons and their precise relationship to the processing of narrative, the theories of Rizzolati, Gallese and others have provided a useful analytic tool in terms of the analogous 'mirror character' effect. Identified by Frank Brandsma, the literary mirror character or characters, sometimes a named individual, very often a group of indistinguishable courtiers or other witnesses, respond to a particular situation with the appropriate emotional response.[44] Malory depicts collectivised emotion in the Arthurian court by listing the 'kynge, duke, erle, barowne, nor knyght, lady nor jantyllwoman', none of whom fail to weep when Sir Launcelot is compelled to depart from the court at Carlisle without persuading Gawain of his heartfelt regret at having accidentally killed his brothers. Such characters school audiences both inside and outside the text in the expression of feeling, modelling normative responses. Drama is created, as in this instance, by the emotionally contrasting character, the dissenter, like Arthur at the beginning of the scene, and Gawain throughout it, or like the unhappy girl, Enide's cousin, in Chrétien's *Erec et Enide* who demonstratively resists the outbreak of rejoicing when the adventure of the 'Joy of the Court' is achieved.[45] The person who does not share the communal emotion must be challenged, negotiated with and persuaded to reformulate their individual feelings for the collective good, so that they may be successfully re-integrated into the community and be seen to perform the emotion that conforms to the ideology of the court, cloister or town. If this fails, tragedy is likely to follow.

Critiquing audience emotion

Medieval authors and readers, such as Ælred of Rievaulx (1110–67) and Peter of Blois (c. 1130–1211), were critical of the superficiality of audiences who responded emotionally to narratives 'de Arturo, Gangano et Tristano' (about Arthur, Gawain, Tristan), whose adventures were recounted in *fabulae* (fictional tales), retold by *joculatores* and *historiones* (troubadours and actors).[46] These authors took their cue from Augustine's discussion in his *Confessions* of his own emotional responses to watching plays.[47] Augustine contrasts the vicarious enjoyment produced by the dramatisation of the sufferings of others with the unhappiness such events would cause if one experienced them in person, asking: 'Sed qualis tandem misericordia in rebus fictis et scenicis? non enim ad subveniendum provocatur auditor sed tantum ad dolendum invitatur, et actori earum imaginum amplius favet cum amplius dolet' ('But what is the real meaning of compassion in imaginary events and stage plays? The audience is not being summoned to assist, but merely invited to feel distress, and the deeper their distress, the more they appreciate the performer of those representations') (Book III, ch. 2, section 2, pp. 92–3). As the audience leaves the theatre, Augustine notes, paradoxically it weeps with joy at the emotional experience it has undergone: *gaudens lacrimat* (Book III, ch. 2, section 2, pp. 94–5). Later in the same book Augustine notes that the grief elicited by drama is entirely superficial: 'et inde erant dolorum amores, non quibus altius penetrarer (non enim amabam talia perpeti qualia spectare), sed quibus auditis et fictis tamquam in superficie raderer' ('This was the source of my love of distresses, not the kind to pierce me to my core, for I had no desire to suffer such things as I used to watch, but the kind of fictions, that when I heard them, would merely graze my surface') (Book III, ch. 2, section 4, pp. 96–7). Augustine's argument chimes both with Tan's distinction between fictive, or F-emotion, and artefact, or A-emotion (pp. 182–3 above) and with Miall and Kuiken's comment that such emotions are 'subtle and fugitive', that they simply 'graze [the heart's] surface'. For Augustine, the contrast between the specious compassion he felt for the characters portrayed by actors, the emotion he should have felt for his fellows suffering in the real world whose misery he had some chance of alleviating, and the enjoyment he gained from watching plays raise important questions about the authenticity of emotion. He resolves the issue by arguing that his emotional lability pointed to an inner emptiness that was subsequently filled by God; his emotional responses would become both licit and authentic when disciplined by Christian doctrine. After his conversion, Augustine maintains that his empathy and compassion ought to be kept for the actors and audience, unthinkingly pursuing pleasure and imperilling their souls, rather than feeling for dramatic characters who suffer the loss of their former happiness within the tragic plot (Book III, ch. 2, section 2, pp. 92–5).

Ælred and Peter of Blois were less concerned about how good the emotion induced by fiction might be for the individual's soul. More crucial was the identity of the individual whose misery was being narrated; the sufferings of Christ could and should call up profound emotional responses, a properly directed compassion that should not be elicited by historical or fictional characters. 'Qui compateris Deo, compateris et Arturo?' (Why do you feel pity both for God and for Arthur?), asks Peter of Blois.[48] True, Jesus's agonies could not be alleviated directly by intervening within the story of the Passion, yet, if hearing about or witnessing the narrative caused individuals to consider their own sinfulness and resolve to amend their lives, Christ could rejoice that his sacrifice had not been in vain.

That Arthur and the other romance heroes might be regarded as real historical figures, as argued for by Radford and Weston, was immaterial to Peter and Ælred's deprecation of weeping in sympathy with Arthur. In the *Speculum caritatis* (composed around 1143)

Ælred represents himself as in discussion with a novice who confesses that he no longer weeps when he hears of the sufferings of Christ. The abbot offers consolation, suggesting that tears are not reliable indicators of a true love of God. In his youth when hearing or reading tales of King Arthur, Ælred had himself been moved 'ad expressionem lacrymarum' (to the point of shedding tears).[49] Such tears are however factitious, he notes; if one is listening to tragedy or epic poetry (*tragœdia* and *carmina*) and weeps at the characters' fates, it would be ridiculous (*per absurdum*) to think that the audience actually cares about (*loves* in Ælred's terms) fictitious personages whom they cannot help. Rather – so argues Peter of Blois – such weeping is sinful: 'tears that would bring those who shed them not to devotion and penitence, but to judgment'.[50] Tears elicited by narrative, even by the Gospel, cannot be regarded as indicative of the depth of an individual's love of God or one's fellow-humans.[51]

Ælred's novice relates how, before entering the monastery, 'ad cachinnos redibam et fabulas' (I kept returning to loud laughter and storytelling). Such fondness for fiction is typical of the twelfth-century aristocratic lifestyle, whether or not the novice himself was Ælred's literary creation.[52] The belief that emotional engagement with *fabulosae*, made-up characters, was somehow sinful or misguided was primarily of concern in the twelfth and early thirteenth centuries; even then it was voiced only by authors who were thoroughly contained within institutional Christianity, and it had no demonstrable effect on noble enjoyment of historical and fictional narratives. Not long after Ælred and William the novice engage in this debate, clerical authors can already be seen making effective use of well-established emotional schemas in order to elicit feelings in their audiences, mobilising the transferability of such schemas across situations and, indeed, genres, through the operation of analogy as Miall and Kuiken observe. The lover-knight, who comes to rescue his beloved in her castle where she is surrounded by besieging enemies, is just such a romance staple. This trope is harnessed in *Ancrene Wisse* (c. 1200), not only as a metaphor for Christ's redemption of the human soul, but precisely to elicit from its audience the loving gratitude that a woman in such a dire plight ought to feel for the champion who not only takes on and routs her enemies but is prepared to sacrifice his life in the process. The fable that *Ancrene Wisse* relates here as 'a tale, a wrihe forbisne' (a tale, a clear exemplum) concludes with the pointed question: 'Nere theos ilke leafdi of uveles cunnes cunde, yef ha over alle thing ne luvede him her-efter?' (Would not this same lady be a scion of an evil lineage if she did not love him more than anything after that?)[53]

Romance furnished both the narratives that made Ælred and William weep and the tropes that were redeployed in the practice of affective piety. Weeping for Christ as if he were an Arthurian knight did not only help to create and teach the value of compunction for religious and lay alike; it must have promoted – not a culture of sentiment for its own sake – but rather a literary culture in which experiencing empathy for the joys and sufferings of secular figures need not always be subordinated to religious ends. As Lee Patterson points out, 'the secular and causal historiography articulated by Geoffrey [of Monmouth]'s *Historia*' initiated an understanding of human activity that was not wholly defined by the project of individual salvation.[54] Before the emergence of humanism in Quattrocento Italy it was 'the legendary histories and romances of the Middle Ages ... these ubiquitous narratives [that] provided the environment in which events could begin to be understood in human terms'.[55] In contradistinction to the learned typologies of emotion promulgated by Latin and clerical writers, native and unofficial psychologies begin to emerge within the genres of chronicle, history and romance with their marked focus on human motivation and human will. It was in these genres that vernacular emotion schemas and scripts were established and refined. Learning from figures of the classical and national pasts not only demanded that audiences engage in the cognitive processing of narrative in order to arrive at the relevant moral conclusions, but also required emotional identification: empathetic engagement with their dilemmas and vicissitudes. Although issues of authority might prioritise such retellings of the past over the kinds of creative invention made possible through the genre of dream-vision, for example, nevertheless Middle English secular literature became the focus for the kinds of imaginative simulations proposed by Oatley and his associates. Alongside the genre conventions and the transferable emotion schemas explored in preceding chapters, various intradiegetic stylistic features functioned to create audience affect. The most significant of these features are considered below.

Intradiegetic features

Sonic effects

Rhythm, alliteration and rhyme, all distinctive characteristics of Middle English poetry, stimulate and intensify feeling in their audiences with their powerful sensory impact.[56] Rhythmic repetition is also a marked feature of devotional Middle English prose; Julian of Norwich's repeated triplets, for example, with their powerfully pulsing beat, urge the audiences to answer Jesus's assurances of his loving care by opening their hearts to him.

> Our Lord Jesus oftentymes seyd: 'I it am, I it am; I it am that is heyest; I it am that thou lovist; I it am that thou lykyst; I it am that thou servist; I it am that thou longyst; I it am that thou desyrist; I it am that thou menyst; I it am that is al; I it am that Holy Church prechyth and teachyth the; I it am that shewed me here to thee.'[57]

Julian goes beyond the triads that she uses so frequently elsewhere in the *Shewings*, daringly extending her parallel structures, even beyond the apparently conclusive 'I it am that is al', with an expansive assurance of orthodoxy and authenticity. Julian was building on earlier vernacular religious styles. Sarah McNamer has called attention to the 'driving, emotion-heightened rhythm' typical of the prose style of the early Middle English Þe Wohunge of Ure Lauerd (*The Wooing of Our Lord*).[58] A group of closely related texts shares Þe Wohunge's passionate rhythmic style. Here is the opening of *On Ureisun of Ure Louerde*:

> Iesu soð god. godes sone. iesu soð goð. soð mon. Mon Maidene bern. Iesu min hali loue min sikere swetnesse. Iesu min heorte. Misel. misaule hele Iesu swete. iesu mi leof. mi lif. mi leome. Min halwi. Min huniter. þu al þat ic hopie. Iesu mi weole min wunne. Min bliþe breostes blisse. Iesu teke þat tu art se softe. 7 se swote. ȝettet to swa leoflic. swo leoflic and swa lufsum. þat te engles. a. biholdeþ þe.[59]

(Jesus, true God, God's son; Jesus, true good, true man; Man, Maiden's child; Jesus, my holy love, my sure sweetness; Jesus my heart; my joy; my soul's health, sweet Jesus; Jesus my love, my life, my light. My balm, my honey-drop, you are all that I hope for; Jesus my pleasure, my joy; my glad breast's bliss; moreover, Jesus, you are so soft and so sweet, yet also so lovely, so lovely and so lovable, that the angels gaze on you for ever.)

The breathless list of caressing blandishments uttered aloud by the reader, just as McNamer suggests of *Þe Wohunge*, sounds as 'sweet terms of endearment [spoken] to her lover in the familiar vernacular', converting the devotee's narrow anchor-hold into an intimate chamber of love.[60] Audiences who heard this work read aloud – particularly the anchoresses for whom it was originally written – must have responded feelingly to the pulsing beat of the repeated, parallel epithets and to the performance of the reader. Judging from the well-worn state of the *Þe Wohunge* manuscript, many a woman must herself have read aloud those very words of passion, naming Jesus as her beloved and calling him to her as her true Bridegroom. Such harnessing of aural tools for emotional effect has come to be particularly associated with texts composed by or for women. We might compare Richard Rolle's evocation of the erotics of devotion in *The Form of Living*, composed in 1348:

> Synguler loue is when al confort and solace is closet out of þe hert, bot of Ihesu Crist only. Oþer delite ne other ioy list hit nat, for þe swetnesse of hym in this degre is so confortable and lestynge, his loue so brennynge and gladynge, þat he or scho þat is in þis degre may as wel feele þe fyre of loue brennynge in har soule as þou may fele þi fynger bren if þou put hit in þe fyre. Bot þat fyre, if hit be hoot, is so delitable and wonderful þat I can nat tel hit. Þan þe sowl is Ihesu louynge, Ihesu thynkynge, Ihesu desyrynge, only in coueitys of him [ondyinge], to hym seghynge, of hym brennynge, in hym restynge.[61]

Although Rolle writes for the recluse Margaret Kirby, mentioned once by her full name or, more often, briefly and allusively across the manuscript tradition, he is at pains here to include male devotees: note the 'he or scho' in the passage above. As Kathryn Vulic has argued, the characterisation of the implied reader as an enclosed woman may simply be a strategy for creating a point of empathetic identification for the text's consumers of either gender, audience members who quite possibly live in the secular world.[62] To argue that such passionate and erotic texts are composed chiefly for women is to fall into the essentialist trap of assuming that women are pre-eminently creatures of the flesh, differentially affected by the techniques of rhyming repetition, as in the repeated participles in the passage cited above. For in fact, this kind of writing is not just typical of material composed for women but is rather a marked feature of mystical writings intended for both genders from the fourteenth century onwards. That our two surviving identifiably female-authored texts composed in Middle English – those of Margery and of Julian of Norwich – recount their autobiographically framed, powerfully personal mystical experiences skews our perception of the kind of audience for whom such writing was intended. Affective piety, however, as the term suggests, functions very much through inviting keen emotional identification with the suffering Christ and his Mother (as we saw in Chapter 2), empathising with Jesus's agony and Mary's sorrow to elicit compunction and to bring about penitence and associated spiritual change. Arousing bodily affect through rhythmic repetition is a key technique in this.

Marked alliterative patterning flags up the sexually aroused give-and-take between Sir Gawain and Lady Bertilak on day three of his stay in Hautdesert – intensified by extending the alliterative pattern to include almost all the major stresses in the line:

Wiȝt wallande joye warmed his hert.
With smoþe smylyng and smolt þay smeten into merþe,
Þat al watz blis and bonchef þat breke hem bitwene,
   and wynne. (lines 1762–5)

(Strong, surging joy warmed his heart, with smooth, sweet smiling they slipped into mirth, so that all was bliss and happiness that was broached between them – and delight.)

The gentle alliterative beats in the first and second lines, on [w]and [sm], suggest how Gawain relaxes into pleasurable conversation, while the thudding b's of the third line might suggest his accelerating pulse, an acceleration effectively arrested by the jolt of the bob: 'and wynne'. In the wheel, the narrator moves away from inhabiting Gawain's subjective estimation of what is going on. In effect, he gives us a cinematic long shot of the pair enjoying themselves, drawing attention to the ethical implications for Gawain: 'Gret perele bitwen hem stod / Nif Maré of hir kny3t mynne' (Great danger stood between them / unless Mary were mindful of her knight) (lines 1772–3).[63] The poem's strongly marked bob-and-wheel metrical patterning functions to both summarise and moralise the emotional fluctuations hidden beneath the flirtatious talk.

The *Gawain*-poet is a master of metrical virtuosity and aural design; in *Pearl*, as McNamer suggests, affective power accrues 'through indirection and allusiveness, tapping into the sensory power of visual and tactile images and patterned sound'.[64] Less self-consciously innovative genres, such as popular metrical romance, also produce emotional effects through chains of sonic similarities. *Sir Perceval of Galles*'s insistent rhythmic beat also harnesses alliteration to intensify such effects within its regular sixteen-line tail-rhyme stanzas. These stanzas alternate rhyming triplets with a fourth line whose rhyme thus recurs four times within the verse unit, and a stressed word in the last line concatenates with another in the first line of the next stanza. The effect is one of 'persistent liveliness', as Mary Flowers Braswell notes.[65] In this stanza, after having achieved remarkable success as a knight and having gained the love of Lady Lufamour, Perceval goes in search of his mother, whom he abandoned when he embarked on the chivalric life. He finds her in a state of madness, roaming in the forest.

> Be that, so nere getis he,
> That scho myghte nangatis fle,   [not at all]
> I say yow full certeynly,
>   Hir byhoved there to byde.
> Scho stertis appon hym in tene;   [grief / rage]
> Wete ye wele, withowtten wene,
> Had hir myghte so mekill bene,
>   Scho had hym slayne that tyde!
> Bot his myghte was the mare,
> And up he toke his modir thare;
> One his bake he hir bare:
>   Pure was his pryde. (lines 2225–36)

Despite the occasional fillers ('I say yow full certeynly'; 'Wete ye wel') the stanza dramatically shows the conflicted mother, who in the previous verse had begun to tremble at the sight of her lost son, as both wanting to run away – and yet she cannot – and then flinging herself violently upon the young man. The marked 'm'-alliteration contrasts her *myghte*, which is not *mekill*, and her son's *myghte* which is *mare*; the alliterative linking continues with *modir*, insisting on the power of the bond between mother and son, even in madness. Grief and rage combined, *tene*, has undone Perceval's poor, deranged mother, provoking her to unmaternal and unfeminine aggression, but with extraordinary tenderness Perceval carries her home to her castle on his back, unconcerned by the humiliation ('Pure was his pryde'). There the porter tends to her until, through the restorative therapy of long, pharmaceutically induced sleep and regular bathing, she recovers her senses. This Middle English Percevaltale is unique in permitting the hero to recuperate his relationship with his mother; in the other versions of the story she dies of grief at his precipitate departure.[66]

Chaucer's 'Tale of Sir Thopas' explicitly invokes *Sir Perceval* – perhaps known to its author in a version very similar to that uniquely preserved in the Thornton manuscript (Lincoln Cathedral Library, MS 91). It is not simply the nonsensical plot, stuffed with romance clichés, driving the Host to interrupt pilgrim-Chaucer's recitation, that annoys the text-internal audience and causes the text-external audience alternately to laugh and groan. The metre itself irritates the ear. Chaucer expands his predecessor's two-stress tail-rhyme to three stresses per line, but the rhyme gets no chance to develop the narrative since the metrical pattern is one of couplets, rather than *Sir Perceval*'s more expansive triplets. Both logic and rhythm are interrupted by the snap of the short line.

> Sir Thopas wax a doghty swayn,
> Whit was his face as payndemayn,
>   Hise lippes rede as rose;
> His rode is lyk scarlet in grayn,
> And I yow telle, in good certayn,
>   He hadde a semely nose. (lines 724–9)

'It has the appearance of rapid motion with very slight real advance, and here and there comes a wonderful flourish, a bit of *bravura* that in a moment communicates the frolicsome mood of the poet, and the joyousness of his self-imposed task', remarked J. M. Manly, more than a hundred years ago.[67] While the modern audience indeed acknowledges the parodic intention and laughs at the clichés, the lack of narrative coherence and the bathos, the text-internal audience seems to concur with the Host's fierce verdict of 'rym dogerel' (line 925). At all events, no one speaks up in pilgrim-Chaucer's defence, for their emotions (both fiction- and artefact-related in Tan's terms) apparently coincide in disapprobation of the poem's style and its incoherent content. The Host receives the fictive-Chaucer's next offering, 'The Tale of Melibee', much more warmly, even if his appreciation rests rather an entirely literal understanding of the moral tale, and on the contrast between Dame Prudence and his own wife (lines 1889–1923).

Imagery and rhetorical devices

Beyond the marked oral and aural qualities particularly found in poetic texts, other narrative and rhetorical techniques encourage affective responses in Middle English audiences. These include pathos, as in Griselde's pleas to the sergeant in 'The Clerk's Tale' that her children be properly buried, and the often noticed repetition of 'lytel' in Dame Eglantyne's account of the murdered schoolboy in 'The Prioress's Tale'. Indeed, after that tale is completed, 'every man / As sobre was that wonder was to se' ('Prologue to the Tale of Sir Thopas', lines 691–2). Apostrophe, whether addressed directly to the audience or to characters within the text, often challenges them to respond empathetically; bathos calls forth a smile. Catalogues suggest plenitude: yet the remarkable series of lists invoked in *The Squire of Low Degree* – uttered by the king who describes a perfect day in order to cheer up his grieving daughter – fail to modify her affect.[68] To his more-than-a-hundred-lines-long catalogue, comprising sub-catalogues of food, wine, materials, jewels, hunting prey, musical instruments and more, the princess simply replies: 'Gramercy, father, so mote I the, / For all these thinges lyketh not me' (lines 853–4).[69] The king lays particular stress on his daughter's possession of, and her contiguity to, the excessive trappings of the aristocratic lifestyle through his repeated use of 'your' – 'Your head shete shall be of pery [jewellery] pyght / With dyamondes set and rubyes bryght' (lines 843–4). The romance may have been composed, as critics have argued and as its late print context suggests, for a non-noble audience. The purpose of the king's endless catalogues 'seems to be to impress an audience with the wealth of a social group to which they themselves do not belong', suggests Erik Kooper.[70] A bourgeois audience would wonder no doubt at the variety, extensiveness and sheer expensiveness of the luxuries itemised so imaginatively by the king who hopes only to give his daughter pleasure; envy would be evoked, and very likely surprise at the deflating effect of the princess's abrupt dismissal of the idea that material pleasures could distract her in any way from her profoundly felt grief.

Conventionalised settings cue audience emotion, signalling the relevant genre and triggering concomitant expectations. The traditional springtime *mise-en-scène* at the beginning of a lyric or a dream-vision suggests to the audience that erotic love will be at the centre of the poem. Such expectations may be fulfilled, as in a good many of the secular lyrics – or subverted. Despite the enamelled artificiality of its aureate language shown to advantage in its May opening, William Dunbar's *The Goldyn Targe* explores the difficult and unsatisfying emotions and behaviours associated with love. There is no erotic fulfilment and release for the dreamer; rather the vision incorporates an accelerated passage through attraction to the beloved, the lover's resistance with the aid of Reason, to yielding, disappointment and unhappiness. Chaucer's *Legend of Good Women* also opens with the bookish speaker impelled outside by the onset of spring:

> ... whan that the month of May
> Is comen, and that I here the foules synge,
> And that the floures gynnen for to sprynge,
> Farewel my bok and my devocioun! (lines 36–9)

Despite the expectations generated by this setting, the Chaucerian narrator goes out to pay his respects to the humble daisy, not the flamboyantly beautiful rose. When he encounters the God of Love, the latter reprehends him thoroughly for his treatment of Criseyde and sets him to more writing – sending him back to his books. In contrast to his conventional treatment of setting in *The Goldyn Targe*, Dunbar makes witty play with tropes of seasonality and love when he elects to set *The Tretis of the Twa Mariit Wemen and the Wedo* on Midsummer's Eve; coming only a short time after the May-time of true, young love, the women's disturbing revelations about the emotions actually in play in contemporary marriage thoroughly unsettle the promises of erotic fulfilment tendered in conventional love visions.

Accounts of the landscape of hell with its lakes of pitch, fiery surges and icy terrains are designed to inspire fear and horror, whether mediated in other-world journey narratives, in descriptions of the next life delivered by unhappy revenants, or in more straightforwardly allegorical texts.[71] The richly descriptive early Middle English prose *Sawles Warde* (c. 1225 in manuscript) offers a vivid vision of hell.[72] Concerned that Will, the unruly housewife who manages the house of the body, is insufficiently obedient to her husband Wit, Warschipe (Prudence), one of the Four Daughters of God, arranges for Fearlac (Fear), an emissary of Death, to visit. The messenger is unattractive: 'lonc he is ant leane, ant his leor deaðlich ant blac ant elheowet, ant euch her þuncheð þet stont in his heaued up' (he is tall and thin, and his face deathly and pale, and unearthly in colour, and each hair on his head seems to stand on end).[73] Fearlac warms to his descriptive task, to warn the household what might await them in the next life. He expounds the terrible stink, 'stench unþolelich'; the impenetrable darkness, 'þicke ... þosternesse'; the devils' ceaseless tossing of souls from icy cold to burning heat and back again; the *helle-wurmes*, toads and frogs that crawl upon and through the suffering bodies, swarming out of their eyes and the nostrils; the cries of the damned, each blaming the other for his agony; the sight of the demons with 'hare grimfule and grurefule nebbes' (their grim and terrifying faces) and the sound of their roaring, *rarunge*; all are brought before the audience's eyes, ears, noses and are felt upon their skins.[74] Fearlac's description culminates in a rhythmic, alliterative and rhyming climax: 'O helle, Deaðes hus, wununge of wanunge, of grure ant of granunge, heatel hame ant heard, wan of alle wontreaðes, buri of bale and bold of eauereuch bitternesse, þu laðest lont of alle' (O hell, house of Death, dwelling of misery, of horror and howling, hateful, harsh home, place of all torments, citadel of sorrow and stronghold of every bitterness, you most hateful land of all).[75] The characteristic style of the AB group, noted above of *Þe Wohunge of Ure Lauerd* and *On Ureisun of Ure Louerde*, with its driving rhythms, insistent alliteration and close-packed rhymes, combined with the direct address of apostrophe, works to intensify the terrors of hell and to move the audience within and beyond the text, to elicits responses of horror and fear.

Fearlac models an appropriate emotional reaction to what he has described; when he thinks of hell, and all that he has seen in it, he reports, each bone in his body trembles. His hair stands on end and pity wells up within him for the suffering sinners. The four daughters of God, and Wit the husband, are not slow to respond to Fearlac's account and even the 'willesfule husewif', the headstrong lady of the castle, Will herself, becomes very quiet. All the members of the household – the senses and the unruly thoughts – turn from her and now attend to Wit.[76] Clusters of images – the snakes and toads, the darkness, the vivid metaphor of souls tossed on pitchforks as if they were pillowslips, the filthy stench – all combine to produce identifiable emotional effects in the text-internal listeners. Both Fearlac, who epitomises in his own body the appropriate emotional response, and the now-subdued Will and her followers who fall silent and into line, demonstrate that the admonitory and didactic text has done its work.

Modern readers tend to privilege the first reading over all other readings. Effects of surprise and suspense are prized; the act of re-reading is usually reserved for particular favourites or part of a programme of systematic study. Medieval readerships and audiences were less at liberty to choose a new narrative or meditation whenever they felt like it. Constrained by the number of manuscripts they possessed or could borrow, or by the repertoire of available oral performers, medieval people enjoyed a deep familiarity with the literary works they consumed, entailing distinctive audience effects. Attention to variations within retellings, appreciation of shifts of emphasis, changes in points of view, amplification and that much under-rated textual pleasure, anticipation, all played a role in audience responses to medieval narratives. The first reading or hearing of *Sir Gawain and the Green Knight* is predicated on suspense – will the Green Knight remain headless? Will Gawain find the Green Chapel? Will he escape Lady Bertilak's blandishments? And not least, will he keep his own head? But these effects, of surprise and admiration as the brilliantly constructed plot with its interlocking games – the Beheading, Temptation and Exchange of Winnings – culminates in Bertilak's revelation of his role in the whole affair, recede on a second or subsequent reading, replaced by attentive listening out for clues, a keener registering of the significance of the 'auncian lady' who proves to be Morgan le Fay, the plot's 'only begetter', as Kittredge terms her, and an appreciation of the skill with which the poet varies the pattern of the exchange of winnings ritual on the third day to imply Gawain's uneasy conscience as he hurries to conclude the final handover.[77] C. S. Lewis suggested of the final book of *Troilus* that it is 'so painful that perhaps no one without reluctance reads it twice'.[78] Indeed, many a listener may have hoped that this time Criseyde will somehow find the courage and opportunity to return to Troy, even if, on repeat hearings, Criseyde's equivocation and the narrator's pose of uneasiness in mediating her behaviour become increasingly apparent.[79] Once again film theory is helpful in highlighting how repeated hearings or readings of a literary text, just like multiple viewings of a film, educate and train an audience in awareness of salient plot details, but also in appreciation of how the work's aesthetic patterning of imagery and structure enhances its cognitive and emotional appraisal of the text's semantic and affective range. User competence and frequency of exposure contribute to a tacit understanding of the emotion repertoires within, and the pleasurable experiences delivered by, the work, whether in film or other media.[80]

Contiguity and contagion

Emotional effects experienced when hearing texts performed would have been amplified through social contiguity. For emotion is contagious; people often unconsciously mimic each other's expressions and movements, an effect that very likely involves the mirror neuron system. Social appraisal is also a key part of emotional contagion; 'person B picks up information about how the other person is feeling about specific circumstances, rather than simply about the nature of the feelings themselves', and responds accordingly.[81] For example, when I realise that I am the only person in the theatre laughing at the play, I rein in my laughter; or when I hear other people in the cinema audibly sniffing at a sad film, I stop trying to suppress my tears.[82] Audience members affect one another emotionally; they inflect and modify one another's responses to narratives in ways that – normally – are expressive of solidarity and empathy with the predominant audience mood. As Brian Parkinson reminds us, 'emotions are active and embodied modes of engagement with the social and practical world. They reconfigure relations between people and objects in the shared environment as well as responding to, and conveying information about, these relations.'[83] As noted above, people who do not conform to the general emotional tenor of the social group call attention to themselves; the consumption of literary texts in homogeneous social groups – the baronial hall, the court – will produce emotional responses that are likely to reflect and maintain social cohesion. Certain Middle English texts are well aware of this effect; the framework of *The Canterbury Tales* is deliberately structured to produce social heterogeneity which must be moulded into consensus in the reception of narratives. The successive versions of *Piers Plowman* may originate in varying (and possibly undesirable) audience reactions: the probable appropriation of the poem's hero by rebels during the 1381 Peasants' Uprising, for example. The A- and B-version scene in which Piers tears the pardon 'in pure tene', excised in the C-version, is a case in point.[84] Whether the pardon-scene was removed because it offered a provocation that was unwise in the post-1381 climate, or because Langland decided that the theology of the tearing was unclear has been a subject of critical debate; indeed both external and authorial factors may have been in play.[85] Either way, the effect of the poem's modification and restructuring was to regulate the ways in which audiences might have responded to this crucial episode.

The imperative to maintain community consensus about what is acceptable as a response to artworks or utterances returns us to

Rosenwein's concept of emotional communities. Rosenwein notes how, in *The Book of Margery Kempe*, many of the clerics and the citizens of Lynn rebuke Margery Kempe for her deviant emotional style, while others fear that Margery's behaviour is intended to persuade their own wives to behave in a like manner, abandoning their husbands to follow her: 'to han awey owr wyvys fro us and ledyn hem with the', claims the Mayor of Leicester (p. 236).[86] A similar allegation is levelled at Margery by a friar at the court of the Archbishop of York (p. 265).[87] Not only do emotional communities police emotional display and reprehend breaches of decorum in community members; they also function as self-sustaining social organisms, controlling the admission of innovative emotion schemas, or repelling behaviours that threaten to the consensual emotion repertoire, those that appear to have undesirable social consequences.

Stories within stories

Medieval narrative art often nests stories within stories. Romance often incorporates micro-narratives, sometimes at the level of allusion, sometimes *in extenso*. In *Emare*, the Emperor is given a beautiful piece of cloth by his vassal, the King of Sicily, encrusted with jewels and made by the Emir of Babylon's daughter. The valuable fabric is 'stuffed wyth ymagerye' (line 168), embroidered with significant and allusive designs. In three corners of the cloth, famous pairs of lovers are depicted: Amadas and Ydoine (whose tale also has an intertextual function in *Sir Degrevant*); Tristan and Isode, and Floris and Blanchefleur. In the fourth corner the Emir's daughter has depicted herself and her beloved, the Sultan. The Emperor's acquisition of the cloth, embroidered with archetypal romance-figures, triggers a sudden, disturbing desire to see his lovely, young daughter, setting in train a chain of events that are explicitly linked to the genre the cloth evokes. As the narrator self-consciously notes, 'in romans as we rede' (line 216), the Emperor invites Emaré to come to his palace; as they feast together he forms the intention to make the girl his wife. Messengers are sent to the Pope to obtain a bull to get around the awkward fact of incest, and once permission is granted the Emperor has a robe made for his daughter from the wonderful cloth. The visual references to the noble lovers of romance operate to make sexual love suddenly salient to the widowed Emperor; his newly rediscovered desire, his 'longyng' (line 188), metamorphoses from the paternal affection of 'he klypped her and kyssed her swete' (line 213) very swiftly to becoming 'anamored' (line 226). Textile and text are closely interwoven, not just within *Emare*'s text in which the artefact figures, for the allusive narrative power of the cloth draws in threads from across the European romance genre.[88] The fabric is not only key in reconfiguring the Emperor's emotions at the start of the romance; it also functions as a classic recognition token to ensure the romance's happy ending through the final family reunion. Through the garment's power the penitent Emperor is brought to occupy his rightful place in the narrative's network of agency, while Emaré's husband recovers his wife and son; the dress's erotic spell is recast to figure faithful and procreative married love. The audience, by contrast, experiences as shocking the emotional disjunction between the narrative expectations of sexual love set up by the cloth's stories and the actors – father and daughter – proposed by the plot.

Romance inset tales may be autobiographical and fictional; the story woven by Sir Orfeo of his own death, imparted to the faithful steward on his incognito return to court, causes the man to swoon and fall to the ground (line 549).[89] This emotional response is treated briefly; the barons present urge him not to give way further to grief as it will not amend the situation. Encouraged by his steward's reaction, Orfeo embarks on a long conditional account of his hypothetical adventures. 'Yif ich were Orfeo the king …' (line 558) he begins, and he continues for a further fifteen lines before revealing his identity. Communal joy breaks out, and the steward himself, in a lively and unconventional move that echoes in part the downward trajectory of his earlier swoon, throws over the tableboard that separates him from his beloved lord and casts himself at his feet. 'Lord! there was grete melody! / For joie thai wepe with her eighe' (lines 590–1). The steward's sorrow is registered, but since the audience knows the truth of the matter, the disjunction between character emotion and audience feeling prevents the poet from dwelling too long on unnecessary misery. Joy, as in the treatment of the 'Joy of the Court' episode in Chrétien's *Erec et Enide*, is essentially a communal emotion, brought into play at the end of the romance when a threat to a community is lifted or a formerly lost or deviant individual can once again be integrated into the group. Or, as Antonina Harbus notes, it can function 'as a sort of resting state or norm of Arthur and his court ... universal and stable social joy', the status quo that must be disrupted at the start of an adventure.[90]

Conversely, in 'The Franklin's Tale', Dorigen rehearses the stories of various classical maidens and matrons who killed themselves rather than face dishonour; the genre conventions of the Breton *lai* suggest quite strongly to the audience that, despite the length of her catalogue of honourable suicides, the Tale's heroine is in little danger of following their example:

> Thus pleyned Dorigen a day or tweye,
> Purposynge evere that she wolde deye.
> But nathelees, upon the thridde nyght,
> Hoom cam Arveragus (lines 1457–60)

'By having Dorigen hyper-trope her trauma, Chaucer disables or at least seriously compromises our tolerance and emotional engagement with her, and at this point in the narrative she is in danger of becoming the object of satire', observes Michael Calabrese unforgivingly.[91] This may be to read her too harshly, but as other critics have noted, Dorigen substitutes speech for action, piling up exempla – all of which point to the same conclusion, as she recognises. And yet through the excessive number of examples and the three-day delay, her resolve is ironically undercut through the deployment of the kind of rhetorical device that normally serves to intensify, rather than complicate, emotional effects.[92]

Chaucer, *par excellence*, opens up gaps – often ironic ones – between how characters profess to feel, how they actually behave and the emotional guidance that generic conventions provide for the well-attuned audiences. So, in 'The Reeve's Tale', Aleyn delivers a well-crafted aubade as he takes leave of the miller's daughter Malyne, whom he had deflowered during the night. The form is classic, even if Aleyn must vary the promises of service he makes to suit his social rank: 'I is thyn awen clerk, swa have I seel!'

(line 4239), swearing devotion as Northern student rather than gentle knight. In another genre, Malyne, poor innocent girl, might be in line for heartbreak, as she prays God to 'save and keepe' her 'goode lemman' (line 4247). Yet the Reeve – or rather Chaucer – skilfully modulates the emotional tone by adding: 'And with that word almoost she gan to wepe' (line 4248). *Almoost* is key here; the emotional gesture that the text suppresses belongs to a different kind of narrative altogether: a moral exemplum, a romance or indeed a tragedy.

One of genre's functions in medieval literature – particularly in genres with as long a history as romance has – is to prime its audience's emotional responses by evoking an emotional repertoire appropriate to the kind of story being related. The expected emotional responses of the first auditors of the different stories within *The Canterbury Tales* – the pilgrims themselves – are frequently recorded, along with marked or deviant reactions to individual Tales. The narrator who promises faithfully to mediate the narratives as he heard them during the journey to Canterbury quickly cedes the right of commentary and interpretation to his fellow-pilgrims, notably to the Host, Harry Bailly, whose role as arbiter of turn-taking modulates into that of literary critic. Harry's feelings about stories are not always reliable; usually the collective response is that endorsed by the frame-narrative. 'The Knight's Tale' meets warm approval from 'yonge [and] oolde ... and namely the gentils everichon' (lines 3110; 3113), though the Miller's response, his promise to 'quite' the tale, indicates his dissent from that collective opinion. So too, in response to 'The Miller's Tale', '[d]iverse folk diversely they seyde / But for the moore part they loughe and pleyde' (lines 3857–8) – except of course for the Reeve, who feels 'ire' and begins to 'grucche' at the depiction of John the carpenter.

If *The Canterbury Tales* are, in part, to be read as an extended exploration of the possibilities of different contemporary literary genres, it is not surprising that Chaucer should also explore the distinction between the fiction-related and aesthetic or artefact-related emotions elicited by his experiment. The Monk's dismal catalogue of tragedies is interrupted by the Knight, who objects to the sad emotions these tales evoke in him. For the 'Monk's Tale' is depressing, the Knight avers in 'The Nun's Priest's Prologue', and: 'litel hevynesse / Is right ynough to muchel folk, I gesse. / I seye for me, it is a grete disese' (lines 2768–70). Rather, the Knight suggests, the Monk should offer uplifting stories, rags-to-riches narratives which begin at the nadir of Fortune's wheel and raise the protagonist so that he 'wexeth fortunat', and there 'abideth in prosperitee' (lines 2776–7). The story should close with the happy-ever-after ending, before the wheel can begin its inexorable downward turn; such tales produce 'joye and greet solas' (line 2774) in their audiences.[93]

Harry Bailly too objects to 'The Monk's Tale', citing the negative aesthetic emotions that its repetitiousness produces. For him, the Tale is incomprehensible, using personification and metaphor that he does not understand, and its teller designates it by an unfamiliar generic term that gives no clue to him as to how he should respond to its conventions: 'He spak how Fortune covered with a clowde / I noot nevere what; and als of a tragedie' (lines 2782–3). To these charges the Host adds that the whole company finds the Monk's offering annoying; it has no merit and is not even entertaining ('it is nat worth a boterflye / For therinne is ther no desport ne game') (lines 2790–10). Asserting his own competence in appreciating literary artistry, Harry claims that he knows that he can listen attentively and with enjoyment 'if any thyng shal wel reported be' (line 2804), but his plea for a tale about hunting finds no purchase with the Monk. The differently nuanced reactions offered by the Knight and Harry to the Monk's catalogue of tragedies thus exemplify two different kinds of audience emotion responses. Both evaluate narratives through their elicitation of two kinds of literary emotion: how the story makes its audience feel and how the audience feels about the story as story.

Other Tales produce emotional effects that are less contested; 'The Prioress's Tale' leaves everyone in the group 'sobre' until the Host breaks the mood by beginning to 'japen' (lines 692–3). 'The Physician's Tale' of Virginius, who kills his daughter Virginia to prevent her defilement by a corrupt judge, provokes the Host to an angry response, swearing violently, although on reflection he characterises the story as a 'pitous tale for to here' (line 302).[94] Expected and appropriate emotional reactions are modelled in the group responses to each of the Tales, offering guidance to the Tales-external audience as to how they should feel about the narratives they hear. Yet Harry Bailly, consistently, and at other times the Knight and the Franklin also intervene within the framework structure with their individual demonstrations of feelings about the stories they have heard. Harry's 'plain man' reactions are sometimes unexpected or unsophisticated, warning audiences that they should listen carefully and reflect on moral meanings, on 'sentence' as well as on entertainment value: 'desport [and] game'. Harry is not necessarily wrong; rather his responses are impetuously instant; his enthusiastic wish that his wife, the redoubtable Dame Goodelief, might have heard the 'Tale of Melibee' (lines 1889–1922) underscores the value of that individual Tale (and of *The Canterbury Tales* in general) in communicating and training in appropriate and disciplined emotional displays.

Audiences and drama

In late medieval cycle drama, play-characters must perform emotion convincingly if they are to elicit appropriate emotion in their audiences. Their gestures, and their spoken references to feelings, must be visible and audible to the crowd, standing at some distance from the locus of performance. In relation to medieval French drama, where detailed stage directions with regard to the actors' physical movements are often recorded, Jody Enders contends that gesture must indeed accompany language in order to be rhetorically effective.[95] Both Quintilian and Cicero, late classical authors of oratory handbooks that functioned as medieval school-texts, argue that gesture is in fact a wordless language; to seek to move audiences by words alone is to miss out on the persuasive potential of appropriate hand movements. Quintilian also comments on the capacity for gestures to bear performative weight, as signifying promising, blessing and other kinds of speech act.[96] Consequently, argues Enders, stage movements and expressions 'do more than teach, move and stir: they could change lives just as much as they could change beliefs'.[97]

Stage directions in English cycle (and morality play) texts provide more limited information about what is occurring on stage. Although, as their editors observe, some directions may be later scribal additions, others may be individual production notes with no 'official' status; their status doubtless varies between manuscripts.[98] The Chester cycle provides extensive Latin stage directions for Simeon in the 'Presentation Play': 'Tunc Simeon sedebit expectans consolationem' (Then Simeon will sit, expecting/looking for consolation) (after st. 15). David Mills comments that Simeon's 'hopeful gaze directs the audience's expectation dramatically; it is then answered by movement and dialogue'.[99] What is not clear here is how looking expectant might have been mediated to the audience. Gesture is often accompanied by commentary, amplifying stage emotion for those audience members who cannot see it clearly from their viewing position. The N-Town Herod tells the audience more than once that he stamps his feet in fury: ('*I stampe*', line 779).[100] After shouting 'Haaa, haaa, haaa!' from below the earth, both damned and saved emerge from their graves in the N-Town 'Judgement Day'.[101] The saved joyfully approach the gates of heaven: 'On kne we crepe, we gon, we glyde' (line 57), imitating the Easter ritual of 'creeping to the cross'. The damned, intuiting their fate before it is declared, cry: 'A, mercy, mercy! We rubbe, we rave!' (line 68). *Rubbe* refers to wringing of the hands. 'Alas for drede sore may we quake' (line 137), cries the first Bad Soul in the York 'Doomsday'; 'sore may we wring our hands and wepe' (line 146), laments his fellow.[102] 'For deole I drowpe and dare' (For sorrow I hang my head and tremble) (line 236), wails a hell-bound emperor in the Chester Judgement; the drooping head is a well-attested sign of sorrow.[103] These gestures may not differ greatly from the expressions of fear and sorrow performed by virtuous characters but, as Davidson claims, were probably performed 'indecorously as we might expect from persons who are inherently bad'.[104] These references do not necessarily enable us to visualise exactly how actors might have moved their bodies in order to express emotion; nevertheless, integrated study of such remarks, along with stage directions where they exist, in the English (and Cornish) medieval dramatic corpus, could expand our understanding of conventional affect displays as envisaged for performances in a community-oriented, late medieval urban context.

If the responses of contemporary audiences to the various plays and interludes performed in medieval England had been reliably captured, they would afford valuable evidence of the ways in which the visual and dramatic combined with the linguistic and other sound effects to evoke feeling in spectators. Late medieval French records offer a few traces of audience reactions; Enders recounts how the Procurator-General of the Parliament of Paris complained in 1542 about the poor acting in community theatrical performances, citing the 'lackluster manipulation of the communication register of gesture'.[105] Incompetent actors 'made gestures contrary to the meaning of what they said, producing derision in the audience so that what was intended as edification became scandal instead', complained the official.[106] Better reviews were received by a young man called Lyotard, recorded in the *Chroniques de Metz* as one who 'was so expert in the actor's complex repertoire of theatrical gestures that, according to the commentators, no one had ever seen the likes of his portrayal of St Barbara'.[107] Hans-Jürgen Diller notes a parallel witness in the York *Memorandum Book*. In 1431 the masons asked to be relieved of having to perform their particular pageant, the Funeral of the Virgin, as it caused 'magis risum et clamorem ... quam deuocionem' (more laughter and clamour than devotion).[108] The humanist Juan Luis Vives, writing in 1515, notes in his critique of a play about the Arrest of Jesus how both actors and spectators laugh uproariously as the disciples flee the soldiers; Peter's severing of Malchus's ear is met with applause, and his denial of Christ with hissing.[109] Vives records his experience in a commentary on a passage from Augustine's *Confessions*, one that occurs later than the saint's discussion on his own theatre-going experience, discussed above. Here Augustine contrasts the veneration of Christian martyrs with the pagan worship of gods or dead heroes, involving theatrical performances,[110] a prompt for Vives to remark on his disgust at the play and the audience's behaviour he had witnessed, most likely somewhere in the Low Countries.[111] 'This is not a reverently quiet audience', notes Sarah Carpenter, 'but one which laughs, hisses, and applauds the shifts of the action, participating noisily in its effects'; similar audience responses can surely be extrapolated for the English play cycles.[112]

These accounts highlight drama's unique mediality; as the fifteenth-century Middle English *Tretise of Miraclis Pleyinge* makes plain, in contrast with the kinds of images that medieval lay-folk would be familiar with, in wall-paintings or manuscript illuminations, 'this is a deed bok, the tother [drama] a quick'.[113] The *Tretise*, for all it mounts an attack on the great civic cycle dramas of the late Middle Ages, offers valuable evidence about the affective nature of biblical narrative when dramatised. Proponents of the mystery plays argue, so the *Tretise* claims, that 'men and wymmen, seinge the passioun of Crist and of his seintis ben movyd to compassion and devocion, wepinge bitere teris', but the *Tretise*-author rejects this kind of weeping as essentially the product of emotional contagion, of unreflecting response to mere spectacle.[114] The viewing of the biblical narratives gives rise to pleasurable empathetic responses, of the kind deprecated by Augustine and Ælred, rather than the kind of introspective and profoundly felt sorrow that leads to true spiritual change, to compunction as properly conceived. The audience weeping produced by the performance of Christ's sufferings in the Passion, from the Scourging to the Crucifixion, is, says the *Tretise*-author, 'not principaly for theire oune sinnes, ne of theire gode feith withinneforthe, but more of theire sight withouteforth, [and] is not alowable byfore God but more reprowable'.[115] Astutely, he notes that it is compassion 'of peyne' rather than 'of synne' that affects audiences; the pathos of Christ's suffering, highlighted by his speeches from the Cross and strongly contrasting with the brutal indifference of the soldiers who crucify him, elicits easy tears that amount only to false weeping, 'for lakkinge of bodily prosperite more than for lakking of gostly, as don dampnyd men in helle.'[116]

By 'lakkinge of bodily prosperite' the author identifies the temporary emotional discomfort that the audience experiences as witnesses; a discomfort that, if it is not accompanied by lasting interior reflection upon the individual sinner's continuing responsibility for Christ's suffering, will not lead to personal change. The types of empathy investigated by Oatley and associates (above, pp. 181–5) in which audiences are enabled to transform their emotions through exposure to literary narratives are excluded in this analysis.[117] The *Tretise*-author's objection, unsurprisingly, in part echoes the arguments made by Augustine in reprehending both the pleasure produced by watching theatrical performances and the superficial emotions elicited by the tragedies enacted on stage. Audience response to the words of the playwright, the *mise-en-scène* of the dramaturge and the acting skills of the performer can, in this argument, be separated from the profound fiction-related emotions that should be elicited by the narrative of salvation itself. Yet if the intentions of the guilds, the civic authorities and the plays' own authors are properly realised, the total emotional experience of watching and participating in the great civic drama cycles should propel the spectators towards a deeply felt compunction with Christ's suffering, an understanding of their own sinful complicity in it and a resolution to repent and reform.

These intended audience effects, even nuanced by individual responses to the didactic and sacramental aims of the cycle plays, go beyond the elicitation of a straightforward empathy with suffering, endemic though that effect is to the Passion sequences and some of the narratives within the story of the Nativity. The cycle plays, however, offer a more capacious emotional repertoire than this, for they frequently contain disturbing comic elements. These might either invite general unthinking laughter, what Diller identifies as Bakhtin's 'laughter of the market-place' as complained of by Vives, or – in some places – 'pious Schadenfreude', such as the laughter elicited by the terror of the damned in Judgement Day pageants.[118] The Wakefield Master's plays in the Towneley Cycle employ and invoke laughter specifically to point up the dangerously foolhardy behaviour of evil characters; 'the Schadenfreude of the audience rests on the knowledge that the tyrant on the stage cannot do them any harm', Diller notes.[119] The proverbial bragging and bravado of the likes of the Wakefield Cain and Herod – invoked as the alter ego of the otherwise ineffectual Absolon in Chaucer's 'Miller's Tale' – produces nervous, even guilty, laughter, a hilarity that knows that the character's condign punishment is only moments away.

The mixed mode of the braggart and his boy, as Diller identifies the folk-play elements in these two Wakefield Master portrayals, is markedly different from the savage comedy in the Massacre of the Innocents plays, instigated by the very Herod whose rashness and folly is shortly to be exposed.[120] In these plays, as Jane Tolmie observes, 'grieving and lamenting mothers are juxtaposed with laughing soldiers'.[121] While the language of game is employed by the soldiers to euphemise their behaviour, those who speak for the dead are the anguished mothers, played, of course, by transvestite men, whose futile attack on Herod's soldiers with distaffs or domestic implements such as ladles 'spreads disorder and invites jokes'.[122] These violent figures offer uncomfortable parallels with the comedy of Noah's wife, who also converts her spindle into a weapon, but whose unruliness is calmed once she enters into her husband's Ark, an enclosure that symbolises Christian salvation, moral obedience and the promise of heaven. The audience are invited to engage in an act of cultural memory, one that remembers proleptically Christ's death, foreshadowed in these plays that follow so soon upon the Nativity. They may also recall other, now unidentifiable, traumas, specific to particular performance contexts.[123]

> Grief, like anger – and the massacre plays are angry too – dependent as they are on the vilification and rejection of Herod and his men – is not contained or solved by art. Quite the contrary. It is preserved and passed on to the reader or audience for specific purposes, didactic, affective and memorialising.[124]

The plays' comedy then was likely to have operated in more complex and disturbing ways than simply signalling foolhardiness and spiritual blindness; it complicates audience affective responses by oscillating between horror and humour and using both for powerful didactic ends. The various tonal shifts, accompanied by gesture in performance, were likely to have evoked a range of powerful and engaged audience responses: 'the emotional variability present in the plays gives a sense of a dramatic strategy at work'.[125]

The cycle plays also offered occasion for social expression of the kinds of behaviours that were concomitant with leisure and enjoyment. The York *Memorandum Book* records the disapproval of a preacher, who was shocked by 'the feastings, drunkenness, clamors, gossipings and other wantonness' that accompanied the play performances.[126] His criticism squares too with the objections found in the *Tretise*, that the mere watching of plays leads to 'yvil continaunse, either stiring othere to leccherie and debatis as aftir most bodily mirthe comen moste debatis, as siche mirthe more undisposith a man to paciencie and ablith to glotonye and to othere vicis'.[127] This critical insight into particular occasions for late medieval emotional expression within the community is evidence for the profound changes in the contexts in which the literary expression of emotion is encountered in the final century of the medieval period.

Conclusion

As these accounts of the reception of civic drama make clear, by the fifteenth century, texts that concern themselves primarily with human feelings are beginning to move beyond the settings familiar in earlier centuries, such as the court and the cloister; now they find their way into a range of new private, coterie, communal and public contexts, reaching audiences whose members comprised a much wider social range. The emerging fourteenth-century interest in the exploration and mediation of interiority becomes more dominant in the following century: ideas about individuals and their relationships with God and one another respond to different kinds of pressure in the wake of complex social change. The techniques for creating audience empathy discussed in this chapter are deployed at greater length, while new approaches to interiority and writing different kinds of self demand fresh strategies for eliciting empathy among expanded readerships. In the next – and final – chapter, I explore the cultural, psychological and stylistic innovations in the fifteenth century that opened up new possibilities for the exploration of emotion, for focusing on this final medieval century allows us to see what has changed – and what has stayed the same – in the conceptualisation of literary emotion by the end of the medieval era.

Notes

1 Jacques de Vitry, *Vita Marie de Oegnies*, Corpus Christianorum Continuatio Mediaevalis 252 (Turnhout: Brepols, 2012), chapter 1.
2 See Anne M. Scott, 'The Role of Exempla in Educating through Emotion: The Deadly Sin of "lecherye" in Robert Mannyng's *Handlyng Synne* (1303–1317)', in Broomhall (ed.), *Authority, Gender and Emotions*, pp. 34–50 at pp. 37–9.

3 Frank Brandsma, 'Mirror Characters', in Keith Busby and Christopher Kleinhenz (eds), *Courtly Arts and the Art of Courtliness* (Woodbridge: Boydell and Brewer, 2006), pp. 275–84.
4 For example, the author of *William of Palerne* often makes use of such exclamatory tags as 'be ȝou sure', here with reference to the emotions of the reunion discussed in Chapter 3; Bunt (ed.), *William of Palerne*, line 4550. He also raises the emotional temperature by directly expressing sympathy with his characters: 'But God now hem helpe! / Slayn worþ þei slepend' (lines 2290–1).
5 Paul Ricœur, *From Text to Action: Essays in Hermeneutics, II*, trans. K. Blamey and J. B. Tompson (Evanston, IL: Northwestern University Press, 1991), p. xiv: 'the mimetic bond between the act of saying and effective action is never completely severed'.
6 Sif Rikhardsdottir, *Emotions in Old Norse Literature: Translations, Voices, Contexts*, Studies in Old Norse Literature (Woodbridge: Boydell and Brewer, 2017), p. 13.
7 Guillemette Bolens, 'La narration des émotions et la réactivité du destinataire dans les Contes de Canterbury de Geoffrey Chaucer', *Médiévales*, 61, special issue 'La chair des émotions' (autumn 2011), pp. 97–117 at p. 99.
8 Oatley, *Best Laid Schemes*; Oatley, 'A Taxonomy'; Raymond A. Mar and Keith Oatley, 'The Function of Fiction is the Abstraction and Simulation of Social Experience', *Perspectives on Psychological Science*, 3:3 (2008), 173–92; Raymond A. Mar, Keith Oatley, Maja Djikic et al., 'Emotion and Narrative Fiction: Interactive Influences Before, After, and During Reading', *Cognition and Emotion*, 25:5 (2011), 818–33.
9 Keith Oatley, 'Why Fiction May Be Twice as True as Fact: Fiction as Cognitive and Emotional Simulation', *Review of General Psychology*, 3:2 (1999), 101–17.
10 Mar and Oatley, 'Function of Fiction', p. 188.
11 Oatley, 'Why Fiction'.
12 Oatley, 'A Taxonomy'; lucidly summarised in Oatley and Djikic, 'Psychology of Narrative', p. 1.
13 Oatley and Djikic, 'Psychology of Narrative', p. 5; cf. also Miall and Kuiken, 'A Feeling for Fiction'.
14 Compare the arguments of Katrina Fong, Justin B. Mullins and Raymond A. Mar, 'What You Read Matters: The Role of Fiction Genre in Predicting Interpersonal Sensitivity', *Psychology of Aesthetics, Creativity, and the Arts*, 7 (2013), 370–6, and the widely reported (but apparently difficult to replicate) David C. Kidd and Emanuele Castano,

'Reading Literary Fiction Improves Theory of Mind', *Science*, 342 (2013), 377–80.
15 Colin Radford and Michael Weston, 'How Can We Be Moved by the Fate of Anna Karenina?', *Proceedings of the Aristotelian Society*, supplementary vols, 49 (1975), 67–93.
16 See Lee Patterson, *Chaucer and the Subject of History* (London and New York: Routledge, 1991).
17 Tan, 'Film-Induced Affect'. See also Ed S.-H. Tan, *Emotion and the Structure of Narrative Film: Film as an Emotion Machine*, trans. Barbara Fasting (Mahwah, NJ: Erlbaum, 1996; repr. New York: Routledge, 2011).
18 Tan, 'Film-Induced Affect', pp. 17–18.
19 Ibid., p. 18.
20 See David S. Miall and Don Kuiken, 'What is Literariness? Three Components of Literary Reading', *Discourse Processes*, 28:2 (1999), 121–38. Miall and Kuiken propose 'defamiliarisation' as one component: this can be cognitive – the introduction of a new fact into an argument – but, in their definition, is equally produced by 'features at the phonetic, grammatical and semantic levels' (pp. 128–9).
21 Andrew and Waldron (eds), *Sir Gawain and the Green Knight*, line 2525, cf. line 1, in Andrew and Waldron (eds), *The Poems of the Pearl Manuscript*. All further quotations are from this edition and cited in text.
22 Summarised in Larrington, 'English Chivalry '.
23 Annick Sperlich, *Family and Friends: Generation in Medieval Romance* (Heidelberg: Winter, 2014) discusses the structural patterns of loss and restoration in ancestral or dynastic romances.
24 Miall and Kuiken, 'A Feeling for Fiction', p. 223; cf. E. W. E. M. Kneepkens and Rolf A. Zwaan, 'Emotions and Literary Text Comprehension', *Poetics*, 23 (1994), 125–38.
25 On aesthetic emotions as distinct from evaluative emotions ('I am enjoying this story'), see further Miall and Kuiken, 'What is Literariness?'; Miall and Kuiken, 'A Feeling for Fiction', p. 223.
26 Miall and Kuiken, 'A Feeling for Fiction', p. 239. Emphasis in original.
27 For a clear account of Giacomo Rizzolati and colleagues' discovery of mirror neurons, see Lea Winerman, 'The Mind's Mirror', *Monitor on Psychology*, 36:9 (October 2005), 48, www.apa.org/monitor/oct05/mirror.aspx (accessed 29 August 2023).
28 An important meta-analysis of the state of play is Vittorio Gallese, Morton Ann Gernsbacher, Cecilia Heyes, Gregory Hickok and Marco

Iacoboni, 'Mirror Neuron Forum', *Perspectives on Psychological Science*, 6:4 (2011), 369–407.
29 Gallese in ibid., p. 395, and compare Vittorio Gallese, 'The "Shared Manifold" Hypothesis: From Mirror Neurons to Empathy', *Journal of Consciousness Studies*, 8 (2001), 33–50.
30 Gallese in Gallese et al., 'Mirror Neuron Forum', p. 395; Hannah Chapelle Wojciehowski, 'The Mirror Neuron Mechanism and Literary Studies: An Interview with Vittorio Gallese', *California Italian Studies*, 2:1 (2011), https://escholarship.org/uc/item/56f8v9bv (accessed 7 September 2023), and Vittorio Gallese and Hannah Wojciehowski, 'How Stories Make Us Feel: Towards an Embodied Narratology', *Californian Italian Studies*, 2:1 (2011), 10.5070/C321008974.
31 Gallese and Wojciehowski, 'How Stories Make Us Feel'.
32 Mar and Oatley, 'The Function of Fiction'; Mar et al., 'Emotion and Narrative Fiction'.
33 Bolens, *The Style of Gestures*, p. 5. Compare Karen Solomon and Lawrence W. Barsalou, 'Perceptual Simulation in Property Verification', *Memory and Cognition*, 32:2 (2004), 244–59.
34 Bolens, *The Style of Gestures*, p. 2.
35 Ibid., pp. 75; 77.
36 Ibid., p. 156.
37 Carolyn Dinshaw, 'A Kiss Is Just a Kiss', p. 211.
38 Ibid., p. 223. See also on touch more generally C. M. Woolgar, *The Senses in Late Medieval England* (New Haven, CT, and London: Yale University Press, 2006), pp. 29–62.
39 McNamer, *Affective Meditation*.
40 Stephen Knight, *Geoffrey Chaucer*, Rereading Literature (Oxford: Blackwell, 1986), p. 123.
41 Jill Mann, *Geoffrey Chaucer*, Feminist Readings (New York and London: Harvester Wheatsheaf, 1991), p. 116.
42 Gallese et al., 'Mirror Neuron Forum', pp. 380–5; 394–6; and Marco Iacoboni, *Mirroring People* (New York: Farrar, Straus and Giroux, 2008).
43 See the extensive discussion of neurophysiological bases of emotion in Plamper, *The History of Emotions*, pp. 219–24; and Nagy, 'The Power', in particular pp. 19–21. See also the comments of Reddy and Plamper in Eustace et al., '*AHR* Conversation'.
44 Brandsma, 'Mirror Characters'.
45 Chrétien de Troyes, *Erec*, trans. Jean-Marie Fritz, in Zink (gen. ed.), *Chrétien de Troyes: Romans*, lines 6184–226.

46 Ælred of Rievaulx, *Speculum caritatis*, II.17, *PL* 195, col. 565D; Peter of Blois, *Liber de confessione sacramentali*, *PL* 207, cols 1088–9. Arthur's historicity was famously questioned by William of Newburgh in *Historia regum Anglicarum*, ed. Richard Howlett, in *Chronicles of the Reigns of Stephen, Henry II and Richard*, 4 vols, Rolls Series 82 (London: Longman, 1884–9), Proemium 1.17.

47 Augustine, *Confessions*, vol. I, ed. and trans. Carolyn J.-B. Hammond, Loeb Classical Library 26 (Cambridge, MA: Harvard University Press, 2014), Book III, ch. 2, section 2 (pp. 92–3). References hereafter are given in text.

48 Peter of Blois, *Liber de confessione sacramentali*, cols 1088–9; translation in Rachel Fulton, *From Judgment to Passion: Devotion to Christ and the Virgin Mary 800–1200* (New York: Columbia University Press, 2005), p. 442.

49 For thoughtful discussion of Ælred, Augustine and Arthur see Jaakko Tahkokallio, 'Fables of King Arthur: Ælred of Rievaulx and Secular Passions', *Mirator*, 9:1 (2008), 19–35.

50 Peter of Blois, *Liber de confessione sacramentali*, cols 1088–9; Fulton, *From Judgment to Passion*, p. 442.

51 Ælred of Rievaulx, *Speculum caritatis*, II.17, cols 565B–565C.

52 Tahkokallio, 'Fables of King Arthur'. See also Ashe, 'Introduction', pp. xix–xxiv; Ashe, '"For love and for lovers"', pp. 16–20.

53 Robert Hasenfratz (ed.), *Ancrene Wisse* (Kalamazoo, MI: Medieval Institute Publications, 2000), Book 7, https://d.lib.rochester.edu/teams/text/hasenfrantz-ancrene-wisse-part-seven.

54 Patterson, *Chaucer and the Subject of History*, p. 96.

55 Ibid., p. 96.

56 Compare Boquet and Nagy, *Sensible Moyen Âge*, p. 154.

57 Julian of Norwich, *The Shewings*, ed. Crampton, Part I, lines 919–23.

58 This text is preserved only in the thirteenth-century manuscript London, British Library, Cotton Titus D. XVIII (127r–133r). See W. Meredith Thompson (ed.), *Þe Wohunge of Ure Laured. Edited from British Museum MS Cotton Titus D.xviii, together with On Ureisun of Ure Louerde; On Wel Swuðe God Ureisun of God Almihti; On Lofsong of Ure Louerde; On Lofsong of Ure Lefdi; Þe Oreisun of Seinte Marie*, EETS OS 241 (London: EETS Press, 1970). See McNamer, *Affective Meditation*, pp. 25–57 at p. 52.

59 *On Ureisun of Ure Louerde*, Lambeth MS 487, in Thompson (ed.), *Þe Wohunge of Ure Laured*, p. 1. See Catherine Innes-Parker, '*Ancrene Wisse* and *Þe Wohunge of Ure Lauerd*: The Thirteenth-Century Female Reader and the Lover-Knight', in Lesley Smith and Jane H. M.

Taylor (eds), *Women, the Book, and the Godly: Selected Proceedings of the St. Hilda's Conference, 1993* (Cambridge: D. S. Brewer, 1995), pp. 137–47.
60 McNamer, *Affective Meditation*, pp. 26–7.
61 Richard Rolle, 'The Form of Living', lines 550–9. See Clare Davidson, 'Erotic Devotion: Richard Rolle's *The Form of Living*', *Limina: A Journal of Historical and Cultural Studies*, 20:3 (2015), special issue 'A Festschrift in Honour of Philippa Maddern', pp. 1–13.
62 Kathryn Vulic, '*De Pater Noster* of Richard Ermyte and the Topos of the Female Audience', *Mystics Quarterly*, 34 (2008), 1–43.
63 See Lawrence Warner, 'Mary, Unmindful of her Knight: *Sir Gawain and the Green Knight* and the Traditions of Sexual Hospitality', *SAC*, 35 (2013), 263–87 for the argument that Gawain's dilemma circles around accepting Bertilak's offer of his wife's sexual favours, and that the lines which immediately follow the quotation need not be emended as editors have consistently done.
64 McNamer, 'The Literariness of Literature', p. 1433.
65 Braswell, 'Introduction: *Sir Perceval of Galles*', in Braswell (ed.), *Sir Perceval of Galles and Ywain and Gawain*.
66 See Carolyne Larrington, 'Learning to Feel'.
67 John Matthews Manly, 'The Stanza Forms of "Sir Thopas"', *Modern Philology*, 8:1 (1910), 141–4 at p. 144.
68 The romance is preserved only in print versions and probably was composed in the late fifteenth century. The whole poem is preserved in a print by William de Copland, from around 1560 (London, British Library, C.21.c.58), and there are three surviving fragments of a print by Wynkyn de Worde (San Marino, CA, The Huntington Library, Rare Books 62181). The romance is also known. after de Worde's title, as 'Undo Your Door'. A highly abbreviated version is also found in the Percy folio. See Nicola Mcdonald, 'Desire Out of Order and *Undo Your Door*', *SAC*, 34 (2012), 247–75.
69 *The Squire of Low Degree*, in Erik Kooper (ed.), *Sentimental and Humorous Romances* (Kalamazoo, MI: Medieval Institute Publications, 2005), https://d.lib.rochester.edu/teams/text/kooper-sentimental-and-humorous-romances-squire-of-low-degree. Further references are given in text.
70 Kooper, Erik, 'Introduction: *The Squire of Low Degree*', in Kooper (ed.), *Sentimental and Humorous Romances* (Kalamazoo, MI: Medieval Institute Publications, 2005), https://d.lib.rochester.edu/teams/text/kooper-sentimental-and-humorous-romances-squire-of-low-degree-introduction. See also Derek Pearsall, 'The Audience

of the Middle English Romances', in Mary-Jo Arn and Hanneke Wirtjes (eds), *Historical and Editorial Studies in Medieval and Early Modern English in Honour of Johan Gerritsen* (Groningen: Wolters-Noordhoff, 1985), pp. 37–47.

71 See Peter Dinzelbacher, *Vision und Visionsliteratur im Mittelalter*, Monographien zur Geschichte des Mittelalters 23 (Stuttgart: Hiersemann, 1981).

72 Preserved in Oxford, Bodleian Library, MS 34; London, British Library MS Royal 17 A XXVII; and London, British Library, MS Cotton Titus D XVIII. Text: *Sawles Warde*, in Bella Millett and Jocelyn Wogan-Browne (ed. and trans.), *Medieval English Prose for Women* (Oxford: Clarendon Press, 1990), pp. 86–109.

73 *Sawles Warde*, p. 88 (my translation).

74 Ibid., pp. 90–2. On the stench of sin, see Woolgar, *The Senses*, pp. 121–6.

75 *Sawles Warde*, p. 94.

76 Ibid., p. 98. See Holly Crocker, 'Affective Politics in Chaucer's *Reeve's Tale*: "Cherl" Masculinity after 1381', *SAC*, 29 (2007), 225–58 at pp. 230–1 for discussion of the exercise of affective masculinity in this text.

77 George Lyman Kittredge, *A Study of Sir Gawain and the Green Knight* (Cambridge, MA: Harvard University Press, 1916), p. 133.

78 C. S. Lewis, *The Allegory of Love* (Oxford: Clarendon Press, 1936), p. 195.

79 See, for example, the readings of Lewis and E. Talbot Donaldson, 'Criseide and her Narrator', in Donaldson, *Speaking of Chaucer* (London: Athlone, 1970), pp. 65–83. See also Gretchen Mieszkowski, '"The Least Innocent of All Innocent-Sounding Lies": The Legacy of Donaldson's "Troilus" Criticism', *Chaucer Review*, 41:3 (2007), 299–310.

80 Tan, *Emotion and the Structure of Narrative*; E. S.-H. Tan and Nico Frijda, 'Sentiment in Film Viewing', in Carl Plantinga and Greg M. Smith (eds), *Passionate Views: Film, Cognition, and Emotion* (Baltimore, MD, and London: Johns Hopkins University Press, 1999), pp. 48–64; Ed S. Tan and Valentijn Visch, 'Genre Scripts and Appreciation of Negative Emotion in the Reception of Film', *Behavioral and Brain Sciences*, 40 (2017), 10.1017/S0140525X17001844.

81 See the useful review article by Brian Parkinson, 'Interpersonal Emotion Transfer: Contagion and Social Appraisal', *Social and Personality Psychology Compass*, 5:7 (2011), 428–39 at p. 434, and Brian Parkinson and Antony S. R. Manstead's more recent summary

article, 'Current Emotion Research in Social Psychology: Thinking about Emotions and Other People', *Emotion Review*, 7:4 (2015), 371–80.
82 Compare Antony S. R. Manstead and A. H. Fischer, 'Social Appraisal: The Social World as Object of and Influence on Appraisal Processes', in K. R. Scherer, A. Schorr and T. Johnstone (eds), *Appraisal Processes in Emotion: Theory, Methods, Research* (New York: Oxford University Press, 2001), pp. 221–32.
83 Parkinson, 'How Social is the Social Psychology of Emotion?', p. 409.
84 Whether the rebels might have been familiar with the A- or the B-version of the poem has been widely discussed. See, as representative of either position, Lawrence Warner, *The Lost History of 'Piers Plowman': The Earliest Transmission of Langland's Work* (Philadelphia, PA: University of Pennsylvania Press, 2011), pp. 10–13, and Kathryn Kerby-Fulton, '*Piers Plowman*', in David Wallace (ed.), *The Cambridge History of Medieval English Literature* (Cambridge: Cambridge University Press, 1999), pp. 513–38 at pp. 520–5.
85 For a useful summary of the debates about the excision of the pardon-scene in the C-version, see Denise N. Baker, 'Pre-Empting Piers's Tearing of the Pardon: Langland's Revisions of the C Version', *Yearbook of Langland Studies*, 31 (2017), 43–72. See also Alastair J. Minnis, 'Piers' Protean Pardon: The Letter and Spirit of Langland's Theology of Indulgences', in Anne Marie D'Arcy and Alan J. Fletcher (eds), *Studies in Late Medieval and Early Renaissance Texts in Honour of John Scattergood* (Dublin: Four Courts, 2005), pp. 218–40, and Traugott Lawler, 'The Pardon Formula in Piers Plowman: Its Ubiquity, its Binary Shape, its Silent Middle Term', *Yearbook of Langland Studies*, 14 (2000), 117–52.
86 Rosenwein, *Generations of Feeling*, pp. 195–9.
87 See Aers, *Community, Gender and Individual Identity*, pp. 100–3.
88 See Tom White, 'Textile Logics of Late Medieval Romance', *Exemplaria*, 28:4 (2016), 297–318.
89 *Sir Orfeo*, in Laskaya and Salisbury (eds), *The Middle English Breton Lays*. Further references are given in text.
90 Antonina Harbus, 'Emotion and Narrative Empathy in *Sir Gawain and the Green Knight*', *English Studies*, 97:6 (2016), 594–607 at p. 599.
91 Michael Calabrese, 'Chaucer's Dorigen and Boccaccio's Female Voices', *SAC*, 29 (2007), 259–92 at p. 286.

92 Compare Jamie Fumo, 'Aurelius's Prayer, *Franklin's Tale* 1031–79: Sources and Analogues', *Neophilologus*, 88 (2004), 623–35, and Stephen Knight, 'Rhetoric and Poetry in the *Franklin's Tale*', *Chaucer Review*, 4:1 (1969), 14–30: 'The series, though improving in its nature, is rather tedious ... the *exempla* grow more and more perfunctory and finally they seem to tail off into *etcetera etcetera*' (p. 27).
93 See Benson's discussion of the variation of ordering of the Monk's stories, in particular the placing of the so-called 'Modern Instances', in *The Riverside Chaucer*, p. 930.
94 Geoffrey Chaucer, 'The Physician's Tale', in Benson (ed.), *The Canterbury Tales*, in Benson (gen. ed.), *The Riverside Chaucer*, pp. 190–3.
95 Jody Enders, 'Of Miming and Signing: The Dramatic Rhetoric of Gesture', in Clifford Davidson (ed.), *Gesture in Medieval Drama and Art* (Kalamazoo, MI: Medieval Institute Press, 2001), pp. 1–25.
96 Ibid., pp. 1–2.
97 Ibid., p. 3.
98 David Mills, 'The Stage Directions in the Manuscripts of the Chester Mystery Cycle', *Medieval English Theatre*, 3:1 (1981), 45–56, and Peter Meredith, 'Stage Directions and the Editing of Early English Drama', in Alexandra F. Johnston (ed.), *Editing Early English Drama: Special Problems and New Directions* (New York: AMS Press, 1983), pp. 65–94. R. M. Lumiansky and David Mills (eds), *The Chester Mystery Cycle*, EETS Special Series 3 (London and New York: Oxford University Press, 1974), p. 108.
99 Mills, 'Stage Directions', p. 48.
100 Margaret Rogerson, 'Raging in the Streets of Medieval York', *Early Theatre*, 3 (2000), 105–25.
101 Douglas Sugano (ed.), *The N-Town Plays* (Kalamazoo, MI: Medieval Institute Press, 2007), http://d.lib.rochester.edu/teams/publication/sugano-the-n-town-plays. All references to this edition are hereafter in text.
102 Clifford Davidson (ed.), *The York Corpus Christi Plays* (Kalamazoo, MI: Medieval Institute Press, 2011); http://d.lib.rochester.edu/teams/publication/davidson-the-york-corpus-christi-plays.
103 Lumiansky and Mills (eds), *The Chester Mystery Cycle*, p. 446. See Clifford Davidson, 'Gesture in Medieval British Drama', in Davidson (ed.), *Gesture in Medieval Drama*, pp. 66–127 for further examples and Maddern, 'Reading Faces', pp. 21–2.

104 Davidson, 'Gesture', p. 81.
105 Enders, 'Of Miming', p. 5.
106 Ibid., p. 5; p. 20, n. 23. L. Petit de Julleville, *Les mystères, Histoire du théâtre en France*, vols 1–2 (1880, repr. Geneva: Slatkine, 1968), vol. 2, p. 190.
107 Enders, 'Of Miming', p. 9; p. 23, n. 48. Petit de Julleville, *Les mystères*, vol. 2, p. 48.
108 Hans-Jürgen Diller, 'Laughter in Medieval English Drama: A Critique of Modernising and Historical Analyses', *Comparative Drama*, 36:1–2 (2002), 1–19 at p. 4. See Alexandra F. Johnston and Margaret Rogerson (eds), *Records of Early English Drama: York* (Toronto: University of Toronto Press, 1979), vol. 1, p. 48 and vol. 2, p. 732.
109 Sarah Carpenter, 'New Evidence: Vives and Audience-Response to Biblical Drama', *Medieval English Theatre*, 31 (2009), 3–12; the passage from Vives is cited on pp. 4–5. My thanks to Sarah Brazil for drawing my attention to this article.
110 Augustine, *The City of God against the Pagans*, vol. III, Book VIII, ch. 27, pp. 138–45.
111 Carpenter, 'New Evidence', p. 6.
112 Ibid., p. 7.
113 Clifford Davidson (ed.), *Tretise of Miraclis Pleyinge* (Kalamazoo, MI: Medieval Institute, 1993), p. 98, line 185.
114 Ibid., p. 98, lines 162–4.
115 Ibid., p. 102, lines 304–06.
116 Ibid., p. 102, line 321; lines 322–3. See on the York Crucifixion Play in particular, Sarah Beckwith, *Signifying God: Social Relation and Symbolic Act in the York Corpus Christi Plays* (Chicago, IL: University of Chicago Press, 2001), pp. 65–70.
117 Oatley and Djikic, 'Psychology of Narrative', p. 5.
118 Diller, 'Laughter', p. 5.
119 Ibid., p. 10.
120 Ibid., pp. 10–11. For a comprehensive account of these plays, see Sarah J. Brazil, 'Modulating Tone in the Early English Slaughter of the Innocents Plays: Between Grief, Vengeance and Humour', *European Medieval Drama*, 22 (2018), 11–35.
121 Jane Tolmie, 'Spinning Women and Manly Soldiers: Grief and Game in the English Massacre Plays', in Jane Tolmie and M. J. Toswell (eds), *Laments for the Lost in Medieval Literature*, Medieval Texts and Cultures of Northern Europe 19 (Turnhout: Brepols, 2010), pp. 283–98, here p. 283.

122 Ibid., p. 289.
123 Jan Assman, *Religion and Cultural Memory*, trans. Rodney Livingstone (Stanford, CA: Stanford University Press, 2006); Tolmie, 'Spinning Women', p. 284.
124 Tolmie, 'Spinning Women', p. 284.
125 Brazil, 'Modulating Tone', pp. 26–8, quote from p. 26. See also Carpenter, 'New Evidence'.
126 Diller, 'Laughter', p. 4.
127 Davidson (ed.), *Tretise*, p. 96, lines 119–23.

5

Fifteenth-century feelings

Changing emotions

The aim of this final chapter is not to adumbrate a further line of approach to literary emotion, but rather to draw together how the depiction and understanding of emotion had changed by the end of the three hundred years of writing that this book addresses. For 'literary texts', so remarks Mary Flannery, here in relation to the particular emotions of shame and shamefastness, 'are something like a controlled environment for literary experimentation, a virtual space', one in which emotional innovation can be explored.[1] The many vernacular texts discussed in this book suggested to their audiences ways in which they might feel and, importantly, how other people might feel. While they reinforced certain emotional norms, they also introduced new styles of feeling and behaving, of performing identity and disciplining body and soul. 'They [texts] are often both diagnostic and willing to challenge traditional forms', suggests Stephanie Trigg.[2] Earlier literary texts had valorised various kinds of expressions of emotion and deprecated others, reacting to, and helping to form, new emotional repertoires and schemas. By focusing on innovative texts, new kinds of authors, audiences, readers alongside the changing modes of textual transmission in the fifteenth century, we can identify changing techniques and formulations in the depiction and evocation of emotion that were produced by that experimentation, now deeply embedded within such fundamental literary concepts as genre, characterisation, plot and figuration.

By the beginning of the fifteenth century much had changed in English literary practice. There was now an acknowledged and recognisable English literary tradition, looking back to Chaucer as its main progenitor, and beyond him to European authors such as Dante, Machaut, Boccaccio and Petrarch. Towards the end of the century the newly introduced technology of the printing press would have an extraordinary impact on an expanded reading public. Changing modes of authorship and of literary consumption, of texts both as heard and as read privately, came into existence; writers whose words, thoughts and feelings would not previously have achieved any kind of general circulation began to find readers. Chaucer's encounters with the new Italian literary humanism, epitomised by the writing of Boccaccio and Petrarch, with their profound curiosity about how men and women thought, felt and behaved, had inspired him to create literary characters who seemed closer to the kinds of people one might meet in daily life, rather than conventional literary types. The individual subject had begun to emerge as a space for exploration and enquiry; audience interest in how other people thought and felt, in what made them tick, increasingly demanded different modes of writing within already established genres.

In her ground-breaking discussion of the ways in which literary characterisation emerges as both authorial tool and a key element in readerly experience, Elizabeth Fowler identifies Chaucer as a pioneer in the literary evocation of interiority, 'offer[ing] poetry as a ... new construction of intentionality and, with it, a new technology for producing interior experience'.[3] Fowler's arguments depend on the concept of the 'social person', the various social identities that are ascribed by readers to textual representations via an understanding of *habitus*, in the Bourdieuian sense elaborated by Monique Scheer: 'Social persons are sets of expectations built into the mind by experience, and they are notions as to what it is to be a person.'[4] What constructs the Chaucerian character in *The Canterbury Tales* is a combination of the individual's social rank, gender, clothing, accoutrements, including the horse they ride, their profession, the details the narrator provides about their past and present, and what they say to the fictive Chaucer, among other elements. These indications build up for the audience an idea of what kind of person this is, a set of assumptions that is always provisional, capable of alteration as new indications of social positioning emerge.

Chaucer's characterisations, as exemplified in *The Canterbury Tales*, depend not only on psychonarrative insights and character utterances and actions of the kinds familiar from earlier literature, but also on the deployment of the 'scrapbook details of characterization' listed above, some of which may seem inconsistent with already established expectations about the social person.[5] Consequently, Chaucer's characters often appear as ambiguous and complex, displaying 'characteriological vivacity'.[6] So, for example, is the Merchant seriously in debt or not? Is the Friar a notorious seducer? How piratical is the Shipman? Thus, Chaucer's Prioress is both nun and courtly lady: identities are placed in tension in the 'General Prologue' description, creating a fuller sense of an individual person. Fowler concludes that poetry can supplant theology in its understanding of the person:

> Chaucer's poetry suggests that fiction-makers – not canonists, or moral theologians, or parsons – are the truly expert analysts of the human character, of human motive, action, passion, belief, and intention. He presents poetic character as a more moving and compelling vehicle for these insights than is the theological discourse about penance.[7]

Chaucer's innovative writing of interiority has been noted throughout this book, particularly in *Troilus and Criseyde*. The fifteenth-century 'Chaucerians' who took him as their master principally admired his rhetoric, and they did not adopt wholesale his methods of characterisation. Nevertheless, as the century progresses, genres adapted to the new engagement with human 'motive, action, passion, belief, and intention' mapped by Fowler, and began to foreground exploration of interiority.[8] Fresh voices are heard, those of both characters and authors; depicting the non-noble affords opportunities for new explorations in emotion contexts. Lower-ranking people are often observed with satiric, parodic or critical intentions, as in Skelton's 'The Tunnyng of Elynoure Rummynge' or the 'Canterbury Interlude' continuation of *The Canterbury Tales*.[9] Nevertheless, growing interest in human interiority and subjectivity also makes space for new kinds of authors and authorship: middle-class people with jobs or businesses, such as Thomas Hoccleve and Margery Kempe, the schoolmaster Robert Henryson and, crucially, the entrepreneur-printer William Caxton and his associates.

This chapter considers in detail two key developments in fifteenth-century literary emotional praxis. The first half discusses the advent of long-form prose fiction which creates more space for emotional elaboration through psychonarration and extended dialogue, anticipating the ways in which the romance would develop as proto-novel in the early modern period. The second half of the chapter discusses the emergence of kinds of autofiction, opportunities for authors to (meta-) represent themselves as emotional subjects, as selves whose interiority is depicted and strategically deployed through the texts they create and circulate. These texts find audiences that are ready to accept the emotional implications 'of assuming a single mind behind the text's stylistic properties and ethical claims, and the availability of the authorial persona for readers' empathetic regard', as Julie Orlemanski writes.[10] Authorial identity, audience receptivity and hopes for the continuing interest of posterity emerge as pressure points for writers: these are textual spaces in which self-reflexive emotion is harnessed to assert the value of literary endeavour.

Long-form romances

Middle English had already produced some texts that were exceptionally long. From Layamon's *Brut* (c. 1200) and the even earlier *Ormulum*, works with their roots in history and chronicle, to stand-alone works such as *Piers Plowman*, certain genres encouraged very long poetic compositions. In historically derived texts, the chronicle structure organises the narrative by aggregating a highly extendable series of diachronic episodes. Story-collections such as *The Canterbury Tales* and *Confessio Amantis* are an expansive series of short-form narratives within a unifying framework, while *Piers Plowman* consists of individual dream-visions narrated in *passus*, literarily 'steps' along a journey that carries the poem's argument forwards, making possible the work's increasing elaboration from the Z-text to the A-, B- and C-texts. In the fifteenth century, however, it was the central secular genre of romance that began to expand in length, multiplying chivalric adventures and the vicissitudes of the main characters, and introducing further protagonists, often within the kind of interlace structure common in French romance. Romances in prose, the best-known of which is Malory's *Morte Darthur*, were composed, translated and finally printed. 'Prose romance itself, long familiar in France, was the century's most distinctive contribution to the genre in England ... the formal freedom of prose, and the increased development it allows for subtly nuanced private scenes, open up the space for the later emergence of the novel', notes Helen Cooper.[11] No longer constrained by the demands of rhyme and metre nor, by the last decades of the century, by the stamina of scribes, these works encouraged more expansive treatment of emotions. Psychonarration is employed more frequently; emotional dialogue allows characters to express their feelings at length, quite often expanding feelings that earlier romances would have left unexpressed. Scenes that might have been omitted in the interests of narrative economy are now fully staged, protagonists explore their own feelings in internal monologues, and, in a significant development, narrators themselves begin to comment not just on the feelings within their texts, but on their own emotional responses to the story they are recounting.[12]

This expansiveness is most evident in prose romances, but it is certainly not limited to them. *Partonope of Blois* (c. 1420), a version of *Partonopeu de Blois*, one of the very earliest twelfth-century French romances, runs to 12,195 lines of poetry. The French original had already been translated into other European vernaculars and it had been expanded (like other twelfth-century French romances) with a *Continuation* that attests to its continuing popularity.[13] *The Romans of Partenay*, a version of Couldrette's 1401–6 poem *Mélusine*, was composed in rhyme royal stanzas, probably between 1440 and 1450; I will return to these two texts below. John Metham's poem of several thousand lines, *Amoryus and Cleopes*, a reworking of the Pyramus and Thisbe story with an oddly miraculous coda in which the protagonists are resurrected, is dated to 1449.[14] The often noted English hybridisation between romance and saints' lives survives, even flourishes, in the fifteenth century; manuscripts such as the two Thornton codices collected religious texts and romances side by side, placing the chivalric and worldly genre in a context that legitimised romance reading alongside devotional study.[15] Moreover, as in the case of 'pious romances' such as the very popular *Sir Isumbras* and *Robert of Cisyle* and the less well-preserved *Sir Gowther*, these compendia brought powerful affects and sensational plotlines, chivalric values, Christian repentance and proper humility into emotional conjunction.[16]

The sheer number of surviving copies of *Sir Isumbras* (9) and *Robert of Cisyle* (10) underscores the popularity of romance in the fifteenth century: older stories were retold and new material was translated from French, just as when the genre came into existence in English two hundred years earlier. Romances were copied and circulated in small local networks, exemplars being shared among the gentry like Robert Thornton or the Norfolk Paston family, and the mercantile and increasingly educated bourgeois: often London-based civil servants and lawyers.[17] Those Continental prose romances which were translated into English in the mid-fifteenth-century were usually treatments of historical 'matters', particularly suited to the long prose form: substantial narratives such as the history of Alexander and the sieges of Thebes and Troy. Caxton's prefaces, identifying his potential readers as 'gentlemen' (and in the case of *Blanchardyn and Eglantyne*, c. 1489, also 'gentlewomen'), were intended to create the market for the histories and romances he was printing, positioning them as available and desirable commodities for new social groups: those who had some disposable income and who were able to read.[18]

Critics have noticed Caxton's general description of his publications as 'history', intended (like other romances deriving from quasi-historical material) to instruct readers in noble behaviour, virtues such as loyalty, truthfulness and courage, and the tenets of chivalry.[19] But alongside these relatively 'public' and exemplary episodes in their heroes' lives, as Cooper points out, 'the subtly nuanced private scenes' provide space for the exploration of emotions: love, sadness, anger and joy, to be sure, but also, notably, they described more complex and nuanced emotional situations, related through the narratorial techniques discussed below.[20] This approach to the treatment of feelings is not Caxton's invention, of course, for long poems such as *Partonope* and *The Romans of Partenay* had already made space for extended emotional scenes, comprising dialogue, psychonarration, action and narratorial comment. The late fifteenth-century *Prose Melusine* based on Jean d'Arras's prose version of 1393 is preserved complete only in London, British Library, Royal MS 18 B II, although Caxton's successor Wynkyn de Worde published fragments of what is probably an abridged version of the *Prose Melusine*, along with long prose romances such as *Valentine and Orson* (1510).[21]

Dialogue

The most direct means for characters to express their interior dispositions is of course through speech. Where in the earlier part of the period, emotional utterances in romance tend to be relatively brief and to the point, dialogue now expands, in both soliloquies and conversational exchanges. The French prose romances, especially the thirteenth-century Vulgate Arthurian Cycle, have always allowed space for long speeches expounding a character's feelings – in particular those of Lancelot and Guenièvre. Malory's *Morte Darthur*, as Helen Cooper comments, draws substantially on the Vulgate and Post-Vulgate Cycles, yet Malory frequently omits 'the psychological or emotional development of the original narratives while keeping the details of tournaments and battles. In matters of the heart he prefers understatement to elaboration.'[22] Towards the end of his work, however, Malory begins to write a great deal more dialogue than earlier in the book; he supplements his principal French source, *La mort Artu*, with the English *Stanzaic Morte Arthur*, rendering the French prose alongside often markedly terser English verse. When Launcelot and the queen are ambushed in her chambers by Aggravaine and his allies, the two lovers realise that they are in mortal danger. The *Stanzaic Morte* gives them a swift exchange in which the queen expresses herself in conventional terms of sorrow and fear:

> 'Wele-away', then said the queen,
> 'Launcelot, what shall worthe of us two?
> The love that hath been us between,

> To such ending that it sholde go!
> ...
> That all our wele is turned to wo!'[23]

Launcelot is even briefer and entirely pragmatic in reply. He tells Guenevere to be quiet, that the game is up, and then asks whether weapons or armour are to hand. The poem then swiftly narrates Launcelot's sequence of actions, killing Aggravaine and some of the other knights, and then reaching safety among his own kinsmen. Launcelot has no time to reassure the queen that he will rescue her: his priority is escape. The *Mort Artu* is also surprisingly brief here: when she hears the noise outside, the queen registers that the king has been apprised of their relationship: 'Ha! Biaus douz amis ... or somes nous honi et mort' (Oh, dear friend, now we're disgraced and doomed).[24] Lancelot briskly assures her that Agravain will perish and enquires about weapons. The queen is given a short speech in which she expresses her fear that they will both die, that Lancelot's life would be a greater loss than hers, and she encourages him to fight his way out: his safety will ensure her survival in the face of juridical condemnation.[25] Malory, in contrast, takes the opportunity to suspend the action. In addition to the discussion of arming and future rescue found in the other sources, he allows the two lovers space for a poignant and heartfelt exchange of farewells.

> Than he [Launcelot] toke the queen in hys armys and kissed her and seyde,
> 'Moste nobelest Crysten queen, I besech you, as ye have ben ever my special good lady, and I at all tymes your poure knight and trewe unto my power, and as I never fayled you in right nor in wronge sythyn the first day kynge Arthur made me knight, that ye woll pray for my soule if that I be slayne. ...
> 'Nay, sir Launcelot, nay!' seyde the queen. 'Wyte thou well that I woll nat lyve long after thy days. But and ye be slayne I woll take my dethe as mekely as ever ded marter take hys dethe for Jesu Crystes sake.'
> 'Well, madame,' seyde Sir Launcelot, 'syth hit ys so that the day ys com that our love muste departe, wyte you well I shall sell my lyff as dere as I may. And thousandfolde', seyde sir Launcelot, I am more hevyar for you than for myself! (I: 875)

The emotion here is powerful yet restrained. Launcelot reminds Guenevere of his long service, hailing her as his queen, not as his love, and soliciting her prayers if he is killed before reassuring her that his kinsmen will see to her rescue if he is slain – by no means a given, considering Bors's earlier reluctance to defend the queen in the affair of the Poisoned Apple.[26] Guenevere's response is more overtly emotional; she makes use of exclamations, slips into the intimate second person ('wyte thou well ... thy days') and asserts that if Launcelot were slain she would prefer to die. That each of the lovers is more solicitous of the other's fate than their own is taken over from the French, but Guenevere's bold alignment of herself with a *marter*, one who willingly dies for love rather than *for Jesu Crystes sake*, is Malory's invention. The rhetoric of sacrifice and martyrdom contains and intensifies the emotion, finally positioning the queen as worthy of Malory's earlier estimation of her as 'whyle she lived ... a trew lover' (I: 842). This remark, made at the beginning of the adventure of 'The Knight of the Cart', signals a change in the author's view of Guenevere. No longer the jealous and difficult woman who resents Launcelot's strategic absences and his service to other women, she is reimagined in this episode as loving, diplomatic and pragmatic, traits that carry through to the end of the *Morte*.

In comparison to the earlier books of the *Morte*, the closing sequence of events from the return from the Grail Quest onwards registers a marked change in the quantity of dialogue and of related emotional expression. Among the most emotionally significant scenes is, as we saw in Chapter 4, the occasion when Launcelot returns the queen to the king and seeks to mend his relationship with Gawain. Others are the various exchanges between Launcelot, the king and Gawain during the Siege of Joyous Gard, and the final heartrending interview between knight and queen at Amesbury (see Chapter 3). These dialogues do not necessarily make direct reference to the emotions in play; more usually they allude briefly to the intensely emotional contexts and are accompanied by clear somatic signs of feeling: weeping, swooning or sighing.

The two English Melusine romances, *The Romans of Partenay* and the *Prose Melusine*, both translate their French originals very closely, rendering the substantial emotional outbursts given to the protagonists at a parallel length.²⁷ Thus, in *The Romans*, once his brother has persuaded him to transgress against the taboo and spy on Melusine in her Saturday bath, Raymounde flies into a rage:

> Then Raymounde gan speke with vois full hautain,
> And hym said, 'therof ye lye vntrewly,
> By your fals throte And youre teeth plain
> In An ill houre here ye entred in surely
> Fro my hous ye goo with your felony
> ...
> Hens, foule rebaude being,
> For, by my faith, full litill is failing
> That presently here that I you not sle;
> Forth depart you hens, by concell of me! (lines 2829–33; 2839–42; p. 101)

Raymounde uses a string of colloquial expressions – *your fals throte, teeth plain, rebaude* – to rebut the public gossip relayed to him by his brother: that Melusine is an adulteress or (with more truth) is *of the fairy* (line 2771, p. 99), insulting him and threatening to kill him on the spot. In the *Prose Melusine*, the translator adds intensifying adjectives, *bitter, contynuel*, to Melusine's lament as she explains to Raymounde the price she must now pay for his transgression. The source's balance of positive and negative emotional outcomes is expanded into triplets: 'hate, doleur & hardnes' and 'solace, playsire & joye'.

> Las, mon amy, or sont noz amours tournees en hayne, noz doulceurs en durté, noz soulage et noz joyes en larmes et en pleurs, nostre bon eur en tresdur et infortuneuse pestilence. Las, mon amy, si tu ne m'eusses fausee je estoy jectee et exemptee de paine et de tourment.²⁸

> (Alas, my friend, now our love has all turned into hatred, our sweetness into hardness, our comfort and joys into tears and weeping, our happiness into a very hard and unlucky plague. Alas, my friend, if you had not been false to me, I would have been left out and exempted from pain and torment.)

> Halas, my frende / now is our loue tourned in hate, doleur & hardnes / oure solace, playsire & joye ben reuersed in byttir teerys & contynuel wepynges, and our good happ is conuerted in ryght hard & vnfortunate pestilence / Halas, my frend! yf thou

haddest not falsed thy feythe & thyn othe, I was putte & exempted from all peyne & tourment.[29]

In earlier English adaptations of French romance, whether Chrétien's poems (as we have seen) or other Insular French material, extended emotional speech and narrative comment were often curtailed. In the fifteenth century however, translators take their cue from the French sources, assuming that their audiences are interested in exploring the high emotions of romance plots. In some earlier 'accused queen' romances, such as *Octavyen* and *Emare*, the dialogue at the key moments of accusation and reunion is typically brief or factual. In *Octavyen*, the queen does not protest her innocence but simply prays for herself and pleads that her children might be christened before they die as she stands by the stake where she is to be burned. At the end of the romance, she relates the salient facts in a single stanza – how she kept one child, while the other was snatched by a wild beast but has now been recovered. She offers no reproach, but simply alludes to 'alle the noye that me was wroghte' (line 1786), a passive that obscures the culpability of the agents of her mistreatment, primarily her husband.[30] In romances from the later fourteenth century onwards, dialogue is often more elaborated. *The Erle of Toulous* is notable for the conversations between the Earl, the knight whom he captures and ransoms, the lady Beulybone and the two wicked knights who plot against her. There is even a verse of inner monologue from the young man who has been tricked into hiding, nearly naked, behind a curtain in the lady's bedroom, wondering why it has taken so long for the conspirators to embark on the 'joly play' (line 728) they have promised he shall participate in; he gradually begins to realise his peril: 'Yf y them calle, sche wyll be adredd / My lady lyeth here in hur bede', he thinks.[31] The long prose romance *Valentine and Orson* similarly elaborates speeches at these key plot points; for example, when the Archbishop importunes the Empress Bellyssant to become his mistress, she firmly rejects him and rebukes him at considerable length. Much later, as we shall see below, when she is restored to her husband by her son, she utters a brief speech of forgiveness, once she has recovered from her swoon.[32]

It is not just conventional set speeches of high emotion that interest the fifteenth-century romance authors; they also innovated dialogue that deals with more complex and diffuse emotions. So in *Blanchardyn and Eglantine*, after Blanchardyn has snatched a flying kiss from Eglantine, a princess who is generally referred to as the 'proud pucelle in love' or 'proud maiden in amours', Eglantine is so shocked by the assault that she faints. When she regains consciousness she expresses her fury, threatening all kinds of retribution against her assailant, relayed in reported speech.[33] Her older female companion, her 'maistresse', tries to calm her down, but to no avail, Eglantine weeps so much that her gown becomes as wet 'as grete shoure of rayne had com doun from the heuens' (p. 43) and seems to be on the verge of suicide. The sensible *maistresse* makes light of the girl's fury and schools her in self-control and common sense, chiding her for an over-emotional reaction: 'I haue right grete merueylle, hou a princes of so grete renounne as ye be of, may make so grete a sorow of a thyng of nought' (p. 43). Other conversations in the romance are equally well observed. One such is Eglantine's careful negotiation with her provost, who is hosting Blanchardyn, and whose daughters are, it is rumoured, greatly taken with their handsome guest. Eglantine warns the provost that his daughters must not indulge in flirtatious behaviour: 'smylynges and fayre shewes of their eyen, whiche wauntonly they caste full often vpon that yonge knyght' (p. 72). The narrator comments shrewdly that this is sound advice, though he also suggests that Eglantine has mixed motives: 'I saye not that Ialousy was cause of this thynge but I leue it in the iugement that in suche a caas can good skyle' (p. 81).

Partonope of Blois, as noted, is a close translation of the French, though it makes significant changes to its source (see below).[34] The heroine Melior has long argumentative exchanges with her sister Wrake, who is striving to restore Partonope to his lady's favour; the shifting emotions in the back-and-forth between the sisters are strikingly well observed. Wrake plays on her sister's fundamental love for the man she has driven away, while Melior oscillates between indignation at Partonope's conduct and pitiable regret for having rejected him. Wrake does not mince her words, working hard to make Melior feel guilty and inviting her to develop some empathy with Partonope's subject position. The queen had drawn him to her castle through 'crafte of false nygromansye' (line 7892), Wrake points out, and demanded that he give her his love, even though she remained invisible; he spent many months totally isolated from any other human contact. Partonope's disobedience was entirely understandable, argues Wrake:

> It greved hym, yis so mote I the,
> All day with-oute company to be,
> And neuer to speke with you but in þe nyght (lines 7898–7900)

Wrake offers a holistic and empathetic view of the intense emotional processes that led to Partonope's 'betrayal', as Melior terms it. Melior has exploited him, treating him as her sexual plaything; consequently, Partonope deserves sympathetic understanding and forgiveness. However, even if Partonope were to regain his wits, Wrake would counsel him to have nothing more to do with Melior, given her treatment of him, 'In love he shuld neuer do you seruyce' (line 7916), she advises. Melior's woes increase when her people demand that she marry the victor of a tournament that is announced in order to find her a husband. Although Partonope recovers from his madness, thanks to Wrake's ministrations, he has a good many other hurdles to leap before he is able to participate in the lengthy round of battles and jousts that will determine Melior's fate.

Action and bodies

The expanded scope of the fifteenth-century romances allowed for the elaboration of scenes of intense emotion. Frequently, more swooning and weeping accompanies the extended dialogues discussed above. The earlier metrical romances could describe such a reunion in a scant three lines, as in *Emare*:

> He toke her yn hys armes two,
> For joye they sowened, both to,
>   Such love was hem bytwene. (lines 934–6)

When in *Valentine and Orson* Bellyssant is finally restored to her husband by her sons, the Emperor approaches the pavilion where his wife and her ladies await,

> Than whan the Emperour apperceiued his wyfe Bellyssant he lepte of his hors in wepyng and syghinge tenderly. And without that he might speke ony worde he embraced the lady the whyche set her vpon both the knees. ... Now it is not to be demaunded yf for to fynd the one the other they were Ioyous, and if that by profounde pyte they had ther heartes touched and oppressed so that by naturall loue they fell vnto the earth in arme togyther in a swowne. (p. 201)

Only when the couple have 'aswaged theyr dolours' (p. 201), tightly locked in embrace, do they regain consciousness and begin to speak. This conventional reunion scene is expanded through the addition of adverbs (*tenderly*) and intensifying adjectives (*profounde, naturall*), lively action (*he lepte of his hors*), and the duplication of verbs (*touched and oppressed*); the narrator lists all the emotions in play: joy, 'natural' love and pity, rather than leaving them to the audience to infer. The reactions of Valentine and Orson, who also weep 'tenderly and pyteyusly' (p. 201) and swoon in sympathy with their parents, are equally elaborated, as are the reactions of Bellyssant's brother, King Pepin, and the mirror characters, the barons and knights who witness the scene.

Partonope too elaborates on its protagonists' emotions, sometimes beyond its source. As Partonope lies in bed for the first time in Melior's castle, he dares not fall asleep, for fear of what might occur in this mysterious environment:

> And as he was In thys a-ffraye,
> And hys herte fulle nere quappynge,
> In þe flore he herde comynge
> A þynge fulle softely what euer hyt were,
> Where-off fully he gan to fere.
> Meruayle he had what hyt myghte be. (lines 1179–84)

Partonope is already in a state of heightened affect, aware of the beating of his heart as he hears something quietly approaching the bed. Suspense is maintained by the line break between *comynge* and *A þynge*, and by the sinister implications of *softely*: whatever it is, is creeping towards him. Partonope's *a-ffraye* develops into full-blown fear, blended with wonder (*Meruayle*), and he hides under the bedclothes, creeping to the far side of the bed. The audience is swiftly reassured: the unknown *euylle þynge* (line 1190), the narrator reveals, is only a young girl. The scene now modulates into comedy; the two lie side-by-side in the darkness, both in states of high emotional arousal. Partonope is possessed by fear, Melior by shame. Melior debates with herself in a long interior monologue, an addition to the French source, wondering how to manage the next move in seducing the young man and debating moral questions of honour and reputation; Partonope has no idea what is happening or how to proceed, but simply lies quaking in terror, in part a legacy from the source where Partonopeu is considerably younger than he is in English: at the start of the action he is only thirteen, while the English text ages him up to eighteen (lines 520–1).[35] The narrator decides to put an end to the stand-off, noting that his source 'telleþe hyt shorteley and noȝt in prose' (line 1294). Melior accidentally stretches out her leg and touches Partonope; she can now pretend to be outraged that there is a man in her bed, thus initiating the conversation and allowing her to claim some moral high ground. Partonope, reassured that his bed-companion is human, female and well-born, is able to ask for mercy and offer his service before sexual contact is initiated. The description of Partonope's foreplay is uncomfortably detailed: Melior 'her legges ... gan to knytte, / And wyth hys knees he gan hem on-shote' (lines 1565–6), before, despite her protests, he penetrates her.[36] The narrator assures us that the pleasure of lovemaking then becomes mutual, though it takes many more lines for Melior to negotiate the social difficulties produced by her initiative in securing her lover and to assure him (and herself) that her behaviour is the result of genuine love.

Narration

Partonope of Blois has a narrator who readily comments on the action, criticising the characters, posing questions to the audience, castigating women in general for their stubborn commitment to chastity and elaborating his own emotional state as 'lyric lover'.[37] He regrets of his own lady,

> In hir can I se no-þing amysse,
> Save oo þing, truly, þat liketh not me:
> In hir herte she can not fynde in noo degre
> Me forto love as I hir truly do (lines 10915–18)

Yet early in the poem (lines 2332–44) the narrator has explained that he is obliged to translate his author, but he himself is 'nouȝt thus in infirmyte' and not in fact even a lover; he prays to be shielded from having to 'hoppe so ferre ynne loue-ys daunce' (lines 2332; 2334).[38] The narrator's position is complicated by his frequent reminders that his work is a translation – and that this 'I' who is invoked is at the same time is not, or not always, the same 'I' who is to be imagined as telling the story. The English narrator's subject position thus becomes highly unstable and calls into question who exactly is speaking whenever the first person is deployed.

Later in the text, the narrator forms views about his characters' conduct, opining that Wrake is cruel to pretend to Melior that Partonope is dead: 'For sothe Wrake, as þinketh me, / Was gretely to blame, when þat she / Se hir suster so grete sorowe take, / And wolde no better chere hir make' (lines 8659–62); he claims he himself would not be so hard-hearted. *Partonope* is also interested in collective emotions, embedded in distinct social contexts and operating to express normative emotional schemas that contrast with the emotional initiatives of the main protagonists. Thus, the narrator gives a detailed account of the shaming of Melior by her women when they enter her bedchamber and find her with Partonope after he has disobeyed her. They reprove her at length for her lustfulness and for taking, as they think, a low-born lover. Their rebukes rehearse, so the narrator implies, the usual time-worn criticisms, and he encourages the audience to discount the women's purported outrage: 'And þes wemmen had well I-ronge / Here belle, wyche was heuy to here' (lines 6139–40). Indeed, once they see how wretched Melior is, they regret what they have said and fall silent; the emotional centre of the scene returns to the princess's feelings of outrage and betrayal. Melior's knights reproach their lady in similarly conventional terms for accepting a pennant from Partonope's spear during the tournament; they openly assert that the anonymous knight must be her secret lover. Again, the narrator discounts their criticism: 'Therfore all men þat be so light of tonge / That as a grete bell þat longe is ronge / Noyse her lesynges' (lines 10137–9). The idiom of 'ringing the bell' (familiar from Criseyde's lament anticipating her future literary reputation

(V: 1058–62)) is conventional, but the poet deploys it with skill, linking together the two scenes of courtly scandal with the suggestion that there is no genuine depth of feeling in the onlookers' reaction. Rather, their performance conforms with ideas of public courtly morality. The readiness with which the courtiers turn to open criticism and rebuke of their sovereign lady highlights the ambivalence felt towards a female ruler. While the women regret their castigation when they see Melior's misery, the male courtiers are silenced only by the narrator's wish that such nasty-minded men should not be allowed to spend any more time among deserving ladies.

Barry Windeatt has thoughtfully analysed how much the *Partonope*-translator owes to Chaucer in terms of idiom, development of narratorial persona, and switching between comedy and high drama.[39] As in *Troilus*, the romance's emotions are distributed across characters, narrator and audience, crafting an involving and complex story in which different emotions are explored at length. The *Partonope*-author is, as he freely admits, following his source closely, and he employs the techniques pioneered at the very birth of vernacular romance in twelfth-century France, techniques which had not generally carried across into earlier English romance. Thus, even though his source is remarkably early in French literary history, in an English context the *Partonope*-translator produces an impression of fifteenth-century modernity in his playfulness, his tone-switching and his interest in emotion and the creation of empathy. Just as Chaucer signals, particularly in *Troilus*, his awareness of women in his audience and Caxton includes 'gentilwomen' among his potential customers for *Blanchardyn*, it seems likely that *Partonope* was intended to have particular appeal to women. Not only does it focus at length on the complex emotional states of Melior and Wrake, as well as Partonope's mother, and Wrake's cousin Persewise, who also falls in love with the hero, but it frequently addresses women directly, praising and regretting their commitment to chastity. Indeed, in a late fifteenth-century will, Isabel Lyston of Norwich left 'an englyssh boke called partonope' to her daughter Margery London: the only known instance of a woman bequeathing a romance written specifically in English to another woman.[40]

The narrator of *Blanchardyn and Eglantine* is also adept at managing the expression of interiority. As Blanchardyn rides towards Eglantine's retinue, he contemplates the vow he has made to kiss the 'proud pucelle in love' in a passage that demonstrates a range of possibilities for emotional expression.

> So thought he moche in hym self by what manere he myght execute and brynge at an ende the werke that he hath undertaken, that is to wyte to kysse the proude mayden in amours. Wherof in this manere of thoughte was his noble herte all affrayed and re-plenysshed wyth grete fere lest he shold faylle of his entrepryse, for wel it was th'advis of Blanchardyn that the thyng ought well to be putte in a proffe syth his promesse was thus made to the knyght. And for this cause entred wythin his thoughte a drede as for to be so hardy that he sholde vaunce hym self for to kysse suche a pryncesse that never he had seen byfore, and wherof th'acquentaunce was so daungerouse. But Love that wyth her dart had made in his herte a grete wounde admonested hym for to procede constantly to his hyghe entrepryse. And after all varyablenes and debates ybrought at an ende wythin the mynde of this newe lover, his resolucion fynall was that he sholde putte peyne for to have a cusse of the proude pucelle in amours al thoughe deth sholde be unto him adjudged onely for this cause. And herupon went Blanchardyn sayenge: 'O veraye God, how well happy shold myn herte be that presently is overmoche pressed bycause of myn enterpryse, yf I myght obteyne that one cussynge. And yf myn infortune or feblenes of corage sholde lette me fro this adventure that so sore I desyre, deth make an ende of me.' (pp. 40–1)

Like other fifteenth-century prose, and as noted above of *Valentine and Orson*, this passage expands its description through the use of doubled pairs of verbs and an increased use of adjectives. It functions primarily through psychonarration, relating Blanchardyn's cogitation about how in practical terms he might fulfil his promise, his fear of how he might fail and shame himself and further anxiety about what might happen if he were to succeed, given the lady's rank and known hostility to amorous approaches. Personified Love has already wounded his heart, encouraging him to proceed; turning over the pros and cons in his mind, he decides that he will indeed try for the kiss. Now he gives utterance to that resolution, balancing the happiness he might obtain against the present state of his heart 'overmoche pressed' by anxiety; should he fail through bad luck or failure of nerve, death may as well take him. This is a complex depiction of interior psychology. Blanchardyn's emotional state oscillates contradictory emotions: love, fear, anxiety, desire and potential shame; and the narrator switches easily between feelings located in the 'mynde' and in the 'herte', the externalised figure of Love and the sentiments that the hero voices in direct speech.

The long-form romance then caters to a marked interest in emotional situations, one that sits alongside detailed descriptions of battles and tournaments. Women's emotions are prominent in the texts discussed here, highlighted in dramatic scenes of courtship, accusation, victimisation, family reunion and marriage. Men too are imagined in intensely emotional situations, not simply as lovers, but as fathers, sons, husbands and brothers – as well as friends, bound in powerful affective relationships with other men. These romance characters are largely conventional, though the 'proud pucelle in love' type is unusual in English, while the immensely effective and likeable Wrake rewrites the idea of the confidante or go-between: her emotional investment in her sister's happiness means that she must strictly school herself, extinguishing through the exercise of reason the desire she begins to feel for Partonope. The emotion scripts that structure the long-form romance's emotion episodes do not generally introduce new elements. The somatic indices of emotion generally remain unchanged – though, unusually, Partonope's hair turns grey during his madness, a symptom rectified by Wrake's application of a herbal remedy. Dialogue, however expands, employing more words and a range of rhetorical techniques to enhance the expression of emotion. Beside the stock scenes of high emotional drama, other feelings are explored: irritation, envy, shame, petty sniping and jealousy. These allow an often dialogue-based exploration of feelings, which is innovative when compared with the earlier metrical romances. Rebecca McNamara and Juanita Ruys suggest that '[t]he concept of emotional communities can thus include genres of written work that center on common issues and experiences'.[41] The romances considered here indeed create their own emotional community, both within and beyond the text, employing genre-specific emotional norms that are legible

Fifteenth-century feelings 247

to its particular audiences. Even if we cannot confidently locate such genre-communities within identifiable real-world emotional communities, given the expansion of romance readership across different social ranks in the fifteenth century, genre-specific emotional systems were communicating evolving emotional schemas and scripts to new audiences and readers. Thus, they perform crucial cultural work, both within their own historical contexts and in our own re-readings of them.

Fifteenth-century life-writing

Medieval authors were fecund writers and theorizers of lives. They reflected on the stages of lives and considered whether body, soul or some collaboration of the two is most responsible for how people act. They experimented with ways of telling life stories, either their own or others.[42]

The late fourteenth century had seen the emergence of literary authors who named themselves in their works. While this enabled them to claim secure authorial status, they would also complicate their self-insertion into their writing in ways that varied by genre. Dream-visions demand the creation of a dreaming 'I' as originator of the material, but the identification of that persona with the poet, named or unnamed, is risky – the *Pearl*-poet, for example, offers apparently autobiographical details of his loss which may or may not reflect his life-situation. The self that speaks as 'I' in *Patience* is not easily identifiable with the *Pearl*-dreamer's voice. The 'I' whose voice unifies story-collections may be a clear persona, as in Gower's *Amans* in *Confessio Amantis*, or may represent some other version of the author, as in Chaucer-the-pilgrim. These writers were no longer exclusively clerics. In London Chaucer combined middle-class professional activities with writing; Gower too may have made his living through legal practice, though the source of his income is not clear. Chaucer's friends and contemporaries included the poet and gentleman Sir John Clanvowe and the unfortunate Thomas Usk, like Chaucer a bureaucrat. Chaucer's fifteenth-century followers likewise belonged to wider social circles, bringing different kinds of life-experience to their writing.[43]

Among these so-called English Chaucerians, the author who gives best insight into the development of new kinds of discourse around emotions and the self is Thomas Hoccleve. Learning from and developing Chaucer's own inventively playful use of an authorial persona, Hoccleve 'adapted Chaucer's self-deprecatory persona as well as his means of insinuating that persona into his works, but he departed from Chaucer by investing his inscribed "self" with the kinds of personal and professional detail that Chaucer scrupulously eschewed', writes Karen Winstead.[44] For most of his working life Hoccleve was a scribe at the office of the Privy Seal, where colleagues and friends formed his emotional community, though he records that he had once had hopes of a priestly benefice.[45] The occupation was steady, but also precarious in terms of regularity of payment.[46] Hoccleve has a good claim to be 'the most strenuously autobiographical poet in early English literature', notes Lee Patterson; he writes in the first person in a number of poems.[47] Whether these passages can be understood as autobiographical in the modern sense is debatable; for, as John Burrow points out, 'the corresponding medieval texts will present themselves as written versions, albeit elaborated and formalised, of an everyday self-referring speech act. They are addressed to particular recipients, and they serve explicitly stated practical ends.'[48] Not only do these passages reflect the emotional scripts appropriate to the particular genre in which they are situated, but they are also strongly aware of the elements of performance associated with the successful performative, the tensions generated by the urgency of writing to change something in the world and the self-conscious emotions elicited by the very act of poetic composition.

Hoccleve's Male Regle

The interrelationship of emotion, genre and persona is strikingly illustrated in the early poem *Male Regle* (1405).[49] The poem is in part a mock-confession, in part a petitional poem to Hoccleve's paymaster, 'my lord the Fourneval' (line 417), a performative that playfully seeks the payment of an annuity. The two generic modes demand different emotional stances, but these positions are complicated by Hoccleve's performance of self-awareness and literary artfulness. Regret, indeed remorse, is appropriate to confession: now he has fallen into ill-health and poverty, Hoccleve claims to realise the folly of his earlier way of living.[50] He blames his youth, which was 'rebel / Vnto reson, and hatith hir doctryne' (lines 65–6). Although the dominant mode is comic, the speaker's emotional tone fluctuates between a performance of penitence – 'my body empty is and bare /of ioie and ful of seekly heuynesse' (lines 14–15) – and his recollection of his dissolute past, the 'hertes gladnesse' (line 13) that the poet used to enjoy. Hoccleve paints a lively picture of the taverns, eating-houses and street-life where he used to amuse himself when he had both health and money.

The traditional topos of the sins of the tavern thus structures the penitential theme, yet the cheerful recollections of the pleasures of London's night-time economy are tempered by social anxiety. Although drinking and eating were unequivocally enjoyable, other pastimes evoke the memory of more complex self-conscious emotions: the embarrassment felt when people spoke of 'loues aart' (line 153) in Hoccleve's presence – 'For shame I wexe as reed as is the gleede' (line 159) – and his avoidance of fights 'for lettynge of my manly cowardyse' (line 174).[51] Hoccleve knows that the taverners and cooks who take for him for 'a verray gentil man' (line 184) because he pays his bills mistake his rank and means, the boatmen who solicit him as a fare to be transported up-river after a night at the tavern flatteringly call him *maistir* (line 201). The speaker's insecurities – abashed by women, cowardly in fights, not rich enough for the life-style of *riot* – now inflect the stance of regret he performs at length, addressing both the god of health and, in the latter part of the poem, his own errant self: 'Be waar, Hoccleue, I rede thee therfore' (line 351), he warns, laying bare the financial straits in which he now finds himself. Anxiety and embarrassment, feelings that are more nuanced, more closely attuned to a model of an interior self, than pride and shame, emerge as dominant emotions in Hoccleve's personal emotional schema. This foregrounding of selfhood encourages an introspection that is uncomfortably aware of the dissonances between an imagined capable and effective social self and an interiority shaped by doubts, failings and the complex operations of memory.[52]

As confession modulates into petition, the tone of bravura recedes, to be replaced by the performance of humility. Yet, in establishing the tone for the new performative, Hoccleve must uneasily negotiate a balance between the acknowledgement of Furnivall's superior rank, with the danger of falling into insincere flattery, and making too bald a request: 'I kepte nat to be seen importune / In my pursuyte' (lines 425–6), he observes. The new performative is managed through the partial elision of the god of health, ostensible addressee of most of the poem, and Furnivall: unless a figure of 'magnificence' 'reewe on myn impotence' (lines 441; 443), the speaker will perish before the day is out, he claims with comic hyperbole. Emotions of momentary defiance and self-abasement inflect the complex interplay between the poem's two 'self-referring' speech-acts: the autobiographical confession and the petition, voiced by a subject who 'to craue moot ... lerne' (line 432). From an emotional perspective, *Male Regle* unites a virtuoso performance and successful performative in, as characterised by Ethan Knapp, 'aggressive self-denigration'.[53]

The Complaint *and autofiction*

Just as Chaucer's persona is broadly consistent across his poems, but bears an unverifiable relationship to Chaucer's self, Hoccleve's persona may be regarded as a kind of 'autofiction', 'a genre that blends fiction and what may appear to be fact into an unstable compound', as Christian Lorentzen has defined it.[54] Lorentzen suggests 'that in autofiction there tends to be emphasis on the narrator's or protagonist's or authorial alter ego's status as a writer or artist and that the book's creation is inscribed in the book itself'.[55] This crucial point about the meta-referentiality of autofiction, that the act of writing the self is made visible as the self is writing, is key to understanding Hoccleve's self-positioning, as we saw above (and is also illustrated in *The Regiment of Princes*).[56] Nowhere is autofiction more strikingly explored than in Hoccleve's *Complaint*, the first work of the late compilation of disparate poems known as the *Series*. The *Complaint* focuses on the poet's current emotional state and its relationship to a past episode of madness, the:

```
... wylde infirmitee
Which þat I hadde / as many a man wel knew
And which me out of myself caste and threew. (lines 40–2)⁵⁷
```

This time, instead of the god of health and (eventually) Lord Furnivall, Hoccleve addresses a more various and unpredictable audience: 'in its various avatars – the *prees*, or crowd, of London; God, to whom he prays; a *frende* who stops by Hoccleve's home; Duke Humphrey, ostensible patron of the *Series*; and a female readership reportedly angry about one of his prior compositions'.⁵⁸ As in *Male Regle*, distinguishing between the 'true' and autobiographical, and a kind of fiction that poses as plausible is pointless. Julie Orlemanski warns that

> the autobiographical conflation of poet and narrator does not mean that what the *Series* recounts is true but rather that readers are constantly referred to the paradoxical figure of the poet-narrator, who flickers between his existence as an effect of the text, brought to life by his diegetic representation, and his role as textual cause and informing principle.⁵⁹

Hoccleve's Prologue to the *Complaint* sets the scene in autumn. As the leaves fall the speaker registers 'þat chaunge / sank into myn herte roote' (line 7). Lying sleepless in bed, 'the thoghtful maladie' (line 21) comes upon him, figured as a dark shower, and making him 'in languor ... swymme' (lines 26–7). This is not the languor of longing that Margery Kempe and the lyric poets cultivated, but rather the paralysis of depression, a recurrent melancholy accompanied by clear physiological symptoms. The verse modulates from the meditative resignation produced by the autumnal mood to a violent spasm of feeling.

```
The greefe about myn herte / so swal
And bolned euere / to and to so sore        [swelled]
Þat needes oute / I muste therwithal.
I thowght I nolde it kepe cloos no more,
Ne lett it in me / for to olde and hore      [grey-haired]
And for to preve / I cam of a woman
I braste out on the morwe and thus began. (lines 29–35)⁶⁰
```

Thus, as Hoccleve says, he embarks on the composition of the *Complaint* as a way of purging his grief: emotion and poetic composition inextricably linked in a therapeutic act of creation. Despite his confidence in his own recovery from his 'wylde infirmitee' through the healing power of God, he remains unhappy: 'haue I be sore set on fyre. / And lyued in greet torment / and martire' (lines 62–3). What grieves him, it emerges, is his treatment by his former companions. These display *desdeyn* (a stronger word than modern English *disdain*, closer to *scorn*), no longer wish to talk to him, avoid catching his eye in public and opine among themselves that his recovery from madness is only temporary: it will return in time or when the weather becomes warm.[61] This verdict is not communicated directly to the speaker; rather he comes to hear of it, 'and thanne my visage / Began to glowe / for the wo and fere' (lines 89–90). These powerful emotions are not the usual feelings of shame and rage that are associated with facial reddening. Rather, they could more accurately be glossed as the self-conscious and socially evaluative emotions of embarrassment and anxiety, as we saw at work in *Male Regle*, and they trigger the renewed onset of 'the thoghtful maladie'.[62] Hoccleve is too anxious to speak (or speak up) to the anonymous Londoners, the *prees*, whom he encounters in daily life. When he returns home, he is afflicted by a 'physicalized anxiety', 'verry shame and fere' (line 151). His heart oscillates between sensations of 'frosty coold' and 'fiery hoot' (line 154).[63] Hoccleve's awareness of how other people shun or insult him produces feelings of shame, fear and sadness, yet he dares not respond directly to those who are hostile to him lest he be accused of relapsing into insanity once more.

 Lasting social isolation and his awareness of being the subject of unkind gossip provoke Hoccleve into trying to reconstruct for himself the experience of his madness, drawing upon what his friends had told him about his behaviour and symptoms. He is incapable of remembering his illness, for then 'the substaunce / of my memorie / went to pleye' (lines 50–1). Worse than the blank in his memory is the loss of his sense of self. Although Hoccleve now knows himself to be well, to have recovered himself, others cannot or will not perceive the self that he feels himself to be. Though some acquaintances kindly enquire about his well-being from his 'felawes / of the priuy seel' (line 296), they refuse to accept assurances about the poet's health. Thus stigmatised, Hoccleve finds himself on the verge of despair, enduring a 'troubly lyf' (line 302). At the heart of the *Complaint* is Hoccleve's vivid depiction of how he repeatedly leaps (*saute made*) in front of his bedroom mirror (lines 155–75), trying to catch his expression, to check whether he looks normal, whether he can pass as such in the community. But even as he gazes at himself, he calls his action into question: is this what he looks like when he is out in the streets? Would reasonable people think this is normal? Can he really 'see' himself as he is? What he sees now before the glass conveys 'noon errour / of suspect look' (lines 164–5); folk who judge by appearances *ought* to judge him sane. And yet their preconceptions about him will skew their perceptions; neither his behaviour nor his appearance can nullify their prejudice. The emotional subject perceives its embodied self in the mirror, but the mirror does not form or project social judgements, as others do. Hoccleve's specular self-scrutiny cannot assuage his anxiety, for as soon as he looks away, that reassuringly sane self is gone, experienced only through the body that he inhabits, whose interiority he – and he alone – apprehends. It is only the act of writing that can capture that elusive self seen in the mirror and display it persuasively to Hoccleve's peers and readers: a 'Hoccleve both written and writing'.[64]

Next, in a quasi-Chaucerian move, Hoccleve seeks authorisation for his self-understanding by taking up a borrowed book. This is a version of Isidore of Seville's *Synonyma*, a work that derives in part from Boethius's *De consolatione philosophiae*.[65] The voice of Reason that speaks to the sufferer in the text seems to offer a model of resignation that puts his anxieties to rest. He resolves to cease caring about others' views of his illness, to 'take it in souffrance'. Emotional consolation is apparently achieved: 'Farwel, my sorwe / I caste it to the cok!' (lines 384; 386), and the *Complaint* ends conventionally with a prayer praising and thanking God. This stoic conclusion rests on 'an unsustainable fantasy of self-sufficient expressive enclosure', writing a self that finds emotional equilibrium only within the privacy of the chamber.[66]

In itself, the *Complaint* offers a uniquely varied and full evocation of mental and emotional states. Hoccleve draws upon a physiological understanding of pathological symptoms (embodied behaviours, mental derangement, memory loss) that accompanies his 'wylde infirmitee' and interweaves his reconstruction of his loss of self with a psychologically complex account of the condition of recovery. Hoccleve tellingly compares his illness with drunkenness – a man may drink so much that 'his wittes / wel ny been reft him fro / and buried in the cuppe', but 'he afterward / Comth to himself ageyn / elles were hard' (lines 229–30). Thus, he positions himself as recuperated, as sober, thanks to God's healing powers; those who observe him from outside see him rather as 'in recovery', ostensibly better but always unstable, always on the verge of relapse. As Knapp writes of the *Male Regle*, 'if there is a systematic poetics at the heart of Hoccleve's work, its essence lies in the attempt to transmute private anxiety into public discourse'.[67]

Through self-scrutiny and readerly recourse to an authorised philosophical discourse of resignation and consolation, Hoccleve has thus achieved a precarious integration of private and social self. Yet the ending of the *Complaint* was always intended as provisional, always to be disrupted by the opening lines of the *Dialogue with a Friend*, which immediately follows the *Complaint* in the *Series* compilation. For, immediately, 'a good freend of fern agoon' (line 8) appears at Hoccleve's chamber door and in a delightfully conversational mode demands to know what he is up to. Patterson suggests, appositely, that 'the setting up of parts of the self as if they were other than the self, only to have them collapse back into the self, or worse, fly apart – is characteristic of Hoccleve'.[68] The well-meaning but provocative arguments of the *freend* externalise and embody certain conflicting emotions still agitating the poet's spirit. Hoccleve invites his friend in and reads him the newly composed *Complaint*, now revealed as already written down in manuscript; it is ready to communicate Hoccleve's new-found self-understanding in circulation to his public. Surprisingly, the friend counsels strongly against sharing the poem; it will be damaging to Hoccleve's reputation, for 'How it stood with thee / leide is al asleepe / Men han foryete it / it is out of mynde' (lines 29–30). Hoccleve responds with vigorous argument: he has heard people making disparaging remarks about him; having been mad is no shame, and God's restoration of his sanity is a blessing that should not be concealed.

The friend's response to the *Complaint* as its first auditor destabilises Hoccleve's apparent achievement in writing himself as re-integrated subject, as creating a version of himself that can step confidently away from the mirror. Are the friend's remarks suggesting that the illness is generally forgotten a comforting fiction, or has Hoccleve radically misunderstood his social milieu, and by extension, is he then wrong about his imagined readership? The *freend* goes on disturbingly to propose that writing is not the answer; indeed it may have caused Hoccleve's madness in the first place and may equally cause a relapse. Although the act of writing apparently brings the poet emotional satisfaction – 'Joie hastow for to muse / Vpon thy book / and therein stare and poure' – yet, warns the friend, this risks adverse mental consequences, 'Til that it thy wit / consume and devoure (lines 404–6). Hoccleve is able to assure his friend that he can exercise moderation and that his writing and study was not the cause of his madness (although he offers no convincing alternative aetiology), and eventually his arguments prevail. With 'the abrupt folding of the friend's resistance', Hoccleve forcibly collapses this externalised self, with its doubts about the curative efficacy of writing and the unpredictable responses of his readership, successfully re-integrating it into his interior state. Now he turns from his principal preoccupation, his own emotions, both subjective and interpersonal, to outline his future writing aims, not without a few further interjections from the *freende*. Hoccleve's plan to translate an *Ars moriendi* is counselled against, his dedication of the work in progress to Humphrey, Duke of Gloucester, considered, and the reception given by women readers by an earlier work of Hoccleve, his *Letter of Cupid*, is discussed: dialogue that signals the disparate following poems that constitute the rest of the *Series*.[69]

Hoccleve's autofiction in the *Complaint* and *Dialogue with a Friend* writes an authorial persona that deploys emotional discourse to communicate on multiple levels. As Sobecki argues, the *Series* may well be a work of mourning, expressing grief for loss, ageing, transience and the urgent task of 'learning to die', at the same time as it makes sophisticated play with questions of authorship, reception and posterity: exactly the questions that Chaucer addresses through his own pioneering autofictional interpellation of the dreaming 'Geffrye' in *The House of Fame*. As Laurie Atkinson argues, in the *Complaint* 'emotion is concealed behind convention, the maker behind his text; but despite Hoccleve's diligent control over the words on the page, as for their interpretation by his audience, that, he must finally concede, "can I nat knowe"'.[70] Hoccleve's writing does not aim 'to talk, really, about himself, sometimes with such raw honesty as to be painful', as Derek Pearsall claimed back in 1966.[71] Rather it works to create an authorial self to explores the phenomena of subjectivity and interiority: the emotions of selfhood and their relationship to the social milieu of his audience.

The Book of Margery Kempe as autofiction

In the final part of this chapter, I consider the autofictional self as site and generator of emotion in *The Book of Margery Kempe*. The *Book* is emphatically *sui generis*: an unparalleled hybrid text whose generic roots lie in the accounts of visions and prayers composed by male and female mystics in England and the Continent, the autobiographical elements that often frame the lives of mystics, composed by their amanuenses, and the well-established genre of saints' lives.[72] 'The *Book of Margery Kempe* is a bold experiment in life-writing. It is radical in its rejection of the centuries-old model of sanctity as manifested through a life of celibacy and suffering', writes Karen Winstead, contrasting the *Book* with the hagiographies and royal biographies that were the primary genres for writing lives in the medieval period.[73] As autofiction, Margery's *Book* indeed offers a highly unstable mixture of plausible fact and unverifiable interior experience, complicated further by questions about authorship and the role played by her amanuenses in the text's formation.[74] Unlike Hoccleve's, though, Margery's writing is not primarily intended to consolidate her position as writer, for the complex circumstances under which the book comes into existence are set out in the 1436 Proem that prefaces the text.[75] This charts how, once she had determined to set down her story, twenty years or more after the onset of her visions, she was assisted by an Englishman who had lived a long time in Germany (possibly her son), a friend of his, and a procrastinating priest. 'Margery had to struggle to find her scribes but she also had the freedom to determine how her memories were set down', suggests Winstead, rather optimistically.[76] The *Book* is not then self-reflexive about the processes of writing, as *The Complaint* is, but rather it is intended to bear witness to God's grace: it is an account of 'hyr felyngys and revelacyons' (p. 47), the sum of Margery's experience, now to be set down at God's command so 'that hys goodnesse myth be knowyn to alle the world' (p. 47). This then is the *Book*'s declared aim.

The *Book* proper begins, like Hoccleve's Prologue, with the recollection of a terrible madness, now cured through the grace of God. Margery suffered a loss of self that saw her bound and watched, after the birth of her first child: 'this creatur went owt of hir mende and was wondyrlye vexid and labowryd wyth spyrytys half yer viii wekys and odde days' (p. 54). This precise record of the illness's duration so early in the text functions to guarantee the accuracy of recollection. Margery is healed when Jesus appears to her as a man, sitting on her bed and quietly asserting his enduring love for her. Margery's own diagnosis of the cause of her madness is her profound fear of dying unconfessed; after Jesus's reassuring intervention, she recovers 'hir wyttys and ... hir reson as wel as evyr sche was beforn' (p. 56). The self to which Margery is restored, however, is a worldly and sinful one, given to 'pride' and 'pompows aray' (p. 57), a woman who quarrels with her husband, envies her neighbours and desires wealth, a depiction that intersects with Langland's Pernele Proud-herte, as we saw in Chapter 1 (pp. 63–4). She goes into business, launching a brewing concern, and when that fails, she takes up 'a newe huswyfre' (p. 59): a horse-powered mill, also a failure. A second encounter with the divine, the sound 'of melodye so swet and delectable, hir thowt, as sche had ben in paradyse' (p. 61), sets her on the path to the realisation of a new self. From this time onwards she no longer feels sexual desire for her husband, though they continue to sleep together, and she bears him children (pp. 62–3). Two years of penitential behaviour, mortification and fasting give her strong confidence in the new orientation of her emotional disposition: 'sche thowt that sche lovyd God mor than he hir' (p. 66); this over-confidence is challenged by the onset of renewed lecherous thoughts and sexual temptation. Rosenwein rightly notes a recurrent pattern in the early part of the book: despair, fear of sin, compunction and joy, through the renewed assurance of God's love.[77]

These initial autofictional elements in the *Book* establish Margery both as an ordinary townswoman, firmly embedded in a social world, and as a regular sinner. Margery, or rather *þis creature* as the subject of the book is described, charts her transformation from young mother and would-be businesswoman to the paradoxical figure at the book's centre: a mother of fourteen who dresses as, and longs to be, a virgin, a laywoman called to devote herself wholly to Jesus Christ in the world, a woman whose passionate feelings for her husband modulate into a horror of marital sex, and then into assiduous care of him in old age, a spousal relationship that is shot through with ambivalences. Margery's emotional self, or rather, as Ruth Evans argues, the *Book*'s divided selves, are depicted as works in progress: 'selfhood as a tension between identity and difference, unity and division'.[78] Even after achieving celibacy and turning wholeheartedly to God, 'she has not arrived at holiness but only begun a journey towards it that continues for many years and never, in fact, reaches entire freedom from temptation', notes Winstead.[79] The emotions of Margery's earlier self are foregrounded through autobiographical and often humiliating detail: her yielding to sexual temptation, only to be told that the man with whom she had agreed to have sex had simply been testing her, is a case in point (pp. 67–8). She learns to school her uglier emotions, overlapping in contemporary analysis with the deadly sins: envy and pride, lust and anger. Intimations of the joy to come in heaven inspire her to an actively Christian way of life.

The *Book* weaves Margery's autofictional emotions throughout the text in four distinct strands. The first of these recounts Margery's feelings of fear, joy, sorrow and anxiety, elicited in response to events that happen in reality. These typically include her interactions with her fellow-citizens, the households of church dignitaries and the churchmen themselves. Sea-voyages are terrifying: when Margery takes ship for Santiago de Compostela she is warned that if there are storms she will be thrown overboard (p. 226), but God grants her safe passage. Not so when she and her daughter-in-law make their tempest-tossed way across the North Sea: 'The sayd creatur had sorwe and care inow; hir thowt sche had nevyr so mech beforn' (p. 396). Threats from the institutional church hierarchy cause her to tremble with fear. Placed in fetters and accused of heresy by the Archbishop of Canterbury, 'hir flesch tremelyd and whakyd wondirly, that sche was fayn to puttyn hyr handys undyr her clothis that it schuld not be aspyed' (p. 249). Margery is willing to deliver 'scharp wordys ... wythowtyn any glosyng er flateryng' (p. 223) to those who stand in need of spiritual correction, including her son, who is addressed 'wyth scharpnes of spiryt' (p. 386). In contrast, kindness from other pilgrims makes her 'rygth glad and mery' (p. 215), while conversation with religious who confirm the holiness of her visions brings the pleasure of shared 'holy dalyawns ... be comownyng in the lofe of owyr Lord Jhesu Crist', here with Julian of Norwich (p. 123). In a similar interview with William Southfield, the Norwich Carmelite 'comfortyd [her] bothe in body and in sowle' (p. 119).[80] Margery also, so she says, takes pleasure in the hostility of others: her chastisement and social ostracism is pleasing to God, demonstrating her capacity to suffer for his love: 'than thys creature thowt it was ful mery to be repreved for Goddes love' (p. 97). As Rosenwein notes, the phrase 'ful mery' is frequently used by Margery to refer to the joys of heaven (pp. 62; 338; 380), but the phrase recurs for the pleasure of worldly friendship (p. 140). Rosenwein also notes the preference that the *Book* has in reporting scorn and rebuke and Margery's isolation, rather than highlighting her affective network of allies.[81]

These terms, *comfort*, *dalliance*, along with *solas*, characterise Margery's emotional responses to her conversations with Jesus, the text's second strand of emotionality. In Rome, for example, where Margery regrets she can gain no 'crumme of gostly undirstondyng' from a sermon that she cannot understand, Jesus speaks to her directly: '[his] melydiows voys swettest of alle savowrys softly sowndyng in hir sowle' (p. 208). Just as heavenly harmonies and sweet odours signalled the promise of heaven in Margery's earliest synaesthetic visions, Jesus's words are intoxicating, yet their effect on Margery is paradoxical: 'Than was hir sowle so delectabely fed wyth the swet dalyawns of owr Lorde and so fulfilled of hys lofe that as a drunkyn man sche turnyd hir fyrst on the o syde and sithyn on the other wyth gret wepyng and gret sobbyng' (pp. 208–9). Emotional arousal, even when positively valenced, emphasises to Margery the distance between her sinful, earthly existence and the eternal joys of heaven, and is expressed with tears and loud vocalisations.

Later in the *Book*, Margery begins to experience everyday life as a palimpsest of the human and the divine – the third distinct context for the elicitation of emotion. Whatever she sees on the workaday streets brings vividly to mind exegetical parallels. When she witnesses a prince, prelate or other worthy man being honoured and respected, 'anon hir mende was refreschyd into owr Lord, thynkyng what joy, what blysse, what worschep and reverens he had in hevyn' (p. 320). Such comforting emotions are counterpointed by the overwriting of others' punishment and suffering with the suffering of Jesus, eliciting feelings of guilt, such that she 'schulde ... criyen, wepyn and sobbyn for her owyn synne' (p. 320). This overwriting is a development from those vividly recounted visions in which Margery interpellates herself into Gospel scenes, elbowing aside the sacred protagonists in order to enact an exemplary role for herself, such as her care for the baby Jesus and the Virgin Mary at the Nativity and after the Crucifixion, seeking out swaddling for the new-born and administering restorative hot drinks (pp. 77; 352). Imaginative devotional texts such as Love's *Mirror of the Blessed Life of Jesus Christ* provided, notes Sarah Salih, 'a ready-made framework of biblical "scripted visions" for Margery's contemplative avatar to step into'.[82]

Margery's visions inscribe her as both witness and actor in the events of the Passion; this allows her to narrate and perform a full range of emotion scripts associated with grief and loss. The sequence is inaugurated by an imagined scene, one with no biblical precedent, in which Margery participates: Jesus's dialogue of farewell with his mother and his parting from her. Mary swoons as he turns to leave her, and Margery dashes forward, catching hold of Jesus's clothes and kneeling at his feet to elicit similar words of command and comfort for herself: she must remain in his service on earth, he tells her, until she is called to heaven. Margery aligns herself with Mary throughout the following series of visions, taking the role of 'hyr unworthy handmaydyn for the tyme' (p. 344). They travel with Christ from Gethsemane via the scourging and buffeting, the Stations of the Cross and Golgotha to the sepulchre; in this journey Margery 'wepte, sobbyd and criyd as thow sche shuld a dyid', her emotional displays surpassing the Virgin's in their vehemence (p. 346). At the deposition, Margery is left at the edge of the scene, unable to touch the Lord's body, as Mary and Mary Magdalen are authorised to do, and the exclusion drives her frantic. '[S]che thowt that sche ran evyr to and fro, as it had be a woman wythouten reson, gretly desyrying to an had the precyows body be hirself alone' (p. 350). The affective power of Margery's repetitive emotional performances in this part of the *Book* derives from their juxtaposition with the most emotive scenes from Jesus's life on earth, the Gospel narrative that is most inextricably linked with the elicitation of compassion and Christian compunction. Margery's foregrounding of herself positions her as onlooker within the narrative frame; in contrast to the images of donors who kneel in sober prayer in the foreground of the Crucifixion in contemporary altarpieces, Margery darts through the successive tableaux of the Passion, stationing herself at the foot of the Cross, lurking at the edge of the burial. Her dynamic performance models an exemplary emotional response that communicates itself to her audience as appropriate to meditation on the Passion story.

Finally, Margery's most extreme emotional script is inaugurated when she experiences a powerful vision at Calvary itself; to her habitual weeping and sobbing is added 'krying and roryng ... so lowde and so wondyrful that it made the pepyl astoynd' (p. 163). This involuntary display recurs over some ten years, triggered by a range of stimuli, from the sight of wounded men, beaten children and suffering animals to male babies and handsome men, recalling the suffering Christ or Christ in his perfect manhood. Artworks, such as crucifixes and pietàs, as well as sermons and rituals elicit some of the most disruptive and disturbing of Margery's emotional displays.[83] Such images are of course intended to function as 'a site of devotional self-fashioning for both the virtuous and sinful, orthodox and heterodox participant'.[84] These images are culturally understood as able to generate emotion in those who look at and mediate upon them ('affective gazing' in Salih's terms); they are objects in spaces where religiously oriented events are expected to happen.[85] In a church in Norwich, Margery views a *pyte* or pietà, the image of the Virgin holding the dead Christ in her arms, as she had held the infant Christ on her lap. This was a relatively new representational form, popularised only from the beginning of the fifteenth century, but already generating lyrics and visual depictions. The image brings the biblical scene so vividly to mind that Margery is compelled 'to cryyn ful lowed and wepyn ful sor, as thei sche schulde a deyde' (p. 286). In response, a priest observes, 'Damsel, Jhesu is ded long sythen', but his employer, a pious lady who intends to invite Margery to dinner, reproves him, 'Ser, it is a good exampyl to me, and to other men also, the grace that God werkyth in hir sowle' (p. 286). Priest and lady thus model opposed responses to Margery's performance; the priest reveals the superficial nature of his faith, while the lady recognises God at work in the world. That Margery's most challenging behaviour is to be regarded as exemplary is discussed further below.

The deep affect that so possesses Margery cannot be subjected to cognitive control, feelings that burst out of her in public performances of devotion both inspire and alienate those who witness them. 'Margery's crying exhibits her lack of ownership of her own body, making visible her usually invisible hosting of Christ within her, producing the fascinating and uncanny spectacle of her as puppet, animated by greater forces', writes Salih, who insightfully analyses the crying emotion-episodes in terms of performance.[86] While the *Book* aims to justify these troubling emotional performances, it also suggests ways in which they are performative: her actions and behaviour change things in the world for Margery herself and those who encounter her. Margery's performances function as self-fashioning, creating and maintaining her religious identity, as pious laywoman, but also as female mystic in the tradition of Marie d'Oignies and Birgitta of Sweden. They challenge the faith, imagination and understanding of those who witness her displays, flushing out hollowness and hypocrisy within the contemporary church and opening up opportunities for ordinary people to recognise and respond emotionally to Margery's holiness, as for example when she travels with a company of women in Italy who have an image of the Christ child that they display to the pious (pp. 177–8) and who show her kindness and respect.[87]

Foregrounding the profound affects, the crying and the gift of tears that she experiences for ten years, Margery's *Book* functions as an exemplary text: not only does it aim to demonstrate to others the goodness of God, as the Prologue states, but it also instructs lay audiences in how they too might assure themselves of salvation and God's love for them, through faith and witness. Emotion is key to this communicative function; the *Book* shows Margery deeply embedding herself in (often) female community wherever she travels.[88] Margery's community is created and sustained through the feelings she engenders as emotional and suffering subject, in response to threat from ecclesiastical authorities and to her spontaneous passionate outbursts of crying and weeping. Exemplarity is thus a product of the *Book*'s own emotionality; within the text Margery triggers affect in, and transmits emotion to, other believers, creating a transnational emotional community of supporters, often women, sympathetic priests and confessors, but equally often ordinary laypeople: 'hir communycacion was so mech in the lofe of God that the herars wer oftyntyme steryd therthorw to wepyn ryt sadly' (pp. 111–12). This loosely formed community exists in opposition to a more normative emotional consensus both in English towns and in her travels across Europe, where Margery is repeatedly confronted and challenged by the other citizens of Lynn, the authoritarian church hierarchy, her fellow-pilgrims and others.[89]

Book II recurs substantially to the biographical mode that initiated Book I. It explains the complex emotions that had characterised the bond between mother and son: her reprehension of his way of life and warning of divine punishment; the son's contracting of disease and its healing through his mother's prayers; his conversion, his marriage and his death while he and his wife are visiting his mother in East Anglia. In Book II the journey becomes the narrative's main organising principle; Margery's communications with God are subordinated to her adventures, travelling with her daughter-in-law to Danzig, and her travails in getting home again. The dominant emotions here are anxiety whenever she is abandoned by one of her travelling companions, fear of sexual assault and terror of crossing the sea, including the humiliation of sea-sickness. There is a striking example of Schadenfreude as she crosses the Channel on her way home; a woman who had reneged on promises of help and had snubbed her is extremely sick, 'whom sche was most besy to helpyn and comfortyn, for owr Lordys love and be charite – other cawse had sche non!' (p. 414). The events in this book occur after the cessation of the noisy 'crying', but Margery's habitual weeping and sobbing still draws both admiration and annoyance, as on her previous pilgrimages.

Unlike Chaucer's and Hoccleve's autofiction, Margery's work is not primarily intended to position the subject within the contemporary literary economy – or at least not within their secular world of patronage, scribal networks and coterie audiences. Yet the *Book*'s frequent citation of the Bible and contemporary authorities, flagged up by its monastic annotators, serves to insert the work – and thereby Margery's self – within a pre-existing nexus of texts and sources, not read by, but read to, Margery. These authorities include other mystical works, religious lyrics and homilies; their presence in the text generates and sustains emotionality in Margery and in her intended audiences: her positioning within the network functions as a key authorising strategy for a vernacular, generically hybrid and female-voiced work.

The surviving manuscript of Margery's text was written by a Norwich scribe, Richard Salthouse, perhaps as part of a wider initiative to disseminate the *Book* after Margery's death. The manuscript is arranged, as Samira Lindstedt notes, as an *ordinatio*, a text designed to make possible 'a more ratiocinative scrutiny of the text and consultation for reference purposes'.[90] The manuscript was preserved at, and was evidently keenly read in, the Carthusian priory of Mount Grace in Yorkshire, finding an elite audience who knew how to read Margery's autofiction, annotating it and commenting on it in at least four hands and authenticating the text as relevant and valuable to a monastic community. The exemplarity of the *Book* to medieval Christians is evidenced by the publication of abridged extracts from it by Wynkyn de Worde (1501) and later by Henry Pepwell (1521).[91] Margery is refigured by Pepwell as 'a devoute ancresse', but both de Worde and Pepwell take pains to identify the book from which their extracts are taken with the name of its author; indeed de Worde 'literally equates Margery and her text', 'a shorte treatyse called Margerie Kempe de Lynn'.[92] The autofiction is largely excised from these versions, and the emotional behaviour toned down. De Worde nonetheless retains one of Margery's most habitual emotional practices: 'whan she sawe the crucyfyxe, or yf she sawe a man had a wounde, or a best, or yf a man bete a childe before her, or smote a hors or another beste with a whyp, if she myght se it or here it, she thought she sawe our Lorde beten or wounded'.[93] This is excerpted from the long chapter 28, which describes the onset of the 'fyrst cry that evyr sche cryed in any contemplacyon' on Calvary and the conditions under which it recurred. De Worde thus identifies that key trope of Margery's emotional schemas, the collapsing of real time and Gospel time into one another and the fusing of emotional responses to Christ's life and redemption with affect in the here and now. Margery's *Book* bears witness to the vital importance of emotion in creating a Christian disposition, one that can learn to weather earthly vicissitudes and to harbour secure hopes of heaven.

The two late medieval innovations discussed in this chapter, the generic innovation of the long-form prose romance and the emergence of autofictional literary accounts of individual interiority, were to prove foundational for the history of literary emotion in the early modern period. The long-form romance, as exemplified by Sidney's *Arcadia*, encouraged the exploration of emotion; prosimetrical narrative combined the expansive possibilities of prose with the intense lyricism of verse. New lyrical forms, most markedly in the sonnet, would create space for emotion as voiced by an introspective speaking 'I', expanding possibilities for expressing interior processes and conditions, when talking about the emotional self. Italian secular and anthropocentric thinking had already reshaped Chaucer's poetic imagination in the late fourteenth century, but in the sixteenth century the ways in which humans feel would be foregrounded as a site for literary exploration without necessarily framing those feelings primarily in relationship to God: consider Chaucer's closing exhortations to the 'yonge fresshe folkes' that each of them 'your herte up casteth the visage / To thilke God that after his image / Yow made' at the end of *Troilus and Criseyde* (V: 1838–40), as contrasted with Hamlet's 'What a piece of work is a man!' New emotional schemas and scripts, deployed in innovative literary genres that would come into being in the sixteenth century such as the sonnet-sequence, the drama and interlude, and the prosimetrum, continued the reshaping of the English literary emotional repertoire, evolving in response to revolutions in religious, scientific, geographic and political conceptualisations.

Notes

1. Flannery, *Practising Shame*, p. 15.
2. Stephanie Trigg, 'Afterword: Reading Historical Emotions', in Marculescu and Morand Métivier (eds), *Affective and Emotional Economies*, pp. 247–51 at p. 249.
3. Elizabeth Fowler, *Literary Character: The Human Figure in Early English Writing* (Ithaca, NY: Cornell University Press, 2003), pp. 1–31 at p. 19.
4. Ibid., p. 3. Compare the Introduction's discussion of Monique Scheer, 'Are Emotions a Kind of Practice' (pp. 26–7 above).
5. Fowler, *Literary Character*, p. 4.
6. Ibid., p. 37.
7. Ibid., p. 36.
8. For the development of English literary humanism, see Daniel Wakelin, *Humanism, Reading, and English Literature 1430–1530* (Oxford: Oxford University Press, 2007), noting his definition of humanism as the study of the classics, distinct from the anthropocentric or secular turn in Chaucer (p. 7).
9. See Fowler's chapter in *Literary Character* on Skelton's 'The Tunnyng of Elynoure Rummynge', pp. 134–78, and John Bowers, 'Introduction to "The Canterbury Interlude and Merchant's Tale of Beryn"', in John Bowers (ed.), *The Canterbury Tales: Fifteenth-Century Continuations and Additions* (Kalamazoo, MI: Medieval Institute Publications, 1992), https://d.lib.rochester.edu/teams/text/bowers-canterbury-tales-fifteenth-century-interlude-and-merchants-tale-of-beryn-introduction.
10. Orlemanski, 'Literary Genre', p. 1258.
11. Helen Cooper, 'Romance after 1400', in Wallace (ed.), *The Cambridge History of Medieval English Literature*, pp. 690–719 at p. 691.
12. See Barry Windeatt, 'Chaucer and Fifteenth-Century Romance: *Partonope of Blois*', in Ruth Morse and Barry Windeatt (eds), *Chaucer Traditions: Studies in Honour of Derek Brewer* (Cambridge: Cambridge University Press, 1990), pp. 62–80.

13 See Penny Eley, *Partonopeus de Blois: Romance in the Making*, Gallica 21 (Cambridge: D. S. Brewer, 2011), 'Introduction', pp. 1–17 for the textual history of *Partonopeus*.
14 John Metham, *Amoryus and Cleopes*, ed. Stephen Page (Kalamazoo, MI: Medieval Institute Publications, 1999), https://d.lib.rochester.edu/teams/publication/page-metham-amoryus-and-cleopes.
15 See Jocelyn Wogan-Browne, '"Bet … to … rede on holy seyntes lyves …": Romance and Hagiography Again', in Carol M. Meale (ed.) *Readings in Medieval English Romance* (Cambridge: D. S. Brewer, 1994), pp. 83–97, and Tracy Adams, 'Printing and the Transformation of the Middle English Romance', *Neophilologus*, 82 (1998), 291–310. On the Thornton manuscripts see Fein (ed.), *Robert Thornton and his Books*.
16 On these romances as read in the political context of the fifteenth century, see Raluca Radulescu, *Romance and its Contexts in Fifteenth-Century England* (Woodbridge: Boydell and Brewer, 2013), pp. 40–86.
17 See for John Paston II's book collection Norman Davis (ed.), *The Paston Letters and Papers of the Fifteenth Century*, 2 vols (Oxford: Clarendon Press, 1971–6), vol. 1, pp. 517–18.
18 Norman F. Blake, 'Investigations into the Prologues and Epilogues of William Caxton', *Bulletin of the John Rylands Library*, 49:1 (1966), 17–46; Norman F. Blake (ed. and intro.), *Caxton's Own Prose* (London: Deutsch, 1973) and John Flood, '"Volentes sibi comparare infrascriptos libros impressos …": Printed Books as a Commercial Commodity in the Fifteenth Century', in Kristian Jensen (ed.), *Incunabula and their Readers: Printing, Selling and Using Books in the Fifteenth Century* (London: British Library, 2003), pp. 139–51.
19 Adams, 'Printing and the Transformation', pp. 295–9.
20 Cooper, 'Romance after 1400', p. 691.
21 On the evidence for the print publication of the work see Tania M. Colwell, 'The Middle English *Melusine*: Evidence for an Early Edition of the Prose Romance in the Bodleian Library', *Journal of the Early Book Society for the Study of Manuscripts and Printing History*, 17 (2014), 254–82, 409–10, and Tania M. Colwell, 'Fragments of the *Roman de Mélusine* in the Upton House Bearsted Collection', *The Library*, 13:3 (2012), 279–315, https://doi.org/10.1093/library/13.3.279.
22 Cooper, 'Romance after 1400'.
23 *Stanzaic Morte Arthur*, ed. Benson and Foster, lines 1816–23.
24 Frappier (ed.) *La mort le roi Artu*, p. 116; Lacy et al. (eds and trans.), *Lancelot-Grail*, vol. IV, p. 121.

25 Frappier (ed.) *La mort le roi Artu*, pp. 116–17; Lacy et al. (eds and trans.), *Lancelot-Grail*, vol. IV, p. 121.
26 See Chapter 2, pp. 120–1.
27 Couldrette, *The Romans of Partenay, or of Lusignen: Otherwise Known as the Tale of Melusine*, ed. Walter W. Skeat (London: N. Trübner for EETS, 1866); Alexander K. Donald (ed.), *Prose Melusine*, Middle English trans. anon. (Millwood, NY: Kraus Reprint, 1981). Further references to *The Romans of Partenay* are given in text.
28 Jean d'Arras, *Melusine: ou la noble histoire de Lusignan*, ed. and trans. Jean-Jacques Vincensini (Paris: Lettres Gothiques, 2003), p. 694. My translation.
29 Donald (ed.), *Prose Melusine*, p. 316.
30 *Octavian*, in Harriet Hudson (ed.), *Four Middle English Romances: Isumbras, Octavian, Sir Eglamour of Artois, Sir Tryamour* (Kalamazoo: MI: TEAMS, 2006), https://d.lib.rochester.edu/teams/text/hudson-octavian.
31 *The Erle of Toulous*, in Laskaya and Salisbury (eds), *The Middle English Breton Lays*.
32 Arthur Dixon (ed.), *Valentine and Orson* (London: EETS, 1937).
33 Leon Kellner (ed.), *Blanchardyn and Eglantine* (London: N. Trübner for EETS, 1890). Further references are given in text. See Anne Clark Bartlett, 'Translation, Self-Representation, and Statecraft: Lady Margaret Beaufort and Caxton's *Blanchardyn and Eglantine* (1489)', *Essays in Medieval Studies*, 22 (2005), 53–66.
34 A. Trampe Bödtker (ed.), *Partonope of Blois* (London: Oxford University Press, 1912). Further references are given in text. See also Brenda Hosington, 'Voices of Protest and Submission: Portraits of Women in *Partonopeu de Blois* and its Middle English Translation', *Reading Medieval Studies*, 17 (1991), 51–75.
35 See Eley, *Partonopeus de Blois*, pp. 19–49 for discussion of Partonopeus's unusually young age, in particular the question of whether 'xviij' is correct in the English manuscripts (p. 21, n. 7).
36 See Amy N. Vines, 'A Woman's "Crafte": Melior as Lover, Teacher and Patron in the Middle English Partonope of Blois', *Modern Philology*, 105:2 (2007), 245–70, particularly pp. 249–53.
37 See Karen A. Grossweiner, 'A Tripartite Model for Determining Narratorial Subjectivity in Medieval Romance: The Composite Subject in *Partonope of Blois*', *Studies in Philology*, 109:4 (2012), 381–408 for a full discussion of the narratorial self in *Partonope*.
38 Ibid., pp. 402–3.
39 Windeatt, 'Chaucer and Fifteenth-Century Romance'.

40 Vines, 'A Woman's "Crafte"', p. 246, n. 3.
41 Rebecca McNamara and Juanita Ruys, 'Unlocking the Silences of the Self-Murdered: Textual Approaches to Suicidal Emotions in the Middle Ages', *Exemplaria*, 26 (2014), 58–80 at p. 75.
42 Karen A. Winstead, *The Oxford History of Life-Writing*, vol. 1: *The Middle Ages* (Oxford: Oxford University Press, 2018), p. 2.
43 Ibid., pp. 131–42.
44 Ibid., p. 132.
45 Kathryn Kerby-Fulton, *The Clerical Proletariat and the Resurgence of Medieval English Poetry* (Philadelphia, PA: University of Pennsylvania Press, 2021), pp. 77–97, makes a strong argument for Hoccleve's knowledge of Langland, noting the similarities between Hoccleve's autobiographical positioning and Langland's 'Apologia' in the C-text. See also Kerby-Fulton, *The Clerical Proletariat*, pp. 110–39 for a close study of the Langlandian echoes in *The Regiment*.
46 For Hoccleve's working conditions see Ethan Knapp, 'Bureaucratic Identity and the Construction of the Self in Hoccleve's *Formulary* and *La Male Regle*', *Speculum*, 74:2 (1999), 357–76.
47 Lee Patterson, '"What is Me?" Hoccleve and the Trials of the Urban Self', in Lee Patterson, *Acts of Recognition: Essays on Medieval Culture* (Indianapolis, IN: University of Notre Dame Press, 2009), pp. 84–109 at p. 84.
48 John Burrow, 'Autobiographical Poetry in the Middle Ages: The Case of Thomas Hoccleve', *PBA*, 68 (1982) 389–412, here pp. 401–2.
49 '*La Male Regle* de T. Hoccleve', in M. C. Seymour (ed.), *Selections from Hoccleve* (Oxford: Oxford University Press, 1981), pp. 12–23, Oxford Scholarly Editions Online, 10.1093/actrade/9780198710837. book. All further references are given in text.
50 I refer to the speaker-persona as Hoccleve, though I am aware that this term designates 'an effect of the text', who narrates the poetic process, as Julie Orlemanski notes, rather than the historical person (see p. 251.).
51 On the strategic nature of Hoccleve's characterisation of himself as a coward, see Andrew Lynch, '"Manly Cowardyse": Thomas Hoccleve's Peace Strategy', *Medium Ævum*, 73:2 (2004), 306–23.
52 See Jessica L. Tracy, Richard W. Robins and June Price Tangney (eds), *The Self-Conscious Emotions: Theory and Research*, 2nd edn (New York: Guilford Press, 2007).
53 Knapp, 'Bureaucratic Identity', p. 373.
54 Christian Lorentzen, 'Sheila Heti, Ben Lerner and Tao Lin, 'How "Auto" is "Autofiction"?', *Vulture*, 11 May 2018, www.vulture.

com/2018/05/how-auto-is-autofiction.html (accessed 29 August 2023).
55 Ibid.
56 See Patterson, '"What is Me?"', pp. 86–8 for a summary discussion of Hoccleve and the self in *The Regiment* and Kerby-Fulton, *The Clerical Proletariat*, pp. 110–39.
57 All quotations from John Burrow (ed.), *Thomas Hoccleve's Complaint and Dialogue*, EETS OS 313 (Oxford: Oxford University Press, 1999); line references are given in text. Sebastian Sobecki has recently made a compelling argument for dating the composition of the *Series* to the spring of 1421, reading the poems as enacting a year of mourning for his friend John Bailey. Sebastian Sobecki, *Last Words: The Public Self and the Late Medieval Author* (Oxford: Oxford University Press, 2019), pp. 65–100.
58 Julie Orlemanski, *Symptomatic Subjects: Bodies, Medicine, and Causation in the Literature of Late Medieval England* (Philadelphia, PA: University of Pennsylvania Press, 2019), pp. 217–48, here at p. 217.
59 Ibid., p. 218.
60 See David Mills, 'The Voices of Thomas Hoccleve', in Catherine Batt (ed.), *Essays on Thomas Hoccleve* (London: Brepols, 1996), pp. 85–107 at pp. 88–9 for thoughtful analysis of this verse.
61 *MED*, s.v. 'disdain(e)'.
62 See Rowland S. Miller, 'Is Embarrassment a Blessing or a Curse?', in Tracy et al. (eds), *The Self-Conscious Emotions*, pp. 245–62 for a useful account of embarrassment, clearly distinguishing it from shame.
63 Orlemanski, *Symptomatic Subjects*, p. 230.
64 Ibid., p. 231.
65 See A. G. Rigg, 'Hoccleve's *Complaint* and Isidore of Seville', *Speculum*, 45 (1970), 564–74, and John Burrow, 'Hoccleve's *Complaint* and Isidore of Seville Again', *Speculum*, 73 (1998), 424–8.
66 Orlemanski, *Symptomatic Subjects*, p. 231.
67 Knapp, 'Bureaucratic Identity', p. 391.
68 Patterson, '"What is Me?"', p. 87.
69 Orlemanski, *Symptomatic Subjects*, p. 242.
70 Laurie Atkinson, '"Why þat yee meeued been / can I nat knowe": Autobiography, Convention, and Discerning Doublenesse in Thomas Hoccleve's *The Series*', *Neophilologus*, 101 (2017), 479–94 at p. 479.
71 Derek Pearsall, 'The English Chaucerians', in Derek Brewer (ed.), *Chaucer and Chaucerians: Critical Studies in Middle English Literature* (London: Nelson, 1966), pp. 201–29 at p. 223.

72 See Linda Olson and Kathryn Kerby-Fulton (eds), *Voices in Dialogue: Reading Women in the Middle Ages* (Notre Dame, IN: University of Notre Dame Press, 2005) for discussion of the female mystic and male amanuensis model, and Felicity Riddy, 'Text and Self in *The Book of Margery Kempe*' in the same volume, pp. 439–43.
73 Winstead, *Oxford History of Life-Writing*, vol. 1, p. 77.
74 '[O]ne cannot help but wonder whether at least some of the events that Margery seems to experience in "bodily wits outwardly" were in fact part of her virtual life', speculates Winstead, ibid.
75 Kempe, *The Book of Margery Kempe*, ed. Windeatt, pp. 41–50.
76 Winstead, *Oxford History of Life-Writing*, vol. 1, p. 78. See also Anthony Bale, 'Introduction', in *The Book of Margery Kempe*, trans. Anthony Bale (Oxford: Oxford World's Classics, 2015), pp. ix–xxiii, at pp. xviii–xix, and note Bale's comment at n. 30.
77 Rosenwein, *Generations of Feeling*, pp. 204–5.
78 The third-person designation is 'a mode of figuration that both inscribes her divided identity and precludes the reader's encounter with a knowable life'. Ruth Evans, '*The Book of Margery Kempe*: Autobiography in the Third Person', in Laura Kalas and Laura Varnam (eds), *Encountering the Book of Margery Kempe* (Manchester: Manchester University Press, 2021), pp. 83–100 at p. 84.
79 Winstead, *Oxford History of Life-Writing*, vol. 1, p. 73.
80 Compare also the comfort taken from the Archbishop of Canterbury granting Margery permission to choose her own confessor and to take the Eucharist every Sunday (*The Book of Margery Kempe*, p. 110).
81 Rosenwein, *Generations of Feeling*, p. 197. Rosenwein also notes the preference that the *Book* has in reporting scorn and rebuke and Margery's isolation, rather than showing her affective network of allies.
82 Sarah Salih, 'Writing Performed Lives: Margery Kempe Meets Marina Abramovic', in Kalas and Varnam (eds), *Encountering the Book of Margery Kempe*, pp. 259–77 at p. 265.
83 See Laura Varnam, 'The Crucifix, the Pietà, and the Female Mystic', *Journal of Medieval Religious Cultures*, 41:2 (2015), 208–37 for an important reading of the affect that comes into play when the devotee encounters an item of religious art.
84 Patterson, '"What is Me?"', p. 219.
85 Sarah Salih, 'Erotica', in Ruth Evans (ed.), *A Cultural History of Sexuality in the Middle Ages*, 2 vols (Oxford: Berg, 2011), vol. 2, pp. 181–212 at p. 208.
86 Salih, 'Writing Performed Lives', pp. 266–7.

87 See Laura Varnam, '"A booke of hyr felyngys": Exemplarity and Margery Kempe's Encounters of the Heart', in Kalas and Varnam (eds), *Encountering the Book of Margery Kempe*, pp. 140–59 at p. 147 for comparable sympathetic responses among Margery's female companions.
88 Patterson, '"What is Me?"'
89 See Rosenwein, *Generations of Feeling*, pp. 195–202 on the emotional communities broadly constituted by those who criticised and reprehended Margery's displays and those who approved, and even participated in, her emotional repertoire.
90 Malcolm B. Parkes, 'The Influence of the Concepts of *Ordinatio* and *Compilatio* on the Development of the Book', in J. J. G. Alexander and M. T. Gibson (eds), *Medieval Learning and Literature: Essays Presented to Richard William Hunt* (Oxford: Clarendon Press, 1976), pp. 113–41 at p. 115, cited from Samira Lindstedt, 'The *Examinacio Dura* of Margery Kempe: Annotation as Authentication in Additional MS 61823', *The Medieval Journal*, 17:2 (2017), 73–102 at p. 77.
91 See Allyson Foster, 'A *Shorte Treatyse of Contemplacyon*: The *Book of Margery Kempe* in its Early Print Contexts', in John Arnold and Katherine Lewis (eds), *A Companion to the Book of Margery Kempe* (Woodbridge: D. S. Brewer, 2004), pp. 95–112.
92 Lindstedt, 'The *Examinacio Dura*', p. 95.
93 'A Shorte Treatyse of Contemplacyon … Taken out of the Bok of Margerie Kempe of Lynn', in *The Book of Margery Kempe*, ed. Windeatt, pp. 429–34 at p. 431.

Conclusion

Emotion is 'an act situated in and composed of interdependent cognitive, somatic, and social components, mixed in varying proportions, depending on the practical logic of the situation in which it takes place', writes Monique Scheer.[1] This book has explored the most important ways in which literary texts composed in Middle English contribute to our understanding of these components within specific genres and changing contexts. The English lexis of feeling expanded enormously from around 1200 when Middle English texts began to be written and preserved, an expansion that continued into the fifteenth century. The semantic field of emotion was remapped as words borrowed from Latin, Old Norse and primarily French were adopted; certain emotional subfields were recalibrated in ways that can be only partially understood using modern emotional lexical systems as an interpretative framework. Yet it is clear from this expansion that writers in Middle English were increasingly interested in emotion. It functioned chiefly as a driver of plot, but it also developed as a key element in the characterisation of individuals. Although we have no word lists of emotion in English until late in the period, analyses of the seven deadly sins serve not only to name emotional states, but very often to embody them, to delineate key emotional behaviours and relate them to the active Christian life. Translation from Insular and Central French was a primary vector for the adoption of new lexis; it also served to recalibrate the native emotional system, particularly by introducing emotions closely associated with courtly identities. The emotion repertoires of French romance were not imported wholesale; rather they were heavily adapted for the new English 'textual communities' that consumed them. Long emotional dialogues and internal monologues are curtailed, authorial comment on emotion – psychonarration – is omitted or rendered only briefly, and accounts of bodily emotion are also reduced. This was typically the case as romance first developed as a genre in early Middle English; by the fifteenth century, as we saw in Chapter 5, extended emotional scenes, staged through both dialogue and narration, were now judged as catering to popular taste and incorporated into romances intended for new audiences. Generic hybridisation is particularly important in expanding the emotional possibilities of certain genres; blending the scripts of hagiography and romance creates a subgenre that explores a gamut of emotions from horror to fear, from joy to spiritual peace. Romance bleeds into devotional literature: tropes such as Christ the Lover-Knight are widely adopted in the service of affectively oriented meditation. Emotional change is facilitated by such lexical, taxonomic and generic innovation; new emotion schemas and scripts become familiar and available to their consumers through the circulation of literary texts.

Emotion is almost always embodied in medieval texts. The bodies of characters are imagined as sites where emotion is displayed and made legible to those who witness it, both within the text and among its audiences. The affect that underlies somatic signs is by no means unambiguous for medieval or contemporary audiences to interpret; colour changes or trembling, for example, may denote different emotions that can be determined only in relation to social – or generic – norms. Although Augustine had distinguished clearly between willed and non-willed bodily indicia of affect, medieval authors are less decisive. The body's expression of emotions may not always be guaranteed as authentic or sincere: women's weeping comes under sceptical scrutiny. Here in the realm of the body questions of interiority and external appearance become critical: does the body betray or conceal emotion? The repertoire of corporeal signs of emotion, whether involuntary or deliberate, does not change much over the period, but the space that authors devote to them expands. As interiority begins to be more consistently narrated, newer, apparently more self-conscious emotions appear: remorse, embarrassment, jealousy, each embodied through somatic and gestural scripts. While these emotions emerge alongside the already well-attested socially oriented feelings of shame and pride, they are only later identified through new lexis. Remorse, of mind or of conscience, is first encountered in fifteenth-century religious, often penitential texts. Embarrassment in the *Oxford English Dictionary*'s sense (3a) of intense emotional shame or awkwardness, occasioned by a social situation, rather than the sense of a material hindrance is first evidenced only in the seventeenth century. Jealousy appears in *Ancrene Wisse*, where it is attributed to God with a different meaning from the later sense. Also mentioned in the penitential manual *Handlyng Synne* from around 1300, it becomes widespread in its current meaning in English only in the very late fourteenth century and fifteenth century. Yet even if jealousy, remorse and embarrassment, along with annoyance and irritation, had no names, authors were well able to depict them as arising in particular social contexts, often subsumed into the broader emotional subfields of shame, anger and fear.

Performativity is emotion's primary function at the scale of the macronarrative. Emotions drive intentionality, underlie utterances and gestures and motivate action. When a character speaks or acts, they or the author may indicate which emotions are in play, but more often the audience is invited to infer the emotional import of what is said or done, and how successful it is at effecting change within the textual world. Performativity is the key point at which emotions intersect with ethics; the character's feelings are powerfully inflected by immediate or more distant goals, and strongly associated with the will. Augustine had emphasised the will's crucial role in determining which object is desired or rejected, and the intensity of the emotion generated by that inclination or revulsion. Medieval authors might sometimes apostrophise their characters, to criticise their behaviour and the feelings which underlie them, while audience judgement is also called for: sometimes explicitly, as in Chaucer's 'Franklin's Tale', for example, but sometimes by implication. Performance proves to be a valuable concept for the analysis of emotions at the level of plot and of thematic development. It is here that literary texts intersect with historians' insights into the roles of ritual and theatricality in medieval contexts: the potential gap between emotions displayed for instrumental purposes and the subject's own emotional position. Awareness of that gap contributes not only to the understanding that exterior display and interiority need not match, but also to the burgeoning fascination, well evidenced already in the fourteenth century, with the individual interiority of literary characters. Now audiences become interested not only in the hero, but in this hero, and how he feels about the latest vicissitude to which he has been subjected. In connection to this new intensified focus on the individual's emotions, Reddy's concept of the emotive turns out to be more useful in medieval literary emotion study than has hitherto been thought. Authors such as Chaucer, the *Gawain*-poet, Gower, Malory and Hoccleve, along with Margery Kempe, use speech to reveal internal emotional states to the speakers themselves; these are utterances that may not succeed as performatives within the textual world, but nevertheless provide significant new insights into interior disposition. That the emotive can function as 'managerial', providing a way to discipline excessive emotion into conformity with relevant social scripts, is an important observation for the extended function of dialogue in later medieval romances, in particular.

The concept of performance, an awareness of who is watching, what they will conclude from what they see and hear and the likely consequences in terms of action, intersects usefully with the expanding field of cognitive theory in medieval studies.[2] Classic cognitive theory engages with the four 'E's: cognition as embodied, embedded, enacted and extended.[3] Minds are contained within bodies, bodies that exist within particular social, cultural and historical environments. They constantly connect external perception to internal process and thus enact behavioural responses. Lastly, minds can be extended beyond the body into other systems: most relevantly, within the processes of textual reproduction, into manuscripts, scribes, publishers and translators. Emotion runs in parallel to these mental processes: mind and feeling coexist even at the extended level, as Margery Kempe's emotions about the writing of her *Book* and the amanuenses who bring it into being bear witness. Theory of mind – the capacity to hypothesise what is occurring in other minds (both real and imagined) – likewise intersects with the notion of empathy: the understanding how and why others might feel about their situations. The consumption of literary texts thus contributes to real-world enhancement of social skills: the capacity to understand how and why others think and feel and to respond accordingly; it thus, if indirectly, answers the criticisms of Augustine, Ælred and the authors of the *Tretise of Miraclis Pleyinge*: that literary emotion is insincere, factitious and a dangerous distraction from the individual's project of salvation.

If medieval literary texts are designed to produce emotion in their audiences, techniques to create empathy and to direct cognitive processing are crucial to their composition. Conventional literary critical methods assist the modern reader in identifying auditory techniques of rhyme, rhythm and alliteration, imagery patterns and rhetorical devices, all of which work to create emotional effects in audiences and readers. Simulation theory, proposing the brain mechanisms by which we construct, participate in and flesh out the details of imaginary worlds, has proved a useful way of thinking about how literary texts generate emotional responses. Theories of social contagion illuminate some of the shared and intensified emotional effects of communal audience experience. Film theory makes possible an understanding of how consumer emotion encompasses three emotional aspects: empathetic feelings produced by the fiction, pleasure or annoyance generated by the artefact's particular aesthetic qualities and the lasting expansion of the individual listener's own set of emotional schemas: the 'teaching how to feel', as McNamer puts it.[4] The kinds of feeling to which McNamer attends are those that underpin the project of devotional self-fashioning: the construction of a Christian selfhood that will bring the reward of salvation. This goal however, as Ashe notes, offers 'no inherent justification ... for individuality, or a belief in uniqueness' for these are irrelevant to the project of Christian conformity.[5] For the secular subject, conscious of their own interior distinctiveness, engaged in seeking 'personal satisfaction and fulfilment', it was romance, par excellence, that provided the tools for emotional growth and self-understanding, and for refining their sense of the individuality of others.[6]

By the beginning of the fifteenth century Chaucer and the *Gawain*-poet had revolutionised the writing of interiority in Middle English literature. The *Gawain*-poet allows intermittent but vivid access to Gawain's emotional state as he seeks to resist the Lady and to prepare himself for the Beheading game, and he delineates Jonah's changing feelings about his prophetic mission and the grief of the Dreamer in *Pearl* with extensive use of psycho-narration, dialogue and bodily indices of feeling to convey changing emotional states. In *Troilus and Criseyde* Chaucer employs these techniques (alongside inset genres such as letters and songs with their own distinctive emotional schemas) to explore the emotions of his principal characters. He also pioneers the cross-textual fictional persona, the 'Geffrye' who both is, and is not, recognisable across the dream-poems, *Troilus* and *The Canterbury Tales*, where he is assiduous recorder of the pilgrims' talk and stories and ill-used taleteller. Yet the narrator-persona's emotions are either concealed or conventional; there is nothing confessional in his first-person writing, not even in his *Retractions*. Langland, in contrast, ventures some personal, if unverifiable, details about his own life in the C-text of *Piers Plowman*; '[t]he conventional nature of medieval autobiography would encourage caution in the interpretation of a poem's biographical details', observes Pearsall.[7] The fifteenth-century development of autofiction is partly rooted in these experiments, partly in the authorising force of the dream-vision genre, and partly, as Burrow suggests, stems from speech-acts, performatives that harness and reproduce apposite emotional styles in order to get things done. Thus enabled, writers write themselves and their feelings into their texts: indeed, in the case of Margery Kempe, herself and her feelings are the principal subject of the work.

New audiences and readers, new possibilities for writing, disseminating and publishing arose in the fifteenth century, enabled by the spread of literacy increasingly to women and to different social ranks. The technology of the printing-press, harnessed by Caxton to create new markets and shape literary tastes, created the space for the expanding interest in emotions. Pre-existing genres such as the hybrid penitential romance continued to be copied and circulated; new literary kinds such as the long-form romance featured extended emotional scenes, narrators who were ready to comment on their own feelings about their material, as well as discussing the feelings of their characters, scripted dialogue that presented emotion head-on or evoked new subtle kinds of emotional sensibility.

Conclusion

The sixteenth century would bring new developments in literary emotion: remarkable lexical innovation and fresh categorisations of bodily indices of emotion. The turn to the classics revitalised the emotional repertoire for writers in the humanist tradition with the rediscovery of the rhetorical potentialities of gesture systems. New social conditions entailed different understandings of performativity: among these were changing conceptualisations of the performance of courtly identity and the work of emotional self-fashioning. The Reformation brought about a fundamental reshaping of the forms through which emotional engagement with God could be undertaken, alongside the development of new mechanisms of religious regulation. The expansion of the commercial sphere and the nascent English colonial projects amid the wondrous potentialities of the New World stimulated the imagination of very different kinds of emotional self, in the city comedies of Ben Jonson or Shakespeare's characters in *The Tempest*, for example. While these radical social changes continued the processes of innovation and obsolescence within the literary emotional repertoire, the foundations for understanding early modern emotion – conceptualisations of bodies and affect, the basic lexis of emotion, interest in the interior person and the gap between that interiority and the outward performance of identity – had already been established in the three centuries preceding 1500.[8]

Notes

1 Scheer, 'Are Emotions a Kind of Practice', pp. 219–20.
2 Juliana Dresvina and Victoria Blud (eds), *Cognitive Sciences and Medieval Studies: An Introduction* (Cardiff: University of Wales Press, 2020) provides an illuminating introduction to the application of cognitive theory to medieval texts and objects.
3 Victoria Blud, 'Making Up a Mind: "4E" Cognition and the Medieval Subject', in Dresvina and Blud (eds), *Cognitive Sciences and Medieval Studies*, pp. 163–82. For a fuller account of 4E cognition, see Albert Newen, Leon de Bruin and Shaun Gallagher (eds), *The Oxford Handbook of 4E Cognition* (Oxford: Oxford University Press, 2018).
4 McNamer, *Affective Meditation*, p. 2.
5 Ashe, 'Introduction', p. xx.

6 Ibid., pp. xxi–xxv. See also Ashe, '"For love and for lovers"', pp. 16–17.
7 William Langland, *Piers Plowman: A New Annotated Edition of the C-Text*, ed. Derek Pearsall (Liverpool: Liverpool University Press, 2008), p. 21. See the 'Author's Apologia' (Passus V, lines 1–108) and most recently on the 'Apologia', Kerby-Fulton, *The Clerical Proletariat*, pp. 77–86.
8 See Broomhall (ed.) *Early Modern Emotions* for the many conceptual continuities between the medieval and early modern periods.

Bibliography

Primary sources

Ælred of Rievaulx, *Speculum caritatis*, PL 195, cols 505–658.
Alcuin, *De virtutibus et vitiis liber ad Widonem comitem*, PL 101, cols 613–38.
Andrew, Malcolm, and Ronald Waldron (eds), *The Poems of the Pearl Manuscript*, 5th edn (Liverpool: Liverpool University Press, 2007).
Augustine, *The City of God against the Pagans*, ed. Jeffrey Henderson, trans. various, 7 vols, Loeb Classical Library (Cambridge, MA: Harvard University Press, and London: Heinemann, 1957–72).
Augustine, *De doctrina christiana*, ed. R. P. H. Green (Oxford: Oxford University Press, 1996).
Augustine, *Confessions*, vol. I, ed. and trans. Carolyn J.-B. Hammond, Loeb Classical Library 26 (Cambridge, MA: Harvard University Press, 2014).
Austin, John L., *How to Do Things with Words*, in Urmson and Sbisà (eds), *The Works of J. L. Austin*.
Benedictine Rule, https://www.intratext.com/IXT/LAT0011/ (accessed 29 August 2023).
Benson, Larry D. (gen. ed.), *The Riverside Chaucer* (Oxford: Oxford University Press, 2008).
Bevis of Hampton, in Herzman, Drake and Salisbury (eds), *Four Romances of England: King Horn, Havelok the Dane, Bevis of Hampton, Athelston* (Kalamazoo: Medieval Institute Press, 1997), http://d.lib.rochester.edu/teams/text/salisbury-four-romances-of-england-bevis-of-hampton.
Blake, Norman F. (ed. and intro.), *Caxton's Own Prose* (London: Deutsch, 1973).
Bliss, A. J. (ed.), *Sir Launfal* (London: Nelson, 1960).
Böddeker, Karl (ed.), *Altenglische Dichtungen des Harl. 2253* (Berlin: Weidemann, 1878).

Bödtker, A. Trampe (ed.), *Partonope of Blois* (London: Oxford University Press, 1912).
Bowers, John (ed.), *The Canterbury Tales: Fifteenth-Century Continuations and Additions* (Kalamazoo, MI: Medieval Institute Publications, 1992).
Braswell, Mary Flowers (ed.), *Sir Perceval of Galles and Ywain and Gawain* (Kalamazoo, MI: Medieval Institute, 1995).
Bunt, G. H. V. (ed.), *William of Palerne* (Groningen: Bouma's Boekhuis, 1983).
Burrow, John (ed.), *Thomas Hoccleve's Complaint and Dialogue*, EETS OS 313 (Oxford: Oxford University Press, 1999).
Caxton, William (trans.), *Book of the Knight of the Tour-Landry*, ed. M. Y. Offord, EETS Special Series 2 (Oxford: Oxford University Press, 1971).
Chaucer, Geoffrey, *Anelida and Arcite*, ed. Vincent J. Dimarco, in Benson (gen. ed.), *The Riverside Chaucer*, pp. 375–81.
Chaucer, Geoffrey, *The Book of the Duchess*, ed. Colin Wilcockson, in Benson (gen. ed.), *The Riverside Chaucer*, pp. 329–46.
Chaucer, Geoffrey, 'The Canon's Yeoman's Prologue and Tale', in Benson (ed.), *The Canterbury Tales*, in Benson (gen. ed.), *The Riverside Chaucer*, pp. 270–81.
Chaucer, Geoffrey, *The Canterbury Tales*, ed. Larry D. Benson, in Benson (gen. ed.), *The Riverside Chaucer*, pp. 3–328.
Chaucer, Geoffrey, 'The Clerk's Prologue and Tale', in Benson (ed.), *The Canterbury Tales*, in Benson (gen. ed.), *The Riverside Chaucer*, pp. 137–53.
Chaucer, Geoffrey, *Compleynt of Mars*, ed. Laila Z. Gross, in Benson (gen. ed.), *The Riverside Chaucer*, pp. 643–7.
Chaucer, Geoffrey, 'The Franklin's Prologue and Tale', in Benson (ed.), *The Canterbury Tales*, in Benson (gen. ed.), *The Riverside Chaucer*, pp. 177–89.
Chaucer, Geoffrey, 'The Knight's Tale', ed. Larry D. Benson, in Benson (gen. ed.), *The Riverside Chaucer*, pp. 37–66.
Chaucer, Geoffrey, *The Legend of Good Women*, ed. M. C. E. Shaner, in Benson (gen. ed.), *The Riverside Chaucer*, pp. 587–630.
Chaucer, Geoffrey, 'The Man of Law's Prologue, Tale and Epilogue', in Benson (ed.), *The Canterbury Tales*, in Benson (gen. ed.), *The Riverside Chaucer*, pp. 87–104.
Chaucer, Geoffrey, 'The Miller's Prologue and Tale', in Benson (ed.), *The Canterbury Tales*, in Benson (gen. ed.), *The Riverside Chaucer*, pp. 66–77.
Chaucer, Geoffrey, 'The Monk's Prologue and Tale', in Benson (ed.), *The Canterbury Tales*, in Benson (gen. ed.), *The Riverside Chaucer*, pp. 240–52.

Bibliography

Chaucer, Geoffrey, 'The Nun's Priest's Prologue and Tale', in Benson (ed.), *The Canterbury Tales*, in Benson (gen. ed.), *The Riverside Chaucer*, pp. 252–61.

Chaucer, Geoffrey, 'The Pardoner's Prologue and Tale', in Benson (ed.), *The Canterbury Tales*, in Benson (gen. ed.), *The Riverside Chaucer*, pp. 193–202.

Chaucer, Geoffrey, *The Parliament of Fowls*, ed. Larry D. Benson, in Benson (gen. ed.), *The Riverside Chaucer*, pp. 383–394.

Chaucer, Geoffrey, 'The Parson's Prologue and Tale', in Benson (ed.), *The Canterbury Tales*, in Benson (gen. ed.), *The Riverside Chaucer*, pp. 287–327.

Chaucer, Geoffrey, 'The Physician's Tale', in Benson (ed.), *The Canterbury Tales*, in Benson (gen. ed.), *The Riverside Chaucer*, pp. 190–3.

Chaucer, Geoffrey, 'The Prologue and Tale of Sir Thopas', in Benson (ed.), *The Canterbury Tales*, in Benson (gen. ed.), *The Riverside Chaucer*, pp. 212–16.

Chaucer, Geoffrey, 'The Reeve's Prologue and Tale', in Benson (ed.), *The Canterbury Tales*, in Benson (gen. ed.), *The Riverside Chaucer*, pp. 77–84.

Chaucer, Geoffrey, *The Romaunt of the Rose*, ed. Larry D. Benson, in Benson (gen. ed.), *The Riverside Chaucer*, pp. 685–767.

Chaucer, Geoffrey, 'The Summoner's Prologue and Tale', in Benson (ed.), *The Canterbury Tales*, in Benson (gen. ed.), *The Riverside Chaucer*, pp. 126–36.

Chaucer, Geoffrey, *Troilus and Criseyde*, ed. Stephen A. Barney, in Benson (gen. ed.), *The Riverside Chaucer*, pp. 471–585.

Chaucer, Geoffrey, 'The Wife of Bath's Prologue and Tale', in Benson (ed.), *The Canterbury Tales*, in Benson (gen. ed.), *The Riverside Chaucer*, pp. 105–28.

Chestre, Thomas, *Sir Launfal*, ed. A. J. Bliss (London: Nelson, 1960).

Chrétien de Troyes, *Erec*, ed. Jean-Marie Fritz, in Michel Zink (ed.), *Chrétien de Troyes: Romans*.

Chrétien de Troyes, *Le chevalier au lion ou le roman d'Yvain*, ed. David F. Hult, in Michel Zink (ed.), *Chrétien de Troyes: Romans*.

Chrétien de Troyes, *Le conte du Graal*, ed. Charles Méla, in Michel Zink (ed.), *Chrétien de Troyes: Romans*.

Conlee, John (ed.), *William Dunbar: The Complete Works* (Kalamazoo, MI: Medieval Institute, 2004), https://d.lib.rochester.edu/teams/publication/conlee-dunbar-complete-works.

Couldrette, *The Romans of Partenay, or of Lusignen: Otherwise Known as the Tale of Melusine*, ed. Walter W. Skeat (London: N. Trübner for EETS, 1866).

Dahlberg, Charles (trans.), *The Romance of the Rose*, 3rd edn (Princeton, NJ: Princeton University Press, 1971).

Dante Aligheri, *Il Paradiso*, Princeton Dante Project, https://dante.prince ton.edu/dante/pdp/commedia.html.
Davidson, Clifford (ed.), *Tretise of Miraclis Pleyinge* (Kalamazoo, MI, Medieval Institute, 1993).
Davidson, Clifford (ed.), *The York Corpus Christi Plays* (Kalamazoo, MI: Medieval Institute Press, 2011), http://d.lib.rochester.edu/teams/publication/davidson-the-york-corpus-christi-plays.
Davies, R. T. (ed.), *Medieval English Lyrics: A Critical Anthology* (London: Faber and Faber, 1999).
Davis, Norman (ed.), *The Paston Letters and Papers of the Fifteenth Century*, 2 vols (Oxford: Clarendon Press, 1971–6).
Dictionary of Old English, https://doe.artsci.utoronto.ca.
Dixon, Arthur (ed.), *Valentine and Orson* (London: EETS, 1937).
Donald, Alexander K. (ed.), *Prose Melusine*, Middle English trans. anon. (Millwood, NY: Kraus Reprint, 1981).
Dunbar, William, *The Golden Targe*, in John Conlee (ed.), *William Dunbar: The Complete Works*, https://d.lib.rochester.edu/teams/text/conlee-dunbar-complete-works-poems-in-the-courtly-tradition#P65.
Eco, Umberto, *The Name of the Rose*, trans. William Weaver (London: Picador, 1984).
Emare, in Laskaya and Salisbury (eds), *The Middle English Breton Lays*, https://d.lib.rochester.edu/teams/publication/laskaya-and-salisbury-middle-english-breton-lays.
The Erle of Toulous, in Laskaya and Salisbury (eds), *The Middle English Breton Lays*, http://d.lib.rochester.edu/teams/text/laskaya-and-salisbury-middle-english-breton-lays-erle-of-tolous.
Fein, Susanna Greer (ed.), *Moral Love Songs and Laments* (Kalamazoo, MI: Medieval Institute Publications, 1998), https://d.lib.rochester.edu/teams/publication/fein-moral-love-songs-and-laments.
Ferguson, Niall, *Kissinger, 1923–1968: The Idealist* (New York and London: Allen Lane, 2015).
Frappier, Jean (ed.), *La mort le roi Artu: roman du XIIIe siècle* (Geneva: Droz, 1964).
Freedman, A. B., and N. T. Harrington (eds), *Ywain and Gawain*, EETS OS 254 (Oxford: Oxford University Press, 1964).
Furnivall, F. J. (ed.), *Early English Meals and Manners*, EETS OS 32 (London: Oxford University Press, 1868).
Gottfried von Strassburg, *Tristan*, https://www.hs-augsburg.de/~harsch/germanica/Chronologie/13Jh/Gottfried/got_tr00.html.
Gower, John, *Confessio Amantis*, vol. I, ed. Russell A. Peck, trans. Andrew Galloway (Kalamazoo, MI: Medieval Institute Press, 2006), http://d.lib.rochester.edu/teams/publication/peck-confessio-amantis-volume-1.

Gower, John, *Confessio Amantis*, vol. II, ed. Russell A. Peck, trans. Andrew Galloway (Kalamazoo, MI: Medieval Institute Press, 2013), https://d.lib.rochester.edu/teams/publication/peck-gower-confessio-am antis-volume-2.

Gower, John, *Confessio Amantis*, vol. III, ed. Russell A. Peck, trans. Andrew Galloway (Kalamazoo, MI: Medieval Institute Press, 2004), https://d.lib.rochester.edu/teams/publication/peck-confession-aman tis-volume-3.

Hasenfratz, Robert (ed.), *Ancrene Wisse* (Kalamazoo, MI: Medieval Institute Publications, 2000), https://d.lib.rochester.edu/teams/publica tion/hasenfratz-ancrene-wisse.

Havelok, in Herzman, Drake and Salisbury (eds), *Four Romances of England*, https://d.lib.rochester.edu/teams/text/salisbury-havelok-the-da ne-introduction.

Herzman, Ronald B., Graham Drake and Eve Salisbury (eds), *Four Romances of England: King Horn, Havelok the Dane, Bevis of Hampton, Athelston* (Kalamazoo, MI: Medieval Institute Press, 1997), https://d.lib. rochester.edu/teams/publication/salisbury-four-romances-of-england.

Hudson, Harriet (ed.), *Four Middle English Romances: Isumbras, Octavian, Sir Eglamour of Artois, Sir Tryamour* (Kalamazoo, MI: TEAMS, 2006), https://d.lib.rochester.edu/teams/publication/hudson-fo ur-middle-english-romances.

Jacques de Vitry, *Vita Marie de Oegnies*, Corpus Christianorum Continuatio Mediaevalis 252 (Turnhout: Brepols, 2012).

Jean d'Arras, *Melusine: ou la noble histoire de Lusignan*, ed. and trans. Jean-Jacques Vincensini (Paris: Lettres Gothiques, 2003).

Johnston, Alexandra F., and Margaret Rogerson (eds), *Records of Early English Drama: York* (Toronto: University of Toronto Press, 1979).

Julian of Norwich, *The Shewings*, ed. Georgia Ronan Crampton (Kalamazoo: Medieval Institute Press, 1994), https://d.lib.rochester.edu/ teams/publication/crampton-shewings-of-julian-norwich.

Kellner, Leon (ed.), *Blanchardyn and Eglantine* (London: N. Trübner for EETS, 1890).

Kempe, Margery, *The Book of Margery Kempe*, ed. Barry Windeatt (Harlow: Longman, 2000).

Kempe, Margery, *The Book of Margery Kempe*, trans. Anthony Bale (Oxford: Oxford World's Classics, 2015).

King Horn, in Herzman, Drake and Salisbury (eds), *Four Romances of England*, https://d.lib.rochester.edu/teams/text/salisbury-king-horn-intr oduction.

Lacy, Norris J., et al. (eds and trans.), *Lancelot-Grail: The Old French Arthurian Vulgate and Post-Vulgate in Translation*, 5 vols (New York: Garland, 1993–6).

Langland, William, *Piers Plowman: A New Annotated Edition of the C-Text*, ed. Derek Pearsall (Liverpool: Liverpool University Press, 2008).
Langland, William, *Piers Plowman: The B-Version*, ed. A. V. C. Schmidt (London and Toronto: Everyman, 1978).
Langlois, Ernest (ed.), *Le roman de la rose*, 5 vols, Société d'anciens textes français (Paris: Firmin-Didot, 1914–24).
Lanval, in *Lais de Marie de France*, ed. Karl Warnke, trans. with notes by Laurence Harf-Lancer (Paris: Librairie Générale Française, 1990).
Laskaya, Anne, and Eve Salisbury (eds), *The Middle English Breton Lays* (Kalamazoo, MI: Medieval Institute Publications, 1995), https://d.lib.rochester.edu/teams/publication/laskaya-and-salisbury-middle-english-breton-lays.
Love, Nicholas, *Mirror of the Blessed Life of Jesus Christ*, ed. Michael G. Sargent, Garland Medieval Texts 18 (New York and London: Garland, 1992).
Lovelich, Henry, *Merlin*, ed. E. A. Kock, Part I, EETS Extra Series 93 (London: Kegan, Paul, 1904).
Lumiansky, R. M., and David Mills (eds), *The Chester Mystery Cycle*, EETS Special Series 3 (London and New York: Oxford University Press, 1974).
Luria, Maxwell S., and Richard L. Hoffman (eds), *Middle English Lyrics* (London and New York: Norton, 1974).
Lydgate, John, *Troy Book: Selections*, ed. Robert R. Edwards (Kalamazoo, MI, Medieval Institute Press, 1998), http://d.lib.rochester.edu/teams/publication/edwards-lydgate-troy-book-selections.
Malory, Sir Thomas, *Le Morte Darthur*, ed. Peter J. C. Field, 2 vols (Cambridge: D. S. Brewer, 2013).
Metham, John, *Amoryus and Cleopes*, ed. Stephen Page (Kalamazoo, MI: Medieval Institute Publications, 1999), https://d.lib.rochester.edu/teams/publication/page-metham-amoryus-and-cleopes.
Octavian, in Harriet Hudson (ed.), *Four Middle English Romances*, https://d.lib.rochester.edu/teams/text/hudson-octavian.
Ovid, *Metamorphoses II*, ed. Jeffrey Henderson, trans. Frank Justus Miller, 2nd edn, rev. G. P. Goold, Loeb Classical Library 43 (Cambridge, MA: Harvard University Press, 1984).
Pecok, Reginald, *The Donet*, ed. Elsie Vaughan Hitchcock, EETS OS 156 (Oxford: Oxford University Press, 1921).
Peter of Blois, *Liber de confessione sacramentali*, PL 207, cols 1077–1092C.
Rolle, Richard, 'The Form of Living', in S. J. Ogilvie-Thomson (ed.), *Richard Rolle: Prose and Verse* (Oxford: Oxford University Press, 1988), pp. 3–25.

Roussineau, Gilles (ed.), *La Suite du Roman de Merlin*, 2 vols (Geneva: Droz, 1996).
Saupe, Karen (ed.), *Middle English Marian Lyrics* (Kalamazoo, MI: Medieval Institute Publications, 1997).
Sawles Warde, in Bella Millett and Jocelyn Wogan-Browne (eds and trans.), *Medieval English Prose for Women* (Oxford: Clarendon Press, 1990), pp. 86–109.
Seymour, M. C. (ed.), *Selections from Hoccleve* (Oxford: Oxford University Press, 1981), pp. 12–23, Oxford Scholarly Editions Online, 10.1093/actrade/9780198710837.book.
Sir Orfeo, in Laskaya and Salisbury (eds), *The Middle English Breton Lays*, http://d.lib.rochester.edu/teams/text/laskaya-and-salisbury-middle-english-breton-lays-sir-orfeo.
Sir Perceval of Galles, in Braswell (ed.), *Sir Perceval of Galles and Ywain and Gawain*, https://d.lib.rochester.edu/teams/text/braswell-sir-pvercev al-of-galles.
Sir Tristrem, in Alan Lupack (ed.), *Sir Lancelot of the Laik and Sir Tristrem* (Kalamazoo, MI: Medieval Institute Publications, 1994), https://d.lib.rochester.edu/teams/publication/lupack-lancelot-of-the-laik-and-sir-tristrem.
Skelton, John, *Bowge of Court*, www.skeltonproject.org/bowge/.
Smiley, Jane, *Golden Age* (London: Picador, 2015).
The Squire of Low Degree, in Erik Kooper (ed.), *Sentimental and Humorous Romances* (Kalamazoo, MI: Medieval Institute Publications, 2005), https://d.lib.rochester.edu/teams/text/kooper-sentimental-and-hu morous-romances-squire-of-low-degree.
Stanzaic Morte Arthur, in Larry D. Benson and Edward E. Foster (eds), *King Arthur's Death: The Middle English Stanzaic Morte and Alliterative Morte Arthure* (Kalamazoo, MI: TEAMS, 1994), https://d.lib.rochester. edu/teams/publication/benson-and-foster-king-arthurs-death.
Sugano, Douglas (ed.), *The N-Town Plays* (Kalamazoo, MI: Medieval Institute Press, 2007), http://d.lib.rochester.edu/teams/publication/suga no-the-n-town-plays.
Thompson, W. Meredith (ed.), *Þe Wohunge of Ure Laured. Edited from British Museum MS Cotton Titus D.xviii, together with On Ureisun of Ure Louerde; On Wel Swuðe God Ureisun of God Almihti; On Lofsong of Ure Louerde; On Lofsong of Ure Lefdi; Þe Oreisun of Seinte Marie*, EETS OS 241 (London: EETS Press, 1970).
Urmson, J. O., and Marina Sbisà (eds), *The Works of J. L. Austin* (Oxford and New York: Oxford University Press, 1976).
William of Newburgh, *Historia regum Anglicarum*, ed. Richard Howlett, in *Chronicles of the Reigns of Stephen, Henry II and Richard*, 4 vols, Rolls Series 82 (London: Longman, 1884–9).

Ywain and Gawain, in Braswell (ed.), *Sir Perceval of Galles and Ywain and Gawain*, http://d.lib.rochester.edu/teams/publication/braswell-sir-percev al-of-galles-and-ywain-and-gawain.
Zink, Michel (ed.), *Chrétien de Troyes: Romans* (Paris: Livre de Poche, 1994).

Secondary sources

Adams, Tracy, 'Printing and the Transformation of the Middle English Romance', *Neophilologus*, 82 (1998), 291–310.
Aers, David, *Chaucer* (Brighton: Harvester, 1986).
Aers, David, 'Christianity for Courtly Subjects: Reflections on the *Gawain*-Poet', in Brewer and Gibson (eds), *A Companion to the Gawain-Poet*, pp. 91–101.
Aers, David, *Community, Gender and Individual Identity: English Writing 1360–1430* (London: Routledge, 1988).
Aers, David, 'A Whisper in the Ears of Early Modernists; or, Reflections on Literary Critics Writing the "History of the Subject"', in Aers (ed.), *Essays on English Communities*, pp. 177–203.
Aers, David (ed.), *Essays on English Communities, Identities and Writing* (Detroit, MI: Wayne State University Press, 1992).
Aers, David (ed.), *Medieval Literature: Criticism, Ideology and History* (Brighton: Harvester, 1988).
Ahmed, Sara, *The Cultural Politics of Emotion*, 2nd edn (Edinburgh: Edinburgh University Press, 2015).
Aird, William M., 'The Tears of Bishop Gundulf: Gender, Religion, and Emotion in the Late Eleventh Century', in Beattie and Fenton (eds), *Intersections of Gender*, pp. 62–84.
Airlie, Stuart, 'The History of Emotions and Emotional History', *Early Medieval Europe*, 10:2 (2001), 235–41.
Akbari, Suzanne Conklin, *Seeing through the Veil: Optical Theory and Medieval Allegory* (Toronto: University of Toronto Press, 2004).
Åkestam, Mia, '"I Felt Like Jumping for Joy": Smiles and Laughter in Medieval Imagery', in Förnegård et al. (eds), *Tears, Sighs and Laughter*, pp. 214–38.
Alexander, J. J. G., and M. T. Gibson (eds), *Medieval Learning and Literature: Essays Presented to Richard William Hunt* (Oxford: Clarendon Press, 1976).
Althoff, Gerd, *Die Macht der Rituale. Symbolik und Herrschaft im Mittelalter* (Darmstadt: Primus Verlag, 2003).
Althoff, Gerd, 'Empörung, Tränen, Zerknirschung: "Emotionen" in der öffentlichen Kommunikation des Mittelalters', *Frühmittelalterliche Studien*, 30 (1996), 60–79.

Althoff, Gerd, 'Ira regis: Prolegomena to a History of Royal Anger', in Rosenwein (ed.), *Anger's Past*, pp. 59–74.

Althoff, Gerd, 'Tränen und Freude: Was interessiert Mittelalter-Historiker an Emotionen', *Frühmittelalterliche Studien*, 40 (2006), 1–11.

Althoff, Gerd (ed.), *Formen und Funktionen öffentlicher Kommunikation im Mittelalter* (Stuttgart: Jan Thorbecke Verlag, 2001).

Anderson, Earl R., 'Malory's "Fair Maide of Ascolat"', *Neuphilologische Mitteilungen*, 87 (1986), 237–54.

Arn, Mary-Jo, and Hanneke Wirtjes (eds), *Historical and Editorial Studies in Medieval and Early Modern English in Honour of Johan Gerritsen* (Groningen: Wolters-Noordhoff, 1985).

Arnold, John, and Katherine Lewis (eds), *A Companion to the Book of Margery Kempe* (Woodbridge: D. S. Brewer, 2004).

Ashe, Laura, '"For love and for lovers": The Origins of Romance', in Krueger (ed.), *The New Cambridge Companion to Medieval Romance*, pp. 14–28.

Ashe, Laura, 'Introduction', in Ashe (ed.), *Early Fiction in England*, pp. xiii–xxvi.

Ashe, Laura (ed.), *Early Fiction in England: From Geoffrey of Monmouth to Chaucer* (London: Penguin, 2015).

Assman, Jan, *Religion and Cultural Memory*, trans. Rodney Livingstone (Stanford, CA: Stanford University Press, 2006).

Atkinson, Laurie, '"Why þat yee meeued been / can I nat knowe": Autobiography, Convention, and Discerning Doublenesse in Thomas Hoccleve's *The Series*', *Neophilologus*, 101 (2017), 479–94.

Auer, Anita, Denis Renevey et al., 'Introduction: Setting the Scene, Interdisciplinary Perspectives on the Medieval North of England', in Auer, Renevey et al. (eds), *Revisiting the Medieval North*, pp. 1–12.

Auer, Anita, Denis Renevey et al. (eds), *Revisiting the Medieval North of England* (Cardiff: University of Wales Press, 2019).

Baker, Denise N., 'Pre-Empting Piers's Tearing of the Pardon: Langland's Revisions of the C Version', *Yearbook of Langland Studies*, 31 (2017), 43–72.

Bale, Anthony, 'Afterword: Three Letters', in Burger and Crocker (eds), *Medieval Affect, Feeling, and Emotion*, pp. 203–17.

Bale, Anthony, 'Introduction', in Kempe, *The Book of Margery Kempe*, trans. Bale, pp. ix–xxiii.

Bartlett, Anne Clark, 'Translation, Self-Representation, and Statecraft: Lady Margaret Beaufort and Caxton's *Blanchardyn and Eglantine* (1489)', *Essays in Medieval Studies*, 22 (2005), 53–66.

Batt, Catherine (ed.), *Essays on Thomas Hoccleve* (London: Brepols, 1996).

Battaglia, Marco, and Alessandro Zironi (eds), *Dat dy man in all landen fry was: studi filologici in onore di Giulio Garuti Simone di Cesare* (Pisa: Pisa University Press, 2017).

Beattie, Cordelia, and Kirsten A. Fenton (eds), *Intersections of Gender, Religion and Ethnicity in the Midde Ages* (Basingstoke: Palgrave Macmillan, 2011).

Beckwith, Sarah, *Signifying God: Social Relation and Symbolic Act in the York Corpus Christi Plays* (Chicago: University of Chicago Press, 2001).

Benson, Robert G., *Medieval Body Language: A Study of the Use of Gesture in Chaucer's Poetry*, Anglistica 71 (Copenhagen: Rosenkilde and Bagge, 1980).

Benton, John F., *Self and Society in Medieval France: The Memoirs of Abbot Guibert of Nogent* (Toronto and London: University of Toronto Press, in association with the Medieval Academy of America, 1984).

Blake, Norman F., 'Investigations into the Prologues and Epilogues of William Caxton', *Bulletin of the John Rylands Library*, 49:1 (1966), 17–46.

Blud, Victoria, 'Emotional Bodies: Cognitive Neuroscience and Mediaeval Studies', *Literature Compass*, 13:6 (2016), 457–66.

Blud, Victoria, 'Making Up a Mind: "4E" Cognition and the Medieval Subject', in Dresvina and Blud (eds), *Cognitive Sciences and Medieval Studies*, pp. 163–82.

Boitani, Piero, and Jill Mann (eds), *The Cambridge Companion to Chaucer* (Cambridge: Cambridge University Press, 2004).

Bolens, Guillemette, 'La narration des émotions et la réactivité du destinataire dans les Contes de Canterbury de Geoffrey Chaucer', *Médiévales*, 61, special issue 'La chair des émotions' (2011), pp. 97–117.

Bolens, Guillemette, *The Style of Gestures: Embodiment and Cognition in Literary Narrative* (Baltimore, MD: Johns Hopkins University Press, 2012).

Boquet, Damien, and Piroska Nagy, *Medieval Sensibilities: A History of Emotions in the Middle Ages*, trans. Robert Shaw (London: Polity Press, 2018).

Boquet, Damien, and Piroska Nagy, 'Pour une histoire des émotions', in Nagy and Boquet (eds), *Le sujet des émotions au Moyen Âge*, pp. 15–51.

Boquet, Damien, and Piroska Nagy, *Sensible Moyen Âge: Une histoire des émotions dans l'Occident médiéval* (Paris: Seuil, 2015).

Boquet, Damien, and Piroska Nagy, with Laurence Moulinier-Brogi (eds), *Médiévales*, 61, special issue 'La chair des émotions' (autumn 2011).

Bourke, Joanna, 'Fear and Anxiety: Writing about Emotion in Modern History', *History Workshop Journal*, 55 (2003), 111–33.

Bowers, John, 'Introduction to "The Canterbury Interlude and Merchant's Tale of Beryn"', in Bowers (ed.), *The Canterbury Tales: Fifteenth-Century Continuations and Additions*, https://d.lib.rochester.edu/teams/text/bowers-canterbury-tales-fifteenth-century-interlude-and-merchants-tale-of-beryn-introduction.

Brandsma, Frank, 'Mirror Characters', in Busby and Kleinhenz (eds), *Courtly Arts and the Art of Courtliness*, pp. 275–84.

Brandsma, Frank, Carolyne Larrington and Corinne Saunders, 'Introduction', in Brandsma, Larrington and Saunders (eds), *Emotions in Medieval Arthurian Literature*, pp. 1–10.

Brandsma, Frank, Carolyne Larrington and Corinne Saunders (eds), *Emotions in Medieval Arthurian Literature: Body, Mind, Voice* (Cambridge: D. S. Brewer, 2015).

Braswell, Mary Flowers, 'Introduction: *Sir Perceval of Galles*', in Braswell (ed.), *Sir Perceval of Galles and Ywain and Gawain*, http://d.lib.rochester.edu/teams/text/braswell-sir-perceval-of-galles-introduction.

Brazil, Sarah J., 'Modulating Tone in the Early English Slaughter of the Innocents Plays: Between Grief, Vengeance and Humour', *European Medieval Drama*, 22 (2018), 11–35.

Brewer, Derek (ed.), *Chaucer and Chaucerians: Critical Studies in Middle English Literature* (London: Nelson, 1966), pp. 201–29.

Brewer, Derek, and Jonathan Gibson (eds), *A Companion to the Gawain-Poet* (Cambridge: D. S. Brewer, 1997).

Broomhall, Susan (ed.), *Authority, Gender and Emotions in Late Medieval and Early Modern England* (Basingstoke: Palgrave Macmillan, 2015).

Broomhall, Susan (ed.), *Early Modern Emotions: An Introduction* (London: Routledge, 2017).

Brown, Amy, 'Lancelot in the Friend Zone: Strategies for Offering and Limiting Affection in the *Stanzaic Morte Arthur*', in Flannery (ed.), *Emotion and Textual Media*, pp. 75–97.

Burger, Glenn, and Holly Crocker, 'Introduction', in Burger and Crocker (eds), *Medieval Affect, Feeling, and Emotion*, pp. 1–24.

Burger, Glenn, and Holly Crocker (eds), *Medieval Affect, Feeling, and Emotion* (Cambridge: Cambridge University Press, 2019).

Burns, E. Jane, 'Courtly Love: Who Needs It? Recent Feminist Work in the Medieval French Tradition', *Signs*, 27:1 (2001), 23–57.

Burrow, John, 'Autobiographical Poetry in the Middle Ages: The Case of Thomas Hoccleve', *PBA*, 68 (1982) 389–412.

Burrow, John, *Gestures and Looks in Medieval Narrative* (Cambridge: Cambridge University Press, 2002).

Burrow, John, 'Hoccleve's *Complaint* and Isidore of Seville Again', *Speculum*, 73 (1998), 424–8.

Busby, Keith, 'Chrétien de Troyes English'd', *Neophilologus*, 71 (1987), 596–613.

Busby, Keith, and Christopher Kleinhenz (eds), *Courtly Arts and the Art of Courtliness* (Woodbridge: Boydell and Brewer, 2006).

Byrne, Aisling, 'Arthur's Refusal to Eat: Ritual and Control in the Romance Feast', *Journal of Medieval History*, 37 (2011), 62–74.

Byrne, Aisling, 'The Intruder at the Feast: Negotiating Boundaries in Medieval Insular Romance', *Arthurian Literature*, 27 (2010), 33–57.

Calabrese, Michael, 'Chaucer's Dorigen and Boccaccio's Female Voices', *SAC*, 29 (2007), 259–92.

Cannon, Christopher, and Maura Nolan (eds), *Medieval Latin and Middle English Literature: Essays in Honour of Jill Mann* (Woodbridge: Boydell and Brewer, 2011).

Carpenter, Sarah, 'New Evidence: Vives and Audience-Response to Biblical Drama', *Medieval English Theatre*, 31 (2009), 3–12.

Carrera, Elena, 'Introduction', in Carrera (ed.), *Emotions and Health, 1200–1700*, pp. 1–19.

Carrera, Elena (ed.), *Emotions and Health, 1200–1700* (Turnhout: Brill, 2014).

Chamarette, Jenny, and Jennifer Higgins (eds), *Guilt and Shame: Essays in French Literature and Cinema* (Oxford: Peter Lang, 2010).

Cheyette, Frederic L., *Ermengarde of Narbonne and the World of the Troubadours* (Ithaca, NY: Cornell University Press, 2001).

Cheyette, Frederic L., and Howell Chickering, 'Love, Anger, and Peace: Social Practice and Poetic Play in the Ending of *Yvain*', *Speculum*, 80 (2005), 75–117.

Clark, David, and Kate McClune (eds), *Blood, Sex, Malory: Essays on the Morte Darthur*, special issue of *Arthurian Literature*, 28 (2011).

Classen, Albrecht, 'Crying in Public and Private: Tears in Medieval German Literature', in Gertsman (ed.), *Crying in the Middle Ages*, pp. 230–48.

Classen, Albrecht (ed.), *Laughter in the Middle Ages: Epistemology of a Fundamental Human Behavior, its Meaning and Consequences* (Berlin, Boston, MA: De Gruyter, 2015).

Classen, Albrecht, 'Laughter as an Expression of Human Nature in the Middle Ages and the Early Modern Period: Literary, Historical, Theological, Philosophical, and Psychological Reflections. Also an Introduction', in Classen (ed.), *Laughter in the Middle Ages*, 1–140.

Clough, Patricia Ticineto, and Jean Halley, *The Affective Turn: Theorizing the Social* (Durham, NC: Duke University Press, 2007).

Cohen-Hanegbi, Naama, and Piroska Nagy (eds), *Pleasure in the Middle Ages*, International Medieval Research 24 (Turnhout: Brepols, 2018).

Colwell, Tania M., 'Fragments of the *Roman de Mélusine* in the Upton House Bearsted Collection', *The Library*, 13:3 (2012), 279–315, https://doi.org/10.1093/library/13.3.279.

Colwell, Tania M., 'The Middle English Melusine: Evidence for an Early Edition of the Prose Romance in the Bodleian Library', *Journal of the*

Early Book Society for the Study of Manuscripts and Printing History, 17 (2014), 254–82, 409–10.

Contzen, Eva von, 'Why We Need a Medieval Narratology: A Manifesto', *Diegesis*, 3:2 (2014), 1–21.

Cooper, Helen, 'Afterword: Malory's Enigmatic Smiles', in Brandsma, Larrington and Saunders (eds), *Emotions in Medieval Arthurian Literature*, pp. 181–8.

Cooper, Helen, 'Romance after 1400', in Wallace (ed.), *The Cambridge History of Medieval English Literature*, pp. 690–719.

Crane, Susan, *The Performance of Self: Ritual, Clothing, and Identity during the Hundred Years War* (Philadelphia, PA: University of Pennsylvania Press, 2002).

Crocker, Holly, 'Affective Politics in Chaucer's *Reeve's Tale*: "Cherl" Masculinity after 1381', *SAC*, 29 (2007), 225–58.

Damasio, Antonio R., *Descartes' Error: Emotion, Reason, and the Human Brain* (New York: G. P. Putnam, 1994).

D'Arcy, Anne Marie, and Alan J. Fletcher (eds), *Studies in Late Medieval and Early Renaissance Texts in Honour of John Scattergood* (Dublin: Four Courts, 2005).

Davidson, Clare, 'Erotic Devotion: Richard Rolle's *The Form of Living*', *Limina: A Journal of Historical and Cultural Studies*, 20:3 (2015), special issue 'A Festschrift in Honour of Philippa Maddern', pp. 1–13.

Davidson, Clifford, 'Gesture in Medieval British Drama', in Davidson (ed.), *Gesture in Medieval Drama*, pp. 66–127.

Davidson, Clifford (ed.), *Gesture in Medieval Drama and Art* (Kalamazoo, MI: Medieval Institute Press, 2001).

Decety, Jean, and Jennifer A. Stevens, 'Action Representation and its Role in Social Interaction', in Markman et al. (eds), *Handbook of Imagination and Mental Simulation*, pp. 3–20.

Demos, E. Virginia (ed.), *Exploring Affect: Selected Writings of Silvan S. Tomkins*, Studies in Emotion and Social Interaction (Cambridge: Cambridge University Press, 1995).

Dietl, Cora, Christoph Schanze, Friedrich Wolfzettel and Lena Zudrell, 'Vorwort der Herausgeber', in Dietl et al. (eds), *Emotion und Handlung im Artusroman*, pp. ix–xx.

Dietl, Cora, Christoph Schanze, Friedrich Wolfzettel and Lena Zudrell (eds), *Emotion und Handlung im Artusroman*, Schriften der Internationalen Artusgesellschaft: Deutsch-österreichische Sektion 13 (Berlin and Boston: De Gruyter, 2017).

Diller, Hans-Jürgen, 'Laughter in Medieval English Drama: A Critique of Modernising and Historical Analyses', *Comparative Drama*, 36:1–2 (2002), 1–19.

Dinshaw, Carolyn, 'A Kiss Is Just a Kiss: Heterosexuality and its Consolations in *Sir Gawain and the Green Knight*', *Diacritics*, 24 (1994), 204–26.

Dinzelbacher, Peter, *Vision und Visionsliteratur im Mittelalter*, Monographien zur Geschichte des Mittelalters 23 (Stuttgart: Hiersemann, 1981).

Dixon, Thomas, *From Passions to Emotions: The Creation of a Secular Category* (Cambridge: Cambridge University Press, 2003).

Donaldson, E. Talbot, 'Criseide and her Narrator', in E. Talbot Donaldson, *Speaking of Chaucer* (London: Athlone, 1970).

Downes, Stephanie, 'How to be "Both": Bilingual and Gendered Emotions in Late Medieval English Balade Sequences', in Broomhall (ed.), *Authority, Gender and Emotions*, pp. 51–65.

Dresvina, Juliana, and Victoria Blud (eds), *Cognitive Sciences and Medieval Studies: An Introduction* (Cardiff: University of Wales Press, 2020).

Dronke, Peter, *Medieval Latin and the Rise of European Love-Lyric*, 2nd edn (Oxford: Clarendon Press, 1999).

Dryden, John, 'Passions, Affections, and Emotions: Methodological Difficulties in Reconstructing Aquinas's Philosophical Psychology', *Literature Compass*, 13:6 (2016), 343–50.

Duncan, Thomas G. (ed.), *A Companion to the Middle English Lyric* (Cambridge: D. S. Brewer, 2005).

Eagleman, David M., *Incognito: The Secret Lives of the Brain* (Edinburgh and New York: Canongate, 2011).

Ekman, Paul, *Emotions Revealed* (New York: Times Books, 2003).

Eley, Penny, *Partonopeus de Blois: Romance in the Making*, Gallica 21 (Cambridge: D. S. Brewer, 2011).

Elias, Norbert, *The Civilizing Process*, 2 vols in 1: *The History of Manners and State Formation and Civilisation*, trans. Edmund Jephcott (Oxford: Blackwell, 1994).

Eming, Jutta, 'On Stage: Ritualized Emotions and Theatricality in Isolde's Trial', *Modern Language Notes*, 124 (2009), 555–71.

Enders, Jody, 'Of Miming and Signing: The Dramatic Rhetoric of Gesture', in Davidson (ed.), *Gesture in Medieval Drama and Art*, pp. 1–25.

Eustace, Nicole, Eugenia Lean, Julie Livingston, Jan Plamper, William M. Reddy and Barbara H. Rosenwein, '*AHR* Conversation: The History of Emotion', *AHR*, 117:5 (2012), 1487–1531.

Evans, Ruth, '*The Book of Margery Kempe*: Autobiography in the Third Person', in Kalas and Varnam (eds), *Encountering the Book of Margery Kempe*, pp. 83–100.

Evans, Ruth (ed.), *A Cultural History of Sexuality in the Middle Ages*, 2 vols (Oxford: Berg, 2011).

Even-Zohar, Itamar, 'Polysystem Theory', *Poetics Today*, 11:1 (1990), 9–94.
Fehr, Beverley, and James A. Russell, 'Concept of Emotion Viewed from a Prototype Perspective', *Journal of Experimental Psychology: General*, 113:3 (1984), 464–86.
Fein, Susanna Greer (ed.), *Robert Thornton and his Books: Essays on the Lincoln and London Thornton Manuscripts* (York: York Medieval Texts, 2014).
Ferm, Olle, 'Laughter and the Medieval Church', in Förnegård et al. (eds), *Tears, Sighs and Laughter*, pp. 166–81.
Feuerhahn, Wolf, and Rafael Mandressi, 'Introduction: les "neurosciences sociales": historicité d'un programme', *Revue d'histoire des sciences humaines*, 25:2 (2011), 3–12.
Finke, Laurie A., and Martin B. Shichtman, 'Magical Mistress Tour: Patronage, Intellectual Property, and the Dissemination of Wealth in the "Lais" of Marie de France', *Signs*, 25:2 (2000), 479–503.
Finlayson, John, 'Definitions of Middle English Romance', in Shepherd (ed.), *Middle English Romances*, pp. 428–56.
Flannery, Mary C., 'Personification and Embodied Emotion', *Literature Compass*, 13:6 (2016), 351–6.
Flannery, Mary C., *Practising Shame: Female Honour in Later Medieval England* (Manchester: Manchester University Press, 2020).
Flannery, Mary C., 'The Shame of the Rose: A Paradox', in Chamarette and Higgins (eds), *Guilt and Shame*, pp. 51–69.
Flannery, Mary C. (ed.), *Emotion and Textual Media*, Early European Research 13 (Turnhout: Brepols, 2018).
Flood, John, '"Volentes sibi comparare infrascriptos libros impressos …": Printed Books as a Commercial Commodity in the Fifteenth Century', in Jensen (ed.), *Incunabula and their Readers*, pp. 139–51.
Fludernik, Monika, 'Through a Glass Darkly: or, the Emergence of Mind in Medieval Narrative', in Herman (ed.), *Emergence of Mind*, pp. 69–100.
Fong, Katrina, Justin B. Mullins and Raymond A. Mar, 'What You Read Matters: The Role of Fiction Genre in Predicting Interpersonal Sensitivity', *Psychology of Aesthetics, Creativity, and the Arts*, 7 (2013), 370–6.
Förnegård, Per, Erika Kihlman, Mia Åkestam and Gunnel Engwall (eds), *Tears, Sighs and Laughter: Expressions of Emotions in the Middle Ages*, Kungl. Vitterhets Historie och Antikvitets Akademien Konferenser 92 (Stockholm: KVHAA, 2017).
Foster, Allyson, 'A *Shorte Treatyse of Contemplacyon*: The *Book of Margery Kempe* in its Early Print Contexts', in Arnold and Lewis (eds), *Companion to the Book of Margery Kempe*, pp. 95–112.

Foster, Meadhbh I. and Mark T. Keane, 'Why Some Surprises are More Surprising than Others: Surprise as a Metacognitive Sense of Explanatory Difficulty', *Cognitive Psychology*, 81 (2015), 74–116.

Fowler, Alastair, *Kinds of Literature: An Introduction to the Theory of Genres and Modes* (Oxford: Clarendon Press, 1982).

Fowler, Elizabeth, *Literary Character: The Human Figure in Early English Writing* (Ithaca, NY: Cornell University Press, 2003).

Frevert, Ute, *Emotions in History: Lost and Found*, The Natalie Zemon Davis Annual Lectures (Budapest: Central European University Press, 2011).

Frijda, Nico, *The Emotions* (Cambridge: Cambridge University Press, 1986).

Frijda, Nico, 'The Laws of Emotion', *American Psychologist*, 43 (1988), 349–58, reprinted in Jenkins, Oatley and Stein (eds), *Human Emotions*, pp. 270–87.

Frijda, Nico, *The Laws of Emotion* (Mahwah, NJ: Lawrence Erlbaum, 2007).

Fulton, Helen (ed.), *Blackwell Companion to Arthurian Literature* (Oxford: Blackwell, 2009).

Fulton, Rachel, *From Judgment to Passion: Devotion to Christ and the Virgin Mary 800–1200* (New York: Columbia University Press, 2005).

Fumo, Jamie, 'Aurelius's Prayer, *Franklin's Tale* 1031–79: Sources and Analogues', *Neophilologus*, 88 (2004), 623–35.

Gallese, Vittorio, 'The "Shared Manifold" Hypothesis: From Mirror Neurons to Empathy', *Journal of Consciousness Studies*, 8 (2001), 33–50.

Gallese, Vittorio, and Alvin Goldman, 'Mirror Neurons and the Simulation Theory of Mind-Reading', *Trends in Cognitive Science*, 2:12 (1998), 493–501.

Gallese, Vittorio, and Hannah Wojciehowski, 'How Stories Make Us Feel: Towards an Embodied Narratology', *Californian Italian Studies*, 2:1 (2011), 10.5070/C321008974.

Gallese, Vittorio, Morton Ann Gernsbacher, Cecilia Heyes, Gregory Hickok and Marco Iacoboni, 'Mirror Neuron Forum', *Perspectives on Psychological Science*, 6:4 (2011), 369–407.

Gaunt, Simon, *Gender and Genre in Medieval French Literature* (Cambridge: Cambridge University Press, 1995).

Gaunt, Simon, 'Marginal Men, Marcabru and Orthodoxy: The Early Troubadours and Adultery', *Medium Ævum*, 59 (1990), 55–72.

Gaunt, Simon, 'Romance and Other Genres', in Krueger (ed.), *The Cambridge Companion to Medieval Romance*, pp. 45–59.

Gertsman, Elina, 'The Facial Gesture: (Mis)Reading Emotion in Gothic Art', *Journal of Medieval Religious Cultures*, 36:1 (2010), 28–46.

Gertsman, Elina, 'Preface: "Going they Went and Wept": Tears in Medieval Discourse', in Gertsman (ed.), *Crying in the Middle Ages*, pp. xi–xx.

Gertsman, Elina (ed.), *Crying in the Middle Ages: Tears of History* (New York and London: Routledge, 2012).

Goldie, Peter, *The Emotions: A Philosophical Exploration* (Oxford: Clarendon Press, 2000).

Goldie, Peter (ed.), *The Oxford Handbook of Philosophy of Emotion* (Oxford: Oxford University Press, 2009).

Greenblatt, Stephen, *Renaissance Self-Fashioning: From More to Shakespeare* (Chicago: University of Chicago Press, 1980).

Gross, Daniel M., *The Secret History of Emotion: From Aristotle's Rhetoric to Modern Brain Science* (Chicago: University of Chicago Press, 2006).

Grossweiner, Karen A., 'A Tripartite Model for Determining Narratorial Subjectivity in Medieval Romance: The Composite Subject in *Partonope of Blois*', *Studies in Philology*, 109:4 (2012), 381–408.

Harbus, Antonina, 'Emotion and Narrative Empathy in *Sir Gawain and the Green Knight*', *English Studies*, 97:6 (2016), 594–607.

Hardman, Phillipa, 'Popular Romances and Young Readers', in Radulescu and Rushton (eds), *A Companion to Medieval Popular Romance*, pp. 150–64.

Herman, David (ed.), *Emergence of Mind: Representations of Consciousness in Narrative Discourse in English* (Lincoln, NE: University of Nebraska Press, 2011).

Hochschild, Arlie Russell, *The Managed Heart: Commercialization of Human Feeling* (Berkeley, CA: University of California Press, 1983).

Hogan, Patrick Colm, *Affective Narratology: The Emotional Structure of Stories* (Lincoln, NE: University of Nebraska Press, 2011).

Hopkins, Andrea, *The Sinful Knights: A Study of Middle English Penitential Romance* (Oxford: Clarendon Press, 1990).

Horobin, Simon, 'J. R. R. Tolkien as a Philologist: A Reconsideration of the Northernisms in the "Reeve's Tale"', *English Studies*, 82:2 (2001), 97–105.

Hosington, Brenda, 'Voices of Protest and Submission: Portraits of Women in *Partonopeu de Blois* and its Middle English Translation', *Reading Medieval Studies*, 17 (1991), 51–75.

Huizinga, Johan, *The Waning of the Middle Ages: A Study of the Forms of Life, Thought and Art in France and the Netherlands in the XIVth and XVth Centuries*, trans. F. J. Hopman (London: Penguin, 2001).

Iacoboni, Marco, *Mirroring People* (New York: Farrar, Straus and Giroux, 2008).

Johnston, Alexandra F. (ed.), *Editing Early English Drama: Special Problems and New Directions* (New York: AMS Press, 1983).

Ingham, Patricia Clare, *Sovereign Fantasies: Arthurian Romance and the Making of Britain* (Philadelphia, PA: University of Pennsylvania Press, 2001).

Innes-Parker, Catherine, '*Ancrene Wisse* and *Þe Wohunge of Ure Lauerd*: The Thirteenth-Century Female Reader and the Lover-Knight', in Smith and Taylor (eds), *Women, the Book, and the Godly*, pp. 137–47.

Izard, Carroll, 'Basic Emotions, Relations among Emotions, and Emotion–Cognition Relations', *Psychological Review*, 99 (1992), 561–5.

Jaeger, C. Stephen, *Ennobling Love: In Search of a Lost Sensibility* (Philadelphia, PA: University of Pennsylvania Press, 2010).

Jaeger, C. Stephen, *The Origins of Courtliness: Civilizing Trends and the Origins of Courtly Ideals, 939–1210* (Pittsburgh, PA: University of Pennsylvania Press, 1985).

Jaeger, C. Stephen, and Ingrid von Kasten (eds), *Codierungen von Emotionen / Emotions and Sensibilities in the Middle Ages* (New York and Berlin: De Gruyter, 2003).

Jager, Eric, *The Book of the Heart* (Chicago: University of Chicago Press, 2000).

James, William, 'What is an Emotion?', *Mind*, 9 (1884), 188–205.

Jenkins, Jennifer, Keith Oatley and Nancy Stein (eds), *Human Emotions* (Oxford: Wiley-Blackwell, 1988).

Jensen, Kristian (ed.), *Incunabula and their Readers: Printing, Selling and Using Books in the Fifteenth Century* (London: British Library, 2003).

Johnston, Andrew James, 'The Exegetics of Laughter: Religious Parody in Chaucer's *Miller's Tale*', in Pfister (ed.), *A History of English Laughter*, pp. 17–33.

Jorgensen, Alice, Frances McCormack and Jonathan Wilcox (eds), *Anglo-Saxon Emotions: Reading the Heart in Old English Language, Literature and Culture* (Farnham: Ashgate, 2015).

Kaempfer, Lucie, 'Drinking Sorrow and Bathing in Bliss: Liquid Emotions in Chaucer', *Open Library of Humanities*, 4:1 (2018), 1–24, https://doi.org/10.16995/olh.227.

Kaempfer, Lucie, 'Finding Joy in *Troilus and Criseyde*' (unpublished DPhil thesis, University of Oxford, 2018).

Kalas, Laura, and Laura Varnam (eds), *Encountering the Book of Margery Kempe* (Manchester: Manchester University Press, 2021).

Karnes, Michelle, 'Nicholas Love and Medieval Meditations on Christ', *Speculum*, 82:2 (2007), 380–408.

Karras, Ruth Mazo, review of William Reddy, *The Making of Romantic Love*, *English Historical Review*, 130 (2015), 958–60.

Kay, Sarah, *Subjectivity in Troubadour Poetry* (Cambridge: Cambridge University Press, 1990).

Kendall, Elliot, 'Chamberlain Danger: The Social Meaning of Love-Allegory in the *Confessio Amantis*', *Medium Ævum*, 76 (2007), 49–69.
Kerby-Fulton, Kathryn, *The Clerical Proletariat and the Resurgence of Medieval English Poetry* (Philadelphia, PA: University of Pennsylvania Press, 2021).
Kerby-Fulton, Kathryn, '*Piers Plowman*', in Wallace (ed.), *The Cambridge History of Medieval English Literature*, pp. 513–38.
Kidd, David C., and Emanuele Castano, 'Reading Literary Fiction Improves Theory of Mind', *Science*, 342 (2013), 377–80.
King, Peter, 'Emotions in Medieval Thought', in Goldie (ed.), *The Oxford Handbook of Philosophy of Emotion*, pp. 167–88.
Kittredge, George Lyman, *A Study of Sir Gawain and the Green Knight* (Cambridge, MA: Harvard University Press, 1916).
Knapp, Ethan, 'Bureaucratic Identity and the Construction of the Self in Hoccleve's *Formulary* and *La Male Regle*', *Speculum*, 74:2 (1999), 357–76.
Kneepkens, E. W. E. M., and Rolf A. Zwaan, 'Emotions and Literary Text Comprehension', *Poetics*, 23 (1994), 125–38.
Knight, Stephen, *Arthurian Literature and Society* (London: Macmillan, 1983).
Knight, Stephen, *Geoffrey Chaucer*, Rereading Literature (Oxford: Blackwell, 1986).
Knight, Stephen, 'Rhetoric and Poetry in the *Franklin's Tale*', *Chaucer Review*, 4:1 (1969), 14–30.
Knuuttila, Simo, *Emotions in Ancient and Medieval Philosophy* (Oxford: Clarendon Press, 2004).
Kooper, Erik, 'Introduction: *The Squire of Low Degree*', in Kooper (ed.), *Sentimental and Humorous Romances* (Kalamazoo, MI: Medieval Institute Publications, 2005), https://d.lib.rochester.edu/teams/text/kooper-sentimental-and-humorous-romances-squire-of-low-degree-introduction.
Kövecses, Zoltán, *Emotion Concepts* (New York: Springer, 1990).
Kövecses, Zoltán, 'Emotion Language: A New Synthesis', in Kövecses, *Metaphor and Emotion*, pp. 182–99.
Kövecses, Zoltán, *Metaphor and Emotion: Language, Culture, and Body in Human Feeling*, Studies in Emotion and Social Interaction (Cambridge: Cambridge University Press, 2000).
Krueger, Roberta L. (ed.), *The Cambridge Companion to Medieval Romance* (Cambridge: Cambridge University Press, 2000).
Krueger, Roberta L. (ed.) *The New Cambridge Companion to Medieval Romance* (Cambridge: Cambridge University Press, 2023).
la Farge, Cathy, 'Launcelot in Compromising Positions: Fabliau in Malory's "Tale of Sir Launcelot du Lake"', in Clark and McClune (eds), *Blood, Sex, Malory*, pp. 181–97.

Langum, Virginia, 'Langland's Diseased Vision', *Avista Forum Journal*, 19:1 (2009), 42–5.

Langum, Virginia, *Medicine and the Seven Deadly Sins in Late Medieval Literature and Culture*, The New Middle Ages (New York: Palgrave Macmillan, 2016).

Larrington, Carolyne, 'English Chivalry and *Sir Gawain and the Green Knight*', in Fulton (ed.), *Blackwell Companion to Arthurian Literature*, pp. 252–64.

Larrington, Carolyne, *King Arthur's Enchantresses: Morgan and her Sisters in Arthurian Tradition* (London: I. B. Tauris, 2006).

Larrington, Carolyne, 'Mourning Gawein: Cognition and Affect in *Diu Crône* and Some French Gauvain-Texts', in Brandsma, Larrington and Saunders (eds), *Emotions in Medieval Arthurian Literature*, pp. 123–41.

Larrington, Carolyne, 'Learning to Feel in the Old Norse Camelot?', *Scandinavian Studies*, 87:1 (2015), 74–94.

Larrington, Carolyne, 'The Psychology of Emotion and Study of the Medieval Period', *Early Medieval Europe*, 10:2 (2001), 251–6.

Larrington, Carolyne, 'Sibling Relations in Malory's *Morte Darthur*', in Clark and McClune (eds), *Blood, Sex, Malory*, pp. 57–74.

Larrington, Carolyne, '"Wyȝe, welcum iwys to þis place!": Emotions in the Schemas for Arrival, Return and Welcome at the Arthurian Court', *Journal of International Arthurian Studies*, 4:1 (2016), 92–103.

Larrington, Carolyne, Judy Quinn and Brittany Schorn (eds), *A Handbook to Eddic Poetry: Myths and Legends of Early Scandinavia* (Cambridge: Cambridge University Press, 2016).

Lawler, Traugott, 'The Pardon Formula in *Piers Plowman*: Its Ubiquity, its Binary Shape, its Silent Middle Term', *Yearbook of Langland Studies*, 14 (2000), 117–52.

LeDoux, Joseph, *The Emotional Brain: The Mysterious Underpinnings of Emotional Life* (New York: Simon and Schuster, 1996).

Lees, Clare A., 'The Dissemination of Alcuin's *De virtutibus et vitiis liber* in Old English: A Preliminary Survey', *Leeds Studies in English*, 16 (1985), 174–89.

Leitch, Megan G., 'Sleeping Knights and "Such Sorow-Makynge": Affect, Ethics and in Malory's *Morte Darthur*', *Arthurian Literature*, 31 (2016), 83–100.

Lewis, C. S., *The Allegory of Love* (Oxford: Clarendon Press, 1936).

Lewis, Michael, Jeannette M. Haviland-Jones and Lisa Feldman Barrett (eds), *Handbook of Emotions*, 3rd edn (New York and London: Guilford Press, 2008).

Liggins, Elizabeth M., 'The Lovers' Swoons in *Troilus and Criseyde*', *Parergon*, 3 (1985), 93–106.

Lindstedt, Samira, 'The *Examinacio Dura* of Margery Kempe: Annotation as Authentication in Additional MS 61823', *The Medieval Journal*, 17:2 (2017), 73–102.

Little, Lester K., 'Pride Goes before Avarice: Social Change and the Vices in Latin Christendom', *AHR*, 76:1 (1971), 16–49.

Lockett, Leslie, *Anglo-Saxon Psychologies in the Vernacular and Latin Traditions* (Toronto: University of Toronto Press, 2011).

Lombardo, Nicholas, *The Logic of Desire: Aquinas on Emotion* (Washington, DC: Catholic University of America Press, 2011).

Lutz, Catherine, and Geoffrey M. White, 'The Anthropology of Emotions', *Annual Review of Anthropology*, 15 (1986), 405–36.

Lynch, Andrew, '"Manly Cowardyse": Thomas Hoccleve's Peace Strategy', *Medium Ævum*, 73:2 (2004), 306–23.

Lynch, Andrew, 'Positive Emotions in Arthurian Romance: Introduction', *Journal of International Arthurian Studies*, 4:1 (2016), 53–7.

Lynch, Andrew, '"What Cheer?" Emotion and Action in the Arthurian World', in Brandsma, Larrington and Saunders (eds), *Emotions in Medieval Arthurian Literature*, pp. 46–63.

McCarthy, Terence, 'Did Morgan le Fay Have a Lover?', *Medium Ævum*, 60 (1991), 284–9.

McCarthy, Terence, 'Malory's "Suete Madam"', *Medium Ævum*, 56 (1987), 89–94.

McCracken, Peggy, review of William Reddy, *The Making of Romantic Love*, *Journal of Asian Studies*, 72 (2013), 681–2.

Mcdonald, Nicola, 'Desire Out of Order and *Undo Your Door*', *SAC*, 34 (2012), 247–75.

McIlroy, Claire Elizabeth, *The English Prose Treatises of Richard Rolle* (Cambridge: D. S. Brewer, 2004).

McNamara, Rebecca, and Juanita Ruys, 'Unlocking the Silences of the Self-Murdered: Textual Approaches to Suicidal Emotions in the Middle Ages', *Exemplaria*, 26 (2014), 58–80.

McNamer, Sarah, *Affective Meditation and the Invention of Medieval Compassion* (Philadelphia, PA: University of Pennsylvania Press, 2010).

McNamer, Sarah, 'Feeling', in Strohm (ed.), *Middle English*, pp. 241–57.

McNamer, Sarah, 'The Literariness of Literature and the History of Emotions', *PMLA*, 130:5 (2015), 1433–42.

Maddern, Philippa, '"It is Full Merry in Heaven": The Pleasurable Connotations of "Merriment" in Late Medieval England', in Cohen-Hanegbi and Nagy (eds), *Pleasure in the Middle Ages*, pp. 21–38.

Maddern, Philippa, 'Reading Faces: How Did Late Medieval Europeans Interpret Emotions in Faces?', *Postmedieval*, 8:1 (2017), 12–34.

Manly, John Matthews, 'The Stanza Forms of "Sir Thopas"', *Modern Philology*, 8:1 (1910), 141–4.
Mann, Jill, 'Chance and Destiny in *Troilus and Criseyde* and the *Knight's Tale*', in Boitani and Mann (eds), *Cambridge Companion to Chaucer*, pp. 93–111.
Mann, Jill, *Geoffrey Chaucer*, Feminist Readings (New York and London: Harvester Wheatsheaf, 1991).
Mann, Jill, 'Troilus' Swoon', *Chaucer Review*, 14:4 (1980), 319–35.
Manstead, Antony S. R., and A. H. Fischer, 'Social Appraisal: The Social World as Object of and Influence on Appraisal Processes', in Scherer, Schorr and Johnstone (eds), *Appraisal Processes in Emotion*, pp. 221–32.
Mar, Raymond A., and Keith Oatley, 'The Function of Fiction is the Abstraction and Simulation of Social Experience', *Perspectives on Psychological Science*, 3:3 (2008), 173–92.
Mar, Raymond A., Keith Oatley, Maja Djikic et al., 'Emotion and Narrative Fiction: Interactive Influences Before, After, and During Reading', *Cognition and Emotion*, 25:5 (2011), 818–33.
Marculescu, Andreea, and Charles-Louis Morand Métivier, 'Introduction', in Marculescu and Morand Métivier (eds), *Affective and Emotional Economies*, pp. 1–16.
Marculescu, Andreea, and Charles-Louis Morand Métivier (eds), *Affective and Emotional Economies in Medieval and Early Modern Europe* (New York: Palgrave Macmillan, 2018).
Markman, Keith D., William M. P. Klein and Julie A. Suhr (eds), *Handbook of Imagination and Mental Simulation* (New York: Taylor and Francis, 2009).
Massumi, Brian, *Parables of the Virtual: Movement, Affect, Sensation* (Durham, NC, and London: Duke University Press, 2002).
Meale, Carol M. (ed.) *Readings in Medieval English Romance* (Cambridge: D. S. Brewer, 1994).
Meecham-Jones, Simon, '"He in Salte Teres Dreynte": Understanding Troilus's Tears', in O'Loughlin, Lynch and Downes (eds), *Emotions and War*, pp. 77–97.
Megna, Paul, 'Langland's Wrath: Righteous Anger Management in *The Vision of Piers Plowman*', *Exemplaria*, 25:2 (2013), 130–51.
Menocal, María Rosa, *The Arabic Role in Medieval Literary History* (Philadelphia, PA: University of Pennsylvania Press, 1987).
Meredith, Peter, 'Stage Directions and the Editing of Early English Drama', in Johnston (ed.), *Editing Early English Drama*, pp. 65–94.
Miall, David S., and Don Kuiken, 'A Feeling for Fiction: Becoming What we Behold', *Poetics*, 30 (2002), 221–41.

Miall, David S., and Don Kuiken, 'What is Literariness? Three Components of Literary Eeading', *Discourse Processes*, 28:2 (1999), 121–38.

Mieszkowski, Gretchen, '"The Least Innocent of All Innocent-Sounding Lies": The Legacy of Donaldson's "Troilus" Criticism', *Chaucer Review*, 41:3 (2007), 299–310.

Mieszkowski, Gretchen, 'Revisiting Troilus's Faint', in Pugh and Marzec (eds), *Men and Masculinities*, pp. 43–57.

Miller, Rowland S., 'Is Embarrassment a Blessing or a Curse?', in Tracy et al. (eds), *Self-Conscious Emotions*, pp. 245–62.

Mills, David, 'The Stage Directions in the Manuscripts of the Chester Mystery Cycle', *Medieval English Theatre*, 3:1 (1981), 45–56.

Mills, David, 'The Voices of Thomas Hoccleve', in Batt (ed.), *Essays on Thomas Hoccleve*, pp. 85–107.

Minnis, Alastair J., 'Piers' Protean Pardon: The Letter and Spirit of Langland's Theology of Indulgences', in D'Arcy and Fletcher (eds), *Studies in Late Medieval and Early Renaissance*, pp. 218–40.

Moi, Toril, 'Desire in Language: Andreas Capellanus and the Controversy of Courtly Love', in Aers (ed.), *Medieval Literature: Criticism, Ideology and History*, pp. 11–33.

Moore, Megan, 'Emotions as the Language of Romance', in Krueger (ed.), *The New Cambridge Companion to Medieval Romance*, pp. 150–66.

Morris, Colin, *The Discovery of the Individual: 1050–1200* (Toronto and London: University of Toronto Press, 1987).

Morse, Ruth, and Barry Windeatt (eds), *Chaucer Traditions: Studies in Honour of Derek Brewer* (Cambridge: Cambridge University Press, 1990).

Müller, Jan-Dirk, and Horst Wenzel (eds), *Mittelalter: Neue Wege durch einen alten Kontinent* (Stuttgart: S. Hirzel, 1999).

Nagy, Piroska, *Le don des larmes au Moyen Âge. Un instrument spirituel en quête d'institution* (Paris, Albin Michel, 2000).

Nagy, Piroska, 'Les larmes du Christ dans l'exégèse médiéval. Du bon usage de la souffrance', *Médiévales,* 27 (1994), 37–50.

Nagy, Piroska, 'The Power of Medieval Emotions and Change: From Theory to Some Unexpected Uses of Spiritual Texts', in Förnegård et al. (eds.), *Tears, Sighs and Laughter*, pp. 13–39.

Nagy, Piroska, and Damien Boquet, *Le sujet des émotions au Moyen Âge* (Paris: Beauchesne, 2008).

Newen, Albert, Leon de Bruin and Shaun Gallagher (eds), *The Oxford Handbook of 4E Cognition* (Oxford: Oxford University Press, 2018).

Newhauser, Richard G., 'The Parson's Tale and its Generic Affiliations', in Raybin and Holley (eds), *Closure in the Canterbury Tales*, pp. 45–76.

Newhauser, Richard G. (ed.), *In the Garden of Evil: The Vices and Culture in the Middle Ages* (Toronto: Pontifical Institute of Medieval Studies, 2005).

Newhauser, Richard G., and Susan J. Ridyard (eds), *Sin in Medieval and Early Modern Culture: The Tradition of the Seven Deadly Sins* (York: York Medieval Press, 2012).

Niedenthal, Paula M., 'Emotion Concepts', in Lewis, Haviland-Jones and Barrett (eds), *Handbook of Emotions*, pp. 587–600.

Nussbaum, Martha, *Upheavals of Thought: The Intelligence of Emotions* (Cambridge: Cambridge University Press, 2001).

Oatley, Keith, *Best Laid Schemes: The Psychology of Emotions* (Cambridge: Cambridge University Press, 1992).

Oatley, Keith, 'A Taxonomy of the Emotions of Literary Response and a Theory of Identification in Fictional Narrative', *Poetics*, 23 (1994), 53–74.

Oatley, Keith, 'Why Fiction May Be Twice as True as Fact: Fiction as Cognitive and Emotional Simulation', *Review of General Psychology*, 3:2 (1999), 101–17.

Oatley, Keith, and Maja Djikic, 'Psychology of Narrative', *Review of General Psychology*, special issue 'Psychology of Narrative Art' (2017), 161–8, http://dx.doi.org/10.1037/gpr0000113 (accessed 29 August 2023).

Oatley, Keith, and Jennifer Jenkins, *Understanding Emotions* (Oxford: Blackwell, 1996).

Ogura, Michiko, *Words and Expressions of Emotion in Medieval English*, Studies in English Medieval Language and Literature 39 (Frankfurt am Main: Peter Lang, 2013).

O'Loughlin, Katrina, Andrew Lynch and Stephanie Downes (eds), *Emotions and War: Medieval to Romantic Literature* (Basingstoke: Palgrave Macmillan, 2015).

Olson, Linda, and Kathryn Kerby-Fulton (eds), *Voices in Dialogue: Reading Women in the Middle Ages* (Notre Dame, IN: University of Notre Dame Press, 2005).

Orlemanski, Julie, 'Literary Genre, Medieval Studies, and the Prosthesis of Disability', *Textual Practice*, 30:7 (2016), 1253–72.

Orlemanski, Julie, *Symptomatic Subjects: Bodies, Medicine, and Causation in the Literature of Late Medieval England* (Philadelphia, PA: University of Pennsylvania Press, 2019).

Orlemanski, Julie, 'Who Has Fiction? Modernity, Fictionality and the Middle Ages', *New Literary History*, 51:1 (2020), 145–70.

Parkes, Malcolm B., 'The Influence of the Concepts of *Ordinatio* and *Compilatio* on the Development of the Book', in Alexander and Gibson (eds), *Medieval Learning and Literature*, pp. 113–41.

Patterson, Lee, *Acts of Recognition: Essays on Medieval Culture* (Indianapolis, IN: University of Notre Dame Press, 2009).

Patterson, Lee, *Chaucer and the Subject of History* (London and New York: Routledge, 1991).

Patterson, Lee, 'On the Margin, Post-Modernism, Ironic History and Medieval Studies', *Speculum*, 65 (1990), 87–108.

Patterson, Lee, '"What is Me?" Hoccleve and the Trials of the Urban Self', in Patterson, *Acts of Recognition*, pp. 84–109.

Parkinson, Brian, 'How Social is the Social Psychology of Emotion?', *British Journal of Social Psychology*, 50 (2011), 405–13.

Parkinson, Brian, 'Interpersonal Emotion Transfer: Contagion and Social Appraisal', *Social and Personality Psychology Compass*, 5:7 (2011), 428–39.

Parkinson, Brian, and Antony S. R. Manstead, 'Current Emotion Research in Social Psychology: Thinking about Emotions and Other People', *Emotion Review*, 7:4 (2015), 371–80.

Pearsall, Derek, 'The Audience of the Middle English Romances', in Arn and Wirtjes (eds), *Historical and Editorial Studies*, pp. 37–47.

Pearsall, Derek, 'The English Chaucerians', in Brewer (ed.), *Chaucer and Chaucerians*, pp. 201–29.

Petit de Julleville, L., *Les mystères. Histoire du théâtre en France*, vols 1–2 (1880, repr. Geneva: Slatkine, 1968).

Pfister, Manuel, 'Introduction: A History of English Laughter?', in Pfister (ed.), *A History of English Laughter*, pp. v–x.

Pfister, Manfred (ed.), *A History of English Laughter: Laughter from Beowulf to Beckett and Beyond* (Amsterdam and New York: Rodopi, 2002).

Philipowski, Katharina, 'Das Gelächter der Cunnewäre', *Zeitschrift für Germanistik*, new series, 13 (2003), 9–25.

Philipowski, Katharina, 'Die Textualität von Gesten: Ein kleiner Beitrag zur Interdisziplinaritätsdebatte', *Journal of English and Germanic Philology*, 101 (2002), 461–77.

Plamper, Jan, 'The History of Emotions: An Interview with William Reddy, Barbara Rosenwein, and Peter Stearns', *History and Theory*, 49 (2010), 237–65.

Plamper, Jan, *The History of Emotions: An Introduction*, trans. Keith Tribe (Oxford: Oxford University Press, 2015).

Plantinga, Carl, and Greg M. Smith (eds), *Passionate Views: Film, Cognition, and Emotion* (Baltimore, MD, and London: Johns Hopkins University Press, 1999).

Poor, Sara S., and Jana K. Schulman (eds), *Women and Medieval Epic: Gender, Genre and the Limits of Masculinity* (London and New York: Palgrave Macmillan, 2007).

Pugh, Tison, and Marcia Smith Marzec (eds), *Men and Masculinities in Chaucer's Troilus and Criseyde* (Woodbridge: D. S. Brewer, 2008).
Purdie, Rhiannon, and Michael Cichon (eds), *Medieval Romance, Medieval Contexts* (Cambridge: D. S. Brewer, 2011).
Radford, Colin, and Michael Weston, 'How Can We Be Moved by the Fate of Anna Karenina?', *Proceedings of the Aristotelian Society*, supplementary vols, 49 (1975), 67–93.
Radulescu, Raluca, *Romance and its Contexts in Fifteenth-Century England* (Woodbridge: Boydell and Brewer, 2013).
Radulescu, Raluca, and Cory J. Rushton (eds), *A Companion to Medieval Popular Romance* (Cambridge: D. S. Brewer, 2009).
Ratcliffe, Matthew, *Feelings of Being: Phenomenology, Psychiatry and the Sense of Reality* (Oxford: Oxford University Press, 2008).
Raybin, David, and Linda T. Holley (eds), *Closure in the Canterbury Tales: The Role of the Parson's Tale* (Kalamazoo, MI: Medieval Institute Publications, 2000).
Reddy, William M., 'Courts and Pleasure: The Neuroscience of Pleasure and the Pursuit of Favour in Twelfth-Century Courts', in Cohen-Hanegbi and Nagy (eds), *Pleasure in the Middle Ages*, pp. 131–64.
Reddy, William M., *The Making of Romantic Love: Longing and Sexuality in Europe, South Asia, and Japan, 900–1200 CE* (Chicago, and London: University of Chicago Press, 2012).
Reddy, William M., *The Navigation of Feeling: A Framework for the History of Emotions* (Cambridge: Cambridge University Press, 2001).
Ricœur, Paul, *From Text to Action: Essays in Hermeneutics, II*, trans. K. Blamey and J. B. Tompson (Evanston, IL: Northwestern University Press, 1991).
Riddy, Felicity, 'Text and Self in *The Book of Margery Kempe*', in Olson and Kerby-Fulton (eds), *Voices in Dialogue*, pp. 439–43.
Rider, Jeff, 'Positive Emotions in the Arthurian *lais* of Marie de France', *Journal of International Arthurian Studies*, 4:1 (2016), 58–68.
Rigg, A. G., 'Hoccleve's *Complaint* and Isidore of Seville', *Speculum*, 45 (1970), 564–74.
Rikhardsdottir, Sif, *Emotions in Old Norse Literature: Translations, Voices, Contexts*, Studies in Old Norse Literature (Woodbridge: Boydell and Brewer, 2017).
Rikhardsdottir, Sif, 'Medieval Emotionality: The Feeling Subject in Medieval Literature', *Comparative Literature*, 69:1 (2017), 74–90.
Rikhardsdottir, Sif, *Medieval Translations and Cultural Discourse: The Movement of Texts in England, France and Scandinavia* (Cambridge: D.S. Brewer, 2012).
Rikhardsdottir, Sif, 'Translating Emotion: Vocalisation and Embodiment in *Yvain* and *Ívens Saga*', in Brandsma, Larrington and Saunders (eds), *Emotions in Medieval Arthurian Literature*, pp. 161–79.

Rizzolati, Giacomo, and Maddalena Fabbri-Destro, 'The Mirror System and its Role in Social Cognition', *Current Opinion in Neurobiology*, 18:2 (2008), 179–84.

Robinson, Jenefer, *Deeper than Reason: Emotion and its Role in Literature, Music, and Art* (Oxford: Clarendon Press, 2005).

Rogerson, Margaret, 'Raging in the Streets of Medieval York', *Early Theatre*, 3 (2000), 105–25.

Rosenwein, Barbara H., 'Worrying about Emotions in History', *AHR*, 107.3 (2002), 821–45.

Rosenwein, Barbara H., *Emotional Communities in the Early Middle Ages* (Ithaca, NY, and London: Cornell University Press, 2006).

Rosenwein, Barbara H., *Generations of Feeling: A History of Emotions, 600–1700* (Cambridge: Cambridge University Press, 2015).

Rosenwein, Barbara H., 'Taking Pleasure in Virtues and Vices: Alcuin's Manual for Count Wido', in Cohen-Hanegbi and Nagy (eds), *Pleasure in the Middle Ages*, pp. 167–79.

Rosenwein, Barbara H. (ed.), *Anger's Past: The Social Uses of an Emotion in the Middle Ages* (Ithaca, NY, and London: Cornell University Press, 1998).

Ruggerini, Maria Elena, 'Alliterative Lexical Collocations in Eddic Poetry', in Larrington, Quinn and Schorn (eds), *A Handbook to Eddic Poetry*, pp. 217–31.

Ruggerini, Maria Elena, 'Word ... soðe gebunden (*Beowulf*, l. 871a): Appreciating Old English Collocations', in Battaglia and Zironi (eds), *Dat dy man in all landen fry was*, pp. 141–64.

Salih, Sarah, 'Erotica', in Evans (ed.), *A Cultural History of Sexuality*, vol. 2, pp. 181–212.

Salih, Sarah, 'Writing Performed Lives: Margery Kempe Meets Marina Abramovic', in Kalas and Varnam (eds), *Encountering the Book of Margery Kempe*, pp. 259–77.

Saunders, Corinne, 'Mind, Body and Affect in Arthurian Romance', in Brandsma, Larrington, Saunders (eds), *Emotions in Arthurian Literature*, pp. 31–46.

Saunders, Corinne, and Charles Fernyhough, 'The Medieval Mind', *The Psychologist*, 29 (November 2016), 880–3, https://thepsychologist.bps.org.uk/volume-29/november-2016/looking-back-medieval-mind (accessed 2 September 2023).

Scheer, Monique, 'Are Emotions a Kind of Practice (and Is That What Makes Them Have a History)? A Bourdieuian Approach to Understanding Emotion', *History and Theory*, 51 (2012), 193–220.

Scherer, Klaus R., and Heiner Ellgring, 'Are Facial Expressions of Emotion Produced by Categorical Affect Programs or Dynamically Driven by Appraisal?' *Emotion*, 7:1 (2007), 113–30.

Scherer, Klaus R., A. Schorr and T. Johnstone (eds), *Appraisal Processes in Emotion: Theory, Methods, Research* (New York: Oxford University Press, 2001).

Schnell, Rüdiger, 'Gefühle gestalten: Bausteine zu einer Poetik mittelalterlicher Emotionsbeschreibungen', *Beiträge zur Geschichte der deutsche Literatur und Sprache*, 138 (2016), 560–606.

Schnell, Rüdiger, 'Medialität und Emotionalität. Bemerkungen zur Lavinias Minne', *Germanisch-Romanische Monatsschrift*, 55:3 (2005), 267–82.

Scott, Anne M., 'The Role of Exempla in Educating through Emotion: The Deadly Sin of "lecherye" in Robert Mannyng's *Handlyng Synne* (1303–1317)', in Broomhall (ed.), *Authority, Gender and Emotions*, pp. 34–50.

Sedgwick, Eve Kosofsky, *Touching Feeling: Affect, Pedagogy, Performativity* (Durham, NC: Duke University Press, 2003).

Seel, Norbert M. (ed.), *Encyclopedia of the Sciences of Learning* (2012), https://doi.org/10.1007/978-1-4419-1428-6_36.

Shepherd, Stephen H. A. (ed.), *Middle English Romances* (New York: Norton, 1995).

Siraisi, Nancy J., *Medieval and Early Renaissance Medicine: An Introduction to Knowledge and Practice* (Chicago: University of Chicago Press, 1990).

Smith, Lesley, and Jane H. M. Taylor (eds), *Women, the Book, and the Godly: Selected Proceedings of the St. Hilda's Conference, 1993* (Cambridge: D. S. Brewer, 1995).

Sobecki, Sebastian, *Last Words: The Public Self and the Late Medieval Author* (Oxford: Oxford University Press, 2019).

Solomon, Karen, and Lawrence W. Barsalou, 'Perceptual Simulation in Property Verification', *Memory and Cognition*, 32:2 (2004), 244–59.

Solomon, Robert C., *The Passions. Emotions and the Meaning of Life* (Indianapolis, IN: Hackett, 1993).

Spearing, A. C., *The Gawain-Poet* (Cambridge: Cambridge University Press, 1970).

Spearing, A. C., *The Medieval Poet as Voyeur: Looking and Listening in Medieval Love Narratives* (Cambridge: Cambridge University Press, 1993).

Spearing, A. C., *Textual Subjectivity: The Encoding of Subjectivity in Medieval Narratives and Lyrics* (Oxford: Oxford University Press, 2005).

Sperlich, Annick, *Family and Friends: Generation in Medieval Romance* (Heidelberg: Winter, 2014).

Starkey, Kathryn, 'Brunhild's Smile: Emotion and the Politics of Gender in the *Nibelungenlied*', in Jaeger and Kasten (eds), *Codierungen von Emotionen*, pp. 159–73.

Starkey, Kathryn, 'Performative Emotion and the Politics of Gender in the *Nibelungenlied*', in Poor and Schulman (eds), *Women and Medieval Epic: Gender*, pp. 253–71.

Stearns, Carol Z., and Peter N. Stearns, *Anger: The Struggle for Emotional Control in America's History* (Chicago: University of Chicago Press, 1986).

Stearns, Peter N., *Jealousy: The Evolution of an Emotion in American History* (New York: New York University Press, 1989).

Stearns, Peter N., with Carol Z. Stearns, 'Emotionology: Clarifying the History of Emotions and Emotional Standards', *AHR*, 90:4 (1985), 813–36.

Stevens, Martin, 'Laughter and Game in *Sir Gawain and the Green Knight*', *Speculum*, 47 (1972), 65–78.

Stock, Brian, *The Implications of Literacy: Written Language and Models of Interpretation in the Eleventh and Twelfth Centuries* (Princeton, NJ: Princeton University Press, 1983).

Stock, Brian, *Listening to the Text: The Uses of the Past* (Baltimore, MD, and London: Johns Hopkins University Press, 1990).

Stone, Rachel, 'Translation of Alcuin's *De virtutibus et vitiis liber* (Book about the Virtues and Vices)', *The Heroic Age: A Journal of Early Medieval Northwestern Europe*, 16 (2015); https://www.heroicage.org/issues/16/stone.php (accessed 7 September 2023).

Straw, Carole, 'Gregory, Cassian, and the Cardinal Vices', in Newhauser (ed.), *In the Garden of Evil*, pp. 35–58.

Strohm, Paul, *Hochon's Arrow: The Social Imagination of Fourteenth-Century Texts* (Princeton, NJ: Princeton University Press, 1992).

Strohm, Paul (ed.), *Middle English*, Oxford Twenty-First Century Approaches to Literature (Oxford: Oxford University Press, 2007).

Tahkokallio, Jaako, 'Fables of King Arthur: Ælred of Rievaulx and Secular Passions', *Mirator*, 9:1 (2008), 19–35.

Tan, Ed S.-H., *Emotion and the Structure of Narrative Film: Film as an Emotion Machine*, trans. Barbara Fasting (Mahwah, NJ: Erlbaum, 1996; repr. New York: Routledge, 2011).

Tan, Ed S.-H., 'Film-Induced Affect as a Witness Emotion', *Poetics*, 23 (1994), 7–32.

Tan, Ed S.-H., and Nico Frijda, 'Sentiment in Film Viewing', in Plantinga and Smith (eds), *Passionate Views*, pp. 48–64.

Tan, Ed S.-H., and Valentijn Visch, 'Genre Scripts and Appreciation of Negative Emotion in the Reception of Film', *Behavioral and Brain Sciences*, 40 (2017), 10.1017/S0140525X17001844.

Taylor, Joseph, *Writing the North of England in the Middle Ages: Regionalism and Nationalism in Medieval English Literature* (Cambridge: Cambridge University Press, 2022).

Tennant, Elaine, 'Prescriptions and Performatives in Imagined Cultures: Gender Dynamics in Nibelungenlied Adventure 11', in Müller and Wenzel (eds), *Mittelalter: Neue Wege*, pp. 273–316.

Tennant, Elaine, 'The Protection of Invention. Printing Privileges in Early Modern Germany', in Williams and Schindler (eds), *Knowledge, Science and Literature*, pp. 7–48.

Tolkien, J. R. R., 'Chaucer as a Philologist: The Reeve's Tale', *Transactions of the Philological Society* (1934), reprinted in *Tolkien Studies*, 5 (2008), 109–71.

Tolmie, Jane, 'Spinning Women and Manly Soldiers: Grief and Game in the English Massacre Plays', in Tolmie and Toswell (eds), *Laments for the Lost*, pp. 283–98.

Tolmie, Jane, and M. J. Toswell (eds), *Laments for the Lost in Medieval Literature*, Medieval Texts and Cultures of Northern Europe 19 (Turnhout: Brepols, 2010).

Tomkins, Silvan S., 'Script Theory', in Demos (ed.), *Exploring Affect*, pp. 295–415.

Tooby, John, and Leda Cosmides, 'The Past Explains the Present: Emotional Adaptations and the Structure of Ancestral Environments', *Ethology and Sociobiology*, 11 (1990), 375–424.

Tracy, Jessica L., Richard W. Robins and June Price Tangney (eds), *The Self-Conscious Emotions: Theory and Research*, 2nd edn (New York: Guilford Press, 2007).

Trigg, Stephanie, 'Affect Theory', in Broomhall (ed.), *Early Modern Emotions*, pp. 10–13.

Trigg, Stephanie, 'Afterword: Reading Historical Emotions', in Marculescu and Morand Métivier (eds), *Affective and Emotional Economies*, pp. 247–51.

Trigg, Stephanie, 'Introduction: Emotional Histories – Beyond the Personalization of the Past and the Abstraction of Affect Theory', *Exemplaria*, 26:1 (2014), 3–15.

Trigg, Stephanie, 'Langland's Tears: Poetry, Emotion, and Mouvance', *Yearbook of Langland Studies*, 26 (2012), 27–48.

Trigg, Stephanie, '"Shamed Be ...": Historicizing Shame in Medieval and Early Modern Courtly Ritual', *Exemplaria*, 19:1 (2007), 67–89.

Trigg, Stephanie, 'Weeping Like a Beaten Child: Figurative Language and the Emotions in Chaucer and Malory', in Burger and Crocker (eds), *Medieval Affect, Feeling, and Emotion*, pp. 25–46.

Turville-Petre, Thorlac, *Description and Narrative in Middle English Alliterative Poetry* (Liverpool: Liverpool University Press, 2018).

Varnam, Laura, '"A booke of hyr felyngys": Exemplarity and Margery Kempe's Encounters of the Heart', in Kalas and Varnam (eds), *Encountering the Book of Margery Kempe*, pp. 140–59.

Bibliography

Varnam, Laura, 'The Crucifix, the Pietà, and the Female Mystic', *Journal of Medieval Religious Cultures*, 41:2 (2015), 208–37.

Verbaal, Wim, 'Bernard's Smile and the Conversion of Laughter', in Förnegård et al. (eds), *Tears, Sighs and Laughter*, pp. 193–21.

Vines, Amy N., 'A Woman's "Crafte": Melior as Lover, Teacher and Patron in the Middle English *Partonope of Blois*', *Modern Philology*, 105:2 (2007), 245–70.

Vulic, Kathryn, 'De Pater Noster of Richard Ermyte and the Topos of the Female Audience', *Mystics Quarterly*, 34 (2008), 1–43.

Wakelin, Daniel, *Humanism, Reading, and English Literature 1430–1530* (Oxford: Oxford University Press, 2007).

Wallace, David (ed.), *The Cambridge History of Medieval English Literature* (Cambridge: Cambridge University Press, 1999).

Warner, Lawrence, *The Lost History of 'Piers Plowman': The Earliest Transmission of Langland's Work* (Philadelphia, PA: University of Pennsylvania Press 2011).

Warner, Lawrence, 'Mary, Unmindful of her Knight: *Sir Gawain and the Green Knight* and the Traditions of Sexual Hospitality', *SAC*, 35 (2013), 263–87.

Webb, Heather, *The Medieval Heart* (New Haven, CT: Yale University Press, 2010).

Weiss, Judith, 'Modern and Medieval Views on Swooning: The Literary and Medical Contexts of Fainting in Romance', in Purdie and Cichon (eds), *Medieval Romance, Medieval Contexts*, pp. 121–34.

Wenzel, Siegfried, 'The Source for Chaucer's Seven Deadly Sins', *Traditio*, 30 (1974), 351–78.

Whetter, Kevin S., *Understanding Genre and Medieval Romance* (Aldershot: Ashgate, 2008).

Whetter, Kevin S., 'Weeping, Wounds and Worship in Malory's *Morte Darthur*', *Arthurian Literature*, 31 (2016), 61–82.

White, Stephen D., 'The Politics of Anger', in Rosenwein (ed.), *Anger's Past*, pp. 127–52.

White, Tom, 'Textile Logics of Late Medieval Romance', *Exemplaria*, 28:4 (2016), 297–318.

Whitehead, Christiania, 'Middle English Religious Lyrics', in Duncan (ed.), *A Companion to the Middle English Lyric*, pp. 96–119.

Widen, Sherri C., and James A. Russell, 'Young Children's Understanding of Others' Emotions', in Lewis, Haviland-Jones and Barrett (eds), *Handbook of Emotions*, pp. 348–63.

Williams, Gerhild Scholz, and Stephan K. Schindler (eds), *Knowledge, Science and Literature in Early Modern Germany* (Chapel Hill, NC: University of North Carolina Press, 1996).

Williams, Graham, *Sincerity in Medieval English Language and Literature* (London: Palgrave Macmillan, 2018).

Windeatt, Barry, 'The Art of Swooning in Middle English' in Cannon and Nolan (eds), *Medieval Latin and Middle English Literature*, pp. 211–30.

Windeatt, Barry, 'Chaucer and Fifteenth-Century Romance: *Partonope of Blois*', in Morse and Windeatt (eds), *Chaucer Traditions*, pp. 62–80.

Windeatt, Barry, 'Gesture in Chaucer', *Medievalia et Humanistica*, new series, 9 (1979), 143–61.

Winstead, Karen A., *The Oxford History of Life-Writing*, vol. 1: *The Middle Ages* (Oxford: Oxford University Press, 2018).

Winerman, Lea, 'The Mind's Mirror', *Monitor on Psychology*, 36:9 (October 2005), 48, www.apa.org/monitor/oct05/mirror.aspx (accessed 29 August 2023).

Wogan-Browne, Jocelyn, '"Bet … to … rede on holy seyntes lyves …": Romance and Hagiography Again', in Meale (ed.) *Readings in Medieval English Romance*, pp. 83–97.

Wogan-Browne, Jocelyn, *Saints' Lives and Women's Literary Culture, 1150–1300: Virginity and its Authorizations* (Oxford: Oxford University Press, 2001).

Wojciehowski, Hannah Chapelle, 'The Mirror Neuron Mechanism and Literary Studies: An Interview with Vittorio Gallese', *California Italian Studies*, 2:1 (2011), https://escholarship.org/uc/item/56f8v9bv (accessed 7 September 2023).

Woolgar, C. M., *The Senses in Late Medieval England* (New Haven, CT, and London: Yale University Press, 2006).

Zumthor, Paul, 'Intertextualité et mouvance', *Littérature*, 41 (1981), 8–16.

Media

BBC Radio 4, *Start the Week*, 12 October 2015.

Web publications

Ashe, Laura, 'The Invention of Fiction', *History Today*, 13 February 2018, www.historytoday.com/miscellanies/invention-fiction (accessed 29 August 2023).

Boquet, Damien, and Piroska Nagy, 'Historical Emotions, Historians' Emotions', in 'Les émotions au Moyen Âge, carnet d'EMMA', https://emma.hypotheses.org/1213#_ftn4 (22) (accessed 29 August 2023).

Gersum Project, www.gersum.org (accessed 29 August 2023).

Johns Hopkins University Middle English Concordance, https://middleenglish.library.jhu.edu/search.

Lorentzen, Christian, 'Sheila Heti, Ben Lerner and Tao Lin: How "Auto" is "Autofiction"?', *Vulture*, 11 May 2018, www.vulture.com/2018/05/how-auto-is-autofiction.html (accessed 29 August 2023).

Old English Thesaurus, https://oldenglishthesaurus.arts.gla.ac.uk.

Smiley, Jane, 'History versus Historical Fiction', *The Guardian*, 15 October 2015, www.theguardian.com/books/2015/oct/15/jane-smiley-niall-ferguson-history-versus-historical-fiction (accessed 29 August 2023).

Index

Note: literary works are indexed under author's name where known.

A-(artefact) emotion 182–4, 192, 209–10
Ælfric of Eynsham 49
Ælred of Rievaulx 191–4, 214
  Speculum Caritatis 192–3
Aers, D. 29, 100
affect 5–6, 17–21, 25–7, 65, 96–105, 112–13, 119, 122, 124–5, 157, 159, 195–200, 241, 262–5, 274–5
affect theory 25–7, 98–101
Airlie, S. 8
Akbari, S. C. 63
Alcuin of York 61–2, 64
Alī ibn al-'Abbās al-Mağūsī 18
allegory 32, 59, 63–6, 101, 161–4, 170–1
alliteration 49–54, 66, 102, 187, 197–9, 202–3, 277
Althoff, G. 15–16, 145–6
Amis and Amiloun 167, 184
Ancrene Wisse 53, 59, 112, 193–4, 275
Andreas Capellanus 169–70
  De arte honeste amandi 169–70
anger, *see also* wrath 16, 19–20, 22–3, 49, 52–5, 62, 64, 66, 94–5, 102–6, 123, 145–7, 149, 162, 216
anxiety 19, 58, 74, 108, 115, 149, 151, 162, 246, 249–54, 263
apostrophe 30, 180, 200, 203
Aristotle 17, 20–1
Arthurian romance 141–2, 148–54, 183–4, 190–1, 234–6
Ashe, L. 28, 277
Atkinson, L. 256
Auchinleck manuscript 68
audience 33, 67–81, 179–217, 277
Augustine 19–20, 100–1, 191–2, 213–14, 274–5, 277
  City of God 19–20
  Confessions 191–2, 213
Austin, J. L. 11, 136–7
authenticity 114, 145–6, 154–60, 192, 195
authorship 229, 231, 247–65
autofiction 34, 250–64, 278
avarice 62
Avicenna (Abu Ali Sina) 17, 20, 24

bathos 200
Benedictine Rule 107
Bevis of Hampton 108–9, 184
Birgitta of Sweden, saint 60–1, 262

Index

Blanchardyn and Eglantyne 233, 239, 244–5
Blud, V. 99
blueness 104–5
blushing see also colour changes 101–3, 123, 143–4
Boccaccio, G. 114, 142, 143
Boethius 50, 253
Bolens, G. 105, 180, 186–7
Boquet, D. 3, 15, 117, 124
Bourdieu, P. 27
Bourke, J. 98
brain 5–7, 18–19, 24–7, 99, 185–9, 277
brain imaging 7, 186
Brandsma, F. 180, 190–1
Breton lai 67, 76–81, 208
Burrow, J. 97, 113, 118, 121, 248, 278

Calabrese, M. 208
catharsis 33, 116
Caxton, W. 120, 166–7, 231, 244, 278
Charles d'Orléans 67
Chaucer, G., see also under individual works 50–3, 106, 229– 31, 244, 247–8, 250, 255–6, 265, 277–8
  Anelida and Arcite 166
  Book of the Duchess, The 104
  'Canon's Yeoman's Tale, The' 53
  Canterbury Tales, The 205, 209, 211, 229–31, 278
  'Clerk's Tale, The' 117, 200
  'Franklin's Tale, The' 148, 189, 208, 275
  House of Fame, The 255–6
  'Knight's Tale, The' 51, 100, 105, 125, 140, 209
  Legend of Good Women, The 120, 161, 201–2
  'Man of Law's Tale, The' 116–17
  'Merchant's Tale, The' 125
  'Miller's Tale, The' 107–8, 119, 123–4, 170, 209, 215
  'Monk's Tale, The' 209–10
  'Nun's Priest's Prologue and Tale, The' 19, 51, 70, 209–10
  'Pardoner's Tale, The' 16
  Parliament of Foules, The 100
  'Physician's Tale, The' 210
  'Prioress's Tale, The' 200, 210
  'Reeve's Tale, The' 51–2, 208–9
  Retractions, The 278
  'Second Nun' Tale, The' 108
  'Summoner's Tale, The' 119
  'Tale of Melibee, The' 200, 211
  'Tale of Sir Thopas, The' 75–6, 199–200
  Troilus and Criseyde 53, 94–7, 99–100, 103–5, 113–16, 119–21, 140, 142–5, 147, 149, 156–8, 160, 166, 188, 204, 230, 244, 265, 278
  'Wife of Bath's Tale, The' 121
Chaucerians 230, 248
Chestre, Thomas 76–81
  Sir Launfal 76–81, 109
Chrétien de Troyes 69–75, 81, 118, 147–8, 151–2, 190–1, 208, 238
  Le chevalier de la charete 118, 151–2
  Erec et Enide 190–1, 208
  Perceval: ou le conte de Graal 73–4
  Yvain 147–8
Cicero 19–20
Cleanness 52–4
cognition 5, 18–22, 33, 99–100, 144, 276
  embodied cognition 180–1, 186–8
cognitive theory 276

colour changes *see also* blushing 101–5, 122, 159, 274
Cooper, H. 111, 121–2, 232–4
compassion 22, 112–13, 191–2, 214, 261
compunction 62, 115, 188, 194, 197, 214–15, 258, 261
concupiscible emotions 20–3
confession 29, 63–5, 102, 156, 248–50
consolation 33, 193, 212, 253–4
Constantine of Africa 18
contagion, emotional 33, 204–6, 214, 277
contiguity 204–6
Contzen, E. von 30
Couldrette 232
  Mélusine 232
courtly culture 13–14, 29, 73–5, 111, 149–50, 159–61, 163–4, 183–4, 187
covetousness 62, 64
Cupid 99–100, 255

Damasio, A. 5
danger 143, 160–71
Dante Alighieri 229
  Il Paradiso 107
Davidson, C. 212
delight 20, 22–3, 110
Descartes, R. 4
desire 20, 22–3, 57–61, 119, 151, 162, 167–70, 206–7, 246, 257
despair 22, 61, 64, 72, 80, 164, 253, 258
dialogue 72, 153–4, 234–40, 246, 254–5, 260
Dietl, C. 30
Diller, H.-J. 213, 215
Dinshaw, C. 119, 188
disgust 49, 51, 65, 124, 190, 213
Dixon, T. 3–4

Djikic, M. 181–2
Downes, S. 67
drama, cycle 188, 211–17
  Chester cycle 212
  N-Town cycle 212
  Towneley cycle 215
  Wakefield master plays 215
  York cycle 212
dream-vision 179–80, 194, 201, 231, 247, 278
Dryden, J. 22
Dunbar, W. 161, 201–2
  Golden Targe, The 161, 201–2
  Tretis of the Twa Mariit Wemen and the Wedo, The 202
Duns Scotus 23, 27

Eco, U. 106–7
Ekman, P. 5
Emare 104, 116, 118–19, 206–7, 238, 240
embarrassment 96, 101–2, 249, 252, 274–5
embodiment 5–6, 17–24, 27, 33, 66, 94–125, 162–4, 180–1, 186–91, 205, 253–4, 274
Eming, J. 146
emotional communities 9–10, 48, 56–7, 67, 205–6, 246–7
emotional change 10–11, 13, 26, 30–1, 122, 217, 274
emotional régimes 9, 13, 139
emotionology 2, 124, 144
emotive 11–12, 32, 139–42, 144, 153, 276
emotive indicia 30, 68–9, 71, 82, 97, 125
empathy 30–2, 180–92, 194, 205, 214–15, 217, 239, 244, 276
Enders, J. 211, 213
envy 62, 64, 66, 210, 246, 258
Erle of Toulous, The 103, 238
Evans, R. 258

Index

Even-Zohar, I. 69
exemplum 107, 208

F-(fictive) emotion 182–3, 192
fear 19–24, 27, 49–51, 72, 95, 98,
    105–6, 123–4, 159, 161–2,
    202–3, 212, 234, 241–2,
    245–6, 257–9, 263
feedback systems 5, 12, 71
Ferguson, N. 1, 8, 28
fictionality 9, 28–31, 158, 229–31
fin'amor 169–70
Flannery, M. 65–66, 162, 167, 228
Floris and Blanchefleur 184, 206
Fludernik, M. 30, 140
focalisation 30, 99, 172, 18, 188–9
folk-psychology 6, 30, 185, 188
Fowler, E. 229–30
Frijda, N. 5–6
Froissart, J. 145–6

Galen 17, 95, 99
Gallese, V. 186, 190
Gaunt, S. 69
genre 10, 25, 28, 48, 66, 69–71,
    81–2, 97, 107, 122, 146,
    154, 194, 201, 207–9, 232–3,
    247–50
gentry 28, 69–71, 74–80, 113, 161,
    170, 233
Geoffrey of Monmouth 194
Gerson, J. 61
gesture 66, 75, 106, 118–25, 138,
    151, 153, 157, 211–16, 279
gluttony 62, 65–6
God 23, 52–4, 59–62, 113, 115,
    142, 156, 184, 192–3, 196,
    217, 257–9, 262–5, 279
Gottfried von Strassburg 115
    Tristan 115, 144, 191

hagiography 113, 116, 158, 184,
    256, 274

Handlyng Synne 275
happiness 49, 62, 72, 109, 116–7,
    123, 157–9, 192, 237, 246
Harbus, A. 208
Hardman, P. 75
hate 21–2, 64, 66, 237
Havelok the Dane 109, 184
heart 17–19, 25, 56, 59, 61, 95,
    99–100, 102, 104–5, 117,
    123, 143, 158, 246, 252
hell 106, 180, 202–3, 212
Henryson, R. 231
Hildemar of Corbie 107
history of emotions 2–3, 8–16
Hoccleve, T. 248–56
    Complaint, The 250–6
    Dialogue, The 254–5
    Letter of Cupid, The 255
    Male Regle, The 248–50
    Regiment of Princes, The 250
    'Series', The 251–4
Hochschild, A. 2
homosociality 80–1, 150
hope 21–2, 61, 140–1, 149
Hopkins, A. 113
Huizinga, J. 7–8
Humphrey, Duke of Gloucester
    251, 255
hybridisation 82, 113, 184, 232–3,
    256, 274, 278
hydraulic model 24, 102, 123

imagination 21, 27–31, 66, 82,
    146, 171, 182, 194, 265
individuality 29–30, 229–31, 265,
    277
inexpressibility 158–9
interiority 12, 28–30, 101, 122,
    135–6, 139–40, 142, 153,
    158, 171, 229–31, 245, 249,
    253, 265, 274–9
irascible emotions 20–4
Isaac of Stella 21

Isidore of Seville 253
Izard, C. 5

Jacques de Vitry 179
Jaeger, C. S. 29
James, W. 4–5
jealousy 94–5, 246, 274–5
Jean d'Arras 234
Jean de la Rochelle 21
Jesus Christ 19, 58–60, 99, 104, 107, 115–16, 188, 192–4, 195–7, 213–16, 257–61
Johnston, A. J. 107–8
joy 19–21, 49, 60–1, 72–3, 79–81, 106–11, 116–17, 144–5, 158–9, 190–1, 207–8, 258–60, 274
Julian of Norwich 60–1, 195, 197, 259
  Shewings 60, 195

Kaempfer, L., 111
Karnes, M. 112
Kempe, Margery 14, 57–61, 99, 104, 112–13, 206, 231, 251, 256–65, 278
  Book of Margery Kempe, The 57–61, 99, 206, 256–65
Kendall, E. 163
kinesis 186–7
King Horn 55–6, 69, 124, 140
King, P. 20
kissing 117–19, 123, 141, 151, 153–4, 239, 245
Knapp, E. 250, 254
kneeling 119–20, 146, 147, 155, 260
Knight, S. 189
Knight of the Tour-Landry 166–7
  Book of the Knight of the Tour-Landry 166–7

Lancelot, Vulgate 151
Langland, William 24, 63–6, 82, 205, 257, 278

Piers Plowman 24, 63–6, 205, 278
laughter 106–11, 121–2, 183, 193, 205, 213, 215–6
lechery 57–8, 62, 119
Lewis, C. S. 204
lexis 8–9, 26, 48–61, 69, 81, 273, 275
Lindstedt, S. 264
long-form prose 34, 231–47, 265, 278
long-form romance 34, 231–47, 265, 278
longing 12, 23, 60, 76, 164
Lorentzen, C. 250
love 12–14, 21–3, 28, 55–6, 58–61, 72–3, 75–6, 80, 94, 96–7, 103, 114, 121, 140–4, 147–54, 160–71, 201–2, 207, 235–6, 239–42
Love, N. 112, 260
  Mirour of the Blessed life of Jesus Christ 112, 260
Lovelich, H. 104–5
  Merlin 104–5
Lydgate, J. 165
  Troy-Book 165
Lynch, A. 82–3
lyric 13–14, 28, 67, 82, 251
  religious 59, 104, 112, 188, 262, 264
  secular 58–9, 113, 201, 265

McCracken, P. 13
McNamara, R, and Ruys, J. 246
McNamer, S. 12, 31, 33, 48, 51, 188, 195–6, 198, 277
Maddern, P. 101, 122–3
Malory, Sir Thomas 111, 115–16, 118, 120–1, 140–2, 149–54, 168–9, 171, 190, 232, 234–6
  Morte Darthur 120–1, 140–2, 149–54, 168–9, 232, 234–6

Manly, J. M. 200
Mann, J. 95–6, 143, 189
Mar, R. 181, 186
Marculescu, A. and C.-L. Morand Métivier 10, 31
Marie de France 67–70, 76–81
　Graelent 76
　Lai de Lanval 76–81
　Lai le Freine 68
Marr, A. 1
Mary Magdalen 60, 261
Mary, Virgin 58–9, 99, 198, 260–2
masculinity 96, 160, 167
Massumi, B. 25, 100
medicine 16–18, 95, 99
Meecham-Jones, S. 113–14
Megna, P. 64
Metham, J. 232
　Amoryus and Cleopes 232
Miall, D. and D. Kuiken 184–5, 192, 193
Mills, D. 212
mind 4–7, 17–18, 24, 181–2, 231, 276
mind-body continuum 4–7, 16, 27–8
mirror characters 180–1, 190–1, 241
mirror neurons 7, 185–90
Moi, T. 169–70
Moore, M. 28
Mort Artu, La 120–1, 152, 234–5
Mount Grace Priory 264
mysticism 57–61, 99, 116, 196–7, 256, 262, 264

Nagy, P. 2, 3, 15, 25–6, 117, 124
narration 242–7
narratology 30, 82, 144, 149, 153, 158, 179
nested stories 206–11
neuropsychology 6–7, 25–6, 27, 189–90

neuroscience 26, 185
Nibelungenlied, Das 137, 138
Northern English 51–4
Nussbaum, M. 6

Oatley, K. 5, 181–2, 186, 194, 214
Octavyen 238
Ogura, M. 50–4
Old English 49–51, 69, 70
Old Norse 49, 52–3, 81
On Ureisun of ure Louerede 195–6, 203
Orlemanski, J. 27–8, 231, 251
Ovid 55, 171

pain 20, 23, 112, 188
pallor 66, 103–4
'paradox of fiction' 181–5
Parkinson, B. 205
Partonope of Blois 70, 232, 234, 239–40, 241–4, 246
Partonopeu de Blois 232, 242
Passion, the 59, 112, 192, 214–15, 260–2
Pastons 9, 59, 233
pathos 200, 214
Patience 52, 54, 186–7, 247
Patterson, L. 29, 194, 248, 254
Pearl 33, 52, 54, 183, 198, 247, 278
Pearsall, D. 256, 278
Pecok, R. 61
Peñaforte, R. 63
Pepwell, H. 264
Peraldus, William 63
perception 5, 21–2, 25–6, 27, 99, 186–7, 197, 276
　visceral perception 25, 26, 97, 100, 186
performance 32, 73, 76, 96, 106, 135–72, 187, 244, 248–50, 261–2, 276, 279

performativity 11, 29, 32, 63, 135–72, 211, 248–50, 262
personification 63–6, 161–4, 170, 210
Peter of Blois 191–3
Philipowski, K. 29, 139
philosophy of emotion 6–7, 16
Plamper, J. 2, 4
polysystem 69, 81
Post-Vulgate Cycle 234
  Post-Vulgate *Suite de Merlin* 169
pretence 32, 124–5, 142, 242–3
pride 62–4, 66, 257–8
printing 34, 229, 233, 278
proprioception 101–2
Prose Melusine 234, 237–8
Prose Merlin 104–5
psychology 5–6, 17–18, 25–6, 181–91
psychonarration 29, 34, 54–6, 76, 106, 123, 143, 158–60, 231, 234, 245, 274

Quintilian 211

Radford, C. and M. Weston 182, 192
reading 68–71, 181–6, 188, 229, 233
reading communities 68–73, 82
Reddy, W. 9, 11–13, 26, 30, 98, 100, 139, 142
religious literature *see also* mysticism; religious lyrics 69, 116, 123, 180, 193–4, 195–7, 233
repertoire 10, 57, 68–9, 73, 75–6, 124, 206, 209, 215, 274, 279
remorse 113, 249, 274–5
rhyme 195–200, 232, 277
rhythm 49, 195–200, 277
Rikhardsdottir, S. 30–1, 67–8, 97, 180

ritual 15–16, 32, 145–50, 154, 275
Robert of Cisyle 233
Rolle, Richard 59, 16, 196–7
  The Form of Living 59, 196–7
Roman de la Rose, La 29, 161–3, 168
romance 28, 34, 56, 68–82, 96, 105, 109, 113, 116, 119, 146–50, 158–9, 168, 180–1, 184, 194, 198–20, 206–9, 231–47, 265, 273–4, 277–8
Romans de Partenay, The 232, 234
Romaunt de la Rose, The 66, 161–2
Rosenwein, B. 2, 8–10, 14, 24, 31, 48, 56–7, 61–2, 99, 206, 257–9

sadness 49–50, 102, 104, 158, 252
Salih, S. 260, 262
Salthouse, R. 264
Saunders, C. and C. Fernyhough 18
Sawles Warde 106, 202–3
Schadenfreude 215, 263–4
Scheer, M. 2, 26–7, 98, 229, 271
schema 3, 10–12, 33–4, 68–9, 274–5, 79, 160, 184–5, 193, 243, 249, 265, 274, 277–8
Schnell, R. 48
Scott, A. M. 179
script 10–11, 27, 34, 68–71, 75–6, 81–2, 95, 122, 124, 141, 147–8, 154, 246–8, 261, 265–6
Sedgwick, E. K. 13
seven deadly sins 50, 61–6, 82
Shakespeare, W.
  Hamlet 265
  Romeo and Juliet 182
  Tempest, The 279
shame 71–2, 77–8, 96, 101–5, 110–11, 115, 123–4, 143–4, 150–1, 155, 161–2, 228, 242, 245–6, 249, 252, 254, 275
shamefastness 164, 167, 228

Index

Sidney, Sir Philip 265
simulation theory 181–6, 277
sincerity 29, 96, 113, 142, 145–7, 154–61, 167, 170
Sir Degrevant 206
Sir Gawain and the Green Knight 52–4, 101–3, 109–11, 118–19, 123, 148, 183–4, 187–8, 197–8, 204
Sir Gowther 233
Sir Isumbras 233
Sir Landevale 76–9
Sir Orfeo 109, 116, 158, 207
Sir Perceval of Galles 73–6, 198–9
Sir Tristrem 70, 156
Skelton, J. 66, 161
  Bowge of Court, The 66, 161, 170–1
  'Tunnyng of Elynoure Rummynge, The' 230
sloth 62, 164, 165
Smiley, J. 1, 3
smiling 121–2, 138, 200
Sobecki, S. 255
social constructivism 5–6, 8
soliloquy 29, 55, 82, 114
Song of Songs, The 58
soul 4, 17, 20–4, 99, 141–2, 192–3, 202–3
Spearing, A. C. 124
speech acts 11–12, 136–7, 139, 211, 248
Squire of Low Degree, The 200–1
Stanzaic Morte Arthure, The 120–1, 152, 234–5
Starkey, K. 138–40, 142, 153
Stearns, P. 2, 8
Stock, B. 9
Stoics 19–20, 25
Strohm, P. 145–6
swooning 94–6, 104, 109, 116–17, 122–3, 141, 153, 159, 207, 236, 238, 240–1, 260

subjectivity 12, 29, 140, 231, 256
surprise 49, 149, 201, 203–4

Tan, E.-H. 182–4, 192, 200, 209
taxonomies 32, 61–6, 82
tears 25, 70–1, 96, 111–17, 122–3, 139, 158, 193, 214, 260, 262–3
Tennant, E. 137–8, 142
terminology 3–4, 6, 50, 136
textual communities 9, 68–9, 273–4
Þe *Wohunge of ure Lauerd* 195–6, 203
theory of mind 30, 276–7
Thomas Aquinas 21–4, 27, 61
Thornton ms., (Lincoln Cathedral 91) 75, 199, 233
Tomkins, S. 11
translation 14, 56, 67–82, 239, 243, 273–4
trembling 25, 98, 101, 105–6, 122–3, 274
Tretise of Miraclis Pleyinge 213–16, 277
Trigg, S. 25, 98, 103, 228
trobaritz 12–14, 28
troubadours 9, 14, 56, 191

universal theory 4–6, 21, 185, 190

Valentine and Orson 234, 238, 240–1, 245
vernacularity 9, 14, 32, 48, 56, 70, 194, 196, 264
Vives, J. L. 213, 215
Vulgate Cycle 234
Vulic, K. 196–7

weeping *see also* tears 59, 75, 96, 111–17, 123, 141, 155, 192–3, 214, 240–1, 261–4, 274

Weiss, J. 96
William of Ockham 23, 27
William of Palerne 52, 55, 70, 154–5, 158–9
Williams, G. 96, 144, 147, 158, 161
Windeatt, B. 121, 244
Winstead, K. 248, 256–7
Wojciehowski, H. 186

wrath 64, 102–3, 145–6, 163
Wulfstan of York 49
Wynkyn de Worde 234, 264–5

York *Memorandum Book* 213, 216
Ywain and Gawain 71–3, 147–8

Zumthor, P. 67

EU authorised representative for GPSR:
Easy Access System Europe, Mustamäe tee 50,
10621 Tallinn, Estonia
gpsr.requests@easproject.com

www.ingramcontent.com/pod-product-compliance
Lightning Source LLC
Chambersburg PA
CBHW051558230426
43668CB00013B/1904